Baseball 7.95

Earl Weaver BASEBALL HALL OF FAME LEAGUE

Kevin Shafer

Osborne **McGraw-Hill**

Berkeley New York St. Louis San Francisco
Auckland Bogotá Hamburg London Madrid
Mexico City Milan Montreal New Delhi Panama City
Paris São Paulo Singapore Sydney
Tokyo Toronto

Osborne **McGraw-Hill**
2600 Tenth Street
Berkeley, California 94710
U.S.A.

For information on translations or book distributors outside of the U.S.A., please write to Osborne **McGraw-Hill** at the above address.

The Sporting News Conlon Collection was produced and provided by Megacards.

Quotations on the opening page of each chapter were reproduced courtesy of the following publications and sources: Chapter 1, *The Sporting News;* Chapter 2, *Curtis Brown, Ltd.;* Chapter 3, *Yale University Alumni Magazine;* Chapter 6, *The Washington Post;* Chapter 7, Contemporary Books, Inc.; Chapter 8, *Baseball Digest;* Chapter 9, Doubleday & Company; Chapter 13, *The Washington Post.* Additional permissions were waived by various authors, publishers, and periodicals for items which fell within that individual or organization's definition of fair use. Every effort has been made to comply with all copyright holders and respect their rights. If any have been infringed upon, the publishers hope that they will be notified of their unintentional error, so that proper credit can be given in future editions.

Earl Weaver Baseball™: Hall of Fame League

1234567890 DOC 998765432

ISBN 0-07-881844-3

To Dori

For your inspiration, your patience, your understanding, and, most of all, for being a baseball fan.

Publisher

Kenna S. Wood

Acquisition Editor

Jeffrey Pepper

Associate Editor

Emily Rader

Technical Editor

Jeffrey Pepper

Project Editor

Kathy Krause

Copy Editor

Paul Medoff

Proofing Coordinator

Nancy McLaughlin Pechonis

Proofreaders

Linda Medoff
Valerie Haynes Perry

Director of Electronic Publishing

Deborah Wilson

Production Supervisor

Barry Michael Bergin

Quality Control Specialist

Bob Myren

Computer Designer

Fred Lass

Typesetters

Jani Beckwith
J. E. Christgau
Peter Hancik
Stefany Otis
Michelle Salinaro
Helena Charm
Marcela V. Hancik
Susie C. Kim
Lance Ravella
Marla Shelasky

Production Assistant

George Anderson

Production Coordinator

Linda Beatty

Cover Designer

Mason Fong

Artists

Mason Fong
Marcela V. Hancik
Susie C. Kim

Contents

Acknowledgments

The Hall of Fame League is the realization of a boyhood dream for the League's original Commissioner, Tim Nelson. He has spent endless hours putting together the League and organizing the data necessary to put this massive operation in motion. On behalf of baseball fans all over the world, I wish to thank him for providing us with so much enjoyment.

Key people at Electronic Arts, Inc., have been instrumental in getting this project off the ground. Special thanks go to Dave Dempsey and Sue Goerss for their support and for providing essential ingredients.

The staff at Osborne/McGraw-Hill deserve special recognition for their professionalism and dedication in seeing this project through the twists and turns of editing and production. Thank you Jeff Pepper, the Acquisitions Editor on the book, for supporting the idea and taking care of the myriad problems that always seem to crop up. I'd like to thank the following people for their editorial work on the book: Emily Rader (Associate Editor), Kathy Krause (Project Editor), Nancy Pechonis (Proofing Coordinator), Paul Medoff (Copy Editor), Linda Medoff (Proofreader), and Valerie Haynes Perry (Proofreader). The following members of the design and production team at Osborne also deserve recognition: Fred Lass (Computer Designer), Mason Fong (Cover and Interiors Designer), Marcela Hancik (Interiors Designer), and Susie Kim (Illustrator and Interiors Designer). Also, thank you Russell Sipe for coming through in a pinch with some difficult photography.

As a loyal franchise owner in the Northern California Hall of Fame League, I'd like to recognize fellow owners Wade Hufford, Rod Divelbiss, Mike Divelbiss, Ray Lynch, Rob Goldstein, and Matt Shier for their stiff competition and for ganging up on me during Draft Day.

Introduction

Many of us remember spending our adolescent summers playing baseball. We'd grab our gloves and bats and saunter over to the local diamond to spend our days playing pickup games with whoever else showed up.

On the days when we couldn't go to the schoolyard, we'd invent ways to play the game around the house. We'd grab a Whiffle ball and bat and challenge each other in the backyard, playing Home Run Derby. When the weather was bad, we'd grab a deck of playing cards or a pair of dice and invent our own ways to play a game of baseball.

As we grew older, we saved our allowances and experimented with "store-bought" versions of the game. We discovered Strat-O-Matic Baseball and plunged into endless hours of rolling dice, keeping score on scraps of paper, and accumulating "season" statistics for our heroes. In fact, long after our youth had passed, many of us secretly still played this board game on weekends with our grown-up friends. We added a whole new level of sophistication to a game designed for children. We created our own leagues, complete with all-star rosters and Major League drafts.

The Computer Age

Today's "store-bought" baseball games are played on computers. Computers have minimized the roles of luck and chance that often dictated those games we invented with playing cards and dice. Statistics, the soul of the game itself, can now be used to determine the outcome of imaginary games played with the heroes of our youth.

Acclaimed by retailers and users as the ultimate computer baseball game, Earl Weaver Baseball II (EWBII) provides fans with a chance to use their home computers to satisfy that inescapable urge to play baseball. Over the years, Electronic Arts has refined EWBII to offer the most realistic computer baseball game on the market today. The program features graphics that emulate a modern televised game, complete with an array of camera angles and replay possibilities. Player statistics provide the basis for performances that produce realistic game results.

Included with EWBII is an Electronic Arts Oldtimers League. This league uses actual statistics for many of the historical stars of the game, and groups them on teams labeled by the eras and leagues in which they played. This league actually signifies the first step toward squaring off historical superstars in mythical games.

But those of us who seek the ultimate enjoyment in baseball are not satisfied with that first step. After all, is it realistic to use the statistics from the turn of the century in conjunction with the statistics of 50 years later? The types of statistics, as well as the methods in which they were recorded, have changed significantly over the decades. To have players from different eras compete against each other, their statistics must be modified in some way to reflect the fact that they are now going to be playing on the same field and in the same league.

The Hall of Fame League

To expand the realism of historical games played with the EWBII program, statistics must be "normalized." If you want to realistically play Ty Cobb in the same league with Mickey Mantle, you must be able to use a set of statistics that takes into account the differences between the way the game was played in the twenties and the way it was played in the fifties.

The creators of the Hall of Fame League have taken that extra step and developed such a set of statistics. The Hall of Fame League is not a product of Electronic Arts. Instead, it uses the Commissioner II utility offered by the manufacturers of EWBII to produce a league of superstars not found anywhere else.

The Players

This league features Hall of Fame stars as well as players who have displayed Hall of Fame caliber playing in posting career years. By normalizing the statistics for the individual best years of 300 of the best players from 1895 to 1990, the creators of the Hall of Fame League have produced a sophisticated enhancement for the Earl Weaver Baseball game.

The Hall of Fame League recognizes the changes in the game over the 125 years of baseball history. The normalization process is based on a concept of putting all of the players in the same league to play under the same conditions with the same rules. After first establishing a set of statistics for an "average player" in the Hall of Fame League, the normalization process then measures the historical best years of players against this "average player." Characteristics such as the quality of league play for a given season, each player's performance relative to league play in a given season, ballparks, and rule changes for the game over the years have all been factored in.

The result of this normalization is a league in which the historical statistics used by EWBII reflect the performance of legends of the game as if they played against each other. Because the statistical manipulation is applied consistently to all players in the league, each superstar still displays his phenomenal performance on the field. Babe Ruth still clouts monstrous home runs, Ty Cobb is still a terror on the basepaths, and Mickey Mantle still puts on a record offensive show. The process normalizes these performances to produce amazingly realistic results with the best players ever to play the game.

The League

The Hall of Fame League entails more than pitting superstars against each other on the field. Drafting and developing your own team can be as fun as playing the games themselves. The Hall of Fame League enables you to run your own franchise just like a Major League ball club and compete against other franchises in realistic league action.

With the information presented in this book, you can compare the players in the League and determine who is the best among the best. By using the total player rating (TPR) this book provides, you can see how each player rates against the other superstars of baseball history. With this rating system as a guide, you can conduct a player draft involving franchise owners who bid against each other for the rights to players. Once franchise owners have selected their teams, you are ready to play a realistic Major League schedule with the best teams ever assembled on a baseball diamond.

About This Book

This book not only provides the data necessary to create the Hall of Fame League, it personalizes the game and its players so that you can maximize your enjoyment of the most realistic computer baseball game on the market today.

Overview

The first four chapters familiarize you with the concepts behind the Hall of Fame League and with EWBII. Chapter 1 provides a brief history lesson showing how the game has changed through the decades, so you can understand why the normalization of statistics is so important. Chapter 2 discusses how to play Earl Weaver Baseball, and Chapter 3 describes the basic structure of the Hall of Fame League. Chapter 4 contains an overview of the statistical manipulations involved with the normalization process.

The next three chapters provide personal profiles of the brightest stars in the League. Chapter 5 introduces you to the some of the best hitters and position players in the history of baseball. Chapter 6 provides profiles of some the greatest pitchers in baseball, and Chapter 7 introduces key players who add bench strength to your roster. Each of these chapters contains a table showing actual and normalized statistics for these players. Thus, these chapters provide not only biographical data on the superstars of the league, but also a statistical reference to show why these players are unparalleled in their performances.

Chapter 8 is an old-fashioned scouting report on about 100 of the remaining players in the league. The report tells you what to look for and what to expect from these players.

The next four chapters guide you through the finer points of running your own Hall of Fame League. Chapter 9 discusses how to prepare for and conduct a player draft. Chapter 10 provides a complete guide for using the Commissioner II Utility program. Chapter 11 describes historic ballparks and teaches you how to construct a ballpark to suit your team. Chapter 12 introduces you to a half-dozen of the game's greatest managers and teaches you how to program your managerial strategy with EWBII.

Chapter 13 provides valuable insight into Earl Weaver, the namesake for EWBII. Here you are will read about the personal history of Earl and his individual managerial style.

The appendixes of this book are comprised of statistical tables containing all the data necessary to program your own Hall of Fame League. These tables show both actual historical statistics and normalized statistics for the 300 players in the Hall of Fame League. Also included are breakdowns for performances by hitters against left-handed and right-handed pitching, as well as for performances by pitchers against left-handed and right-handed hitting.

Margin Icons

Appearing in the margins are several icons next to profiles and scouting reports of various players. These icons can be used for quick reference to find information about certain players whose skill levels might be higher in certain aspects of the game. These icons (and their corresponding areas of emphasis) are as follows.

Right-handed outfielder (defense)
Left-handed outfielder (defense)
Right-handed infielder (defense)
Left-handed infielder (defense)

Catcher
Right-handed pitcher
Left-handed pitcher
Right-handed hitter (offense)
Left-handed hitter (offense)

The Commissioner II Utility

The Commissioner II Utility, an add-on program from Electronic Arts that must be purchased separately from EWBII, is not required for enjoying the Hall of Fame League. However, this utility must be used to enter statistics for the players in the League, to align players on teams in your league, to modify ballparks, and to program managerial strategies. Together with the information presented in this book, you can use the Commissioner II Utility set up your own Hall of Fame League and conduct a player draft.

If you do not have a copy of the Commissioner II Utility, you can still participate in the Hall of Fame League. All you need is a copy of the teams and players in the League, and you can still enjoy playing games with the Earl Weaver Baseball program. However, you will be limited to using the preprogrammed managerial strategies and preset ballpark statistics that come with the Earl Weaver Baseball program.

If you choose to enter the data for all these players, be prepared to spend some time doing so. If you do not want to manually enter the statistics for the players in the League, or if you do not own a copy of the Commissioner II Utility program, you can purchase a disk copy of the league.

Hundreds of hours have been spent deriving the more than 20,000 statistics for the players in the Hall of Fame League. The creators of the Hall of Fame League are offering a magnetic disk containing all the players and sample teams for the League. This offer is not made anywhere else. The sale of the disk is made independently of Osborne/McGraw-Hill, and is not a product of Electronic Arts.

To order your disk copy of the Hall of Fame League, fill out this order form and mail it to the address indicated.

Order Form

To order the data disk containing player statistics for the Hall of Fame League (DOS format only), please provide the following information and include a check or money order for the appropriate amount:

Hall of Fame Data Disk:	**$19.95**
for California Residents:	**$21.40** ($19.95 + 7.25% sales tax)
Shipping and Handling:	**$ 2.00** (all U.S. orders)
Foreign Orders:	**$24.95** ($19.95 + $5 shipping & handling)

Number of Copies:________ Amount Enclosed: $________

Method of Payment: _____Check _____Money Order

Disk Format: _____5 1/4" _____ 3 1/2"

Name:____

Street Address:____

City:__________________________State:_______ ZIP:__________

Country (if not USA):____________________________________

Please send this form, along with your check or money order, to:

Kevin Shafer
Hall of Fame Data Disk
Box 1395
Lafayette, CA 94549-1395

This offer is subject to change or cancellation at any time.

This is solely the offering of the author. Osborne/McGraw-Hill takes no responsibility for the fulfillment of this offer. Please allow four to six weeks for delivery.

ALL TIME LEADER
TY COBB
HIGHEST CAREER BATTING AVERAGE – .36

HOF - 19
CHICAGO
ROGERS HORNSBY
CHICAGO CUBS – 2ND BASE
1929

MOST VALUABLE PLAYER
JIMMIE FOXX
A.L. MVP – BASEBALL WRITER'S ASSOCIATION
1932

CHAPTER 1

Why a Hall of Fame League?

"Baseball? It's just a game—as simple as a ball and a bat. Yet, as complex as the American spirit it symbolizes. It's a sport, business—and sometimes even religion."

—Ernie Harwell in his essay, "The Game for All America"

"Oh what a ball game we have going here at beautiful Shafer Stadium on just a perfect day for baseball. Bottom of the ninth, Hughie Jennings on second, Johnny Bench on first, with two out and the home team down by two. Ruth steps out of the box to gather himself. He swung right through that last pitch by Gossage. The Goose, coming on in relief of Lefty Grove here in the ninth after Grove walked two in a row, is throwing nothing but heat. Ruth steps back in, takes a couple of those familiar practice swings. Here's the stretch. The shortstop, Wagner, bluffs toward Jennings, but the real out has to be Ruth. He represents the winning run. Here's the 3-2 pitch..."

Wait just a minute! What is this, the impossible dream? Hughie Jennings, Johnny Bench, and Babe Ruth all on the same team? That's three Hall of Famers who played in different eras. What do you mean, Goose Gossage in relief of Lefty Grove?

This may be a dream team, but Hall of Famers playing with and against each other is not impossible, not in this era of computerized technology. With a computer, you can even bring back your favorite Hall of Fame superstars and have them play against the stars of today. In fact, you can do better than that. You can have them play under your tutelage, with your strategy, with your lineup, in your very own cornfield that you have customized into the perfect ballpark for your club. Dreams *do* come true with Earl Weaver Baseball and the Hall of Fame League.

As youngsters, many of us spent those hot, dusty, summer afternoons on a playground ball diamond. We'd play pickup games, two against two, announcing each batter as though it were a Major League ball game. We fantasized that we were our heroes stepping to the plate or making the fantastic catch diving toward the line in the outfield. We'd play Little League, Pony League, and American Legion ball to hone our skills as future Hall of Famers. We slept with our mitts nearby and our bats not far away. Those who were lucky enough to live in a Major League city could go to a game and watch and dream about how someday that would be us out there in front of millions of fans.

In 1976, Bill Veeck defined the baseball season: "The true harbinger of spring, not the crocuses or swallows returning to Capistrano, but the sound of the bat on the ball."

As we grew older, very few of us ever realized that dream, but our love for the game has never paled, and empathy for the stars has never faded. We read the box scores more carefully, study the stories of the heroes before our time, and are true connoisseurs of the game. Our appetite for baseball begins weeks before spring training and is insatiable well into the football season. We can't get enough baseball. As a wise old White Sox fan once said, "Baseball is life. Everything can be equated to baseball."

The Earl Weaver Baseball game allows you to enjoy the game any time you want. It takes you beyond the box score. It allows you to manage a team and make decisions in key situations. But rather than physically playing on those dusty playground diamonds, with Earl Weaver Baseball you can participate intellectually, in the comfort of your own home, and participate with the legends of the game to boot!

By playing in the Hall of Fame League, you will learn about the stars who have spanned 120 years of baseball history. You'll learn the importance of starting pitching, the role of the stopper, when to sacrifice, when to hit and run, where to bat the greatest hitters of all time, and how to counter a lineup that boasts a .340 team batting average.

With the Hall of Fame League, you become a mogul among moguls. You learn how to deal with other general managers, how to appease the Commissioner, how to draft a team from a pool of players so talented you very likely will become dazed with decisions on whom to pick to be part of your club. You'll learn the value of each player so that you can bid against other moguls for the rights to a superstar. You'll learn how to design your home ballpark to take advantage of awesome power, blazing speed, or superior pitching.

All this becomes possible by combining the Earl Weaver Baseball game with state-of-the-art statistical analysis. This combination allows you to normalize statistics from the 1800s through the Roaring Twenties until today. By using this process, you can actually put Babe Ruth at the plate to face Goose Gossage and enjoy a realistic result (did he hit one out or didn't he?).

Henry B. Chadwick was the first person to record a statistical summary of baseball games. As a New York newspaper reporter in the 1840s, he established standards still used to record the results of games played 150 years later. He is the only baseball writer ever to be elected to the Hall of Fame.

Equalization of statistics is at the heart of the Hall of Fame League. By using an array of functions and formulas, you can put players from one era in the same league as players 50 years later. It may sound confusing, but don't worry—the Hall of Fame League is a total package. All the statistical analysis, all the number crunching, and all the equations have been done for you. Your role in this league is to enjoy.

The importance of the statistical equalization is best illustrated, perhaps, by an understanding of the evolution that the game of baseball has undergone. By seeing in a capsule how the game of the 1880s differed so much from that of the 1960s, you can get a feel for how complicated the equalization process really is.

Looking into the Mirror

Accept, for the moment, that the White Sox fan was correct in asserting that "baseball is life." You would naturally assume that something so all-encompassing must be affected by the society and culture around it. Baseball historians maintain just that.

Baseball today is as different from baseball at the turn of the century as our society and culture today are from those bygone days. The price of a bleacher seat has risen astronomically. Players no longer ride the rails to play their road games. Parades through the middle of town are reserved for World Series champions rather than a visiting ball club on the way to the park for the opening of a critical series. The cost of operating a franchise (including salaries that are now measured in seven-figure packages) has driven up the price of admission. Team jets have replaced public railroads as the chosen mode of transportation. Television, with its instant replay and massive coverage in prime media markets, has increased fan exposure immeasurably. The game that was never played at night or on Sunday is now broadcast on television in the form of doubleheaders or tripleheaders—even on holidays.

During a September 1879 meeting in Buffalo, presidents of National League clubs agreed to an annual "reserve list" that gave each club the exclusive rights to sign players from season to season. The reserve list was the forerunner to the "reserve clause" in player's contracts, a provision that restricted the rights of players for the next 90 years.

Adjustments in the way our society approaches life are reflected on the baseball field of play. Consider the collapse of the National Association in 1875 after only five years of existence: A moderately temperate society of the mid-1870s would not tolerate open betting on games (some of it purportedly by players themselves), suspected bribery among players and officials, and open selling of liquor at the ballparks. The game of 1908 was one of a rather prudish society, a game in which more bunting and fewer home runs (a rather gentlemanly or conservative game) were accepted as the norm. By contrast, the game of the 1890s was a violent game marked by dirty play and devious tactics. During the Roaring Twenties, the Sultan of Swat, Babe Ruth, dominated the game and the headlines with his skill and off-field antics. Ruth's drinking became almost as legendary as his explosive home runs.

Baseball has changed through the decades as our society and culture have changed. Our heroes have changed, the rules have changed, the conditions have changed. But through the past 120 years, it's still the same basic game. This is a subtle distinction—baseball has changed, but the game remains the same. The game itself is still played with eight fielders, a pitcher, and a hitter. Changes in rules, changes in conditions, changes in equipment, and even changes in the player pool have affected the *way* the game is played—that is, the strategy used to play the game. For example, changes in baseball from 1900 to 1925 spelled the dawning of the long ball and the disdain of the sacrifice bunt by most managers. The introduction of artificial surfaces with the 1965 opening of "the Eighth Wonder of the World," the Astrodome, shifted more emphasis to speed and athleticism. These examples show but a few of the changes that have affected the way the game was played, the strategy that is necessary to win.

The Evolution of Strategy

Comparing heroes past and present cannot be accomplished without first understanding the way the game has been played through the years, how strategies have been invented and discarded, and how baseball itself has aged. By understanding why Nig Cuppy pitched so many complete games in 1896, why Ty Cobb's stolen base totals were so high in 1911, how Babe Ruth altered the course of history in 1920, why Ted Williams had such an impact in 1941, or why Mickey Mantle was so special in 1957, you can begin to appreciate why these players are in the Hall of Fame League.

Before the Turn of the Century

The game of baseball before the turn of the century probably could be characterized as hard on the players. The game was played in the 1870s without gloves, pitchers delivered their offerings underhanded, batters would tell the pitcher to pitch either high or low, and nine balls were required for a walk. Without the comfort of fielding gloves, players' hands would swell by the end of a game and catching line drives could be hazardous to a player's health. A game in the 1870s was typified by numerous fielding errors (little wonder!) to the tune of about three or four an inning.

Rules were changed in the 1880s. The number of balls required to walk a batter fluctuated throughout the decade until finally in 1889 the rule was set at four. The pitcher's box was moved back from 45 feet to 50 feet and, by the end of the decade, pitchers were finally allowed to throw overhand. A standard strike zone from the shoulders to the knees was established in 1887. And gloves began to catch on, so total errors were starting to diminish.

Another rule change instituted in 1887 was the result of excessive rowdyness by several clubs, most notably the St. Louis team of the American Association managed by Charles Comiskey. Teams would launch constant verbal abuse at the opposing pitcher in an effort to disrupt the pitcher's concentration. Players acting as coaches would run up and down the baselines yelling at the pitcher to get him rattled. For obvious reasons, a rule defining the coach's box was put into effect in 1887.

In the mid-1800s, the Knickerbocker Base Ball Club of New York was playing a game featuring fixed batting orders, four bases in a diamond configuration 40 paces apart, and a pitcher delivering a ball underhanded to a batter 15 paces away. Often considered the forerunner to baseball in America, the game was commonly known as the "New York Game."

During the 1880s, schedule changes went into effect requiring clubs to play 90 to 130 games per season. The expanded schedule had a direct effect on what has become known as the pitching staff.

Because until 1891 no substitutions were allowed for anyone but the pitcher (except, of course, in cases of injury), ball clubs of this era had no reason for reserve players. The only reserve players they really ever used were pitchers. Most clubs during the mid-1800s, such as the Chicago White Stockings, got by with just one pitcher. In 1876, three clubs used two men of equal talent and alternated them. One club (Boston) actually had three pitchers it used that year.

Some historians credit Jack Chapman with being the first manager to use a multipitcher staff. In 1884 while managing Detroit, Chapman rotated five men throughout the course of the season and would not allow any of them to pitch more than 30 percent of the games. But his team finished last. In fact, no team using more than one pitcher ever won the pennant until 1887. That year, Detroit (this time under the

During a championship series between Cleveland and Baltimore in 1895 (a series that featured dirty play by both clubs), fans in Baltimore showered the visiting club with seat cushions, beer bottles, vegetables, and anything else they could get their hands on. Fans in Cleveland retaliated by barraging the visiting Baltimore team's horse-drawn bus with rocks, bricks, and dirt clods.

reins of Bill Watkins) featured five pitchers, none of whom was allowed to be used in more than a third of the total games.

In most cases, those teams during this period who were using multipitcher staffs were actually trying to hide a weakness. Because the weaker team could not match a great pitcher against a stronger team's great pitcher, the weaker team would counter with several mediocre pitchers instead. When the names of Watkins' Detroit pitchers began showing up at the top of several league-leading categories in 1887, many other teams began the following year by drifting away from the one-pitcher approach in favor of multipitcher staffs.

In addition to the emergence of multipitcher staffs, other strategic developments during the 1870s and 1880s included backing up fielders, backing up throws to the infield, instituting pregame batting practice, and using the sacrifice bunt.

One of the most innovative clubs of this era had to be the Baltimore Oriole teams of the 1890s managed by Ned Hanlon. These teams won three consecutive titles (1894-1896). They had team batting averages of .343 in 1894, .324 in 1895, and .328 in 1896. They stole about 48 percent more bases than any other National League team of the era. This team could hit and they could run. They combined their exceptional skills with innovative strategies (such as the hit and run, the Baltimore Chop, and the bunt single) that are still recognized today. Other innovators of the 1890s included the Brooklyn club (credited with coming up with the cutoff play) and the Boston Beaneaters (who were credited with devising the double steal). Tommy McCarthy of Boston has also received credit for instituting runner-to-batter signals.

But oh, those pesky Orioles—they became almost as famous for the innovations that were barred from the game as they did for their accomplishments. One of the most famous tactics was holding runners at first—literally. The first baseman would physically grab the runner by the belt to delay his departure. Other tactics included hiding extra balls in the tall outfield grass, the catcher dropping pebbles in the shoes of the batter or shielding the umpire from the shenanigans taking place on the field. These tactics often resulted in violence on the field.

Rule changes that were instituted included moving the pitching distance in 1893 to the present 60 feet 6 inches, which precluded a dominance of pitchers over the early part of that decade.

The Turn of the Century and the Twenties

When Ban Johnson took over as American League president in 1901, he made it clear that dirty tactics no longer would be tolerated. He cleaned up play on the field and the National League was forced to follow suit.

A rule change adopted in 1901 by the National League and in 1903 by the American League dictated that a foul ball was counted as a strike. This change benefitted the pitchers, and thus runs became scarce and outs became plentiful. Bunts became the weapon of choice as clubs chose to give up those cheap outs in order to score that one important run.

The game at the turn of the century still emphasized baserunning (stealing) and one-run ball games. The period from 1901-1920 is referred to by many historians as the *dead-ball era.* This was a time when the dominant pitchers were keeping the opposition from scoring. League ERA totals during this period were between 2.30 and 2.70.

Teams also began relying on their superstars to get them precious runs. Men like Ty Cobb, who signed with the Detroit Tigers at age 18 in 1905, and Hughie Jennings began their journeys into the Hall of Fame.

Following his retirement as an active player, Hughie Jennings managed a successful Detroit Tigers team in 1907-1909. With Cobb (who went on to win 12 batting titles in 13 seasons) as his major offensive weapon, Jennings was adhering to the style of the times. He relied on his pitching staff and his superstar to win championships. Because the Tigers had an offensively weak catcher in Boss Schmidt (who was considered a good defensive player with an excellent arm), Jennings began a platooning system by using Schmidt only against left-handed pitchers. Some reports suggest that Jennings' predecessor at the helm, Bill Amour, may have used platooning before Jennings' arrival, but it was Jennings who popularized the strategy.

Jennings' former teammate, John McGraw, took over managing the New York Giants after retiring as an active player. McGraw had a pitcher in 1908, Otis "Doc" Crandall, who lacked overpowering speed and stamina. Crandall seemed to get hit hard in the later innings of a ball game, but he also seemed to be most effective when he took over for starting pitchers. McGraw designated Crandall as baseball's first "relief pitcher" in 1909. This bold strategy came at a time when starting pitching seldom failed to complete a game—about two-thirds of all starts that year were complete games.

In 1909, Ben Shibe invented the cork-centered baseball, which was adopted by both leagues in 1911. The new ball signaled a jump in offensive levels for the first couple of years. However, pitchers again became dominant by 1913.

In 1902, John McGraw signed a four-year contract to manage the New York Giants for $11,000 per year. That salary was more than any manager or player had ever received.

The 1920s were the era of Babe Ruth. On the heels of the 1919 Black Sox scandal, owners were desperate to find a way to reinstate integrity in the game. They needed some way to rekindle fan interest and support. The answer was Babe Ruth.

Ruth was a player like none before or since. The owners decided to give him free rein and let him take the game wherever he wanted to go. His style of play, particularly his offensive skills, changed the way the game was played. His consistent power and ability to go deep changed the strategy of the era.

Before 1920, the record for most runs scored by a player in a season of the 1900s was set by Ty Cobb at 147 (set in 1911). Ruth broke that record in 1920 by scoring 158 runs and broke it again in 1921 with 177. In all, Cobb's record was topped 13 times between 1920 and 1940.

The record for total runs scored by the entire league for a 16-team, 154-game schedule was set in 1911 at 11,164. In 1921, that record was broken and a new mark set at 11,935, set again in 1922 at 12,059, in 1925 at 12,592, in 1929 at

12,747, and yet again in 1930 at 13,695. Figure 1-1 shows by decade the fluctuation in total runs scored per game.

Power records, often reflected in the slugging percentage statistic, also surged. Tris Speaker's 1912 record for doubles (53) was broken by Speaker himself in 1923 (59) and broken eight more times in the 1920s and 1930s. Babe Ruth's home run record (29), set in 1919, was raised three times by Ruth himself by 1927. The league slugging average ranged between .310 and .340 in the dead-ball era, but in 1930 had risen to .421 in the American League and .448 in the National League. Figure 1-2 shows the explosion in slugging percentage in the 1920s. Figure 1-3 shows how the number of home runs hit by teams has increased throughout the decades (until 1970). By the early 1930s, the dead-ball era was deceased.

Thanks to the offensive shows put on by Babe Ruth during the 1920 season, the New York Yankees became the first Major League club to draw a million fans in a single season.

Some critics attributed this offensive explosion to a *rabbit ball,* a ball that featured the cork-cushioned center. However, investigations into the construction of the balls showed that the only difference was in the quality of the yarn used and that the ball was no livelier than balls used previously.

By the time World War I ended in 1918, the number of professional baseball players serving their country was 247. By January of 1945, more than 5400 professional baseball players had served their country during World War II.

Ruth's prowess at hitting home runs clearly had the most impact during the 1920s. However, a couple of rule changes and some new policies also had an effect. The spitball, commonly used as a weapon by pitchers, was outlawed during the 1920s. Odd deliveries by pitchers were similarly banned. Whereas before the turn of the century a game could be played with just one ball (even if a foul ball went out of play, the ushers retrieved it so that it could be returned to play), owners became concerned about safety of the hitters. Thus, during the 1920s, rules were instituted dictating that clean balls (notice the plural) must be kept in play.

Pitchers began complaining that they were being too restricted. They said the gloss on the new balls was making it too difficult to throw curve balls. In 1921, umpires began "rubbing up" balls that would be used during a game, a practice that is still followed today.

To counter all this offense, pitchers were forced to consider walks not as a sign of weakness, but a strategy. The

Figure 1-1.

Comparison of runs scored per game in the National League and American League from 1875 to 1990

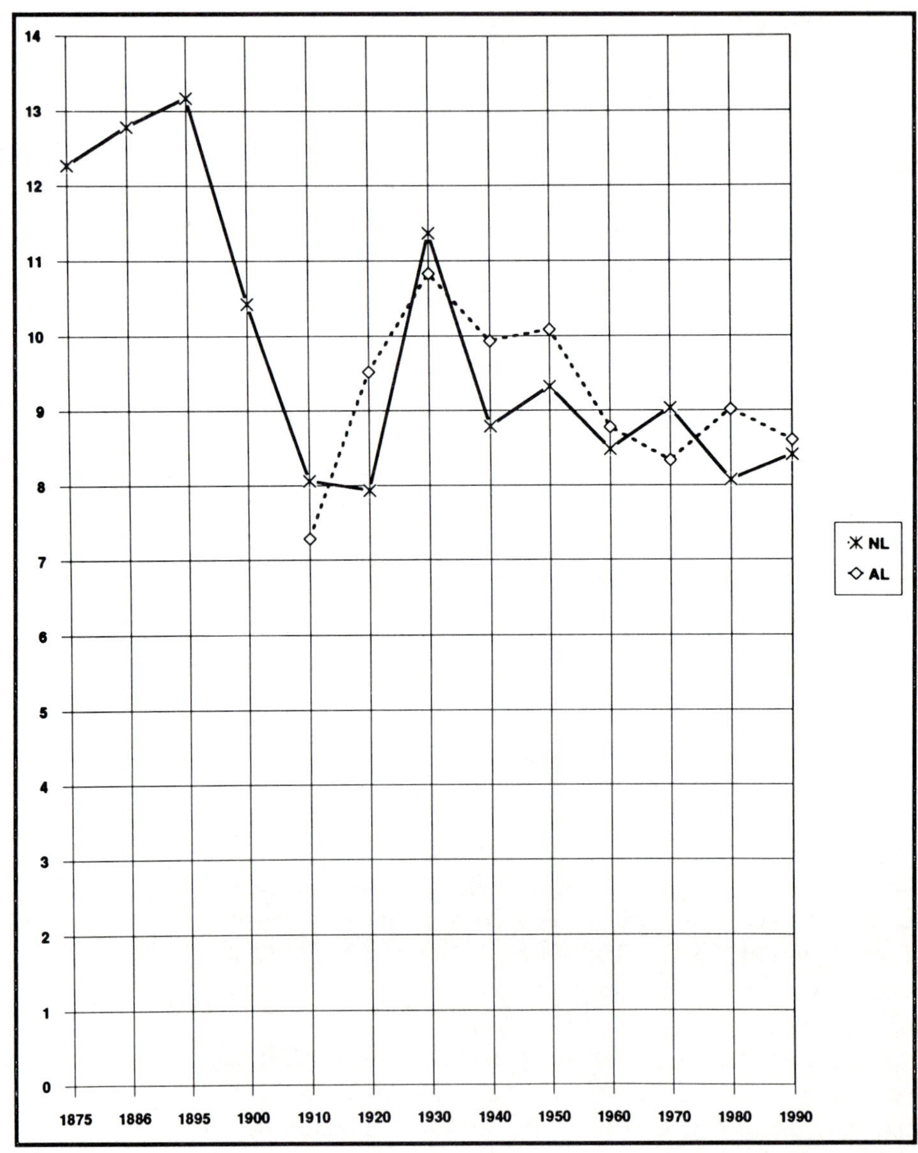

walk became a pitcher's way of working around the big sluggers of the day. Relief pitchers became more prominent during the early 1900s, as reflected in the percentage of

Figure 1-2.

Comparison of slugging percentages in the National League and American League from 1875 to 1990

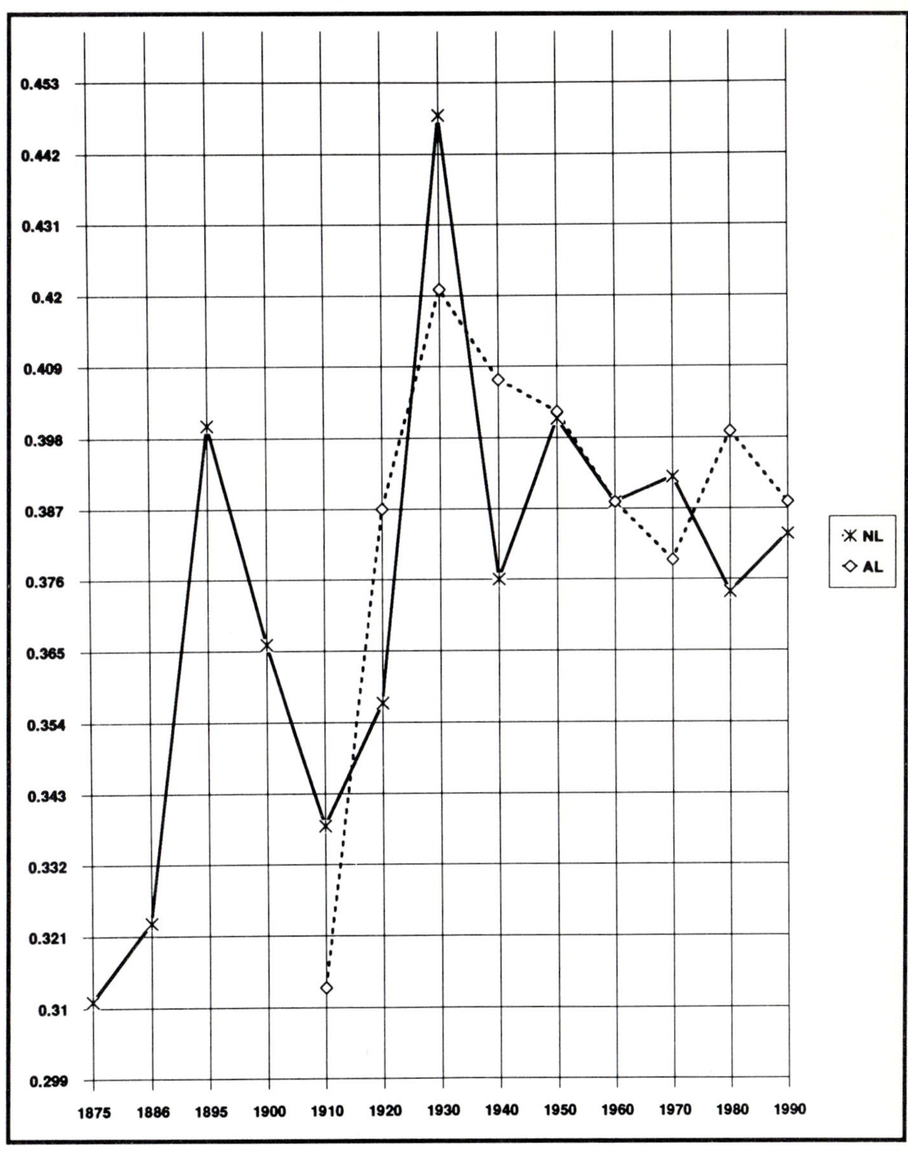

complete games pitched. In 1901, National League starting pitchers completed 90 percent of their games. By 1919, that figure had dropped to 60 percent, and by the end of the 1920s,

Figure 1-3.

Comparison of home runs per team in the National League and American League from 1875 to 1990

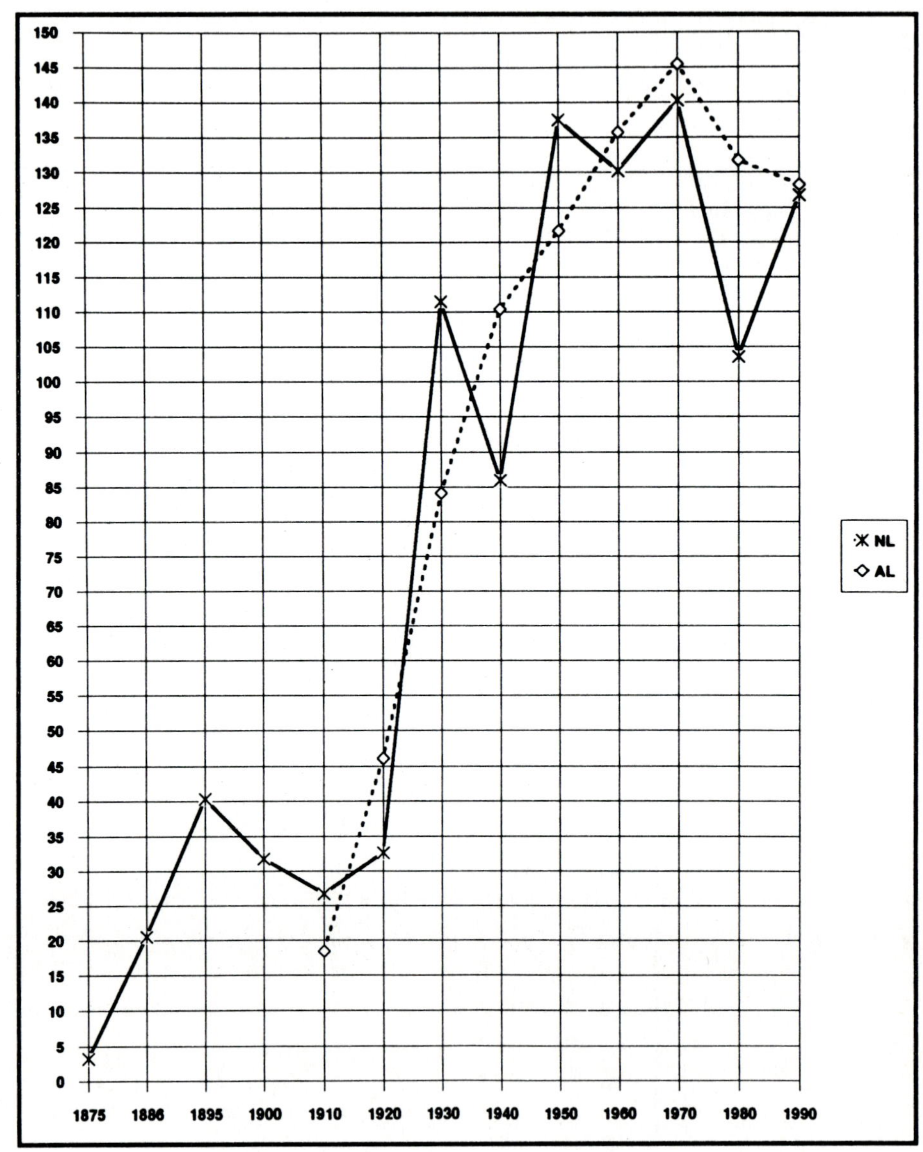

the figure stood at 43 percent. That percentage stayed almost even through the 1930s and 1940s.

The Depression and the War Years

As the country was gripped by the Depression of the Thirties, baseball, like the economy, stagnated. The war years of the Forties similarly affected the game, as many of the top players were called to serve their country. A wartime economy forced manufacturers to use lesser materials when making the baseballs. Thus, the game saw little change until after the fighting had stopped.

In the early 1940s, manager Leo Durocher came up with the concept of a bullpen ace. Until then, the relief pitcher really did not have much prominence in the game. This was the first indication that a manager really didn't expect his starter to finish a game. Joe Cronin used this strategy in 1946 to get Boston the pennant with a bullpen ace named Bob Klinger. After that, the trend in the game leaned more and more away from complete games by starters. In 1947, relievers led their teams in appearances on 10 of the 16 pitching staffs in the league. Five years later, 13 of 16 staffs could claim that stat.

Player platooning, first introduced in the early 1900s, had lain dormant for almost 40 years. In the late 1940s, however, manager Casey Stengel won three world championships using platooning strategy at third base, first base, the outfield, and even utility fielders. Other managers, eager to realize Casey's success, soon began to follow suit.

After the war was over, many of the big stars of the day returned to baseball. Ted Williams gained prominence as a hitter who would wait for a pitch to hit and uppercut it out of the park. Batters began taking more pitches and the number of walks issued around the leagues increased. The threat of the long ball returned to the game.

The Baby Boom Years

The long ball continued to dominate the strategy of the game throughout the 1950s. Stars like Mickey Mantle emerged with that rare combination of speed and power. But the stolen base was not a common occurrence in the Fifties, as managers seemed willing just to get men on and wait for the big shot out of the park. Stars of the era included players like Ted

Kluszewski, who ripped the sleeves from his uniform to make room for his massive upper arms.

During the early 1960s, speed began to emerge as a viable offensive weapon. Stars like Mantle and Maury Wills, who stole 104 bases and caused many distracted pitchers to serve up fat pitches in 1962, were making the headlines. Of the top 19 base stealers of all time, 13 of them played their careers since 1960. The emergence of the weapon of speed during the Sixties at the same time as some significant rule changes during the decade was no coincidence. The strike zone, which had been set at the armpits to the knees, was redefined from the shoulders to the bottom of the knees. This expanded strike zone had a dramatic effect on offensive output. Home run totals began to plummet, batting averages dropped, and total runs scored decreased. The new dead-ball era had begun. Pitching again dominated the game.

Dodger reliever Mike Marshall had a physical education graduate degree from Michigan State University and was known for his exhaustive conditioning program. In 1974, Marshall's conditioning paid off as he appeared in 106 games, which broke his previous record of 92 appearances set the previous season.

The role of the bullpen changed from that of rescuing a struggling starter to a viable defensive weapon designed to ensure victory in late innings. The importance of bullpen strategy is reflected in the list of Cy Young award winners during the 1970s and early 1980s. In 1974, Mike Marshall became the first relief pitcher to win the coveted pitching accolade (106 games, 21 saves, 15 wins). Sparky Lyle grabbed Cy Young honors in 1977 (13 wins and 26 saves) and Bruce Sutter followed suit in 1979 (6 wins, 37 saves). Perhaps even more indicative were two pitchers who not only won the Cy Young award, but also were named Most Valuable Player. Rollie Fingers accomplished that feat in 1981 with 6 wins and 28 saves, and Willie Hernandez repeated that accomplishment in 1984 with 9 wins and 32 saves.

Attendance in the American League declined during this era of the pitcher. To counter the dominance on the mound (and to generate more fan interest), the American League owners adopted the Designated Hitter (DH) rule in 1973. Under this rule, managers could substitute a better hitter for the pitcher in the batting order. The DH, some historians claim, provided a refuge for older, perhaps slower, ballplayers who could not perform at their peaks defensively, but still had threatening offensive punch.

The emergence of base stealing as an offensive weapon during the mid-1960s coincided with the introduction of a new playing surface—artificial turf. Owners were recognizing more and more the significant effect a ballpark could have on the success of their clubs.

The Ballparks

The domed and multipurpose stadiums of today bear little resemblance to the playing fields of the 1800s. Diamonds back then were, literally, playing *fields* that seldom had outfield fences and had ruts worn by the players to signify the base paths. One such park was home to the National Association's Forest City team of Rockford, Illinois, in 1871. Trees lined the base lines, third base was on a hill, home plate was in a depression, and the outfield was framed by a gutter that drained an adjacent horse-racing facility. The first outfield fences appeared at Brooklyn's Union Grounds, which, by the way, served as an ice skating rink in the off-season and was actually flooded during the winter. The early fences could be as close as 180 feet or as far away as 500 feet.

The original stadiums were constructed of wood. Wood posed many structural and fire hazards, but was the accepted structural material of the day. The wood stadiums were often abandoned when they became too dilapidated, and the gradual transition from wooden to more permanent structures coincided with increased fan acceptance of the game. This occurred around the turn of the century. The average fan attendance climbed from 100,000 per franchise in 1890 to about 362,000 per franchise in 1905.

Around this time, concrete and steel became the structural materials of choice and added to the permanence of the facilities. One example was the construction of Shibe Park in Philadelphia by owner Ben Shibe to replace the old wooden Columbia Park in 1909. This new park seated 20,000 with grandstands and bleachers following along the first- and third-base lines. In Pittsburgh, Barney Dreyfuss replaced old Exposition Park with Forbes Field. This state-of-the-art facility actually featured elevators, lighting in the grandstands, telephones, and maids in the ladies' rooms. It also included a unique ramp system for access to the triple-decked grandstand, a system that is still employed today in stadium construction.

Forbes Field and Shibe Park were the first modern baseball "stadiums" to be constructed of concrete and steel and to accommodate large numbers of fans in the stands.

Those ballparks constructed between 1909 and 1923 boasted individuality. When Charles Comiskey decided to build what is now called Old Comiskey Park, he solicited the aid of his star pitcher Ed Walsh in designing the park. It's not surprising that the dimensions of that facility were 363 down the lines, 382 in the power alleys, and 455 to dead center field. This was designed to be a pitcher's park. However, the center field distance was still meager when compared to the bathtub-shaped Polo Grounds in New York where the dimensions were 260 down the lines and a whopping 500 feet to center field!

Night baseball was first introduced late in the 1930s. However, acceptance of night baseball did not really gain much prominence until the 1960s. In fact, some old parks were kept in their classic, nonlighted state for many years. The oldest holdout was Wrigley Field in Chicago. Opened in 1914, that park did not host any night games for nearly 75 years.

Because the league was attempting to devalue runs scored and promote pitching in the 1960s, the trend toward construction of more pitchers' parks is not surprising. During this period, the stands were moved back away from the field, thus creating more foul territory—an advantage for pitchers and a disadvantage for hitters.

Stadium construction in the 1950s began a trend of franchise shifts. The cities of Baltimore and Milwaukee constructed new facilities that prompted the move of the St. Louis franchise in the American League to Baltimore and the Boston franchise of the National League to Milwaukee. Two of the most celebrated moves during the 1950s, of course, were the

Dodgers leaving Brooklyn for Los Angeles and the Giants abandoning the Polo Grounds for San Francisco.

More shifts occurred during the 1960s when the Washington Senators (AL) moved to Minnesota and became the Twins, the Braves uprooted from Milwaukee to a new home in Atlanta, and the Kansas City Athletics left the confines of Municipal Stadium to plant their roots in the new Oakland-Alameda County Coliseum.

Probably the most profound impact on stadium construction, and on the game itself, occurred with the opening of the Astrodome in Houston in 1965. The advent of indoor baseball signaled the birth of the artificial surface, or Astroturf as it eventually became known.

In 1909, George Cahill attempted to convince Major League baseball to use a portable lighting system he invented for playing games at night. He traveled across the country demonstrating his invention, but night baseball would not be accepted for another 20 years.

The turf became the most copied aspect of new stadiums. The cities of Philadelphia, Pittsburgh, and Cincinnati all were completed in 1970 and all featured artificial surfaces. St. Louis even replaced natural grass in Busch Stadium in 1970 with what has been described as a "very fast" artificial surface. Of the 14 municipally funded stadiums constructed since the opening of the Astrodome in 1965 and still in use today, only 5 (Atlanta-Fulton County Stadium, Anaheim Stadium, Oakland-Alameda County Coliseum, Jack Murphy Stadium, and Arlington Stadium) have natural grass and dirt. In the National League, half the 12 teams in the league play their home games on an artificial surface.

The advent of artificial turf, coupled with moving back the fences in newer parks, ushered in the era of the speed game. Because the surface was much faster than dirt and grass, more agile players, speedier athletes, became the weapons of choice for teams playing on the turf. In other words, speed replaced brawn as the attribute most coveted by teams playing on artificial surfaces. The introduction of the artificial surface added a whole new dimension to the home-field advantage. Consider "Rickeyball," where Rickey Henderson leads off with a walk, steals second, steals third, and has three opportunities to get knocked in (if he doesn't simply steal home).

Equipment Controversies

No one would argue that the ballplayers in the 1800s who braved the ridicule of teammates and opponents to wear fielding gloves definitely gained an advantage in the field. In fact, the history of baseball is sprinkled with new ideas that players, owners, and manufacturers devised to gain the upper hand in baseball equipment. Some of these innovations are still with us today. Some have had an impact on the way the game is played and some have been banned by changes in the rules. Fielding gloves, bats, and, of course, the ball are the basic tools of the trade.

Players at the turn of the century would often tuck their fielding gloves in their hip pockets while they took a turn at bat.

When gloves were first introduced in the late 1800s, they lacked webbing or lacing. They were worn simply to protect the hands. Some players of that time even wore gloves on both hands. By cutting out the fingers on the glove they wore on their throwing hands, they could still grip the ball. Today's gloves are so technologically advanced in the construction of webbing, lacing, and pockets that some purists claim they replace the functionality of the hands themselves.

"It used to be you had to catch the ball two-handed because the glove was so small," said Casey Stengel, who played in the early 1900s. "You know how small they were? Well, I used my baseball glove to get married. Didn't have any dress gloves, so I put my baseball glove on. That took care of my right hand and I kept my left hand in my pocket."

Over the years, rule book changes have gradually defined such things as the material used in the construction of fielding gloves, the size of the pocket, the size of the overall glove, and the weight of the glove. These rules came as a result of players using equipment that gave them what were deemed as unfair advantages over their competitors. One specific example was Hank Greenberg, a first baseman in 1939 who had a special netting on his glove that was soon banned. Today's rule book contains a page and a half describing the dimensions, materials, lacings, and webbings of fielding gloves—13 size limitations in all.

Baseball Bats

Other than the fact that today's bat is round and not flat like some bats in the 1800s, very few modifications have been made over the past century. Today's bats may be cupped at the end, may be constructed of more than one piece of wood (the advancement of lamination caused that rule change—several pieces of wood can be laminated into one piece), and may have a gripping substance applied to the handle. Controversies have cropped up in recent times, however, concerning *corked bats,* which have the center hollowed out and filled with cork to allow the ball to jump off the bat surface, and the use of aluminum bats at the Major League level (they are widely used throughout the college and minor league levels).

The size of bats has remained relatively the same throughout the history of the game. Although a length limit is now in the books, the bats in use today are seldom longer than 36 inches, the same length used at the turn of the century.

The diameter of a baseball is 2.87 inches and the diameter of a bat cannot exceed 2.75 inches. The area in which a bat can meet the baseball squarely and result in a straight line drive is less than half an inch.

The weight of the bat and the style of the bat have always been personalized by the players. *Barrel* or *bottle bats,* whose diameter was almost the same from end to end, were popular in the 1800s. Babe Ruth reportedly used a 48-ounce bat, and at times a 52-ounce bat, but required tapered handles to fit his smallish hands. Today's power hitters seem to prefer a thinner handle than today's contact hitters.

Bat speed is the term of the 1990s. Today, hitting coaches are professing that the force with which a ball is hit (rather than the bulk of the weapon used to hit it) will determine how far the ball will go. Because of this theory, bats today rarely exceed 33 ounces in weight or 35 inches in length.

But what if that ball had been "juiced," livened up to spring off the bat and travel greater distances? Would bat speed be as important, or would bulk be as important as it was during the Roaring Twenties?

The Baseball

The controversy over the "rabbit ball" did rear its ugly head during the era of the long ball. However, the rules governing the construction of the ball have changed little in the past century. Today's ball is slightly smaller than the early days of baseball, it contains the cork center introduced in 1909 to replace the old rubber center, and the stitching is now required to be tight (a resiliency factor if nothing else). So why do the balls used today travel greater distances?

Some analysts (and there have been many) claim the ball used today could, in fact, be replaced by the ball used in 1861. One factor cited for increased power production is that baseballs are changed more often today during the course of a game. In the old days, the ball was kept in play until it became mushy or was lost. Another reason cited for a "livelier" ball today is the fact that the yarn is wound tighter than it was in the past. Whatever the reasons, league officials and official investigators have decided that the baseball has never been "juiced up" throughout the history of the game.

Putting It All to Good Use

Now that you have that brief history lesson firmly tucked away, what's your next play? You may have noticed some of the trends of the game during that trip through time and can appreciate the strategies that make the game of baseball so timeless. Consider this chapter as the time you've spent kicking around the minor leagues—you've made it through AA ball and AAA ball, and now it's your turn to come up to The Show.

In the chapters that follow, you will learn how statistics for players who provided so much entertainment for fans generations apart can be used to pit heroes against heroes on the same field, in the same game. You will learn how to mold your team from a talent pool like no other. You will learn how to rate your players, how to spot the everyday player, how to reinforce your lineup with role players and a strong bench, what to look for when constructing a starting rotation, how to use a bullpen effectively, and more. You'll learn what it's like to go through an actual Hall of Fame draft, an experience that some veterans claim is almost as much fun as the game itself. You'll learn how to design that special ballpark to complement the wonderful talent you have drafted as your team. And, because Earl Weaver Baseball is designed around the philosophies of the famous Oriole skipper, you will be briefed on how Earl views the various strategies of the game.

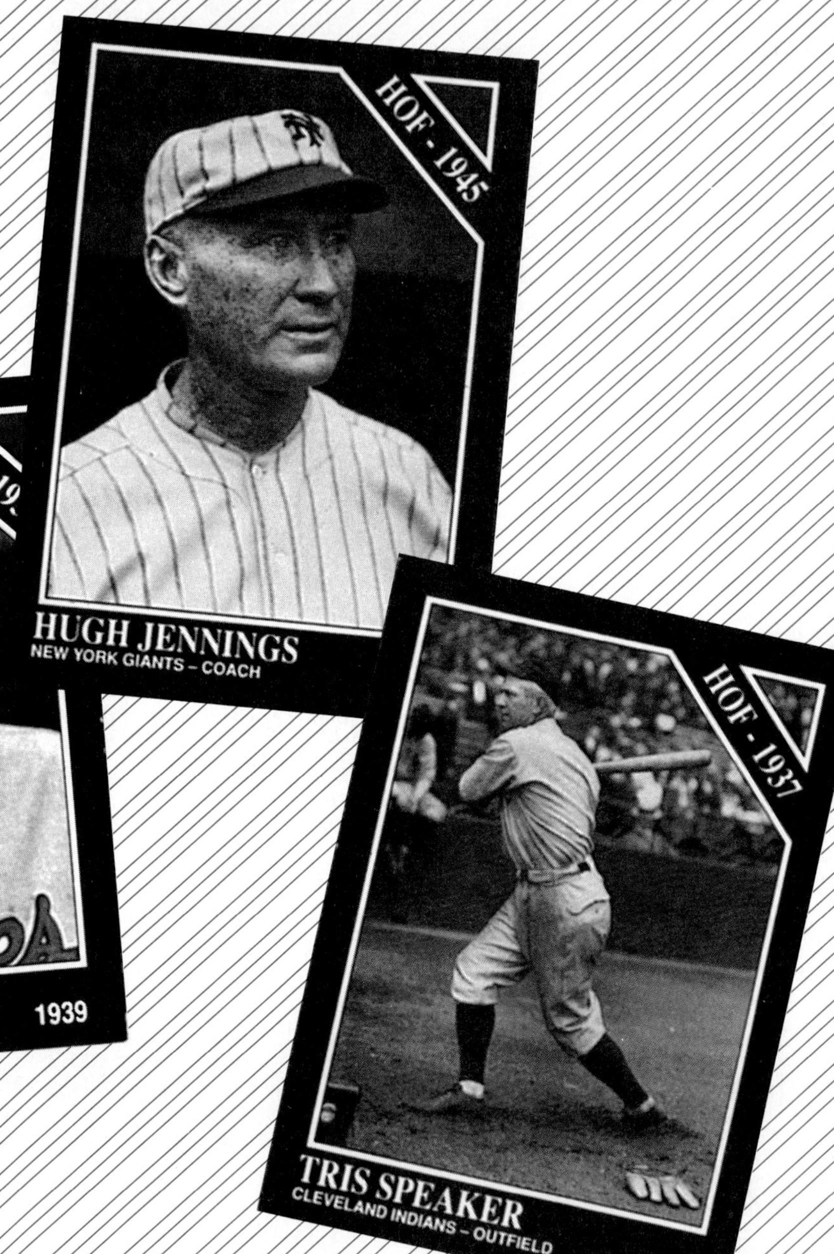

HOF - 1945
HUGH JENNINGS
NEW YORK GIANTS – COACH
HONUS WAGNER
PITTSBURGH PIRATES – COACH
1939
HOF - 1937
TRIS SPEAKER
CLEVELAND INDIANS – OUTFIELD
1924

CHAPTER 2

Playing the Game

All winter long I am one for whom the bell is tolling;
I can arouse no interest in basketball, indoor
fly casting or bowling:
The sports pages are strictly no soap;
And until the cry of Play Ball! I simply mope.

—Ogden Nash

The evolution of the Earl Weaver Baseball game is similar to the evolution of baseball itself. With the introduction of Earl Weaver Baseball II in the fall of 1991, Electronic Arts created a whole new level of computer baseball. The interaction between player and computer has been so refined with EWBII that all you are missing for your days at the ballpark are the smell of hot dogs and freshly cut grass, the sound of vendors hawking their wares, the crack of the bat, and the roar of the crowd.

Comparing previous versions of Earl Weaver Baseball to EWBII is like comparing baseball at the turn of the century to baseball in the 1990s. The changes introduced with EWBII are the culmination of years of feedback from actual users of the game. Among the improvements are a more sophisticated, user-friendly menu system and the ability to program managerial strategies. This book addresses EWBII, but before playing the new game, you should be aware of some of these improvements.

Versions of Earl Weaver Baseball previous to EWBII used a single main menu for establishing system settings and game features. EWBII uses a menu system that begins with the Main Menu and traverses numerous submenus to attain the results gained from the cumbersome old main menu. These menus are designed so that you can make your choices with a minimal amount of typing. As the manual for EWBII states, this game challenges your baseball ability and managerial strategy, not your typing skills.

Older versions of the game frustrated users who would establish settings for a session, but were unable to save those settings. EWBII allows you to save your game settings from game session to game session and to change game settings while a game is in progress. Key commands appear at the bottom of most screens, so you are not required to have the manual handy to look up how to change various settings. To return to the game in progress, you simply press a single key.

The capability of programming managerial strategies adds a whole new dimension to computer baseball. Although Earl Weaver does possess Hall of Fame cunning, and his strategies are widely respected throughout the baseball world, not everyone agrees with all Earl's strategies in key situations. With EWBII, you select a manager for your team, a feature not available in previous versions of the game. In fact, EWBII actually allows you to program your managerial strategy so that when you choose to allow the computer to play your games, you are still actively involved in the decision-making process. Managerial programming is discussed in detail later in this book.

Before you can appreciate how much fun you will have with EWBII and the Hall of Fame League, you must first get the game on your system and establish some perspective on what all the menus and settings really mean.

Installation

The original disks that are shipped with Earl Weaver Baseball contain *compressed* data. That is, you may not play the game with the original disks. You must follow the installation procedures whether you will be playing from a hard disk or from a floppy disk. The installation program decompresses the information while preparing the game for play on your system. The installation process is an easy, menu-driven program in which you supply information about where you want the game installed, what graphics card your system contains, and what, if any, sound board your system employs.

You must run the installation program in order to play Earl Weaver Baseball II.

The material presented in this chapter pertains to installing Earl Weaver Baseball II on the following computer systems: IBM AT and compatibles, PS/2, and Models 30+; the Tandy 1000, 3000, 4000, or 5000 computers; and Compaq. The game requires at least 512K of RAM (640K for the Tandy computers) and an EGA or better graphics board. You may play the game using the keyboard or a joystick, and your playing enjoyment can be enhanced if you have a sound board such as those manufactured by Roland or AdLib.

The game includes three 5 1/4-inch 360K floppy disks or two 3 1/2-inch microfloppy disks. The floppy disks are labeled Program Disk, Graphics Disk 1, and Graphics Disk 2. The microfloppy disks are labeled Program Disk and Graphics Disk. These disks are not copy protected.

Once you begin the installation process, you are asked a series of questions. Do not press the ENTER key while answering most of these questions. The designers specifically warn you not to press ENTER during the installation process unless you are instructed to do so.

To begin the installation program, boot your system with DOS and insert the Program Disk in drive A. Type **A:** to make this the active drive and press ENTER. Type **INSTALL** (you can use upper- or lowercase letters; DOS isn't case sensitive) and press ENTER again. A dialog box appears offering you the following options:

1. Make Back Up Copies of EWB II
2. Install Earl Weaver Baseball II

If you have not backed up your original disks, choose option 1. You are asked which drive will be your target drive and then you are asked to insert the EWBII disks. When you are asked to insert a target disk, you must use three blank formatted 5 1/4-inch floppy disks or two blank formatted 3 1/2-inch microfloppy disks. Label your floppy disks as the Program Disk, Graphics Disk 1, and Graphics Disk 2. You should label the microfloppy disks as the Program Disk and the Graphics Disk.

After you have backed up the original disks, you are returned to the DOS prompt for drive A. Type **INSTALL** to get back into the dialog box, and you are ready to begin the installation process. Once you select option 2, another dialog box appears with the following options:

1. Install EWBII on floppy disks
2. Install EWBII on a hard disk

Always be sure to make backup copies of the original Earl Weaver Baseball II disks and keep them in a safe storage area.

If you choose to install EWBII on a *floppy disk*, the installation program asks you the letter of the drive to which you want to install the game. If, for instance, you want to install the game on a floppy disk in drive B, press B. You are asked to confirm that B is correct. If you press Y, the installation program continues. If you press N, you are again asked to enter the correct drive letter. To install EWBII on a floppy disk, you must use a disk that can contain more than 500K of data. The program disks can be read in a 360K floppy drive. If you are using 360K floppies, the installation program will prompt you to use more than one disk.

If you choose to install EWBII on a *hard disk* (it uses about 500K, depending on your configuration), the installation program asks you the letter of the drive to which you want to install the game. For example, if you want to install the game on drive D, press D. After you confirm your drive selection, the program asks for a path name for EWBII. The default path name (or subdirectory where the game is installed) is called EWB20. If you want to use the default subdirectory, press ENTER. If you want to use a different path name, type it in without using spaces, and press ENTER.

A third dialog box appears and asks you to select a graphics mode from the following options:

1. EGA
2. EGA or MCGA
3. MCGA
4. TANDY GRAPHICS

If you are using a VGA system, select MCGA (option 2 or 3). If you later change the graphics mode on your system, you must reinstall the game.

After you have selected the graphics mode, a dialog box then asks you to select the sound mode from the following options:

1. No Sound Board (IBM speaker)
2. Roland
3. Adlib compatible
4. TANDY sound

Warning: The screen (assuming your hard drive is D) tells you to type **cd D:\EWB20** <return *to change to the newly installed directory, but if you do this you will get an "Invalid directory" error message, because of the last backslash. Instead, use the normal DOS procedure of typing* **D:** *to change drives and then typing* **cd\EWB20** *to change directories.*

Again, if you later change sound boards in your system, you must reinstall the game.

The installation program now has all the necessary information and prompts you to begin inserting disks so that data can be decompressed and copied to the appropriate target drives. During this final step, you are prompted to insert the Program Disk and either one or both of the Graphics disks, depending on which graphics mode and sound board you have chosen.

To start the game on a *hard disk,* change directories to the proper path name where the game has been installed. To start the game on a *floppy disk,* log onto the drive in which the disk containing the game is located. The command that you type to begin the game from either the hard disk or the floppy disk is **EWB2**. If you have installed the game on two 360K floppy disks, you are prompted to change disks before you can begin to play.

The Code Wheel

The green *code wheel* included with the game is a security measure from Electronic Arts to ensure that your copy of the game is legitimate. Near the beginning of the first game of a playing session, you are asked to enter a number from the code wheel. The outer rim of the wheel contains team names and the inner wheel contains years. The dialog box says, "Please find the yearly salary for *this position* on *this team.*" Another box then appears listing the team, year, position, and the words "Enter Salary: $" with a + cursor. This "yearly salary" is actually a code number that you must enter to continue playing this game (or other games in this session). To find the correct number, match the correct team with the correct year and read the number in the cutout box corresponding to the designated position. Type this number and press ENTER.

You have three chances to enter the correct number. If you fail after three attempts, the game is aborted, and you are returned to DOS.

Two Games in One

The Earl Weaver Baseball II game is actually two games in one. You have a choice of playing an arcade version of the game or the regulation version of the game.

The arcade version of the game is called the *action mode.* While playing the game in this mode, you control the pitcher, the batter, and the fielders. You actually determine what kind of pitch the pitcher will deliver and the location of the pitch. You position your fielders to defense against particular hitters. While on offense, you actually control the batter's swing and the runners on base (that is, you determine lead-offs, when to run, and how to slide). All these actions are controlled either by specific keys on the keyboard (and numeric keypad) or by a joystick. Managerial decisions are limited in the action mode.

The regulation version of the game is the *manager mode,* designed for managerial maneuvering and strategy. This version requires more strategy and cunning because you are assuming the role of the manager, rather than the role of the player as you do in the action mode.

Both versions of the game make use of set lineups and rosters, which are accessed through a series of menus discussed later in this chapter. Because the Earl Weaver Hall of Fame League is designed more for managing a team, the regulation game is the mode of choice. For that reason, the discussions of menus and settings presented in this chapter address only the regulation game in detail. For more information on the action mode, see the manual that accompanies the game.

Controlling the Game

To maneuver through the menu choices while using the keyboard, each player has a set of keys designated for a direction of movement. The default settings for the game require the home team to use the keyboard and the visiting team to use the numeric keypad.

The Earl Weaver Baseball II program will not allow both players to use the same set of keys for input.

For the home team player using the keyboard, the following keys determine direction of movement:

Q	W (↑)	E
A (←)	S (accept)	D (→)
Z	X (↓)	C

For the visiting team player using the numeric keypad, the following keys determine direction of movement:

7	8 (↑)	9
4 (←)	5 (accept)	6 (→)
1	2 (↓)	3

The arrows indicate the direction of movement created by these keys and the "accept" indicates that you are accepting the option currently on the menu.

The Quick Start Menu

Whenever you start EWBII, the Quick Start Menu is the first menu you see. This menu, which is shown in Figure 2-1, allows you to bypass all other menus and get straight to playing a game. You will find that the Quick Start Menu is convenient

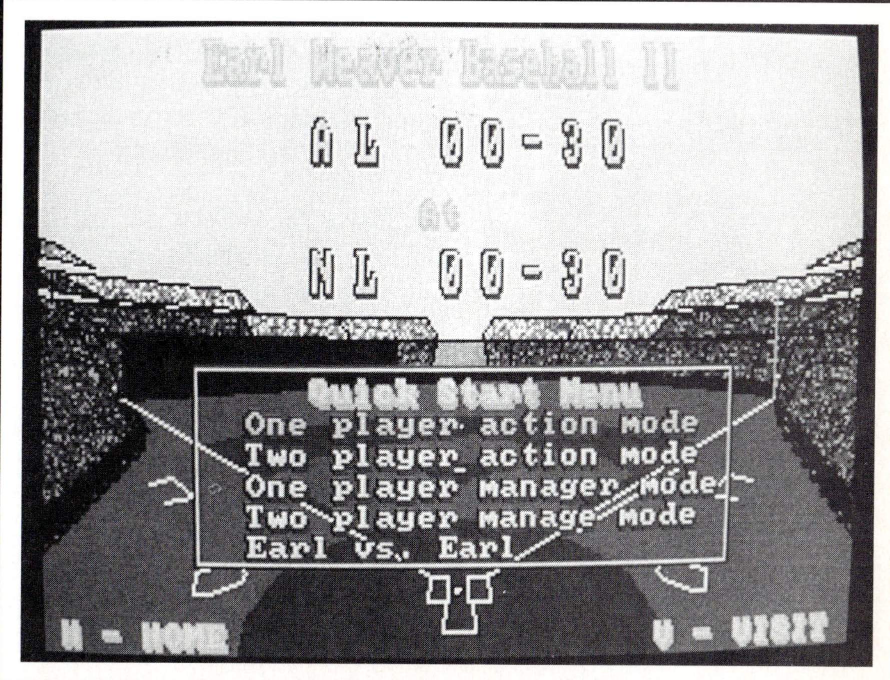

Figure 2-1.

The Quick Start Menu

only after you have customized settings presented in other menus discussed later in this chapter. However, because it is the first menu that you see, this section describes what all the information you are seeing really means.

The last league you played becomes the default league, and thus the last file path you used becomes the default file path.

The top of the screen displays *Team A* At *Team B*, which means that the visiting team is always listed first and the home team second. When you first play, the screen shows "AL 00-30 at NL 00-30", which means that the American League All-Stars of the years 1900-1930 are visiting the National League All-Stars of the years 1900-1930. To change the home team, press H and the program scrolls forward through all the teams available in the current subdirectory or on the active floppy disk. To scroll backward, press SHIFT-H. To change the visiting team press V, and to scroll backward press SHIFT-V.

The Quick Start Menu lists the following five game modes available for playing EWBII:

One Player Action Mode The player is the home team and controls the fielders, pitchers, and batters on the team. Primarily an arcade version of the game, the player is allowed to make some managerial decisions, but mostly tells the pitcher when to pitch, the batter when to swing, the runners when to run, and the fielders where to play.

Two Player Action Mode This mode is similar to the one player action mode, except that two players are involved. Player One is the home team and Player Two is the visiting team. Just as with the one player action mode, this is an arcade version of the game.

One Player Manager Mode The player is the manager of the home team and the computer is the manager of the visiting team. This mode allows purists to exercise their managerial skills, because in the manager modes, the player does not directly control the pitcher's actions, the batter's swings, or the fielder's performance. However, managerial decisions are more extensive in the manager mode than in action mode.

Two Player Manage Mode This mode is similar to the one player manager mode, except that two players are involved. Player One is the home team and Player Two is the visiting team. As in the one player manager mode, the player does not directly control the pitcher's actions, the batter's swings, or the fielder's performance. Again, managerial decisions are more extensive in the manager mode than in action mode.

Earl vs. Earl In this mode, the computer controls both teams. If you are anxious to see how the game is played and cannot wait to wade through the various menus to customize the game, you can access a demonstration game from the Quick Start Menu. If you press D from this menu, the program will begin playing a series of three-inning games matching various teams against each other. These games are played in the Earl vs. Earl mode. If you do not make a choice from the Quick Start Menu, the demonstration game is automatically invoked after a few seconds.

To end the demonstration game, or to get out of the Quick Start Menu, press ESC or F10. Pressing ESC from almost any point in the game returns you to the Main Menu.

You can also load any two EWBII teams and have Earl manage both squads by selecting the Earl vs. Earl mode.

The Main Menu

The Main Menu, shown in Figure 2-2, consists of the following nine options:

User Settings (F1)
System Settings (F2)
Team Selection (F3)
Ballpark Selection (F4)
Change League File (F5)
Ground Rules (F6)
Features (F7)
Advanced Features (F8)
Quit to DOS (F10)

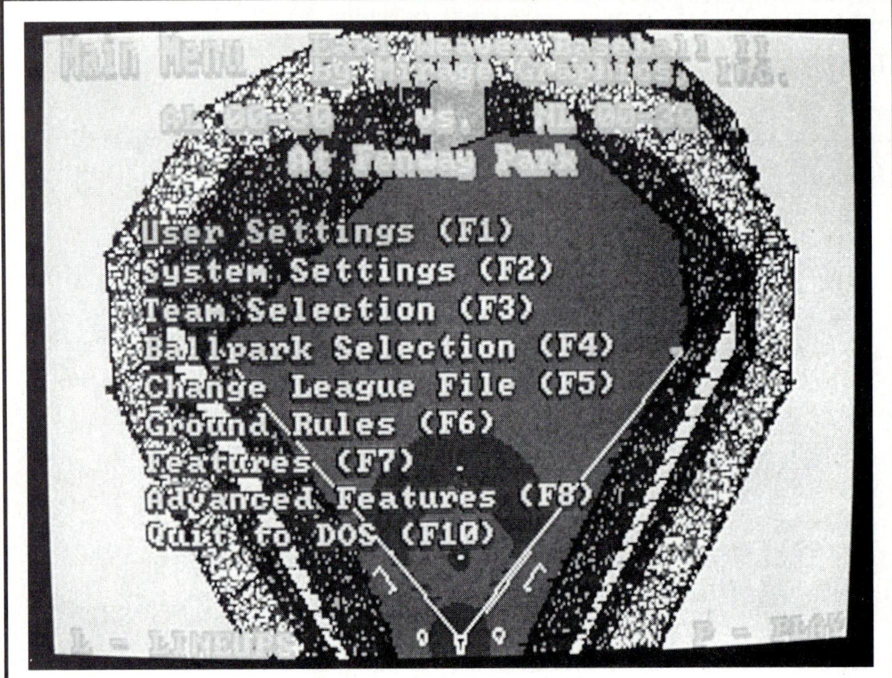

Figure 2-2.

The Main Menu

At the bottom of the menu are the words "Lineups" and "Play." The Lineup option is discussed in the next section, and the Play option, logically, begins a game.

You may either use the control keys from the keyboard to highlight an option and press ENTER to select it, or you may press the corresponding function key shown in parentheses following the option. Each option leads to a submenu with more options and settings.

User Settings (F1)

The User Settings menu, shown in Figure 2-3, has two sets of options that correspond to the home team and the visiting team. On each side of the screen, you see a list of options, which are detailed here.

Figure 2-3.

The User Settings menu

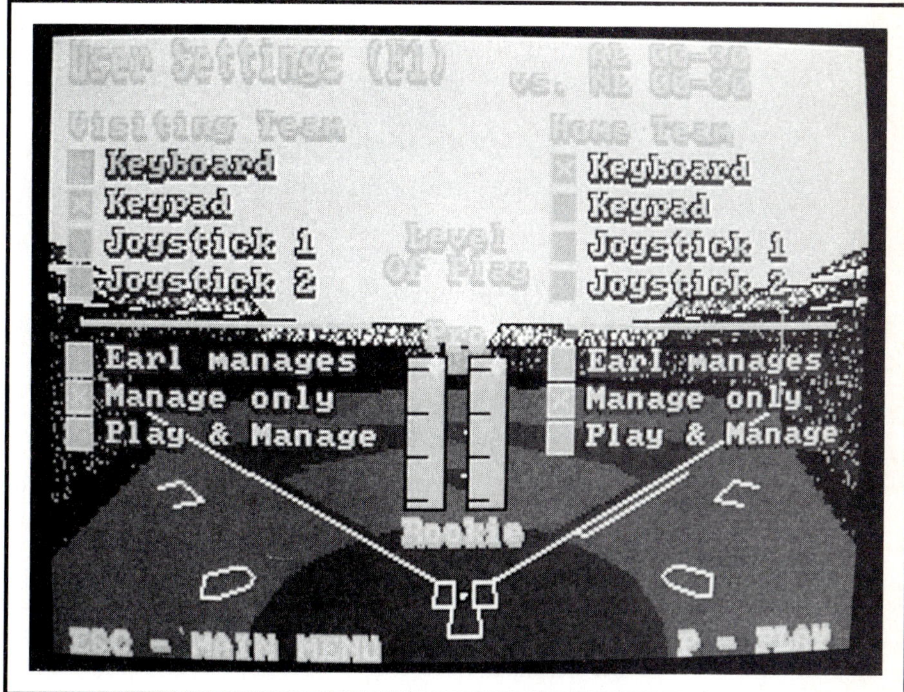

Control Options: Visiting Team and Home Team These tell the program how you will interface with the computer (that is, whether you will be using the keyboard, the numeric keypad, joystick 1, or joystick 2). Note that when two players are involved, EWBII prevents both players from using the same source of input (for example, both players are not allowed to use the same joystick).

Level Of Play The four available levels of play indicate your expertise and range from Rookie to Pro. Of course, all managers in the EWBII Hall of Fame League have set this option to Pro.

Play & Manage Options Be sure to set these options for both the home and visiting teams. These options determine who will be managing or playing the home and visiting teams. You may select Earl manages (the computer manages the team in all aspects of the game), Manage only (you manage the team but do not control the pitchers, batters, base runners, or fielders), or Play & Manage (you make managerial decisions and also control the pitchers, batters, base runners, and fielders). Use the Earl manages and Manage only selections to play the regulation game, and use the Play & Manage selection to play the arcade game.

The Hall of Fame League uses only the Earl manages and the Manage only modes of play.

System Settings (F2)

The System Settings menu shown in Figure 2-4 determines what "bells and whistles" will be in effect while games are in

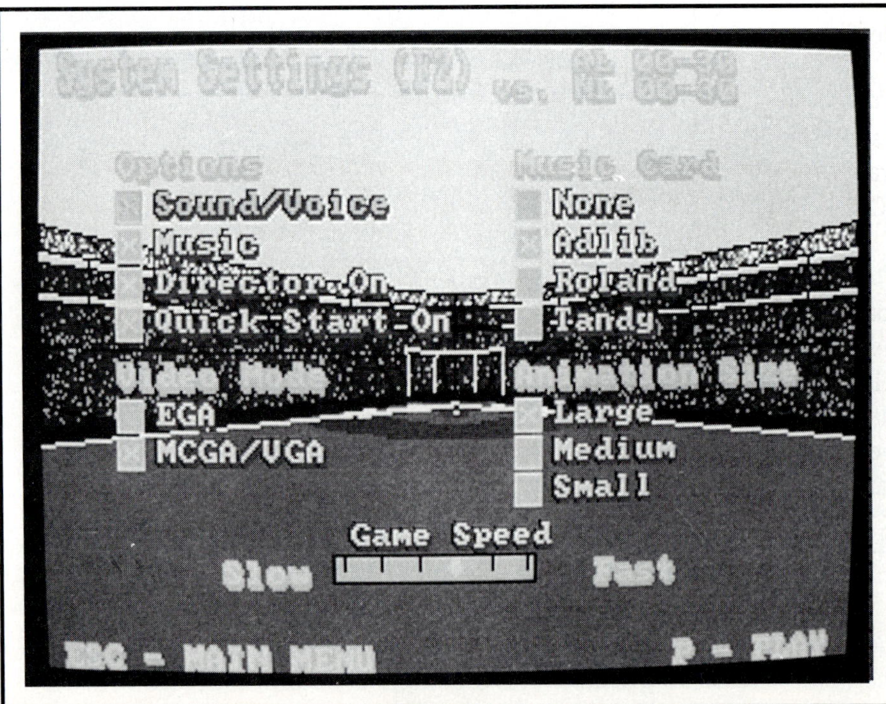

Figure 2-4.

The System Settings menu

progress. You may change these settings at any time during the game. The system settings consist of the following:

Sound/Voice This option toggles on and off the umpire's voice, the stadium organ music, and sound effects that accompany the game.

Music EWBII has its own built-in theme song that will play any time you are making menu selections or when the game is not in progress. Again, this option is toggled on and off.

Director On This option toggles on and off the Director feature used to adjust camera angles for watching the game unfold. The Director feature is discussed in more detail later in this chapter in the section entitled "The Camera."

Although you can alter the system settings for the video mode of your computer, if you change graphics cards in your system you will have to reinstall EWBII.

Quick Start On This toggle allows you to enable the Quick Start Menu so that you do not have to go through the Main Menu each time you start up EWBII.

Video Mode Just as you selected a video mode during the installation of the game, this option allows you to select which graphics card your computer is using. Your choices here are EGA or MCGA/VGA.

Music Card This option allows you to specify the sound board in your computer. The default setting is None, which indicates your computer has no add-on sound board. You may select one of the other options: AdLib, Roland, or Tandy. Note that without a sound board, your computer can still generate the sound/voice and music provided by EWBII. The Music Card option merely allows you to enhance the audible features of the game, if you have a computer equipped with a sound board.

Animation Size Use these options to set the size of the animated players on the screen. The Large option produces a full-screen batter and large fielder animations. The Medium option produces a full-screen batter and medium-sized fielder animations. The Small option produces small batter animations and medium-sized fielder animations. The smaller the animation size setting, the less memory is required to produce the graphics, and thus the faster the game is played. The default setting for Animation Size is Large. If your computer has insufficient memory to load the animation graphics, EWBII automatically plays the game in the Stats & Physics mode (see "Ground Rules (F6)" later in this chapter for an explanation of modes of play).

Game Speed The six game speed selections range from slow to fast. Obviously, the speed you choose will be limited by your computer hardware configuration.

Team Selection (F3)

Choosing this option produces the menu shown in Figure 2-5, which allows you to select the teams that will play the game. By default, EWBII looks in the subdirectory containing the program to find the list of available teams. If you want to access another subdirectory or another disk, you must use the Change League File (F5) option discussed later. You cannot change teams after a game has started. The program will not allow you to access this menu once you have started a game.

Use this menu to select home and visiting teams, view a team's roster (by pressing R), view the current team's lineup (by pressing L), or start a game (by pressing P). The Roster screen and the Lineup screen are discussed in detail later in this chapter. To select a home team, highlight the team and press H. To select a visiting team, highlight the team and press V.

If you highlight a team and press ENTER, a box containing Home, Visitor, Roster, and Cancel options appears. Highlight and select Visitor or press V to designate the selected team as the visitors. Highlight and select Home or press H to designate the selected team as the home team. Highlight a team and select Roster or press R to view the players on that team. These

Figure 2-5.

The Team Selection menu

keypresses are listed at the bottom of the screen. To exit the Home-Visitor-Roster dialog box, highlight and select Cancel.

Ballpark Selection (F4)

You can select the ballpark in which to play your game by selecting this option. EWBII comes with 32 ballparks to choose from, including 30 contemporary or historical parks and two fantasy parks (Weaver Stadium and Homer Heaven). The Ballpark Selection screen, shown in Figure 2-6, provides an overhead and center field view of the stadium. Also included are the stadium dimensions for the distance from home plate to left field (LF), left center field (LC), center field (CF), right center field (RC), and right field (RF). The heights of the fences at these locations are also provided.

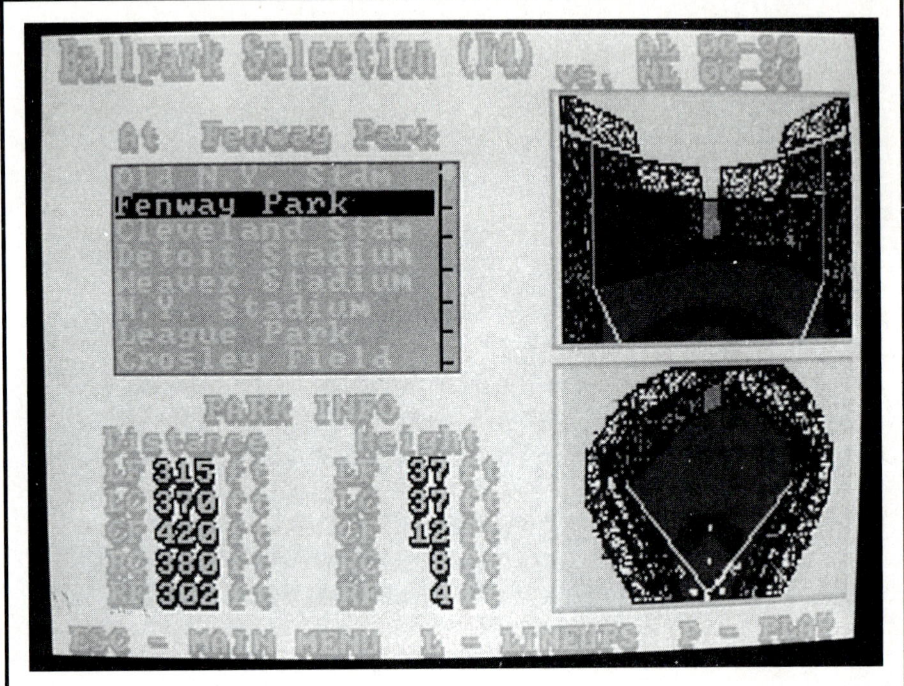

Figure 2-6.

The Ballpark Selection screen

You can choose the stadium from this menu, but once a game has started, you are not allowed to change the stadium. To select a ballpark, scroll through the list of available parks and when you have highlighted the stadium of your choice, press ENTER. The screen then changes to display the name of the stadium at the top, the views of the stadium to the right side, and the dimensions on the left side.

EWBII also allows you to use the Commissioner II Utility to customize your ballpark to fit your team. For more information on customizing ballparks, including specifications on the ballparks supplied with EWBII, see Chapter 11, "Building the Perfect Ballpark." The Commissioner II Utility is discussed later in this chapter.

Change League File (F5)

When this option refers to a "league," it actually refers to a file containing a group of teams designated for a traditional league. This option allows you to specify where the program can find this alternate file. Although EWBII is shipped with a sample league, the Commissioner II Utility allows you to create new leagues that are made up of different teams.

When you select this option, the current path is displayed at the top of the screen shown in Figure 2-7. On the left of the screen is a display box containing the files (or "leagues") in this default path. On the right of the screen is a box that contains optional directories. Use the movement control keys to either select a file from the box on the left or to move the cursor to the directory box on the right. Highlight the file of your choice and press ENTER.

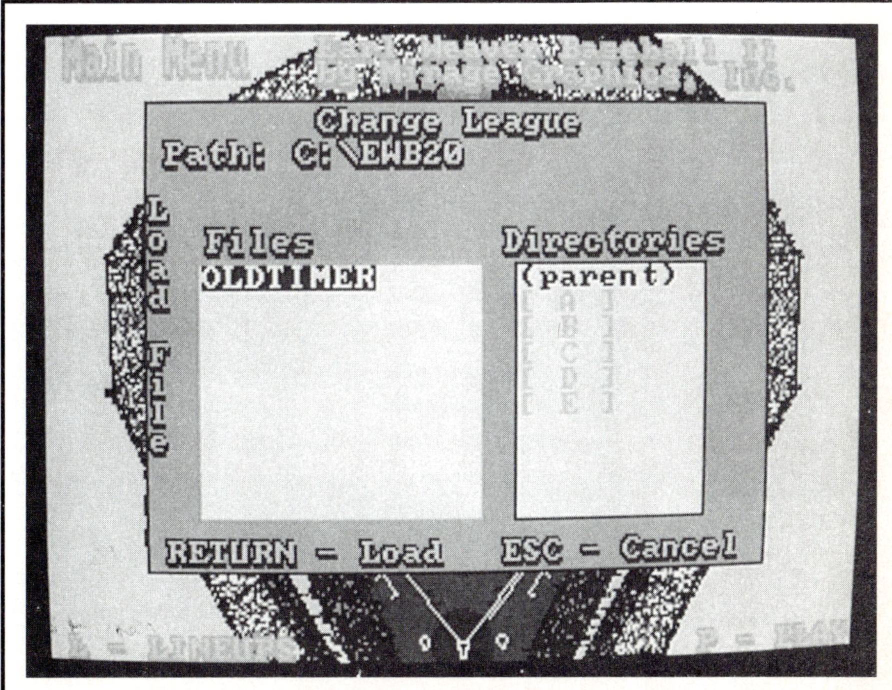

Figure 2-7.

The Change League File screen

Ground Rules (F6)

Ground rules dictate how your game will be played. Consider this option to be your meeting at home plate with the umpires and the opposing manager. When you select Ground Rules (F6), the groups of options shown in Figure 2-8 become available, each with its own group of settings.

Game Play Options (On/Off)

For the game play options, the following settings are available:

One Pitch Mode The One pitch mode displays only one pitch per at-bat. This mode shows the most significant pitch in the at-bat (such as a third strike, a fourth ball, or the batter making contact), so you should watch the ball-and-strike indicator at the bottom of the screen to keep track of the count. This mode is only available in the regulation game.

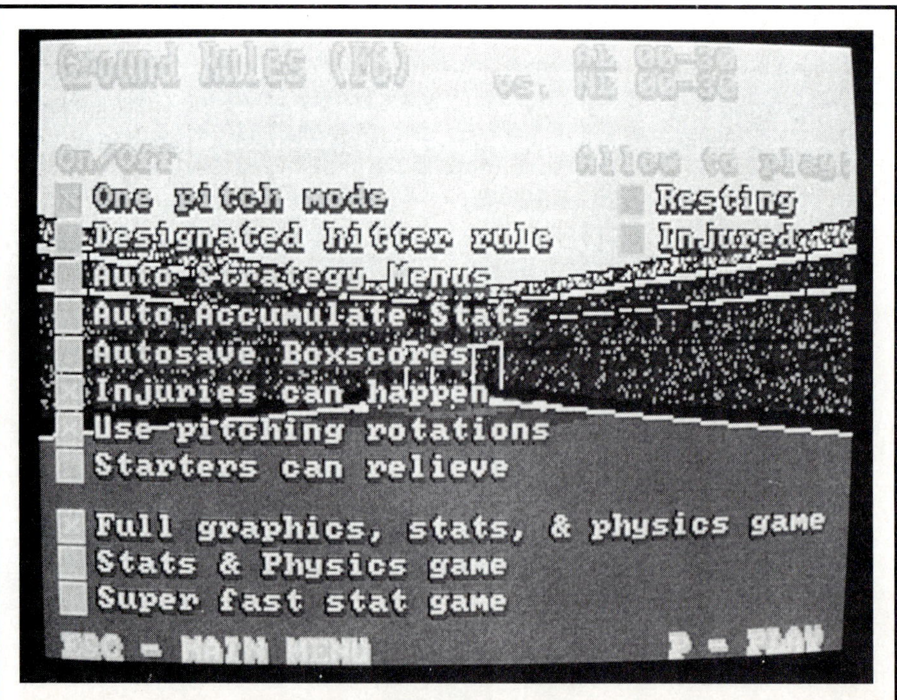

Figure 2-8.

The Ground Rules screen

Designated Hitter Rule The Designated hitter (DH) rule means that teams may substitute a hitter in the pitcher's spot in the batting order. In other words, using the DH means that pitchers do not bat, even though they are still in the game as pitchers.

Auto Strategy Menus If you turn on this selection, the strategy menus (discussed later in this chapter) are automatically displayed for every significant game situation and at the beginning of each of your team's at-bats.

Auto Accumulate Stats When turned on, this selection will automatically accumulate all player statistics at the end of each game.

Autosave Boxscores When turned on, this selection automatically saves a box score of the game to a disk file. Each file is given a .BOX file extension. You may view or print these files from a text editing program.

Injuries Can Happen This is not a warning, but rather a feature that, when turned on, means that a player can be injured during the course of a game. Unless you choose the Allow to play: Injured option explained later, the injured player must come out of the game.

The Designated hitter (DH) is designed to add more offense to a baseball game by allowing a manager to substitute a hitter for the pitcher in the batting order.

Use Pitching Rotations Turning on this option invokes a five-man pitching rotation for the teams.

Starters Can Relieve If you turn on this option, you are telling the program that pitchers who are normally starters (and subject to the starting rotation, with appropriate days of rest) can be used as relievers. If you turn off this option, starting pitchers who are in the five-man starting rotation cannot be used in a relief role.

Game Mode Options For the game mode options, you have the following choices:

Full Graphics, Stats, & Physics Game This option invokes the full EWBII game, complete with all the game action, animations, and statistics.

Stats & Physics Game This option tells the program to keep all the statistics for the game, but suppress the animations. Rather than seeing the animations on screen, you see brief descriptions of the game action. Games played under this mode still use the player stats, wind effects, park configurations, and player attributes, but the graphics are not used. Because of the suppression of the graphics, games played under this mode are much faster than the Full graphics, stats, & physics games. Games played under this mode can be finished in 45 to 90 seconds on most computers.

Super Fast Stat Game For those who are playing leagues and are interested only in the statistical outcome of games, this is the mode for you. This mode invokes Earl vs. Earl, one-pitch games without animations, without wind effects, and without play descriptions. Games played under this mode take about 30 to 90 seconds on most computers.

Allow to Play: For the Allow to play: options, you have the following selections to choose from:

Resting If you turn on this feature, resting pitchers can be used as starters or relievers.

Injured If you turn on this feature, injured players are allowed to stay in a game.

Features (F7) This option provides a help menu of the features supplied with EWBII. You can access these features by typing a key during the course of the game. In other words, to make use of these features, you need not access the Features menu each time you want to activate a feature.

Instant Replay (i) You can review the most recent play of the game by using this feature. You cannot use the Instant Replay to reverse an umpire's call (after all, this is baseball, not the NFL). To freeze the action during an instant replay, press F. To see an instant replay in slow motion, press SHIFT-I.

Home Team Advice (h) When you select this feature, you are asking Earl Weaver to advise the home team concerning the current game situation. To accept Earl's words of wisdom, select Accept on the dialog box and press ENTER. To ignore Earl, select Reject.

From this menu you can also access Home Team Manager's Advice by pressing ALT-H. This feature functions the same as Home Team Advice, except that you are asking for advice from the manager of the home team rather than from Earl.

Visiting Team Advice (v) When you select this feature, you are asking Earl Weaver to advise the visiting team concerning the current game situation. To accept Earl's words of wisdom, select Accept on the dialog box and press ENTER. To ignore Earl, select Reject.

From this menu you can also access Visiting Team Manager's Advice by pressing ALT-V. This feature functions the same as Visiting Team Advice except that you are asking for advice from the manager of the visiting team rather than from Earl.

Improved digitized graphics introduced with EWBII allow you to freeze the action during an instant replay.

End Game in Progress (F10) At any point during the game, you may abort the game by pressing F10. This option has a "safety net" prompt that asks you if you want to save the game.

Save Game in Progress (k) If you are interrupted during a game, fear not. You can use this option to save the game and resume it later. You will be asked to name the file in which the game will be stored. Be sure to keep your filenames simple and *do not* use an extension. The program automatically adds the .SAV file extension to games saved in progress.

Radar Gun (r) Use this feature to find out the speed (in miles per hour) of the last pitch. This is a handy feature if you want to see if your pitcher is losing his "stuff."

Wind (@) This feature tells you the current wind velocity and the direction the wind is blowing. EWBII emulates real-life conditions, and the wind can change during the course of a game.

The Pitcher/Batter Stats option provides you with important information to make key managerial decisions during a game.

Time Out (t) This pauses play of the game. Pressing any key resumes action.

Umpire's Call (u) Be sure not to argue with the boys in blue, but this feature tells you how the home plate umpire called the last pitch–a ball or a strike.

Pitcher/Batter Stats (p) The pitcher's stats are given in his ERA and the number of pitches he has thrown during the course of the game. This feature also tells you if someone is warming up in the bullpen or the name of a pitcher who has just been relieved. The batter's stats are given for his batting average, his running speed, and how he has hit during the course of the game. If this batter has not yet batted during the game, this feature tells what position the batter plays. If this is a pinch hitter, the name of the player being replaced is displayed. The number of runners on base and their running speeds are also shown when invoking this feature.

Open Strategy Menus (Space Bar) Selecting this feature or pressing the SPACEBAR opens the Strategy Menus, which are described in detail later in this chapter.

You can create your own "highlight film" by using the Save Play option. This option allows you to review certain plays of a game by using the Load Play option.

Boxscore (b) This feature allows you to display the box score at any point during the game. The box score is automatically displayed at the conclusion of a game. Included in the box score are the runs scored each inning, the winning and losing pitchers, the save, the number of home team and visiting team double plays, who got the game-winning RBI (GWRBI), the elapsed time of the game, and the predominant wind speed and direction. By selecting "How They Scored," you will be given summaries on game action and player statistics. You can print the box score or you can save it to a disk file. You should not specify a file extension for the disk file since the program automatically assigns a .BOX extension. These files can then be viewed or printed from a text editor.

Save Play You can actually put together your own highlight file for later viewing by using this feature. Immediately after a play occurs, access the Features menu by pressing F7. Highlight this option and press ENTER. Then select a directory to which you want the play saved, enter the name of the play (such as PLAY1), highlight the Save Now option, and you will have created a saved play file. Do not use a file extension for your filename because the program automatically assigns a .PLY extension to the file.

Load Play This feature allows you to load the saved play file so that you may view your highlights. The two teams involved must be loaded in order to load a saved play, the same ballpark must be loaded, and you must start a game between these two teams at this location. After the first pitch, you should be able to access the Features menu and load the saved play file.

Advanced Features (F8)

The following options are included in the advanced features of the game:

Grant a Day Off This option allows days off to be granted to players in the currently loaded league.

Clear Accumulated Stats All stats of the players and all team won/lost records for the currently loaded league are erased. This is a permanent erasure and cannot be reversed.

Round Robin You can play a 162-game (81 home games and 81 road games) round-robin tournament between the currently selected home team and all other teams in the currently loaded league. All games are played under the Stats & Physics game mode (that is, no animations). All stats for players and teams are automatically saved at the end of each game. In order to save box scores, you must turn on the Autosave Boxscores option in the Ground Rules menu before the tournament begins.

Continue a Saved Game This option allows you to resume play of a game that was interrupted and saved.

Batting Practice Primarily a tool for sharpening your arcade skills, this option allows you to take batting practice to improve your hand-eye coordination.

Save Settings and Rules If you want to save the settings and rules for a game, choose this option, and a file will be created to load with the game. You are asked to name the file, but do not provide a file extension. The program automatically assigns a .SET extension to the file.

Load Settings and Rules This option loads a previously saved file of settings and rules.

Utility Programs (u) The only utility program available for EWBII is the Commissioner II Utility, which is discussed later in this chapter.

Quit to DOS (F10)

This option exits EWBII and returns you to DOS. You are asked to confirm that you indeed want to exit EWBII.

The Lineup Card

At the bottom of the Main Menu screen is an option for viewing a team's lineup. By pressing L from the Main Menu, you invoke a screen shown in Figure 2-9 that displays the lineup for the currently selected team. In the upper-left corner of the screen you will see the starting lineup. In the upper-right corner of the screen you will see a list of fielders on the bench, and in

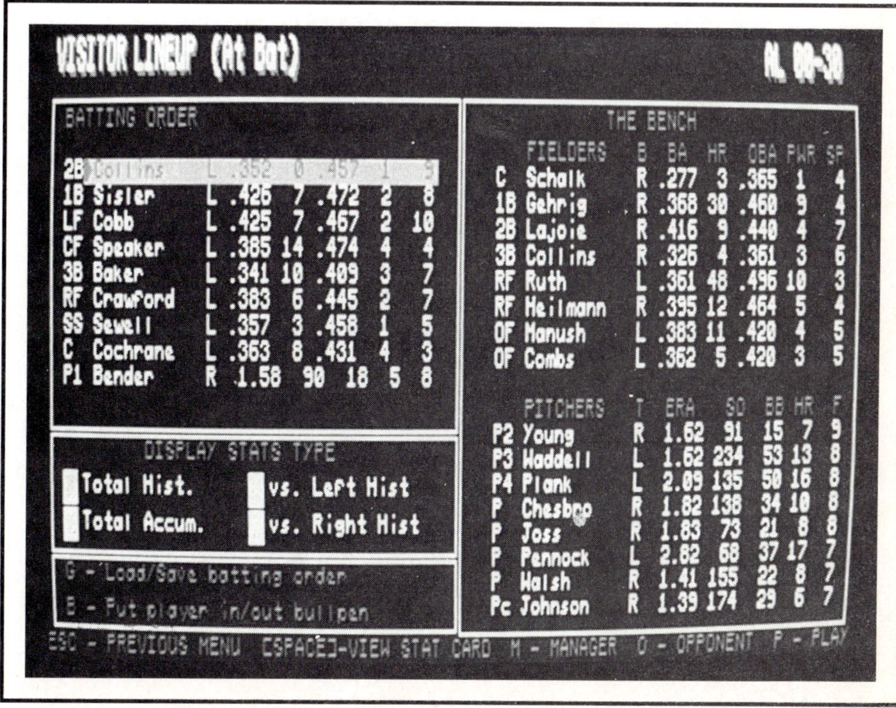

Figure 2-9.

The Lineup screen

the lower-right corner of the screen is a list of pitchers on the bench.

From this screen, you can leave the starting lineup as is or make changes to it. You can rearrange the players in the lineup to create a new batting order or insert players into the starting lineup. After a game has begun, you may still insert players into the lineup, but you cannot change the batting order. That is, once a game has begun you can substitute players into the lineup, but the only changes you can make to the batting order are through substitutions.

If you have not completed your lineup by assigning players to every defensive position, you cannot begin playing a game.

To rearrange players in the lineup, first highlight and select one of the players, and then highlight and select the other player. The program then switches their positions in the batting order. To insert a player into the lineup, highlight the player you want to insert. Then highlight and select the player for whom you are substituting, and the lineup change is made. Before a game can begin, you must have a complete lineup, or a lineup that includes all defensive positions and the DH (if applicable). The program will not allow a game to begin if one team has an incomplete lineup.

The defensive position of a player can only be changed if that player is in the starting lineup. To change a player's defensive position, highlight the position to the left of the player's name and press ENTER. A dialog box appears listing all defensive positions. Highlight the new position and press ENTER. Be sure that all defensive positions are filled and a DH is included (if you are using the DH), because a game cannot begin without a complete lineup.

If you want to view the stats of a player, highlight his name and press the SPACEBAR. A box appears in the middle of the screen with a summary of the chosen player's statistics. You can choose which statistics are displayed by selecting an option in the Display Stats Type box in the lower-left of the screen. You can choose to view the player's total historical statistics (Total Hist.), his total accumulated statistics from games played in the League (Total Accum.), his historical stats against left-handed pitching (vs. Left Hist.), or his historical stats against right-handed pitching (vs. Right Hist.). To select one of the display options, move the cursor to the box next to the option and press ENTER. You may select only one of these stat types.

Other options available from the Lineup screen (but not shown on it) include the following:

Previous Team's Lineup (ALT-P) While you are viewing the lineup of the current team, you may choose this option to view the lineup of the team that precedes the current team on the list of available teams for the currently selected league. Because this "league" actually contains files of teams, the files are listed in alphabetical order. Thus, the "previous" team is the team that appears immediately before the current team on this alphabetical list.

If you are confused about how to set your starting lineup, you can ask Earl to make suggestions on how to set up your batting order.

Next Team's Lineup (ALT-N) This option is the same as viewing the previous team's lineup except that you are able to view the team following the current team in the alphabetical list.

Toggle DH Rule (ALT-D) Use this option to toggle on and off the use of the designated hitter (DH).

Clear Saved Lineups (ALT-C) This option allows you to clear any lineups that have been saved to disk.

Earl's Lineup Suggestion (M) You can use Earl's expertise in selecting a lineup by choosing this option. Earl will examine the starting lineup and suggest a batting order. You have the choice of accepting Earl's expert advice or rejecting it.

Team Manager's Lineup Suggestion (ALT-M) The manager of your team may have his own way of thinking when it comes to the batting order for the starting lineup. Use this option to see what he thinks is the best way to bat your starting lineup. You have the choice of accepting the team manager's suggested batting order or rejecting it.

Earl's Lineup Suggestion/Entire Roster (SHIFT-M) This option lists what Earl thinks is the best starting lineup and the best batting order. You can accept or reject the suggested lineup.

Team Manager's Lineup Suggestion/Entire Roster (ALT-SHIFT-M) See what your team manager thinks are the best lineup and batting order by selecting this option. You can accept or reject the suggested lineup.

Pitching Rotations

The default pitching staff for EWBII consists of five starters (in other words, a five-man rotation). The Lineup screen shows you the starting pitcher in the lineup for that game and, in the pitcher's section of the screen, the next four starters in the order that they will appear in the rotation. Starting pitchers are designated on the Lineup screen with position symbols P1 through P5, which indicate that they are starting pitchers and which spot in the rotation they occupy.

To alter your pitching rotation, select the first starter and press ALT-1. Then select the second pitcher in your rotation and press ALT-2. Continue this process until you have established the order of your rotation. Although you can designate more than one pitcher as your number one starter or number two starter or any other starter, this practice is not recommended. If you prefer to use a four-man rotation, designate only four starting pitchers.

You can use as many as five pitchers in your pitching rotation. You designate the order of your pitchers in your starting rotation. The sixth pitcher is designated as a closer.

Your bullpen will consist of *closers* and *general-use pitchers*. For a more detailed discussion on closers and relievers, see Chapter 6, "The Pitchers." To designate a pitcher as a closer, highlight that player's name and press ALT-6. Closers are indicated with a Pc beside their names on the roster. To designate a pitcher as a general-use pitcher, highlight the name and press ALT-0. General-use pitchers have a P beside their names on the lineup card.

Creating and Saving Lineups

A new feature of EWBII is the capability to set and save lineups for specific teams, opponents, and situations. You can save lineups to face right-handed pitching or left-handed pitching.

To save a team's lineup, go to the Team Selection (F3) option on the Main Menu and designate the team as either home or visiting. Before the game begins, go to the Lineup screen (by pressing L) and make the changes you want. Press G to bring up the Load/Save dialog box. You can now use the saved lineup to override the default lineup of the team.

The Roster Screen

Although many of the same functions available on the Lineup screen are available on the Roster screen, several advanced functions also appear here, as shown in Figure 2-10.

Figure 2-10.

The Roster screen

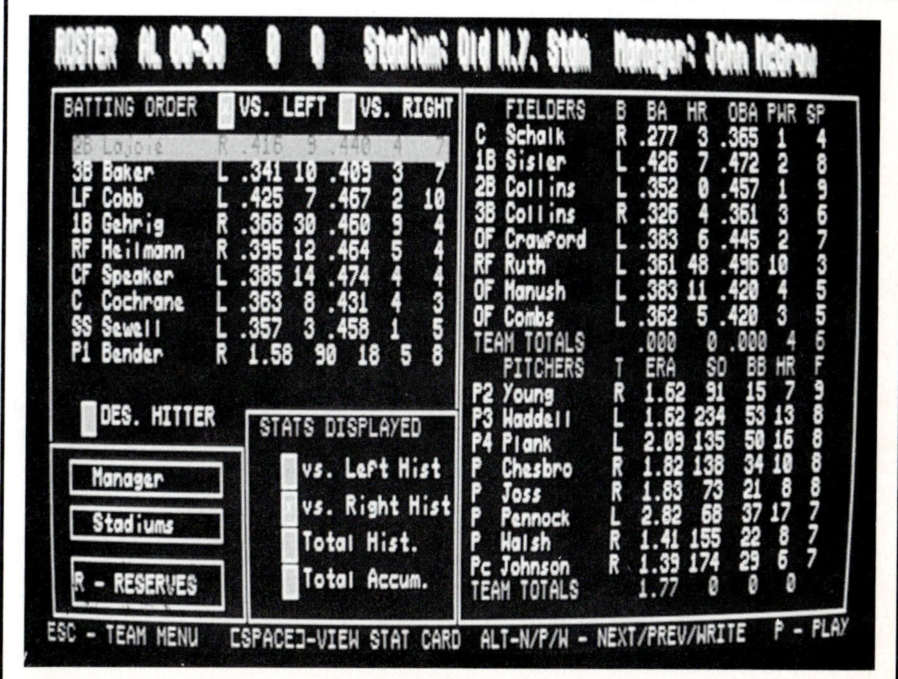

To view a team's roster from the Main Menu, select the Team Selection (F3) option and then press R. To view the roster of the next team, press ALT-N, or to view the roster of the previous team, press ALT-P. From this screen, you can view statistics and lineups, view a team manager's suggested lineup, view a team's reserve players, change the manager or stadium, or save the roster to disk.

To view an individual player's statistics, highlight the player's name and press the SPACEBAR. Pressing the SPACEBAR a second time returns you to the main Roster screen. In the lower portion of the screen you have the options to view a team's historical statistics against left-handed pitching, a team's historical stats against right-handed pitching, a team's total historical statistics, or a team's accumulated statistics from games played with EWBII. To select one of these options, highlight and select the corresponding box.

The Roster screen allows you to view all the players on your team (or any other team) and to examine their individual statistics.

To view a team manager's suggested batting order against right-handed pitching or against left-handed pitching, select the corresponding box. Note that players with an asterisk (*) beside their names are either resting or injured.

To view a team's reserve players, press R. This shows the first 15 reserves on the team. If you have more than 15, press M to show the rest of your reserve players.

If you want to change managers, highlight and select the Managers box or press M. When you find the manager you want, highlight the name and press ENTER. Press ESC to exit the Managers selection box.

To change stadiums, highlight and select the Stadiums box. Choose the stadium you want and press ENTER. Press ESC to exit the Stadiums selection box.

To save a roster to a disk file, press ALT-W. Type in the filename without an extension (and do not include spaces in the name). The program automatically saves these files without a filename extension.

Strategy Menus

The Strategy Menus are used to impose a specific strategy for a specific situation. If you have selected the Auto Strategy Menu option in the ground rules, the menus appear automatically at every strategic point in the game. Otherwise, you invoke them by pressing the SPACEBAR during a game.

Two strategy menus are available to you: one for offense and one for defense. Use the control keys for your team to move up and down through the menu. To select a strategy, press the "accept" key and a ■ appears next to the option. Once you have selected all your options, select READY at the top of the menu or press P. If you have selected Hide, the ■ will not appear next to your selection.

The offensive and defensive options available from the strategy menus are shown in Table 2-1. Chapter 12, "Molding the Perfect Manager," provides a detailed discussion of how Hall of Fame managers react in many of these strategic situations, and Chapter 13, "Earl's Strategy," discusses in detail Earl Weaver's theories on these strategies.

Table 2-1.

Strategy Menu Options

OFFENSIVE STRATEGIES	
Option	**Action**
READY	Returns to play
Lineup	Opens Lineup screen
Earl	Asks Earl for his advice
Aggr	Aggressive base running
Bunt	Tells the batter to bunt
H&R	Hit and run (not available in arcade mode)
R&H	Run and hit (not available in arcade mode)

Table 2-1.

Strategy Menu Options (continued)

OFFENSIVE STRATEGIES *(continued)*	
Option	**Action**
Take	Tells batter not to swing
Leadoff	Tells the runner to take a longer leadoff from base (arcade only)
Steal 2	Attempts to steal second base (not available in arcade mode)
Steal 3	Attempts to steal third base (not available in arcade mode)
Steal H	Attempts to steal home (not available in arcade mode)
D Steal	Attempts a double steal (not available in arcade mode)
Squeeze	Attempts a squeeze bunt
Run 3RD	Runner on third should try to score if batter makes contact
Hide	Masks the selection of options
DEFENSIVE STRATEGIES	
Option	**Action**
READY	Returns to play
Lineup	Opens Lineup screen
Earl	Asks Earl for his advice
Confer	Questions pitcher and catcher on pitcher's status
Guard	First baseman and third baseman play close to foul lines
Hold	Moves infielders closer to lead base to reduce leadoffs by baserunners

Table 2-1.

Strategy Menu Options (continued)

DEFENSIVE STRATEGIES *(continued)*	
Option	**Action**
IF Shft	Shifts infielders left or right
IF Dpth	Shifts infielders in or out
OF Shft	Shifts outfielders left or right
OF Dpth	Shifts outfielders in or out
P Arnd	Pitches around the hitter
P Out	Pitch out
Chg 1ST	First baseman charges home in anticipation of a bunt
Chg 3RD	Third baseman charges home in anticipation of a bunt
Give Run	Infielders allow runner from third to score on infield grounder in order to get force out or attempt a double play
Hide	Masks the selection of options

Converting Previous Versions of the Game

If you have leagues or teams that you created with versions of Earl Weaver Baseball previous to the latest release, you must convert these games to a format recognizable by EWBII. A conversion program included with the game translates the old files so that EWBII can read them.

To convert old versions of the game, first copy the EWB2CONV.EXE file (included on the EWBII program disk and installed with your game) into the subdirectory or onto the floppy disk containing the old versions. This subdirectory (or floppy disk) must also contain the PLAYERS, LEAGNAME, and PARKS files from the old version. Type **EWB2CONV** and press ENTER.

You must convert teams created with older versions in order to play games involving these teams in Earl Weaver Baseball II.

The conversion program asks you to supply a new name for your new EWBII file. Type in the name and press ENTER. Be sure to keep the name simple and do not supply a filename extension. When the files have been converted, you see two new files in the subdirectory or on the floppy disk. These new files have the extensions .EWB and .FRM. You are now ready to use your old league and old teams in EWBII.

The Camera

The graphics animations in EWBII are designed to simulate views from various television cameras located throughout the stadium. Generally, the playing field is divided by an X axis running from first base through third base and a Y axis running from home plate through second base. When the camera is moved, it is usually moved along these axes. You may also raise and lower the camera for different viewing angles. The default settings use these six camera angles: behind home plate, behind first looking to third, behind third base looking to first, looking in from left field to home, looking in from center field to home, and looking in from right field to home. Two types of cameras are used. Camera 1 rotates up and down and camera 2 rotates left and right. Camera 1 is the default camera.

The Director, which is toggled on and off using the System Settings (F2) option from the Main Menu, functions just like a director of a television broadcast. When this feature is turned on, the Director selects camera angles and positions to show the play-by-play. The Director follows a play around the field and provides the best view of the action from the different camera angles and positions. Because each play can be viewed from different angles from different cameras, the Director switches cameras throughout the game.

When the Director feature is turned off, the view of the game is supplied by only four cameras (the three preset overview cameras and the full batter camera). With the Director disabled, each play is viewed from one of these camera angles and the Director does not switch to different cameras during the course of the action.

You can adjust the cameras yourself to move them to different positions for different viewing angles. Press / as a play is taking place or during an instant replay. The play pauses and you see the words "Adjust Cameras" in the upper-left corner of the screen. You can use the key commands listed in Table 2-2 to move the camera around the field. When you have finished adjusting the camera, press / to return to the game.

Only advanced users should change the camera angles used to show games. Without an advanced knowledge of the game, you might alter the graphic display of the action on the field too much and miss some of the key plays during a game.

Because of the dynamic nature of the Director feature, and because of the unlimited camera angles available, be sure to use caution when adjusting cameras. You can easily lose track of where you are. The algorithms used for this feature are extremely complicated, and adjusting the cameras should only be attempted by advanced users. Be sure you do not use this feature with the full batter screen—your program will crash.

If you find an angle and position you like, you can *lock* that angle and position so that the Director can use it during the course of the game. To lock a camera angle, press L when you are in the Adjust Camera mode. A dialog box appears confirming that you have locked the camera angle.

The Director remembers only the most recently locked angle. Thus, if you lock a camera angle, it is displayed after every pitch and the Director does not switch to any other camera angle during play. Once you lock a camera angle, it overrides all previously locked camera angles. If you do not lock a camera angle, the Director takes control of the "broadcast" and switches to the preset camera angles and positions.

To unlock a camera angle, press U while you are in the Adjust Camera mode. A dialog box appears to confirm that the camera angle has been unlocked. Once camera angles are unlocked, the Director resumes control and uses the preset angles and positions.

Whenever you exit the game, camera data is saved in the settings file. You can also save this data by selecting the

Table 2-2.

Camera Options

MISCELLANEOUS OPTIONS	
Option	**Action**
/	Adjusts the camera. While you are adjusting the camera, play is paused during the game. Press / again or press ESC to return to the game
L	Locks the current camera angle
U	Unlocks the camera and returns control to the Director
CAMERA ADJUSTMENTS	
Option	**Action**
-	Zooms out
=	Zooms in
Z	Distorts vertical perspectives by shrinking heights. This distortion may provide better viewing of some plays or situations
T	Toggles between camera 1 and camera 2
[	Toggles left field stands on and off
]	Toggles right field stands on and off
\	Toggles outfield bleachers and fence on and off
I	Raises the level of camera 2
M	Lowers the level of camera 2
1 or 2	Views from behind home plate
3 or 4	Views from first base
5 or 6	Views from third base
7	Views from left field bleachers
8	Views from center field bleachers

Table 2-2.

Camera Options (continued)

CAMERA ADJUSTMENTS *(continued)*	
Option	**Action**
9	Views from right field bleachers
RIGHT ARROW	Moves camera right along X axis
LEFT ARROW	Moves camera left along X axis
UP ARROW	Moves camera up along Y axis
DOWN ARROW	Moves camera down along Y axis
SHIFT-	Using SHIFT plus any camera adjustment makes camera movements in large increments
CHANGING CAMERA FOCUS	
Option	**Action**
ALT-RIGHT ARROW	Moves right along X axis
ALT-LEFT ARROW	Moves left along X axis
ALT-UP ARROW	Moves up along Y axis
ALT-DOWN ARROW	Moves down along Y axis
ALT-I	Raises focus of camera 1
ALT-M	Lowers focus of camera 1
SCROLLING CAMERA FOCUS (EGA ONLY)	
Option	**Action**
CTRL-RIGHT ARROW	Scrolls right along X axis
CTRL-LEFT ARROW	Scrolls left along X axis
CTRL-UP ARROW	Scrolls up along Y axis
CTRL-DOWN ARROW	Scrolls down along Y axis
QUICK CHANGING CAMERA FOCUS	
Option	**Action**
ALT-1 to ALT-9	Changes camera focus to different fielders
ALT-0	Focuses on ball

Save Settings and Rules feature from the Advanced Features (F8) menu. If you want to save a locked camera angle, select Advanced Features (F8) from the Main Menu and then select the Save Settings and Rules option. You can then use the Load Settings and Rules option to later invoke your new camera angles.

The Commissioner II Add-On Utility

The Commissioner's Disk II contains add-on utilities to EWBII. The utilities supplied on this disk enable you to edit statistics of players, sort and display league leaders, view and print out baseball cards, combine accumulated stats from a league, download current stats for present-day Major League players, grant days off for your league, customize ballparks, create and edit leagues, draft teams, waive players, and sign free agents.

Although not essential for enjoying EWBII, the Commissioner II Utility is highly recommended for organizing and managing the EWBII Hall of Fame League. Because many of the features available on the Commissioner's Disk II are an integral part of organizing your Hall of Fame League, some of the features are discussed in greater detail in later chapters of this book. This section provides instructions on how to install the utility and a brief overview of many of the features on the Commissioner's Disk II.

Installation

The Commissioner's Disk II (CDII) comes on two 5 1/4-inch floppy disks or one 3 1/2-inch microfloppy disk. The floppy disks are labeled Program Disk and Import Disk, and the microfloppy disk is labeled Program Disk. Because the files on these disks are in a compressed format, you must install the CDII on your system in order to decompress the data. As with the EWBII program, most installation commands are given without pressing the ENTER key. Do not press ENTER unless instructed to do so.

After booting your system with DOS, insert the Program Disk in any drive and type the drive letter corresponding to that drive. For example, you could place the Program Disk in drive A and type **A:**. Type **INSTALL** and press ENTER. At any point during the installation process, you can exit the program by pressing ESC.

The first dialog box to appear is the Copy/Install box. The following four options are available:

1. Make Back Ups of the Commissioner
2. Install Commissioner and Import
3. Install Commissioner Only
4. Install Import/Download only

Be sure to make backup copies of the original Commissioner II disks and keep them in a safe storage area.

If you have not backed up your original disks, choose option 1. You will be asked which drive will be your target drive and then you will be asked to insert the CDII disks. When you are asked to insert a target disk, you must use two blank, formatted 5 1/4-inch floppy disks or one blank, formatted 3 1/2-inch microfloppy disk. Label your floppy disks as the Program Disk and Import Disk. Label the microfloppy disk as the Program Disk.

The Import and Download programs are used to obtain current statistics provided by Stats, Inc. This company provides an online service (that is, a service accessed by modem through your computer) to provide current statistics about current players in the Major Leagues.

To install the CDII Utility and the Import program, select option 2 from the Copy/Install dialog box. You will be prompted for the drive letter to which you want to install CDII. For example, if your hard disk is drive D, press D. The program asks for confirmation of this drive letter, and you press Y to confirm or N to enter a different letter.

The program then asks for a path name on the designated drive. This path name tells the program in which subdirectory to install CDII. The default path name is EWB20, the same default subdirectory that contains the EWBII game. Press ENTER to accept the default subdirectory. You are then asked to insert the Program Disk and press any key to continue.

After CDII has been installed in the designated subdirectory, a dialog box appears asking you for a path name in which to install the Import program. Again, this path name is the name of the subdirectory in which the Import program will be installed. The default path name is IMPORT, so press ENTER to accept the default, or type in a different name. You are then asked to insert the Import Disk and press any key to continue.

To install only CDII, select option 3. The procedures will be the same as those for installing CDII under option 2. To install the Import and Download programs only, select option 4. The procedures will be the same as those for installing the Import program under option 2.

After the installation is completed, you can access the Commissioner II program from the Advanced Features (F8) submenu of the Main Menu by pressing U and highlighting COMM2 in the Load Utility dialog box. Press ENTER to accept your choice. You can also access the Commissioner II Utility directly from DOS by typing **EWB2 C**, which bypasses the game and takes you right into the Commissioner II Utility. Figure 2-11 shows the opening screen for the Commissioner II Utility.

Editing

The Editing features are used to adjust teams and players, rosters, managers, ballparks, and league/division names. Most of the features are covered in detail in Chapter 10, "The Commissioner's Tools."

Edit Teams and Players For teams, you can edit the name, historical won/lost record, accumulated won/lost record, team color, home field, computer manager, designated hitter rule, and team abbreviation.

The Player Stats option under the Edit Teams and Players option can be used to edit individual statistics of players on a team.

Figure 2-11.

The Commissioner II Utility opening screen

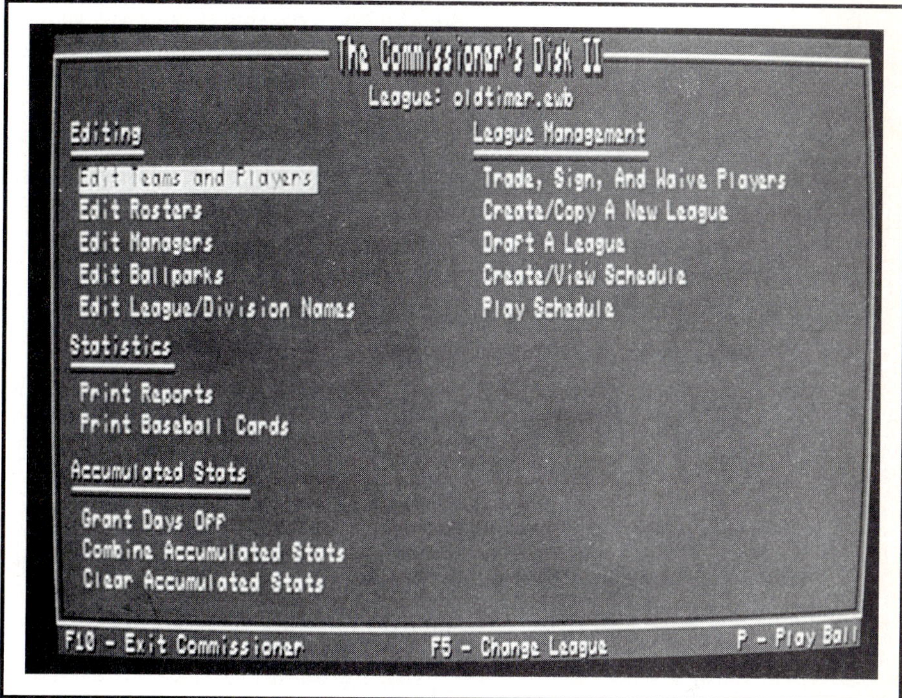

Edit Rosters This option allows you to set starting lineups and active rosters for teams.

Edit Managers Use this option to edit strategies used by the manager of your team in critical situations throughout the game. In effect, using this feature allows you to set the default strategy for your manager so that your games can be played by the computer. This option is discussed in detail in Chapter 12, "Molding the Perfect Manager."

Edit Ballparks This option allows you to customize your ballpark for your team's characteristics. See Chapter 11, "Building the Perfect Ballpark," for more details on this option.

Edit League/Division Names Use this option to change your league name, your division name, or your team names.

Statistics

The Statistics features are included to allow you to print out statistical reports on your teams or to create baseball cards. The two options for Statistics are Print Reports and Print Baseball Cards.

Print Reports This option allows you to display on screen or print (to the printer or a disk file) accumulated and historical statistics for your hitters, pitchers, and fielders. A variety of sort options enables you to view data (or print data) in several different ways to provide lists of league leaders in different categories.

Print Baseball Cards You can display on-screen baseball cards for your players, or you can print the cards to a disk file or a printer.

Accumulated Stats

The Accumulated Stats features enable you to manipulate statistical data for your teams. The following options are available:

Grant Days Off This option grants days off to a team, a few selected teams, or all the teams in a league.

Combine Accumulated Stats Use this option to combine accumulated statistics for players in different leagues, newly downloaded statistics for a player with existing statistics, or won/lost records of teams in different leagues.

Clear Accumulated Stats Use this option to clear all the accumulated statistics for a team, a few selected teams, or all the teams in a league.

League Management

Use the League Management options to manage the player movement in your league, to create or copy a league, to draft a league, to create a schedule for your league, or to play a preset schedule for your league.

Trade, Sign, And Waive Players This option allows you to trade players between teams, sign free agents, waive players, assign players to a reserve status, or copy teams.

Create/Copy A New League This option allows you to create a league from scratch.

Draft A League This option is designed to help you conduct a draft of players in a player pool for teams in your league. The Earl Weaver Hall of Fame League conducts a separate draft and does not incorporate this option.

Create/View Schedule Use this option to set up a schedule for your league. Once the schedule has been set up, you can print the schedule for distribution among your teams.

Play Schedule This option allows you to play the set schedule. You may play the entire schedule or part of that schedule. This option also enables you to automatically save statistics and box scores for your games.

Stats Download Program and Import Program

These programs are included on CDII for those who will be using the Stats, Inc. online statistical service. Generally, these programs are included for those users who are involved in Rotisserie leagues and require up-to-the-minute statistical information about players and teams for seasons in progress or those seasons recently completed. For more information about this service, call Stats, Inc. at (708) 676-3370, Monday through Friday, 2 P.M. to 5 P.M. (Central Time).

Making It All Work for You

Now that you have a perspective on how to play EWBII, it is time for you to learn how to set up your Hall of Fame League, decide who will be participating in the league, and discover how some of the best players of all time can go to work for you. Before you do all that, you should meet a few of the people in charge and see how this organization is run.

HOF - 1938
GROVER ALEXANDER
ST. LOUIS CARDINALS – PITCHER
HOF - 19
CARL HUBBELL
NEW YORK GIANTS – PITCHER
1929
ALL TIME LEADER
ED WALSH
LOWEST CAREER ERA – 1.82
1912

CHAPTER 3

The League

"It [baseball] breaks your heart. It is designed to break your heart. The game begins in the spring, when everything else begins again, and it blossoms in the summer, filling afternoons and evenings, and then as soon as the chill rains come, it stops and leaves you to face the fall alone."

–Bart Giamatti, former Commissioner of Baseball, in his essay, "The Green Fields of the Mind"

One of the most appealing aspects of playing computer baseball is having fictional players face off in actual league competition. By using a pool of "fantasy" players, you can create a "fantasy league" in which your team can face off against other teams in the league. Fantasy league baseball fans discovered the ultimate computer game with the introduction of the Earl Weaver Baseball II program in 1991. Considered by some to be the best computer baseball game on the market, Earl Weaver Baseball II lets you enjoy seeing fantasy teams compete with realistic results.

When Electronic Arts released the first version of the Earl Weaver Baseball program several years ago, a group of Northern California fans decided to take advantage of programmable features in the game to create their own players. The latest version of the program, Earl Weaver Baseball II, retained the capability to create your own players, draft them onto your own teams, align these teams into your own league, build your own stadiums, and, in fact, create your own manager. These fans decided to create the ultimate fantasy league with the ultimate computer game.

By poring through the statistical annals of baseball, these fans were able to re-create the best players ever to play in the Major Leagues. The result of the research and programming of the players has been the development of a computer fantasy league that offers its own league rules, its own front office, its own team franchises, and its own player pool. The birth of the EWBII Hall of Fame League marked the introduction of a fantasy league that could be found nowhere else. Although a similar league is provided with the EWBII game, the similarity ends with the names of the players involved.

The Hall of Fame League allows you to play legends from baseball history in the same league with superstars of today.

The Hall of Fame League can be enjoyed by any computer baseball fan who is looking for an enhancement to the EWBII game. As you read through the chapters in this book, you'll gain valuable insight on how to establish your own Hall of Fame League. You can use this book as a guide to establishing your own league and experiencing the ultimate enjoyment of fantasy league computer baseball.

The Hall of Fame League played its inaugural season several years ago using the original version of Electronic Arts' Earl Weaver Baseball game. The concept of the league is simply to step up the level of enjoyment when managing a Major League baseball team. Rather than managing mere mortals, the founders of the Hall of Fame League devised a system by which you can actually manage a team of mortals and immortals alike.

Just like in the real Major Leagues, the Hall of Fame League consists of franchise owners who sit down every spring and draft the perfect ball club from a pool of more than 150 of the best hitters and fielders the game has ever known (more than 40 percent of whom have already been elected into the Hall of Fame) and more than 100 starting and relief pitchers (more than 20 percent of whom have been inducted into baseball's home of immortality). Those players who have not been elected to the Hall of Fame are stars of today and of the recent past. The criteria used for selecting players to be included in the Earl Weaver Hall of Fame draft pool are as follows.

* A player must have played ten years in the Major Leagues.
* A player must have had a superstar year that was of Hall of Fame caliber (this means the player must have had one of the best seasons of all time at his position, which is used for his statistics in the League).

Once the rosters have been set, the League plays a full 162-game season with a World Series in October (just like in real life!). Games are played either one-on-one with real people managing their teams or franchise owners managing their teams with Earl managing the opponent's team (that is, setting up the computer to automatically play the games).

The Hall of Fame League is not designed to be a gambling game, although both real money and play money are involved. The philosophy of the League is to have fun. A competitive drive provides the wheels on which the League operates. Any money involved merely greases those wheels. After all, history has proven that real Major Leaguers and gambling are like oil and water—they simply do not mix.

Your league can be modified to suit the whims and wishes of the franchise owners. By definition, that's how a league operates. What is presented here merely shows how the original EWBII Hall of Fame League was produced. The guidelines presented in this chapter have worked out well throughout the short life of the League. Always remember, the beauty of the game of baseball is that it is adaptable to the conditions and to the people around it.

Ground Rules

Owning a franchise is as simple as making a commitment, knowing the game of baseball, loving the game of baseball, and paying a nominal entry fee. The Hall of Fame League presented here charges $50 (real money) to purchase ownership rights and admission to the player draft. Enough players are in the pool to set up 10 teams consisting of 25 players on each roster. Each franchise owner automatically inherits $400 in play money, which is used to purchase players during Draft Day.

To the victors go the spoils. Awards are offered from the pot of money collected from each of the franchise owners. In addition to top prizes for the World Series winner (35 percent of the pot) and the World Series loser (25 percent of the pot), individual awards are handed out for being the top dog in a variety of categories. Each of the individual title winners gets 5 percent of the pot for being the League's best in home runs, batting average, runs batted in, stolen bases, earned run average, wins (by a pitcher), and saves.

You must be familiar with Earl Weaver Baseball in order to participate in the League. This is not to say that you must own a computer to become a franchise owner (as indicated in the ownership options discussed next), but familiarity with the game is a must. Knowing how the game is played, and even how Earl manages a team, are tools you'll come to appreciate.

Ownership Options

The original Hall of Fame League charter offered three options of ownership for franchises:

* *Option A: Draft a Team, Set a Lineup, Play Your Games* Choosing this option, a franchise owner commits to playing at least 81 of the 162 games for that team and submitting to the Commissioner, whom you'll meet shortly, a disk containing all the statistics from those games. The Commissioner, whom you'll really like after you've met, will run off any remaining games using the Earl manages option in the game.

* *Option B: Draft a Team and Set a Lineup* This option is designed for those without a computer or without access to a computer. Under this option, franchise owners may draft their teams, set a pitching rotation to match the league schedule, set the batting lineups, and rely on the Commissioner, who's already heard a lot about you,

to play the games. Again, the Earl manages option is used to play these games.

* *Option C: Draft a Team, Set a Lineup, Play Some of Your Games, Cut a Deal with the Commissioner* This option has a lot of appeal to those who want to participate as much as possible, but, because of factors beyond their control, are unable to make the commitment required in Option A. Some franchise owners who opt for Option C actually own computers and *really* want to play the games. Others do not own a computer but are able to gain access to one and use it as often as possible. Whatever the case, the key to Option C is the fourth step—cutting a deal with the Commissioner, who is the heart and soul of this league. Sometimes future considerations are involved in that deal, but more than one franchise owner has entered the Hall of Fame League under Option C.

Variations with Earl Weaver Baseball II

The introduction of Earl Weaver Baseball II in the fall of 1991 created new possibilities for managing your team, possibilities previously unavailable with earlier versions of the game. Although the Play & Manage options of the game remain the same as in earlier versions (that is, you can choose to manage your Hall of Fame League team or have Earl manage both your team and your opponent's team), new Game Mode options have been instituted that could change the way your league is played.

With the newest version of the Earl Weaver Baseball game, you can now choose one of three options for playing your games:

* *Full graphics, stats, & physics game* This option allows you to enjoy the full Earl Weaver Baseball game action, animation, and gathering of game statistics.

* *Stats & Physics game* This option allows you to see all of the game statistics and simple descriptions of the game action without seeing any of the player animation. The games still employ the player statistics, wind effects, park dimensions, and player attributes, but the animation of the game is missing. Thus, these games can be played on most computers in 45 to 90 seconds.

* *Super fast stat game* Choosing this option means you have selected Earl to manage both teams and the games are played with no animation, no wind effects, and no player descriptions. This is the fastest way to play games. On most computers, games can be completed in 30 to 90 seconds.

If your Hall of Fame League is set up to use Earl Weaver Baseball II, the first and third ownership options become more appealing for your franchise ownership. By using the Super fast stat game option, you can now enjoy watching your team march to the pennant while not spending an inordinate amount of time in front of your computer. Purists of the game, however, will probably find that selecting a combination of the game mode options will provide a compromise between time commitment and enjoyment of the game.

Partners and Multiple Ownership

League play can be very time consuming, especially if you've committed to playing at least half your games and you enjoy using the Full graphics, stats, & physics game option. Having a partner can make running your team more efficient because you can split duties. But notice the word "partner" was used and not "co-owner." You might have a capital investor, a bankroller, a consortium, or even a silent partner. But a co-owner will be anything but silent. Experience has shown that someone—and again notice the "one"—must be in charge to have a successful franchise. Two people trying to call the shots merely causes unneeded friction. This is not to say that two people cannot pool their resources and their knowledge of the game. However, someone must have the final say. Once you have established a principal owner and a secondary owner, you have the makings of a successful partnership.

Partnerships can increase the fun of the League by providing you a confidante with whom you can discuss who to draft, how much to spend on which players, how to set the batting order, how to set the pitching rotation, who to trade, and with whom you can make the deals. This interaction might even resemble the day-to-day operation of a real Major League team.

Your league is only as good as the people who are involved and the people who run it.

Trading between franchises can be a traumatic experience or it can be fun. Trades involving partners can also contain an unfair advantage in more ways than just the obvious two-against-one odds. Partners can work another franchise owner by using the old good guy/bad guy routine. While one partner balks at a particular trade, the other partner whispers in the ear of the prospective pigeon, "I like this trade, but my partner obviously has some problems with it. If you throw in so-and-so, I'll give you so-and-so, and I think he just might go for it."

Playing games can be most time consuming. With a partner, this time could be split up. Be forewarned, however, that this split will take careful strategic planning. While you may stick with a starting pitcher through eight innings, for instance, your partner may give him the hook in the fifth. If you plan on splitting playing time, be sure both partners are "working off the same page."

Franchise owners may choose to invest in more than one team. This obviously magnifies the preparation for the draft. However, trades between these franchises are prohibited by order of the Commissioner.

It's about time you met this institution called the Commissioner.

Administration

Walking down the halls of the imaginary headquarters of the Hall of Fame League, one thing you notice is that all the executive offices have gold nameplates on the oak doors. This is by design, for the administrative powers that be are what make the League tick.

The Commissioner

The Commissioner must generate interest among potential franchise owners and keep that interest going throughout the long season. The Commissioner must be committed to the League, have a sense of fair play, and be able to keep track of what is going on in the League day after day, week after week.

A commissioner with a flair for the game, a feeling of the excitement generated every spring, and the ability to maintain that excitement for several months is invaluable. The Commissioner of the original Northern California league has such a flair. Consider this 1991 letter mailed out by him to solicit franchise owners:

THE COMMISSIONER IS BACK!

And a few of the boys of summer have come out of the cornfield with him. They're restless. They've been tossing it around, takin' some BP. They're loose but the summer's gettin' on. They need somebody to choose 'em up and play ball.

THAT SOMEBODY COULD BE YOU!

Face it, you'll always be a kid at heart about baseball. You still can't believe you weren't signed to play Double A ball. Well, now you can do better than that.

YOU CAN HAVE YOUR OWN FRANCHISE!

And these guys are good. They're the best there ever was, maybe the best there ever will be. Your team is certain to be the finest nine you ever put on the field. You can hit, run, steal, and go deep. You've got stoppers and glove men and bullpen aces.

BUT ARE THEY GOOD ENOUGH?

These other guys are good, too. There's only one way to find out. Head to Head, 162 games and a World Series. Then you'll know. But the journey has other rewards...

Once interest has piqued and franchise owners are begging for an opportunity to participate, the real work begins. The Commissioner must distribute the current statistics on the player pool and set up Draft Day. Fees must be collected from the franchise owners. Once the draft has been conducted, all trades consummated, and the rosters set, the Commissioner must use the Commissioner's disk to generate a schedule (see Chapter 10). After the schedule has been distributed to the franchise owners, pitching rotations must be set and submitted to the Commissioner, along with batting orders and lineups. The Commissioner, of course, sets deadlines for all these events and makes sure the franchise owners meet the appointed dates. The Commissioner then distributes a disk containing the set rosters and information about pitching rotations, batting orders, and lineups to all franchise owners. After all that, it's time to play ball!

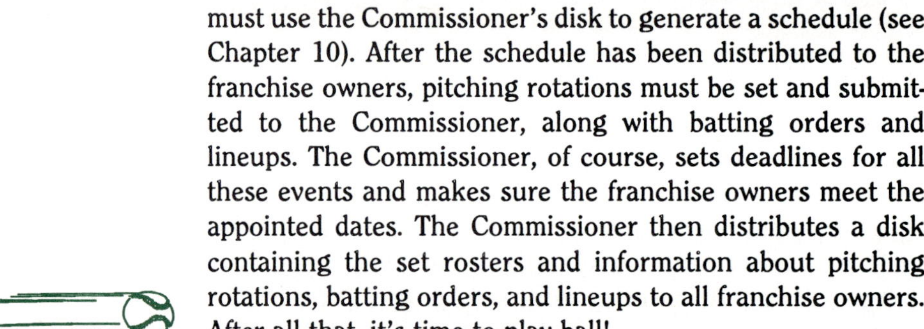

The Commissioner is the focal point of activity for the Hall of Fame League. Organizational and motivational skills are requirements for this administrative position.

The Commissioner's office is the collection point. Not only must fees be collected, current information on roster changes and adjustments must be sent to the Commissioner. All trades are subject to "approval" of the Commissioner, but this is really another way of saying the Commissioner must be notified of all trades so that adjustments can be made at the League office for any roster moves.

Trades are made directly between franchise owners, usually by means of a series of telephone calls. In reality, the Commissioner's involvement in trades is rubber-stamping the moves and adjusting franchise rosters. In a manner of speaking, the Commissioner is merely keeping track of which players are ending up on which teams. Franchise owners are not allowed to trade back players. That is, owners may not trade a player for part of the season under the condition that the player be returned later in the season. This rule eliminates unfair player movement during the final days of the pennant race. No future transactions are allowed. All deals must be consummated and finalized by the trading deadline.

As the season progresses, the Commissioner's organizational skills will have to be complemented by exceptional motivational skills. Teams that are not winning must be encouraged to keep playing–after all, it is a long season and anything can happen. If a franchise owner files for bankruptcy and drops out of the League, the Commissioner is responsible for seeing that the season is played out.

Because of all these responsibilities, some leagues may decide that this is too much for one person to handle. One option would be for the franchise owners to vote on a Commission (comprised of, say, three owners) rather than the single Commissioner. This divides the huge responsibilities that would otherwise be placed on one person.

All statistics from league play must end up on the Commissioner's desk. The Commissioner, after all, controls the pot of prize money and is responsible for distribution of awards to the individual title winners. The Commissioner must also set the date for the World Series and let the League know who the participants are. This all requires accumulation of statistics–as if the Commissioner didn't have enough to do. The League might consider using a statistician for accumulation of all the data.

Statistician

Although the Commissioner may choose to retain control of statistical accumulation, the use of a statistician has a lot of appeal. The League should be notified on a regular basis (ideally biweekly or, at the very least, monthly) how everyone is doing. The honor system is in effect while owners are playing games. That means the owners are responsible for adhering to the preset lineups and pitching rotations as distributed by the Commissioner.

A designated statistician could concentrate on strictly accumulating data and distributing information to the League. Having one person responsible for this duty ensures a more consistent distribution of information, which, in turn, keeps owners playing games. After all, a cellar dweller doesn't get tired of looking up unless he knows he's resting on the bottom. By the same token, looking down from the top is a lot more fun when you know that you are doing it.

League President

This position is really that of a social chairman. This person has nothing to do with the actual running of the League per se, but instead adds a personal touch to the League. The League President is responsible for gathering all the franchise owners at least twice or three times a season so that the owners meet face-to-face sometime other than on Draft Day. Parties are always a welcome addition to any league.

One of the best times to have a party is shortly before the trading deadline. Having all the owners at one place at one time not only cuts down on telephone bills, it provides an opportunity to do some downright horse trading. Refreshments are served, the owners begin to relax, ideas are tossed about as to who has the strongest team and why, who needs what and why, and the next thing you know, deals are being struck in the back room, in the hallway, out on the porch—wherever.

The League President is also responsible for scheduling the formal playing site of the World Series. At that time, the Commissioner could make awards to the individual title owners and each owner could root for the team of choice to take it all. This also provides an opportunity for those who did not win it all to at least participate in the season finale.

Ideas to Consider

For those old-timers who remember Strat-O-Matic baseball days, reach back among the cobwebs for just a second. Strat-O-Matic baseball is basically a dice-oriented baseball game. In fact, the roots of the EWBII Hall of Fame League can be traced back to some old Strat-O-Matic baseball leagues. Way back then, baseball fanatics would draft their teams and gather periodically at someone's house to play off a series of games against their opponents. This, of course, was before the days when you could have Earl manage your opponent's team and you could manage your team. In those days, your opponent had to sit right there with you and roll his or her own dice.

The concept of gathering owners to play games face-to-face has not lost its appeal through the years. After all, playing against a real person, as opposed to the computer, can be a lot more enjoyable. In the old Strat-O-Matic days, the league would gather on a Sunday afternoon at an owner's home or office and simply eat, drink, and play games all day. It was truly a sight to behold. It was also a lot of fun.

Consider having league get-togethers to play several series. This, of course, would require more than one on-site computer, but the effort is truly worth it. Many games are played, much food and drink are consumed, and the enjoyment is worth the effort.

The more often you meet other owners face-to-face, the more enjoyable the league will be.

Your life as you have always known it may be affected during the course of a season. Attention may be diverted from home life to preparing for the draft, tying up the telephone for hours trying to make the perfect deal, sitting in front of the computer for hours on end trying to catapult your team into first place. Try including your family members in the action. A spouse might make the perfect partner in a franchise. This idea works especially well for those who are lucky enough to have family members intimately familiar with the game.

If your league uses Earl Weaver Baseball II, the Commissioner may decide not to risk letting franchise owners play their games over a span of several months. Sometimes family commitments, job commitments, and even social commitments can interfere with owners getting their games played within a reasonable time span. Using Earl Weaver Baseball II, your Commissioner may decide that all games should be played by the front office, using the faster game modes instituted with EWBII. The games could be played in clumps with results distributed at certain intervals, such as every quarter. At the end of these intervals, owners would be allowed to make lineup changes, make trades, and generally fine-tune their teams for the pennant race. You could also institute awards for individual leaders at the end of these intervals.

At the end of a season, most leagues choose to throw all players back into the player pool and conduct a brand new, complete draft. (See Chapter 9, "Draft Day," for more details on conducting the draft.) However, one alternative is to conduct a partial draft. In order to conduct this partial draft, the Commissioner must notify all franchise owners before the *original* draft about plans for the following season. Franchise owners will want to know what will happen during the present season as well as the next season when planning their draft strategies.

Retaining portions of your roster from season to season provides an interesting twist to participating in the Hall of Fame League.

Under this scenario, franchise owners are allowed to protect three "Plan A" players. These players remain on the same teams and cannot be drafted by another team. The initial cash allotted to a team is reduced by the total amount paid for "Plan A" players during the original draft. The owners are also allowed to declare seven "Plan B" players. These players would be subject to drafting by other teams. The initial cash allotted to a team is similarly reduced by the total amount paid for "Plan B" players. However, "Plan B" players can be drafted by another team and the amount paid during the draft will be credited directly to the original franchise owner's team cash. (See Chapter 9 for more details on conducting a draft.)

Notifying League owners of results of games played and updating the League on the standings, the League leaders, the winners, and the losers can be the perfect opportunity to add some class to the League. After all, this is the computer age. Consider devising a newsletter, complete with capsule versions of key series, as a means for keeping the League informed. Figure 3-1 shows a sample newsletter. This task could be assumed by the Commissioner, the statistician, or even the League President. You could even make up stories about antics of the players off the field (the kind of behind-the-scenes stuff we all love to read).

Speaking of players, it's about time you met some of the mortals and immortals who want to work for you. You have some interviews to conduct, some resumés to consider, and some information to digest before beginning to formulate your draft strategy.

Figure 3-1.

Sample newsletter notifying franchise owners of league results

Hall of Fame News

Earl Weaver Baseball Hall of Fame League

Tim Nelson, Commissioner *Kevin Shafer, Editor*

ROOKIES STREAK INTO WORLD SERIES

Playing in their rookie seasons for the Hall of Fame League, Matt Shier and Mike Divelbiss have shot their teams into the 1991 World Series. Both managers kept their teams playing .500 ball throughout the season and posted strong finishes to streak ahead of the pack by season's end.

With the season only a quarter old, Shier made some key lineup changes that kept his team rolling to their first pennant.

Divelbiss, who is known across the league as "Trader Mike," used a conservative draft strategy last spring but earned his nickname before the beginning of the season by making numerous key trades to put together his winning club.

Shier's ballclub posted a solid .251 team batting average behind Babe Ruth's leading .313 average, 44 home runs, and 129 RBI. First baseman Jimmie Foxx was the defensive star all season with only two errors. Lefty Gomez was a 20-game winner for Shier with solid bullpen support from Dennis Eckersley and Sparky Lyle.

Final Standings

	W	*L*	*PCT*
Shier	86	76	.531
M. Divelbiss	84	78	.519
Nelson	83	79	.512
Goldstein	83	79	.512
R. Divelbiss	82	80	.506
Shafer	82	80	.506
Hufford	74	88	.457
Lynch	73	89	.451

Al Simmons, perhaps a lesser known outfielder during draft day, paced Trader Mike's club with a solid .304 season and collected 107 RBI. The solid double-play combo of Miller Huggins at second and George Davis at short committed only seven errors between them all season. On the hill, left-hander John Antonelli led Trader Mike's club with 19 wins.

The Leaders

CATEGORY	*PLAYER*	*TOTAL*	*TEAM*
Home Runs	Gehrig	47	Nelson
Batting Avg.	Jennings	.334	Shafer
Runs Batted In	Gehrig	140	Nelson
Stolen Bases	Cobb	43	Shafer
Wins	Johnson	25	Nelson
Saves	Fingers	15	M. Divelbiss
Earned Run Average	Grove	2.52	Lynch

EWBII Makes Debut

The latest version of Earl Weaver Baseball has hit the market and will be used in the 1992 Earl Weaver Hall of Fame League.

Earl Weaver Baseball II has improved considerably over previous versions of the games. An extensive new menu system, digitized graphics that allow freeze-frame instant replays, managerial programming features, and streamlined user interface are among the improvements.

The 1992 season will be played with computer managers that are programmed to make decisions based on franchise owner strategies. New playing modes introduced in EWBII will allow games to be played in 90 seconds or less.

The player draft for the 1992 season will be conducted December 8. Only 10 teams will be allowed in the league.

For more information and to confirm you spot in the league, contact Commissioner Tim Nelson at (501) 601-5555 or (501) 937-5555.

Gehrig Tops in Two

Managers Tim Nelson, Kevin Shafer, Mike Divelbiss, and Ray Lynch had strong leadership from top performers to collect individual titles during the season. Lou Gehrig might have been the biggest surprise of all when he just edged out Babe Ruth for the HOF League home run title. Gehrig finished the season with 47 round-trippers and Ruth collected 44. Gehrig used his awesome power to collect 140 RBIs for the Nelson club. Hughie Jennings posted a solid .334 season to lead all hitters. Ty Cobb was his usual terror on the basepaths and recorded 43 thefts for the season.

Walter Johnson led the league with 25 wins and Lefty Grove topped all starters with a solid 2.52 ERA. Rollie Fingers took top Fireman honors.

November 1, 1991

HOF - 1979
HACK WILSON
CHICAGO CUBS – OUTFIELD
HOF - 19
TED LYONS
CHICAGO WHITE SOX – PITCHER
1932
HOF - 1985
ARKY VAUGHAN
PITTSBURGH PIRATES – SHORTSTOP
1935

CHAPTER 4

The Statistics

"Say you were standing with one foot in the oven and one foot in an ice bucket. According to the percentage people, you should be about perfectly comfortable."

–Bobby Bragan, former Braves manager

This will be your office. Granted, it's not as plush as the administrative offices upstairs, but this will seem like home to you in no time. The door sticks a little when you try to open it, but just kick it right about *here* when you turn the doorknob. You'll have to excuse the mess–baseball managers are not the neatest people in the world. Don't pay any attention to those dents in the side of this metal desk. Those are just signs of frustration from days when things didn't go according to plan.

Your files (and the tables in the appendix section of this book) contain the statistics the players in the Hall of Fame League produced in their best years. Learning about these great seasons could take the better part of the day. In fact, just understanding the categories (not to mention the numbers themselves) could give you your first managerial headache. Before your head starts throbbing and your stomach ties itself into a knot, let's discuss what you can learn from this mountain of paper.

Baseball is a game of numbers. One for three is a good day at the plate. The pitching mound is 15 inches high and 60 feet 6 inches from the plate. The right-field line in Yankee Stadium is 309 feet long. After the games are played, numbers are the measure of who won and how they won, who lost and why. The numbers in box scores hold the history of the game–the stuff of legends.

In order to gauge the ability of your club or to size up the quality of your opposition, you must understand baseball statistics. The information in the appendixes for the 300 players in the Hall of Fame League provide all you need to know about each player's abilities in order to assemble a winning team.

The Hall of Fame League statistical information provided in this book is based on the historical records of the players. You can enter the information in a data file that can be used to play Earl Weaver Baseball II (see Chapter 10 for instructions on how to do this). The data files for the Hall of Fame League are NOT supplied with the game.

The statistics in this book can be broken down into two major categories: *actual statistics* and *normalized statistics.* Actual statistics represent historical numbers posted by a player for a given year. Normalized statistics, for reasons explained in detail later in this chapter, convert the actual statistics into those the player would be expected to produce in a modern 1990s baseball game.

In the next few chapters you will meet the stars of the League, you will learn how to place a dollar value on the talent you need in order to draft a ball club, and you will learn how to input the statistical information so that the season can begin. But first you must learn about baseball statistics and how games are won.

Putting Together a Winner

As the manager of your ball club, your job description reads "Win baseball games." That sounds simple enough. Since the team scoring the most runs wins the game, all you have to do is put together a team that scores more runs than it gives up. Runs translate into wins. In spite of the times you win 4-3 and lose 12-1, usually the team that scores more runs than it gives up over a season wins more baseball games than it loses.

Over the history of Major League baseball, each team has averaged about 4.5 runs per game. How many runs are necessary to add a victory to the win column of a .500 ball club (one that wins 81 and loses 81)? Analysis establishes that, over the course of a season, for every 9 runs a team can score in excess of the runs scored by its opponents, it chalks up one victory more (and one loss less) than a .500 ball club.

You have many weapons at your disposal to achieve a positive run margin. For example, your team might have great power hitters who can knock the ball out of the park, a stellar pitching rotation with pitchers who give up few runs per game, a great defensive club that makes the opposition earn every run, or a team with great speed on the base paths to take advantage of all possible scoring opportunities.

Your team philosophy dictates the character of your team. By establishing what character you want your team to assume, you determine which players to include on your roster.

You may not have a team that possesses all of these traits, but you certainly can have a team with more than one of them. For example, you might field a team that boasts great hitting and good pitching, such as the Yankee teams of the 1920s. Or you might have a team that has great pitching, superior defense, and blinding speed, such as the Dodger teams of the 1960s. You could have a squad resembling Earl Weaver's Oriole teams of the 1960s, characterized by great pitching and great power at the plate.

Winning championships in the Earl Weaver Hall of Fame League is not easy. The differences between teams in the League is slight. Because of the level of talent in the player pool, a full 162-game season is necessary to determine a champion. Even after playing 162 games, the difference in the standings between the League champion and the team occupying the cellar is rarely more than 15 victories. That means that coming up short in your close games could prove to be the difference between winning the pennant and coming in second.

In order to put together a winner, you must fulfill four objectives. First, you must establish a team philosophy. That philosophy provides the character of your team—will you stock up on pitching, hitting, speed, or fielding? Second, you must draft the best players available to fit into your team philosophy. Your top 6 or 8 players are more important to your team than your last 10 to 12 players because they will figure in the outcome of more plays per game. You should not, however, minimize the importance of bench strength, as discussed in Chapter 7. Third, you must design a ballpark that is consistent with your team philosophy. Chapter 11 teaches you how to customize your ballpark to take advantage of your team's strengths or minimize its weaknesses. Finally, you must manage your team according to your team philosophy. Chapter 12 examines different managing styles and how to customize a manager to fit your team.

Fulfilling all four objectives is the key to fielding a winning ball club. Falling short on any of the four may cost you the pennant. These objectives, however, are merely strategic. Your tactical goal is to win ball games. In order to do that, you must understand how runs are created and how they are prevented.

Run Production

In the game of baseball, 16 different events advance a runner at least one base and ideally produce runs.

The batter can advance one or more bases in the following seven ways:

* Hitting a home run
* Hitting a triple
* Hitting a double
* Hitting a single
* Walking
* Being hit by a pitch
* Being awarded first base because of the catcher's interference

A base runner can advance one or more bases by

* Earning an extra-base advancement
* Stealing a base

* Advancing on a balk by the pitcher
* Advancing on a wild pitch by the pitcher
* Advancing on a passed ball by the catcher
* Advancing because of a fielder's indifference

Both the batter and the base runner can advance one or more bases because of

* A fielding error
* Interference
* Obstruction

Nine of these events (catcher's interference, an extra-base advancement, a balk, a wild pitch, a passed ball, fielder indifference, a fielding error, interference, and obstruction) occur so infrequently that they are insignificant. The remaining seven events (home runs, singles, doubles, triples, walks, hit-by-pitch, and stolen bases) result in nearly all the runs that are scored.

In its most basic form, baseball is a game in which the team scoring the most runs before recording a predetermined number of outs wins the game. Runs scored and outs are the two elements common to all games of baseball.

Remember those summer afternoons when you and your buddies would grab a Whiffle ball and bat, gather in someone's backyard (preferably one with a fence), and crank up a game of Home Run Derby? That sandlot game was based on a 1950s television show in which Major League sluggers would compete to see who could hit the most home runs. The rules of Home Run Derby reflect baseball at its simplest–hit a home run and you score a run; anything else is an out. The one to score the most runs wins. Sound familiar?

The two basic components of Home Run Derby are runs and outs, just as in the regular game of baseball. Outs are the currency of the game. You have 27 outs to spend in a regular nine-inning ball game. The number of runs you score (and obviously your ability to win) is determined by how frequently you make outs. Thus, the runs created (produced by the seven events mentioned previously) and the number of outs you make while creating them are the real measures of success and failure in baseball.

Linear Weights

In 1978, baseball statistician Pete Palmer ran a computer simulation of every Major League baseball game played since 1901. His purpose was to establish a unified system of values for the average amount of runs produced by each base-advancing event in the game. This massive simulation established each event's relative value in terms of runs scored. Those values are as follows:

Event	Average Runs Scored
Home run	1.40
Triple	1.09
Double	0.78
Single	0.47
Walk	0.33
Hit by pitch	0.33
Stolen base	0.30

In other words, a home run (which, remember, can be a solo shot or with men on) produces an average of 1.40 runs per game, a single produces an average of 0.47 runs per game, and so on.

To complete his analysis, Palmer then considered the run-preventing value of outs. Over baseball history, the average cost of an out has fluctuated depending on the conditions of play. For example, an out made in a hitter's year costs a team more runs than an out made in a pitcher's year. Palmer's analysis showed that, over the history of Major League baseball, an out cost a team 0.27 runs per game.

Through this computer analysis, Palmer succeeded in relating the two basic components of the game—runs and outs—and he did so using historical statistics of actual games. His next step was to use these values to devise the *linear weights system*, a system that baseball statisticians can use to measure the relative performances of ballplayers from year to year.

In the linear weights system, an average ballplayer is defined as producing zero runs per game. In other words, if you add the values of all the base-advancing events in which the average player was involved and subtract the value of all the outs in which he was involved, the sum would be zero. This means that if a ballplayer is below the league average, he actually costs his teams runs and, therefore, wins.

By defining the performance of an average ballplayer, you can then use the linear weights system to evaluate the performance of other ballplayers as they relate to the performance of the average ballplayer. The four categories in the linear weights system are batting runs, stealing runs, fielding runs, and pitching runs. Since the average ballplayer is defined as zero, a positive number in any of these four categories reflects how far above average a player has performed. The players of the Hall of Fame League produced more linear weight runs at the positions they played than anyone else in the history of the game.

Batting Runs

In order to find the number of batting runs produced by a player, you first must calculate his positive run production. This is determined by multiplying the base-advancing events achieved by a batter by each event's linear weights value. The linear weights runs produced for each type of base-advancing event are then added together to establish the player's positive run production. The formula for that number is

$$(.47)1B + (.78)2B + (1.09)3B + (1.40)HR + (.33)BB + (.33)HBP$$

where 1B is the number of singles hit, 2B is the number of doubles, 3B is the number of triples, HR is the number of home runs, BB is the number of times the player walked, and HBP is the number of times the player was hit by a pitch.

Unfortunately, our player also made outs, which cost his team runs. To determine the number of runs that the player cost his team, you use the following formula:

(AVO)(AB–H) - .50(OOB)

where AVO is the average value of an out in the league and year of the season chosen, the number of at-bats (AB) minus the number of hits (H) is the actual number of outs he made, and OOB is the number of outs made while he was on base (such as being the front end of a double play or the victim of a fielder's choice). The average value of an out is computed as the positive run production of the entire league divided by the total number of outs made during the season. The data for OOB is extremely hard to find in historical baseball statistics. Therefore, this part of the formula is generally disregarded.

Armed with the number of positive runs produced by a player's base-advancing events and the number of negative runs attributable to the outs the player made, you can now calculate his batting runs. Simply subtract the negative runs from the positive runs, and you know how well your particular player performed at the plate.

Stealing Runs

The linear weights system says that a base stealer must be successful more than two-thirds of the time in order to help his team. If a player is successful less than two-thirds of the time, he is actually costing his team more runs by making outs than he creates by stealing successfully.

The number of bases stolen is not a true measure of a player's performance as a base runner. You must penalize the player for failing to steal because the out costs your team runs. The formula for stealing runs takes this into consideration by assigning a negative run value to the number of times caught stealing. The formula for stealing runs is as follows

(.30)SB - (.60)CS

where SB is the number of stolen bases and CS is the number of times the player was caught stealing.

Back in the early days of baseball, the times that a player was caught stealing were often not recorded. Because of this missing data, the stealing runs for some of the players from these days have been estimated.

Fielding Runs

This linear weights fielding measure is somewhat complicated. It is designed to identify the runs that were saved by good fielding, and then compare that number to the average number of runs saved by an average fielder at a particular position. The complexity arises when you consider that certain positions require different levels of fielding skill. The formula is designed, therefore, to take into account the differing demands of the various positions on the field.

For second basemen, shortstops, and third basemen, the formula to determine the league average is

$$\text{Avg. pos. league} = (.20(PO + 2A - E + DP)_{\text{league at position}}) / (PO_{\text{league total}} - K_{\text{league total}})$$

where PO is putouts, A is assists, E is errors, DP is double plays, and K is strikeouts.

You then determine the total innings in which a player participated. To derive that number, you use an estimate based on his fielding record and his number of plate appearances.

Once all that information is determined, you are now able to calculate the fielding runs for the most skilled positions on the field—the second baseman, shortstop, and third baseman:

$$\text{Fielding runs} = .20(PO + 2A - E + DP)_{\text{player}} - \text{avg. pos. league} * (PO_{\text{team}} - K_{\text{team}})(I_{\text{player}} / I_{\text{team}})$$

where PO is putouts, A is assists, E is errors, DP is double plays, K is strikeouts, and I is innings.

Because these positions are considered more skilled than other positions, the assists number is doubled. That is, the fielding skill required to get an assist at these positions is greater than the skill at other positions necessary merely to record a putout.

To figure out the fielding runs for first basemen, the formula is modified so that putouts and double plays are simply eliminated (after all, most double plays end at first base). For outfielders, the formula is adjusted to weigh assists heavier because good outfielders can prevent runs through the mere threat of a good arm. For catchers, strikeouts are removed from the formula, errors are subtracted, and the number of passed balls is also factored in. For pitchers, the total number is weighted less than other infielders because a pitcher's style may produce fewer ground balls.

Pitching Runs

The role of the pitcher is primarily to keep the other team from scoring runs—a defensive position.

Instead of measuring the number of runs above or below average a pitcher contributed to his team, you must measure how many runs above or below average a pitcher saved his team. A pitcher's performance is measured by how well he kept the opposition from scoring. Unfortunately, the statistical record for pitchers is flawed. In what baseball statisticians view as the crime of the century, you cannot find a record of how many doubles or triples a pitcher gave up in a given season. This means that you cannot compute the linear weight runs caused by base-advancing events involving a pitcher. Thus, you cannot compare such runs to the league average to see how many runs a pitcher may have saved.

Because of this, the best statistical measure available for a pitcher is his earned run average (ERA). By using the ERA, factoring in the total number of innings he pitched (IP), and using the ERA for the league that year, you can estimate pitching runs. The formula for pitching runs is

IP * (League ERA/9) - earned runs allowed

Park Effects

The pitchers, fielders, base runners, and even the batters are all affected by the environment in which the game is played. The ballpark has such a significant effect on a performance that you cannot ignore its effects on a player's accomplishments.

Because each team plays 81 games at home and 81 games on the road, the effect the dimensions and conditions of its home park have on run production can be measured. The mathematics of adjusting for park effect are complex. But generally they involve increasing or decreasing a player's batting runs or pitching runs to adjust for the effects of the home park.

Total Player Rating

Whew! That is a lot of number crunching. You'll notice that not all the mathematical calculations were thrown at you here. That would be like starting a rookie in the World Series. Luckily, the statistics in the appendixes show the results of these formulas. Probably the most important number of all appears in the column Total Player Rating or TPR.

For the hitters, this number adds the batting runs, stealing runs, and fielding runs to produce a figure that measures overall ability relative to the other players in the league. This is the grand slam of the stats on the sheets in front of you.

The TPR number for pitchers adds the batting runs, fielding runs, and pitching runs to produce a figure that is the best basis for comparison of the pitchers in the league.

Normalization of Statistics

Now you know how far above or below average a player is in terms of runs scored or saved. You may have thought this painful process of understanding baseball statistics was over, but wait—you're not finished yet.

With Earl Weaver Baseball II, you can ask Mickey Mantle to re-create his 1957 season in a new league that will pit him against stars such as Hack Wilson, who will be asked to re-create his phenomenal 1930 performance. But is it realistic for Mickey Mantle to play against Hack Wilson when they played at different times under different conditions and even slightly different rules?

In order to test their abilities fairly and accurately, you must find a way to compare the performances of all these great players in their greatest seasons. You must have a way to get Mantle out of Yankee Stadium and Wilson out of Wrigley Field and into the 1990s to play in an Earl Weaver Baseball stadium of your design, against each other, and under the same conditions. You accomplish this through a process known as *normalization.*

Comparing the raw statistics posted for Hack Wilson in 1930 with those for Mickey Mantle in 1957 creates a statistical illusion as to who was the better offensive performer.

In 1930, Hack Wilson played in 155 games, had 585 at-bats, scored 146 runs, had 208 hits, 35 doubles, 6 triples, 56 home runs, 190 RBI, 105 walks, and 84 strikeouts. That year Wilson set the NL record for most home runs and most home runs per at-bat (9.6). His RBI total of 190 set a Major League record that is yet to be broken. His batting average was .356, his slugging percentage was .723, his on-base percentage was .454, and his isolated power percentage was .367.

In 1957, Mickey Mantle played in 144 games, had 474 at-bats, scored 121 runs, had 173 hits, 28 doubles, 6 triples, 34 home runs, 94 RBI, 146 walks, and 75 strikeouts. His batting average was .365, his slugging percentage was .665, his on-base percentage was .515, and his isolated power percentage was .300. He led the league in runs scored and walks. His performance that year won him MVP honors.

Figure 4-1a and Figure 4-1b show how each player compared to the average player in his league for the given year. As shown in Figure 4-2a, it appears that, based on raw statistics, Mickey Mantle was a slightly better hitter than Hack Wilson. But the linear weights system says that Mantle was a far better hitter, as illustrated in Figure 4-2b. If Mantle's best season was that much better than Wilson's best season, you can't tell it from their actual statistics. How can you adjust the statistics for Wilson and Mantle to correct this statistical illusion?

Figure 4-1a.

Performance of Hack Wilson in 1930 versus the 1930 National League average

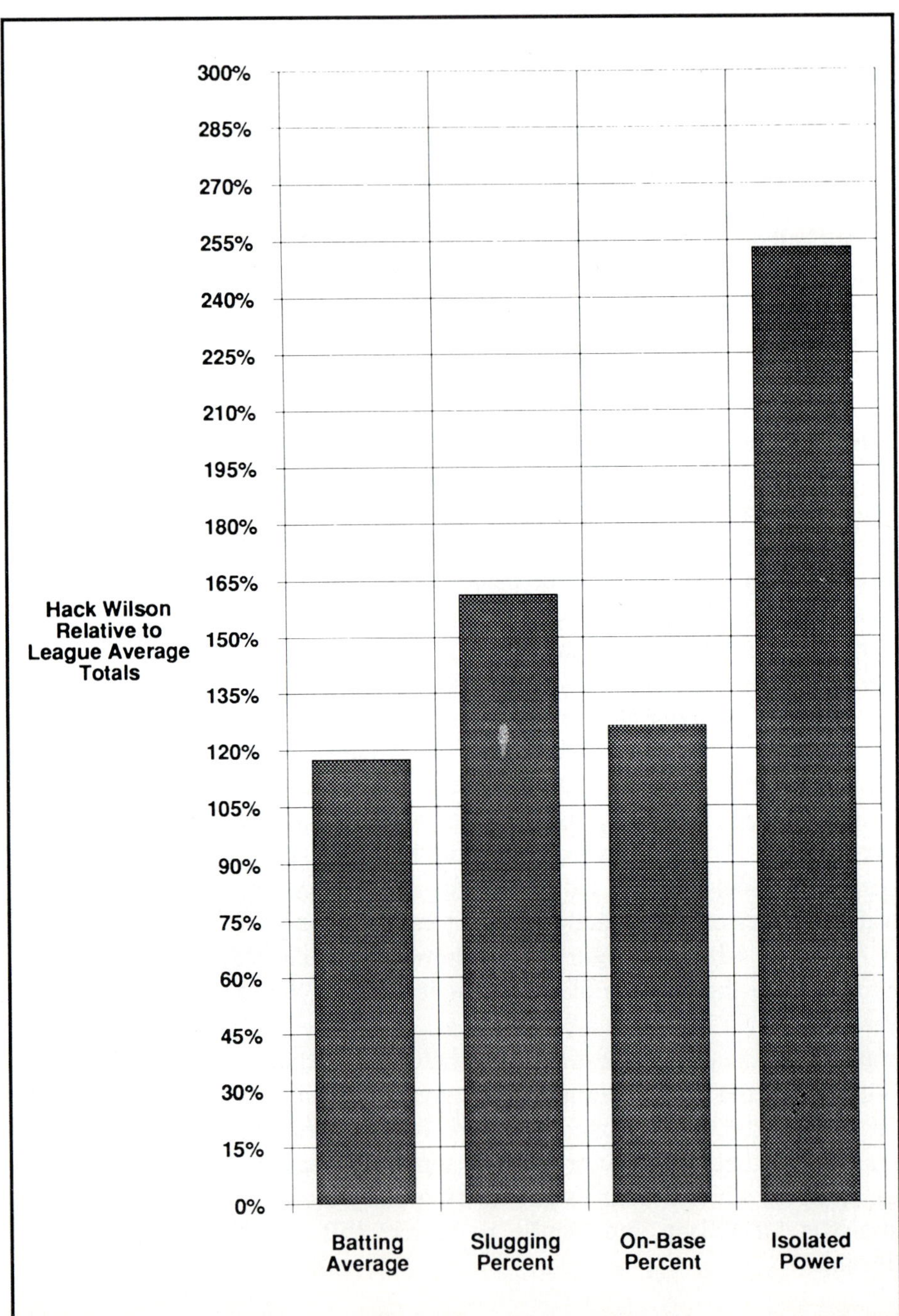

Figure 4-1b.

Performance of Mickey Mantle in 1957 versus the 1957 American League average

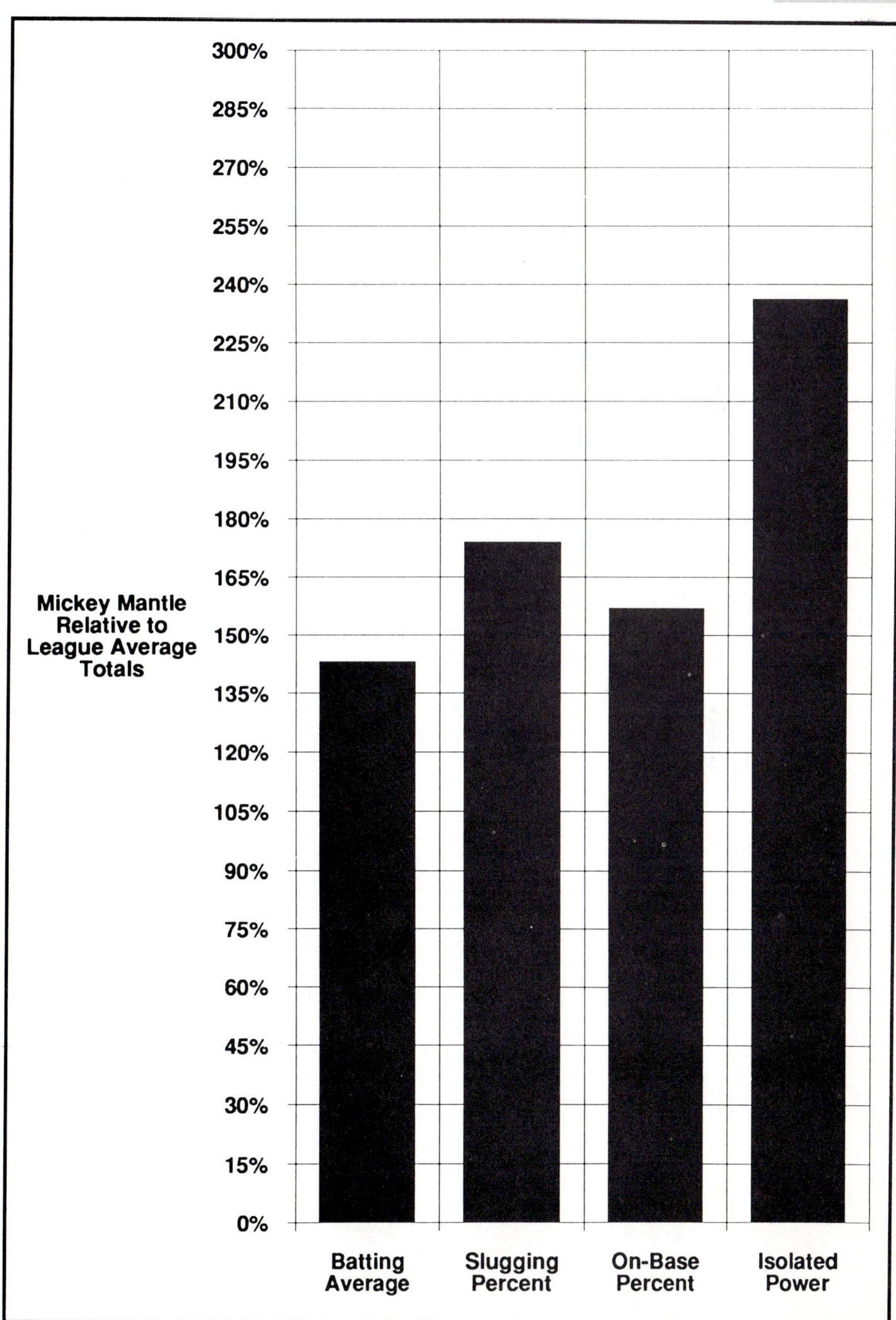

Figure 4-2a.

Comparison of Hack Wilson and Mickey Mantle in raw statistics relative to league average totals

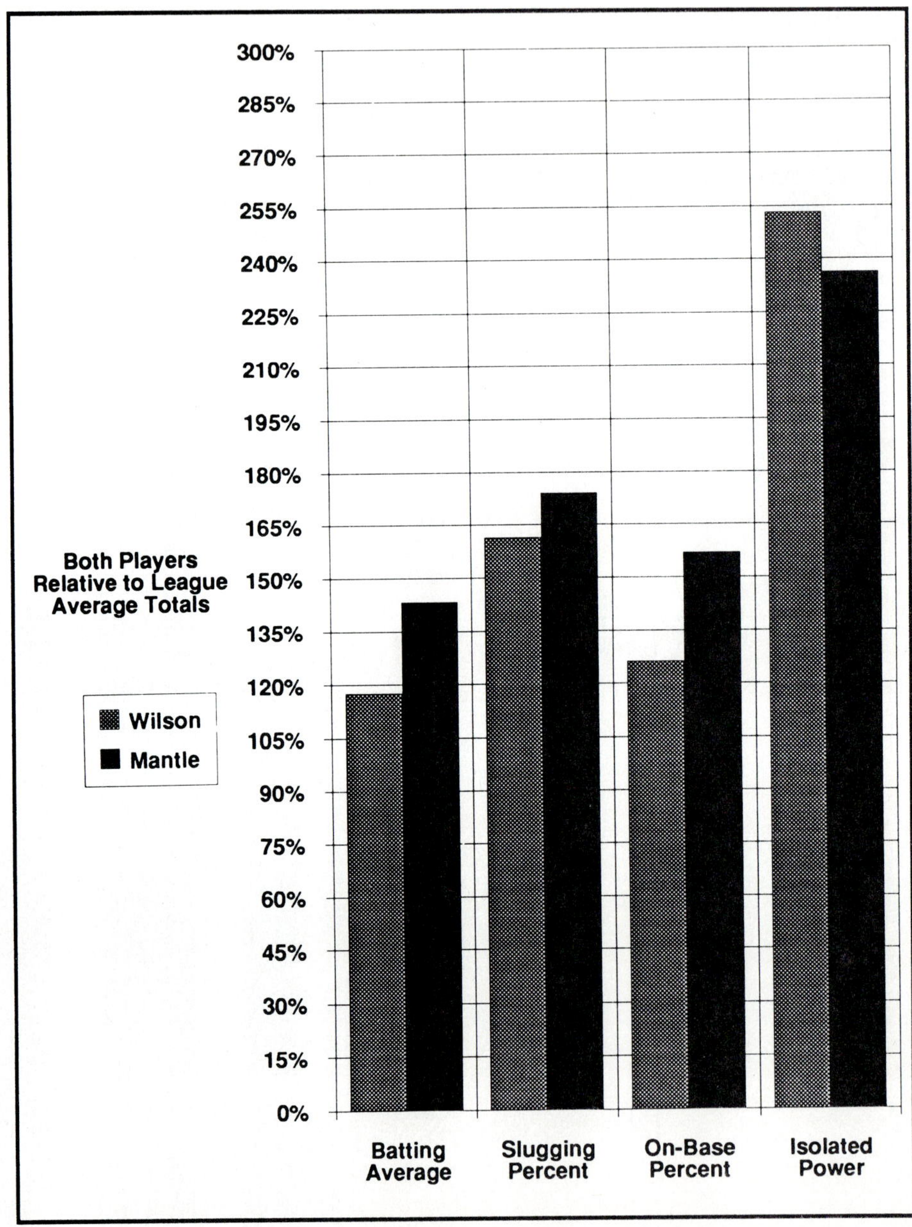

Figure 4-2b.

Comparison of Hack Wilson and Mickey Mantle after normalization

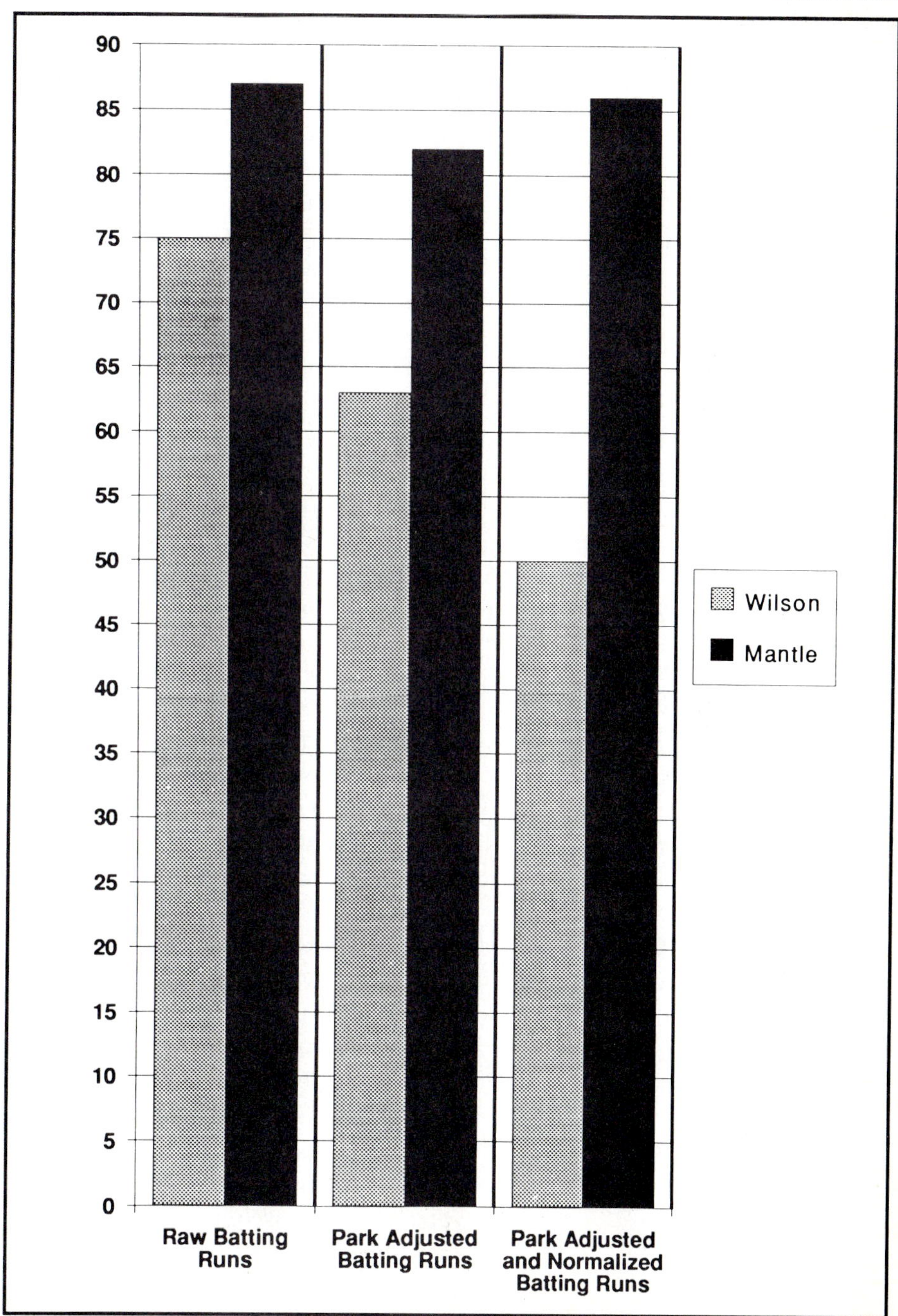

The first step in this process is to come up with a common denominator between the new league and the leagues the stars from different eras played in. Just as the value of the dollar has fluctuated over the past 100 years, the value of an out—the currency of baseball—has also fluctuated. Using Palmer's computer simulation as a model, Figure 4-3 shows how the value of an out has changed over the history of baseball.

The process of normalization used to create the player statistics for the Hall of Fame League is based on the fact that, since all of the players in the Hall of Fame League are playing in the same league, the cost of an out must be the same for each player. That seems fair, doesn't it? As you learned previously in this chapter, runs lost from outs made are part of the measure of a player's performance. Batting runs, for example, are computed by subtracting the runs lost by making outs from the runs created by producing base-advancing events.

Normalization of statistics for the Hall of Fame League means comparing all players to a common denominator.

Remember that a player's linear weights runs represent how many runs that player produced above or below the runs an average player would produce. The normalization process is designed to ensure that a player will perform equally far above or below average in the new Hall of Fame League as he performed in the league in which he actually played.

By assuming that each player's runs created by base-advancing events are unchanged from his actual statistics, hypothetical statistics for a normalized season with a common baseline (the value of an out) for all players in the new league can be computed. Each player's runs lost from outs made are calculated by multiplying the run-preventing value of an out by the total number of outs made. Since each player's runs created by base-advancing events are unchanged and the value of an out is the same for each player, the only way to keep the player's linear weights runs unchanged is to adjust (or normalize) his actual statistics by increasing or decreasing the number of outs he made. The player's new statistics then produce linear weights runs exactly equal to the linear weights runs he originally achieved in the league in which he actually

Figure 4-3.

Historical fluctuation in value of an out

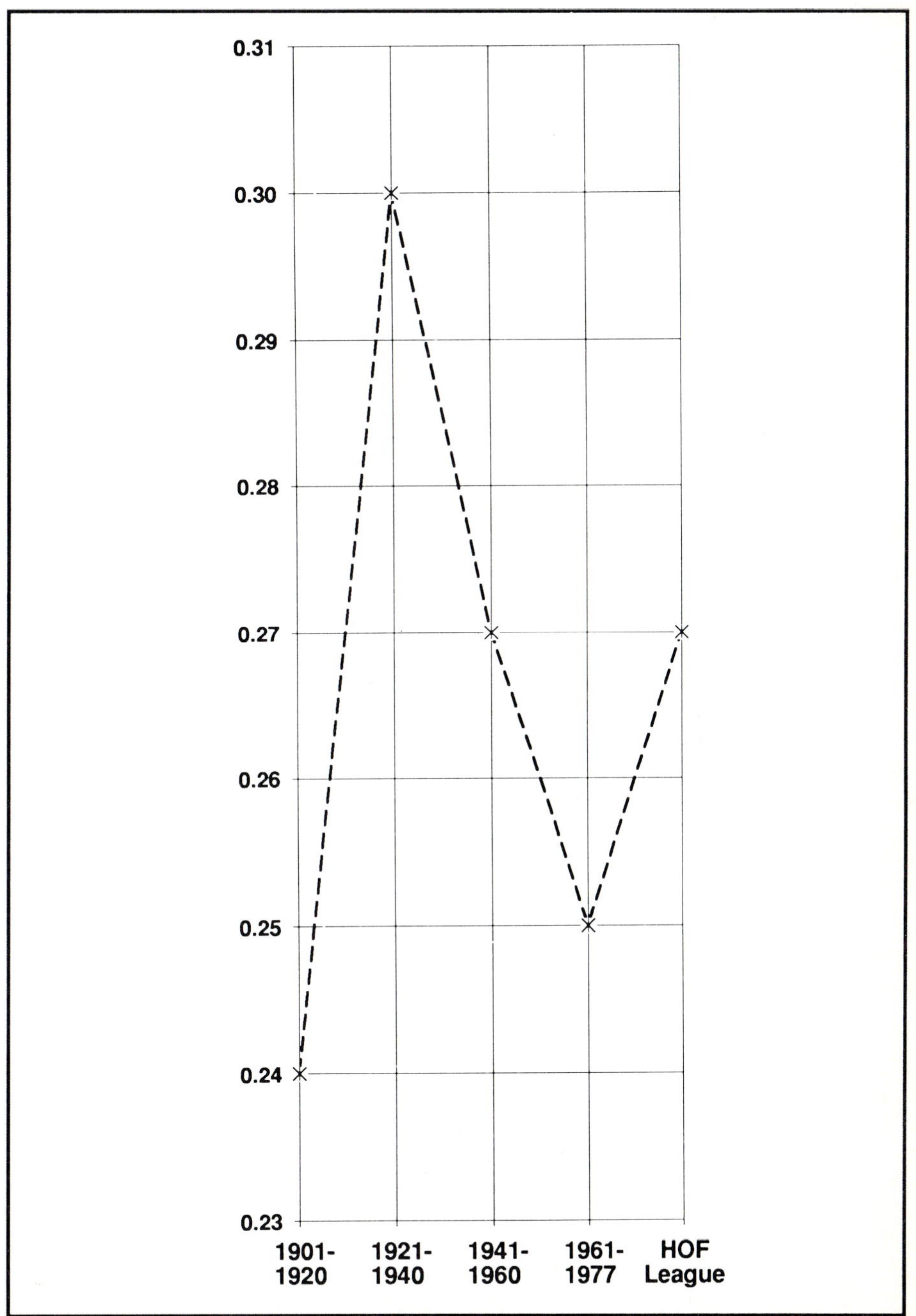

played. The practical effect of this computation is that outs are added to the statistics of players whose best seasons are from hitters' years and subtracted from players whose best seasons were achieved in pitchers' years.

Without normalizing raw statistics, comparing players from different eras of baseball history can produce distorted results.

Without normalization, looking at the statistics of players from different eras is comparing apples to oranges. You have to be able to compare the players in the same offensive context in order to see who is actually the better performer. To compare the players, you first derive a raw total player rating (TPR). In order to compare them under the same conditions, you must first adjust the TPR to put them in the same ballpark. Then you must remove the effects of the league and year in which each man played so that all players can be compared in the same league. The Hall of Fame League is based on the offensive context of the late 1980s and the early 1990s (8.0 to 8.5 runs per game in a league not using the designated hitter rule). The result of this process is a normalized TPR and the normalized statistics for the players in the Earl Weaver Baseball Hall of Fame League. Figure 4-4 compares the batting statistics for Wilson and Mantle, after adjustment to a common ballpark, and after adjustment to the Hall of Fame League. As you can see from this normalization process, Mickey Mantle was a far better hitter than Hack Wilson, despite the fact that Wilson posted superior raw numbers in 1930.

Appendixes A and D show the raw statistics and the normalized statistics for each player in the League. Linear weights runs reflected in the appendixes are adjusted to show the runs a player would have produced or saved had he played in a full season.

Statistical Breakdown

In order to examine the statistical breakdowns for the players in the Hall of Fame League, you need to know the meanings of the abbreviations used in the tables contained in Appendixes A through F.

Figure 4-4.

Comparison of Hack Wilson and Mickey Mantle in normalized raw statistics

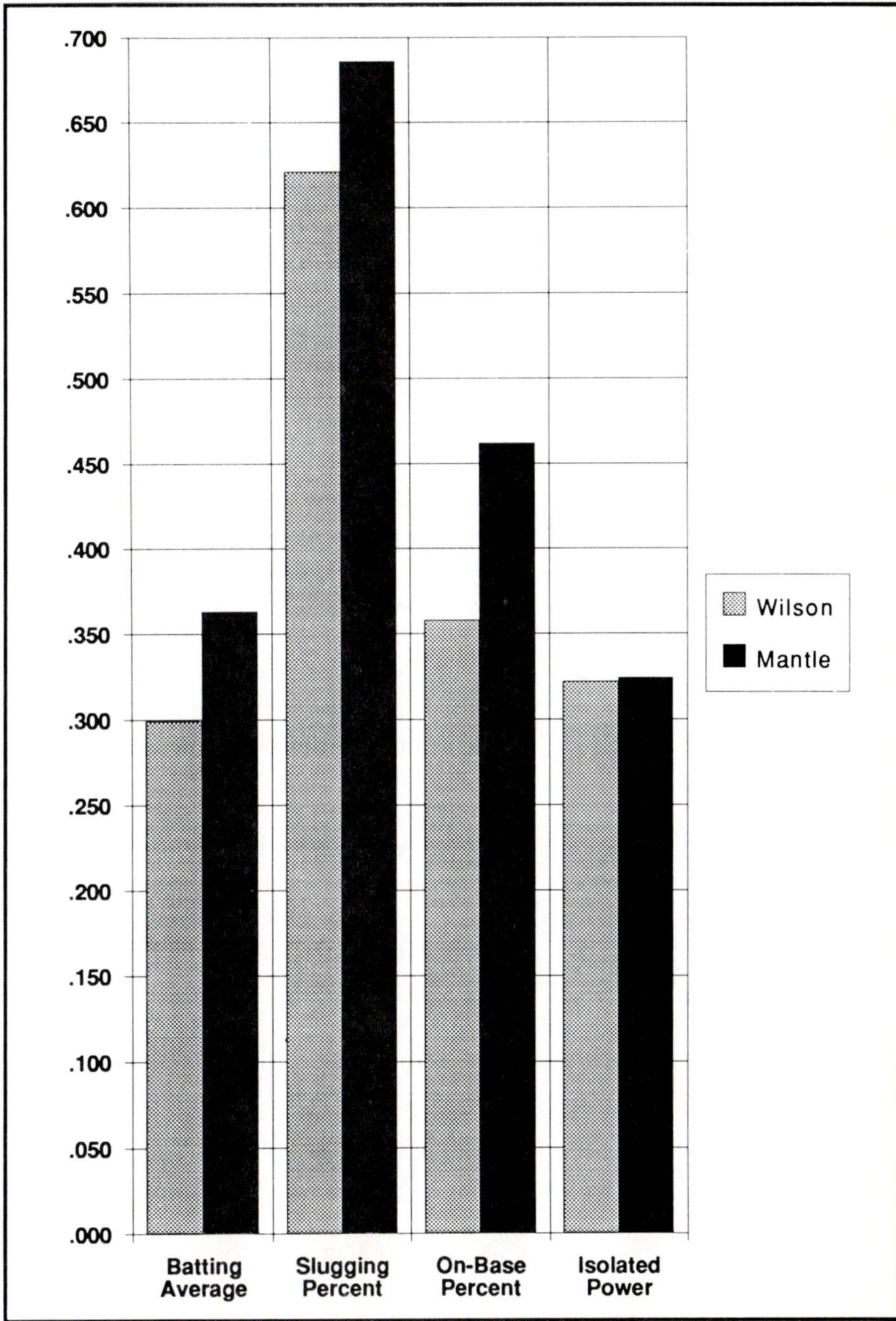

Hitters

Some of the categories are familiar to you. You'll recognize the historical data beside the player's name, listing how he bats (right-handed versus left-handed hitter), the position he plays, the year he played, and the league in which he played. The number of games played (G), runs scored (R), runs batted in (RBI), stolen bases (SB), and caught stealing (CS) represent the actual season totals for the player's best year. The figures for at-bats (AB), hits (H), batting average (BA), doubles (2B), triples (3B), home runs (HR), walks (BB), and strikeouts (K) are represented in two lines. The top line represents the actual season totals for that category and the bottom line represents the normalized total.

As you read in Chapter 1, "Why a Hall of Fame League?," the game has changed considerably in the past 100 years and, not coincidentally, so has the way statistics have been kept. You may notice some blanks in the caught stealing category. This data simply has not been found in the box scores of baseball history.

The percentage totals in the next few columns are measures of various success ratios at different aspects of the game. The slugging percentage (SL%) shows the total bases accumulated (one for a single, two for a double, three for a triple, four for a home run) divided by the number of at-bats. This statistic measures the ability to get the extra-base hit. Since the relative values used are greater than what the linear weights system says they should be, SL% slightly overvalues power hitters.

The on-base percentage (OB%) reflects how often a player reached base. This statistic is calculated as the number of hits, plus the number of walks, plus the number of times hit by a pitch (each way of reaching base safely) divided by the total number of at-bats plus walks plus times hit by a pitch. The flaw in OB% is that, according to the linear weights system, hits and walks are not equally valuable in producing runs. The OB% overvalues getting on base by walking or being hit by a pitch.

The statistic for on-base-times-slugging percentage (OTS%) is the product of the slugging percentage and the on-base percentage. The flaws in the SL% and OB% tend to cancel out in this statistic, which is a good measure of offensive ability.

The isolated power statistic (ISO PWR) is a measure of the hitter's pure power. The statistic is derived by taking total bases, subtracting hits, leaving only extra bases earned, and dividing that figure by the number of at-bats. Simply put, isolated power is the slugging percentage minus the batting average.

The numbers for SL%, OB%, and ISO PWR show normalized statistics.

Pitchers

Again, some of the categories in this statistical breakdown are familiar to you. You'll recognize the historical data beside the pitcher's name, listing the arm with which he throws, whether he is a starter or reliever the year he played, and the league in which he played. Figures for wins (W), losses (L), total games (TG), games started (GS), and complete games pitched (CG), and saves (SV) represent the actual season totals for the player's best year.

Some of the next few categories have a top-line number (actual statistic) and a bottom-line number (normalized statistic). These categories include innings pitched (IP), hits allowed (H), home runs allowed (HR), walks allowed (BB), strikeouts recorded (K), earned runs (ER), and earned run average (ERA). Note that of these categories, only the ERA is a calculation (number of earned runs multiplied by nine, and the product divided by the total innings pitched). The opponent's batting average (OPP BA) and opponent's on-base percentage (OPP OB%) reflect how effective the pitcher is against the hitters he faces.

What To Look For

Looking at all those categories to discover the best player for your team at different positions may bring back that managerial headache. However, certain categories provide a good feel for what a player can do.

After batting runs, the two most important categories for the hitters are the OB% (on-base percentage) and the SL% (slugging percentage). These two categories tell you how often a player reaches base and how much punch he has in his bat. A player's ability to hit is also reflected in his batting average (BA), and his power is reflected in his isolated power (ISO PWR) statistic.

Like batting runs, the OTS (on-base-times-slugging) number is valuable because it shows a player's overall hitting ability. The OTS is an excellent quick indicator of hitting prowess.

For pitchers, you can get a quick feel for how good the player is by looking at four categories: earned run average (ERA), opponent's on-base percentage (OPP OB%), opponent's batting average (OPP BA), and homers per plate appearance (HR/PA).

The Hall of Fame League adjusts a pitcher's ERA so that it corresponds to a pitcher's normalized pitching runs saved per plate appearance. The opponents' on-base percentage and batting average give you an idea of whether he is a power pitcher or a control pitcher and how good he is. Power pitchers have low OBA% and high OOB%.

Since statistics for doubles and triples given up by pitchers are not available, the homers per plate appearance statistic is the "power" number for pitchers. For pitchers, both outs made and home runs given up are normalized. The home run adjustment attempts to remove the impact of the lack of home runs during the dead-ball era in baseball history. Pitchers, but not hitters, from this era were adjusted for home runs on the theory that the hitters "chose" not to try to hit the ball out of the park.

Special Features in EWBII

Although the guys you will meet shortly are unquestionably great, any Major League manager will tell you that right-handed hitters hit left-handed pitching better than left-handed hitters do (some more so than others), and vice versa. In order to accommodate this well-known fact, you should be aware of how your hitters fare against righties and against lefties. Although they loathe to admit it, right-handed pitchers fare better against right-handed hitters (some more so than others), and vice versa. In order to come up with an effective batting order and to bring in the proper reliever, you must know how a hitter performs against both right-handed and left-handed pitching.

Chapter 6, "The Pitchers," addresses the logic behind these phenomena. In the EWBII game, statistics for players reflect this breakdown of hitting or pitching versus right and versus left. Historical data is not always available to show how well a pitcher or hitter did against right-handed or left-handed opponents. For that reason, the left/right breakdowns in the Earl Weaver Hall of Fame League are estimated to conform to conventional wisdom. Appendixes B and E show the hitters' and pitchers' abilities versus right and versus left (and, amazingly, vice versa).

The Earl Weaver Baseball II game uses several categories of its own to summarize the statistics for each player in the League. Table 4-1 shows the statistics that EWBII uses to play the game. (See Chapter 10 for a discussion on entering statistics for players.)

The EWBII game also uses its own measurements for certain abilities. These categories (Power, H&R, Bunt, Runs, Range, Arm, and Durability) assign a number from 1 to 10 to denote how good a player is. The higher the number, the higher the skill level. For example, the Power category reflects a player's skill at hitting for extra bases. The H&R (hit-and-run) category shows how good a contact hitter a player is. The number under Bunt reflects how well a player is able to execute a sacrifice or squeeze. Runs shows how fast the player can run the bases both to steal and to advance on a batted ball. Range and Arm are factors that measure the fielding prowess of a player. Durability indicates how often a player gets injured.

Just as for the hitters, the EWBII game uses a series of measurements for the abilities of pitchers. These categories

Table 4-1.

Statistics from the Edit Players Utility in the Commissioner II Program

HITTERS			
Biographical	**Statistical**	**Weaver/Fldg**	
Name	Games	Power	
Bats	AB*	H&R	
Pos	Runs	Bunt	
Skin	Hits*	FB%	
Status	2B	Runs	
Year	3B	Range	
ID#	HR	Arm	
	RBI	Durability	
	Sacrifice Hits	FA 2	
	BB*	E	
	K*	PO	
	SB	Ast	
	CS		
PITCHERS			
Biographical	**Statistical**	**Weaver/Fldg**	**Batting**
Name	W/L	Speed	AB
Bats	Games	Control	H
Pos	Games Started	Fatigue	HR
Skin	Comp. Games	FB%	Sac
*Normalized statistic			

Table 4-1.

Statistics from the Edit Players Utility in the Commissioner II Program (continued)

PITCHERS *(continued)*			
Biographical	**Statistical**	**Weaver/Fldg**	**Batting**
Status	Saves	Bunt	
Year	IP*	Hold	
ID#	AB	Durability	
	Hits*	FA	
	Earned Runs*	BK	
	HR*		
	BB*		
	K*		
	HB		
RATING NUMBERS			
Hitters	**Pitchers**		
SL%*	ERA*		
OB%*	Opp. BA		
ISO PWR*	Opp OB%		
SB Rtg	Pitch Runs*		
Fld Rtg	Bat Runs*		
Stl Runs*	Field Runs*		
Fld Runs*	Plyr Rtng*		
Bat Runs*			
Plyr Rtg*			
*Normalized statistic			

(Speed, Control, Fatigue, Bunt, Hold, and Durability) assign a number from 1 to 10 indicating how good a pitcher is. Again, the higher the number, the higher the skill level. For example, a pitcher with a Speed rating of 10 equates to a pitcher who has a fastball with a speed of 89 to 96 m.p.h. until he gets tired. The Control rating is based on a pitcher's strikeout-to-walks ratio. The Fatigue rating is based on the average innings pitched per game played. This rating defines number of pitches a pitcher can deliver before his effectiveness begins to diminish. Once a pitcher becomes fatigued, his speed and control ratings go down, and the batter's on-base percentage and home runs per at-bat increase. Again, durability indicates how often a pitcher gets injured.

Normalized batting statistics for a pitcher are included (pitchers from leagues incorporating the designated hitter rule are assumed to be average). These numbers reflect the number of at-bats (AB), hits (H), home runs (HR), and batting average (BA) of a pitcher. The bunts rating (B) indicates the pitcher's ability to advance a runner by means of a sacrifice bunt. This number has been estimated based on the pitcher's batting ability.

Appendixes C and F contain all of the EWBII ratings for players in the Hall of Fame League.

Fielding Statistics

Raw fielding data is of mystical significance to baseball statisticians. Because of the varying playing conditions of different eras, historical fielding statistics can be deceiving. For example, outfield assists before the turn of the century were four times greater than they are today. This can be attributed to the "dead ball" at the turn of the century that permitted outfielders to play shallow and accumulate enormous assist numbers. Another example is the use of gloves, which obviously lowered error totals after they came into common use.

Despite the apparent elegance of the linear weights system, many baseball statisticians believe it is impossible to separate a player's fielding ability from that of his teammates, particularly the pitcher. Despite such qualms, fielding statistics are supplied in the Hall of Fame League. These statistics include numbers for errors (E), putouts (PO), and assists (AST). These three numbers are used to calculate a player's fielding percentage. That percentage is derived by adding putouts plus assists, and dividing that total by the sum of putouts plus assists plus errors.

The Hall of Fame League estimates these EWBII values based on the players' normalized fielding runs. The ratings for a hitter's arm, range, and his fielding percentage have been adjusted to conform to his normalized fielding runs ratings.

Appendixes C and F contain all of the fielding ratings for players in the Hall of Fame League.

Time Out on the Field

That was a healthy dose of information to digest all at once. That commotion you hear outside your door means that activity out on the field is starting to wind down, and players are starting to mill back into the locker room. Now that you are familiar with the statistical information before you and you understand what all those numbers mean, it's time to meet a few of the ballplayers who would like to go to work for you.

1927 YANKEES
LOU GEHRIG
NEW YORK YANKEES – 1ST BASE
1927 YANKEES
BABE RUTH
NEW YORK YANKEES – OUTFIELD
1927
MOST VALUABLE PLAYER
EDDIE COLLINS
A.L. MVP – CHALMERS AWARD
1914

The Hitters

"I don't like to sound egotistical, but every time I stepped up to the plate with a bat in my hands, I couldn't help but feel sorry for the pitcher."

–Rogers Hornsby

Sitting here in the manager's office reviewing all these stat sheets and resumés of the players you are about to meet may seem a bit confusing, intimidating, and downright overwhelming. Try not to let your nervousness show–you know how important first impressions can be during job interviews.

Speaking of impressions, perhaps you'd better take a moment to consider what you are about to see. Down the runway, outside your door making all the noise in the clubhouse, and gathered out on the field (tossing the ball around and playing a little pepper) are 26 of the greatest hitters and position players the game has ever known. As they are brought into your office, try not to stare at their uniforms.

Keep in mind that the players of the 1890s were big on sweating (they thought that the more they sweated, the better they played). The players of that era will come in here dressed in heavy wool uniforms with quilted knickerbockers and hip-length wool sweaters. Guys who played around the turn of the century will be decked out in loose-fitting shirts bearing high collars with long T-shirts underneath, and a more baggy look than the players of the 1890s. The guys who played in the early 1900s will reflect more of the look you are used to, but will be wearing uniforms with collars that resemble those Nehru jackets worn in the 1960s. Except for the players who performed during your lifetime, most of these guys will look like they are wearing more clothing than you have in your closet at home. Just remember, thanks to the passage of time and the introduction of new fashions, the heroes of today in their skintight double-knits will look much different from those early-day players.

Twenty-Six Picks to Click

You are about to come face-to-face with 26 of the greatest ballplayers in the history of the game of baseball. Try not to laugh at the way these guys are dressed, and please excuse some of them if they seem to be perspiring profusely underneath those heavy wool garments.

Rather than simply quoting to you statistics for the career years that got these men into the Hall of Fame League, this will be an opportunity to let you get to know each player as an individual. Complete books have been written on the lives of some of these guys, and you certainly do not have time to read the whole library of baseball biographies and autobiographies.

Some encapsulated information will help you associate the personalities with names and numbers. The time capsules in this chapter contain a selection of anecdotes, quotations, and lore about these historical men.

Table 5-1, located at the end of this chapter, provides the actual (top line) and normalized (bottom line) statistics for each of the players introduced in this chapter. (Refer to Chapter 4, "The Statistics," for an explanation of each statistical category.) Table 5-2 (also located at the end of this chapter) provides normalized statistics representing the player's overall offensive performance, his performance against left-handed pitching, and his performance against right-handed pitching.

By looking at the Total Player Rating (TTL PLYR RTG) in Table 5-1, you can see the rankings of the players at their positions. Although these tables show only offensive numbers, these players were all-around stars, both at the plate and in the field. Appendixes A and B display complete listings for all the non-pitchers in the league. Appendix C shows their defensive statistics and their EWBII ratings.

If you are anxious to see the Hall of Fame League in action, these players will provide a good starting point. Combined with the pitchers presented in Chapter 6 and some of the platoon players presented in Chapter 7, the players presented here will give you a couple of really good teams for a really good game. The players (in the order that they appear in the tables) and their representative years are as follows:

Outfielders George Ruth (1920), Ed Delahanty (1896), Ty Cobb (1911), Tris Speaker (1913), Ted Williams (1941), Joe Jackson (1912), Mickey Mantle (1957), Stan Musial (1948), Willie Mays (1955)

Shortstops George Davis (1899), Hughie Jennings (1896), Honus Wagner (1905)

Third Basemen Mike Schmidt (1981), George Brett (1980), Ron Santo (1966)

Second Basemen Napoleon Lajoie (1910), Eddie Collins (1910), Rogers Hornsby (1924)

First Basemen Norm Cash (1961), Jimmie Foxx (1933), Lou Gehrig (1927), Willie McCovey (1969)

Catchers Carlton Fisk (1972), Joe Torre (1966), Roy Campanella (1951), Johnny Bench (1972)

Try to keep in mind that these players represent baseball from just about every decade over the past century.

George Ruth ("The Babe")

When George Herman Ruth broke into professional baseball, he played with the minor league Baltimore Orioles. The owner of that team was Jack Dunn, who had played professional baseball for Ned Hanlon and John McGraw (two men instrumental in the development of baseball at the turn of the century). During his first game, an intrasquad workout, Ruth hit a prodigious home run. The next day, the *Baltimore American* newspaper splashed the headline "Ruth Makes Mighty Clout." His teammates, who obviously noticed the attention the young Ruth was getting in his debut, started calling him "Dunnie's Baby." By the third week of training camp, newspapers began calling him Babe Ruth.

Ruth was young and innocent when he started playing professional baseball. His trip to spring training that year marked the first train ride of his life. It was just the beginning of the greatest career baseball has ever known. No other player before or since has affected the game more than Ruth. No other man could play the game the way Ruth played it. And no other could play off the field the way Ruth played. "I guess I could have written two books of my life," Ruth once said, "one for the adults and one for the kids."

As a pitcher, Babe Ruth completed 107 of the 148 games he started. His lifetime pitching record was 94 wins, 46 losses, and a 2.28 ERA.

As his home run totals grew and as he set (and broke) records year by year, Ruth established a mythical image. But as great as his offensive performance was, few baseball fans realize that Ruth actually broke in as one of the game's great pitchers.

Because of economic competition in Baltimore from the Federal League during Ruth's rookie season, the Orioles' owner wanted to gain Major League status for his ball club. He was unable to get that status from the league, and so he began selling his best players in order to raise cash. On July 19, 1914, Dunn sold Ruth (who had won 14 games as a pitcher, lost 6, and was batting a meager .200) along with pitcher Ernie Shore and catcher Ben Egan to the American League Boston Red Sox for a total of $30,000.

Ruth's first day in uniform for the Bosox marked his Major League debut as a pitcher. Their opponent was the Cleveland club, and Ruth pitched seven strong innings for the victory. That year he was 18-8. Ruth established himself as the best pitcher in baseball by the middle of the 1916 season. That year he was 23-12 and outdueled Walter Johnson, one of the great pitchers of all time, four times. His manager, Bill Carrigan, wanted to use Ruth as an everyday outfielder

In Game Two of the 1916 World Series, Ruth was a 2-1 victor in a record 14-inning affair. He started the game by allowing a first-inning homer and then hurled 13 scoreless innings for the win.

because he was still poking home runs even as a pitcher. However, the manager decided that playing the outfield would disrupt Ruth's pitching. That 1916 season Ruth posted the best ERA (1.75) in the American League.

Ruth was married at age 19 to Helen Woodford, and they made their home in an apartment in Boston. But when Ruth was on the road, he had a reputation as being a bit on the wild side. Carrigan tried to keep Ruth in line while on the road and always made sure his hotel room was next to Ruth's. Carrigan kept Ruth on a strict allowance by drawing Ruth's paycheck of $3500 for the season and giving Ruth a little bit each day. That little bit, according to Carrigan, lasted about five minutes.

Carrigan had his hands full with Ruth. During a road trip to Washington, the Red Sox were about to enjoy an off-day on Sunday. Ruth asked permission from Carrigan to visit his parents in Baltimore. The Babe laid it on thick, telling Carrigan that he hadn't seen them in a long time. Permission was granted. The following Monday, Carrigan decided to surprise Ruth by having Ruth's father sit in box seats directly behind the Red Sox dugout. The manager wanted to be nearby when Ruth discovered the surprise.

As Ruth came from the clubhouse and emerged from the dugout, his father rang out, "Fine son you are, George. You never came to see your Ma and Dad." Obviously caught in his own little scheme, Ruth glanced at his father, glanced at Carrigan, and quietly slipped away.

Ruth was often characterized as "living in his own little world." Once during a road trip to Philadelphia, he was in the hotel lobby following a game in which he had pitched. Stuffy McInnis, a star first baseman for the Athletics who had played on four pennant winners, went up to Ruth and said, "Babe, that was a hell of a fine game you pitched this afternoon." "Thanks, that's very nice of you," Ruth said. "Glad you were able to come out and watch us play."

In 1918, Ed Barrow was managing the Red Sox. Barrow was used to working in the front office and not as familiar as he should have been with the skills of his players. He relied heavily on his outfielder, Harry Hooper, for advice on who to play and where to play them. Hooper suggested that Ruth be put in the lineup as a regular everyday player. On May 6, 1918, Barrow started Ruth at first base, the first time in his career that he had done anything in the Major Leagues except pitch and pinch hit. And, of course, he hit a home run that day.

Carl Mays, a pitcher on the club, deserted the team in 1919. Ruth was again asked to pitch. He complied, but at the same time he began his first run at the record books. By the end of July, Ruth had tied the American League record for home runs with 16. He set his sights on the Major League record of 27 set in 1884 by Ned Williamson of the Chicago Colts. Ruth ended the year with 29 home runs at the ripe old age of 24.

Babe Ruth is the only player to have hit three home runs in two World Series contests. He did it during the 1926 and the 1928 Fall Classics.

During the off-season that year, owner Harry Frazee, who was a producer and always needed cash for his Broadway shows, became strapped for money. After long negotiations that winter, he finally agreed to sell Ruth to the New York Yankees for $100,000 and a loan of $300,000. Ruth was given a two-year contract at $20,000 per year with a $1000 signing bonus. That trade is the basis for what has been called "The Curse of the Bambino" at Fenway Park—a curse that legend says has prevented the Red Sox from winning a World Series since 1918.

Naturally, Boston fans were outraged. Frazee, in a public relations move to soften the blow, said, "Ruth had become simply impossible, and the Boston club could no longer put up with his eccentricities. I think the Yankees are taking a gamble. While Ruth is undoubtedly the greatest hitter the game has ever seen, he is likewise one of the most selfish and inconsiderate men ever to put on a baseball uniform."

That statement may have been true in the sense that Frazee never wore a baseball uniform. The Boston owner was known for his penny-pinching ways. During Ruth's last season with the Red Sox, Frazee honored the Bambino with a "Babe Ruth Day" at Fenway Park. Ruth said, "I had to buy my wife's ticket to the game. Fifteen thousand fans show up and all I got was a cigar." Ironically, this was the day that Ruth tied Williamson's home run record, pitched into the sixth inning, and won the game in the ninth inning with a long blast out of the park.

Ruth's arrival in New York coincided with what has been described as the "lively ball era" in baseball. That season for the Yankees he hit 54 home runs in 458 at bats and boasted an impressive batting average of .376. The next year, Ruth caught fire: 59 home runs, 171 RBI, 177 runs scored, batted .378, and had a phenomenal slugging percentage of .846. For the next 40 years, only one Major League hitter would top the 59-home run mark—Ruth himself in 1927 when he hit 60 home runs in a single season.

Many baseball fans associate Babe Ruth with the number 3. However, he played 15 seasons before he even wore a number on his uniform. The number 3 signified that he batted third in the order.

Behind those unbelievable numbers was still The Babe, living in his own little world. During a game against the White Sox in 1923, the Yankees were clobbering the Pale Hose. In the ninth inning, a puppy wandered onto the field and Ruth, playing in the outfield, dropped his glove, dropped to his knees, and began chasing the puppy on all fours. The White Sox hitter launched a fly ball in Ruth's direction and The Babe reached up and caught the ball barehanded.

Ruth's girth (which was the purpose for the traditional Yankee pinstriped uniforms—the pinstripes made him look thinner) was acquired because of a tremendous appetite. For breakfast he would often eat an 18-egg omelet, three slices of ham, a half-dozen slices of toast, and two bottles of beer. For dinner he might eat an entire chicken, potatoes, spinach, corn, peas, beans, bread (with butter), pie, ice cream, and a small pitcher of coffee.

He especially liked a restaurant in St. Louis where he would order hundreds of barbecued spareribs to take on the road with him. He would set up shop in a washroom on the train and sell the ribs to his teammates for 50 cents each. But, of course, he supplied free beer.

Ruth was simply the greatest player the game of baseball has ever known. In all, he set 192 Major League records, 53 of which have yet to be broken. He was voted into the Hall of Fame in 1936.

Ed Delahanty ("Big Ed")

Ed was the oldest of seven boys in the Delahanty clan. Four of his brothers (Frank, Jim, Joe, and Tom) also played in the big leagues, but Big Ed was the star of the bunch. "We were given bats instead of rattles," he once said.

Big Ed broke into big league ball in 1887 with Mansfield of the Ohio State League. That year the tall right-hander hit .355 and played the next season for Wheeling of the Tri-State League. He was hitting .408 after just 21 games when the Phillies bought his contract for $1500. He played in only 74 games for the Phillies in 1888, mostly at second base, and hit a scant .274. Perhaps out of frustration, Delahanty jumped to the Player's League in 1889, but returned to the Phillies in 1890.

By 1892 he was tearing up the league with his bat. He led the league in triples with 21 that season. The following year, he just missed winning the Triple Crown with a .368 batting average, 19 home runs, and 146 RBI. Hitting 19 home runs in 1893 was phenomenal and, in fact, was one of the highest season totals for home runs in the nineteenth century.

Ed Delahanty, who once went 6 for 6 in a game, was the first Major League ballplayer to clout four home runs in a game.

By 1894, Big Ed was hitting his stride. He managed to hit .400, but it wasn't until five years later that he would win his first batting title with a .408 average. In 1902, Delahanty jumped from the National League Phillies to the American League Senators. By hitting .376 and winning the American League batting title, he became the first man to lead both leagues in hitting. In all, he won three slugging titles in the National League and one slugging title in the American League. You must keep in mind, however, that 1893 was the year baseball moved the pitcher's mound back ten feet and required the pitcher keep his foot on the pitching rubber until delivering the pitch.

Delahanty was a notorious "bad ball" hitter. Legend claims that he would step across the plate to smash a fat pitch. Legend also says that he once hit a baseball in half with his awesome power. Turkey Mike Donlin once congratulated him on hitting a tremendous home run against St. Louis. "That's one you can be proud of, Ed," Donlin said. "Hell, no. If I could have cut that hit into singles, I'd lead the whole damn league," Big Ed retorted.

Like many of his contemporaries, Delahanty was a drinking man. His disdain for team training rules resulted in his suspension in June 1903. He left the Senators and took a train bound for New York. As was his custom, Delahanty got drunk, so drunk that the train's conductor kicked him off the train at Niagara, Ontario. Canadian law required the conductor to turn the drunk and disorderly Delahanty over to a Canadian constable, but the law was not obeyed. One account said that Delahanty was wandering toward a drawbridge near Niagara Falls at about midnight. When a watchman approached him swinging a lantern, Delahanty panicked and fell into the Niagara River. His body wasn't found until a week later. He was 35 years old.

Big Ed Delahanty was inducted into the Hall of Fame in 1945.

Ty Cobb ("The Georgia Peach")

If you have this fellow on your team, be prepared for fireworks. Ty Cobb was described by his Detroit teammate Sam Crawford as suffering from "a persecution complex." Later in life, Cobb described his youthful demeanor as "a snarling wildcat." Although recognized as one of the best players in the game (he was the first player elected to the Hall of Fame), he was also one of the most violent and one of the most hated.

One incident that may have contributed to Cobb's irascible demeanor occurred when he was 18 years old. His mother shot and killed his father, whom Cobb held in high esteem. His father, suspecting that his mother was being unfaithful, set a trap by saying he would be away for a few days. The elder Cobb returned late one night in an effort to catch his wife cheating on him. He was sneaking in through a bedroom window when his frightened wife shot and killed the intruder.

No other player in the history of the game had such a violent tone to his career, and chief among the irritants for his violent temper was an unabated racism. Cobb was accused of slapping a black elevator operator, quarreling with a black groundskeeper in Detroit and then attempting to choke the groundskeeper's wife, pistol-whipping a black butcher's assistant, and punching a black groundskeeper while in Philadelphia for a game.

In New York in 1912, Cobb was enraged by a crippled heckler who often had insulted him. The heckler, Claude Lueker, reportedly called Cobb a "half-nigger" and Cobb went after him in the stands. He knocked Lueker down, kicked and stomped him viciously. A bystander yelled at Cobb that the man had no hands and Cobb replied, "I don't care if he has no feet" and continued to stomp the man with his spikes.

The practice of sharpening spikes was not done solely by Ty Cobb. Players of his day often used the spikes to counter defensive infielders who would block the bag to prevent a runner from reaching their base.

On the field, his violence was masked by his competitiveness. He often spiked opposing infielders in his quest to be the best. In the 1909 season, Cobb thought Boston pitcher Cy Morgan was throwing at his head and decided to retaliate. Cobb was on second when Morgan let go with a wild pitch. Cobb decided to come all the way around, anticipating that Morgan would be covering home and he could get his revenge on the pitcher with a violent collision. In his autobiography, Cobb described how, when he was a few steps past third, Morgan was covering the plate as planned. "As I came down the line and went whipping at him with my steel showing, Morgan...turned and actually ran away from the plate. I scored, and Morgan was released by Boston that night."

Most of the players in the league despised Cobb. In 1910, he was battling with Cleveland's Nap Lajoie for the batting title. As the season came down to the last weekend, Cobb was leading the batting race and so he decided to sit out the final two games on the schedule. Cleveland was playing a doubleheader at St. Louis on the last day of the season and Lajoie needed almost a perfect day to overtake Cobb. St. Louis manager Jack O'Connor told his third baseman to play on the outfield grass all day, and Lajoie was able to safely bunt for seven of his eight hits that day (he smacked a triple his first time up before he recognized his opponent's strategy). He ended the doubleheader going 8 for 9. The next day, eight players—all of them Cobb's teammates—sent Lajoie a telegram of congratulations.

Cobb used an unusual batting stance of keeping his hands apart and then choking up or swinging from the end of the bat, depending on the pitch. During his career he won ten American League batting titles and still boasts the game's highest career batting average (.366). He hit over .400 three times, won the stolen base title six times, and led the league in runs scored five times. Cobb hit .300 or better for 23 consecutive seasons (which still stands as a Major League record). He simply got on base, stole bases, and scored. He only hit 118 home runs during his 24-year career (47 of those were inside the park), but remember that he played all but the last few years during the dead-ball era. Cobb was the first man elected to the Hall of Fame in 1936.

Tris Speaker ("The Gray Eagle")

A native Texan with premature gray hair (thus the nickname The Gray Eagle), Speaker was best known for how shallow he played center field. In essence, he was so shallow that he was comparable to a rover in slow-pitch softball or, some say, a fifth infielder. Speaker would frequently spear line drives over the infield that everyone assumed were hits and then throw out unsuspecting base runners for double plays. Occasionally he made unassisted double plays by catching a low line drive and actually running in and touching second base himself. In fact, Speaker remains the only man to have made this play in a World Series. Astonishingly, Speaker was the pivot man on 4-8-3 double plays! And, hard as it is to believe, this center fielder even took pickoff throws from the pitcher.

Speaker fell off a horse at a young age and broke his right arm. Because of the injury, he was forced to learn to do things with his left hand. Although he threw left-handed, he was basically ambidextrous. Known for his dedicated work ethic, Speaker never lost his self-confidence even when things were not going well. Throughout his 22-year career, he worked to improve his game. "When I was a rookie, Cy Young used to hit me flies to sharpen my abilities to judge in advance the direction and distance of an outfield-hit ball," he said. Some historians credit Speaker with being the first outfielder to test the wind by throwing up blades of grass and watching them fall to the ground.

The Gray Eagle could go back as well as he could come in. He once said the few balls that did go over his head for triples were far less damaging than the many singles he took away from the hitters. During the years 1910 to 1915, Speaker was flanked in the outfield by Duffy Lewis and Harry Hooper to form what many baseball historians consider one of the best defensive outfields the game has ever known. Speaker was the leader of that trio and made 161 of their record 455 assists. As Lewis said, "Speaker was the king of the outfield...It was always 'Take it,' or 'I got it.' In all the years we never bumped into each other."

Because he played in the American League against such great hitters as Ty Cobb, Babe Ruth, and George Sisler, Tris Speaker only won one batting title. Had he played in the National League, however, his numbers would have won him four or five batting titles.

Speaker worked just as hard on his hitting as he did on his fielding, and he was just as successful. He did not appreciate any criticism, not even from his manager. In 1910 he was suffering an early-season batting slump and manager Patsy Donovan suggested that Speaker temporarily move out of his traditional third spot in the batting order. "Like hell I will!" was Speaker's reply. That season he was Boston's best hitter with a .340 average.

During his career, Speaker established 49 records as a player. He ranks second in total lifetime putouts in the outfield and first in assists. He batted well over .300 for 18 consecutive years, but he won only one batting crown. He topped a .375 batting average six times and had a lifetime average of .344. He still holds the record for most lifetime doubles (793). Primarily a line drive hitter, no one has ever hit more triples in World Series competition.

Speaker almost never struck out and stole 433 bases throughout his long career. He was named MVP in 1912 (the Red Sox won the pennant that year) and again in 1915.

In 1937, Tris Speaker became the seventh player elected to the Hall of Fame.

Ted Williams ("The Splendid Splinter")

The mother of Ted Williams was known throughout his hometown of San Diego as "Salvation Mary" because she was an active missionary in the Salvation Army. She often would take the young Williams along with her on her appointed rounds. She did allow him to play baseball, and play baseball he did. He was offered his first professional contract by a semi-pro team that was sponsored by the Texas Liquor House. "I came home and told my mother about the money, and she said that was fine. 'Who will you play for?' 'Uh, the Texas Liquor House.' If I had said Murder, Inc., I wouldn't have gotten a quicker refusal," Williams recalled.

He eventually broke into the minors with the San Diego Padres of the Pacific Coast League. The Padres were getting shelled by ten runs late in one game when Williams volunteered to pitch. He was inserted in the lineup as a pinch hitter and promptly got a hit. During his first inning of pitching he survived unscathed. His next time up he doubled and the Padres put together a rally to come within one run. When he went to the mound following the rally inning, he got hammered and the Padres lost the game. He told his manager he thought he was playing the wrong position. From that point on, Ted Williams became one of the best left fielders the game has ever known.

A visit to spring training the following year did not earn him a spot on the Major League roster. He played for the minor league Minneapolis team that year and hit .366 with 142 RBI and 43 homers. He also began displaying his now famous temper by throwing several tantrums in the clubhouse.

Ted Williams made it to The Show in 1939. One day in Detroit during his first at-bat of the day, the count was 3-0. Tiger catcher Rudy York said, "You're not hitting, are you, kid?" Williams replied emphatically, "I sure as hell am," and cranked a shot into the upper deck of right field in Briggs Stadium.

"I got to first base and Greenberg was still looking where the ball had gone. I reached second and Gehringer, who hadn't said a word to anybody in 20 years, was still saying nothing. Frank Croucher at short just looked, and Billy Rogell, playing third base didn't say anything either, but I could see him watching me closely. I got home, and York said, 'You weren't kidding, were you?' "

"The next time up there were two men on, and this is the one I hit out of Briggs Stadium. I got to first base and Greenberg was still looking, and Gehringer still hadn't said anything to anybody in 20 years, and Croucher at short was scraping the ground. Then I got to Rogell at third base and he said, 'What the hell you been eating?' "

What he was eating probably had less to do with his success than his work habits. "There has always been a saying in baseball that you can't make a hitter. But I think you can improve a hitter. More than you can *improve* a fielder. More mistakes are made hitting than in any other part of the game," Williams once told *Sport Magazine*.

At the beginning of the 1941 season, Williams suffered an ankle injury that limited him to pinch-hitting duties. He spent his time taking extra batting practice off pitcher Joe Dobson. "Dobson had a hell of a curve and a good overhand fastball and he always bore down. Every day that his arm held out and the blisters on my hand held out, we'd go at it there like it was all-out war, one-on-one," Williams described. "Well, for me, it was great fun, and I was about as sharp as I could ever be." That year he had 185 hits, 37 home runs, walked 145 times, and batted .406. It was first time in a decade that anyone had topped .400, and no one has done it since.

The last day of the 1941 season, Boston was playing a doubleheader against Philadelphia. The Splendid Splinter's batting average was at .39955. Manager Joe Cronin offered to let him sit out, since the average would round out to .400. Williams said that if he couldn't hit .400 all the way, he didn't deserve the honor. He went six for eight that day with a homer and a double.

Despite the fact that Ted Williams slugged an amazing 31 homers as a rookie and collected 145 RBI, few people realize that he walked 107 times that season (a 20th century rookie record). Throughout his career he walked more than 100 times in more than half the seasons he played, and because of that, never had a season in which he collected 200 hits.

Williams had a tremendous reputation as being nasty and hard to get along with. Once, he checked into a motel in Fort Myers, Florida, on a fishing trip. He signed the register as G.C. Luther. The clerk glanced at the register and then said, "For a minute I thought you were Ted Williams." Williams replied, "Yeah, a lot of people say that. I think Williams is actually a much older man." The two chatted amiably for a few minutes and then the clerk said, "I have to admit I had my doubts when you signed in, Mr. Luther. I thought you really were Ted Williams. But I can see you're not. You've got a much nicer disposition."

Shortly before he retired, Williams dropped by Ty Cobb's house in Arizona for a visit. The two chatted about hitting and hitters, a friendly discussion among experts. Then they decided to name their all-time all-star teams. Williams suggested putting Rogers Hornsby at second base. Cobb wavered and Williams reasoned "Hornsby out-hit you a couple of years." Cobb, who hated Hornsby, went into a rage and kicked Williams out of the house. Cobb and Williams never spoke to each other after that.

Throughout his career, Williams won six American League batting championships, four home run titles (his personal best was 43 in 1949), led the league in runs scored six times, was league leader in RBI four times, led in walks eight times, and nine times led the league in slugging percentage. He was voted into the Hall of Fame in 1966.

Joe Jackson ("Shoeless Joe")

Joe Jackson was the product of the poverty-ridden cotton belt of South Carolina. He was an illiterate millhand when he signed his first pro contract and debuted as a 19-year-old rookie with the 1908 Philadelphia Athletics. Jackson's country ways and his lack of education made it almost impossible for him to adapt to city life. Throughout his career, he never seemed to acquire the sophistication usually associated with a ballplayer of his incredible talent.

Stories abound of how Jackson would go to restaurants with his teammates and wait for one of them to order. Since he couldn't read the menu, he would simply say to the waiter, "I'll have what he's having."

Once, on the morning of a game, Philadelphia manager Connie Mack wandered by Jackson's dining-room table at the team's hotel. Jackson was busily eating from a plate piled high with fried eggs. "How do you expect to play ball after eating a meal like that?" Mack demanded. "I didn't order them, Mr. Mack," Jackson said. "I just asked for two eggs. Honest." His curiosity got the best of him and Mack pressed the star outfielder for details. Jackson explained that the dining room staff asked the guests to write down their orders. "I didn't know how to make a two, so I put down two ones," Jackson explained. The waiter had taken the order and delivered 11 fried eggs.

When Joe Jackson played his first full season with the Cleveland Naps in 1911, he set a Major League record by hitting .408 as a rookie. He still holds the record for the highest season average for both Cleveland and the Chicago White Sox.

Shoeless Joe's lack of sophistication and education were well-known by the fans. In fact, hecklers would try to break up his usually stellar performances by openly ridiculing him from the stands. In one game he hit a monstrous triple and was standing on third base when a fan yelled, "Hey Joe, can you spell 'cat'?" Jackson sent a stream of tobacco juice in the direction of the heckler and retorted, "How about you, big shot, can you spell 'triple'?"

His teammates on the Athletics were just as merciless on Jackson. Constantly the butt of ridicule from his teammates because of his lack of education, Jackson became sullen and ineffective as a ballplayer. The Athletics then traded him to Cleveland in 1910 for a mediocre outfielder named Bris Lord.

Jackson's Cleveland teammates accepted him for the supernatural baseball player he was and kept the personal ridicule to a minimum. Much happier with his new club, Jackson responded with some of the best years of his career. During his first full season with Cleveland in 1911 (technically his rookie season, since he only played a few games with Philadelphia) he hit .408 but finished second to Ty Cobb in the race for the batting title. (Cobb posted a .420 season.) The next season, Jackson hit .395, but finished second again to Cobb's .410. The next two seasons he hit .373 and .338. Using his favorite bat, "Black Betsy," Jackson posted the third highest lifetime batting average ever (.356). Babe Ruth once said he patterned his swing after Jackson, which is ironic when you consider that many historians credit Ruth with rescuing the game of baseball from the devastating effects of the 1919 "Black Sox" scandal, with which Jackson was supposedly involved.

Joe Jackson earned the nickname "Shoeless Joe" because once during a game in the Carolina Association league he removed his tight-fitting shoes and played the game in his stocking feet.

In 1915, the Cleveland franchise became financially troubled and unloaded Jackson to the White Sox for three unknowns and $31,500. Jackson immediately entered troubled waters. He resented the well-educated star second baseman of the White Sox, Eddie Collins. He wasn't the only one. The team was divided among the Collins followers and a group of malcontents who were unhappy about their salaries, unhappy about the money they were getting out of baseball. The latter group accepted Jackson. They didn't make fun of his country ways or his country drawl. This was the group that would be known in baseball history as the "Black Sox."

The White Sox won the pennant in 1917. The following year, 1918, several key players were serving their country during the war and were absent from the team. In 1919, when everyone returned, the Sox again won the pennant and were heavy favorites to take the World Series from the Cincinnati squad. Jackson had a fine season in 1919 and posted a .351 batting average with 96 RBI.

According to baseball history, a group of gamblers got to the disgruntled players on the 1919 White Sox and promised them $20,000 if they would throw the World Series. Jackson allegedly was part of that group and was promised between $5000 and $8000 to participate in the fix. If Jackson did try to throw the World Series, he did it while hitting an amazing .375!

A jury acquitted the group on criminal charges, but Judge Kenesaw Mountain Landis, the commissioner of the league, banned the eight ballplayers accused of fixing the games and prohibited them from playing Major League baseball for the rest of their lives.

Jackson's amazing lifetime batting average reflects the fact that he hit .300 or better in 10 of his 13 Major League seasons. His extraordinary offensive output was complemented by a powerful, strong arm and solid defensive play. Because of his banishment, Jackson has not been eligible for the Hall of Fame, but in the Hall of Fame League a player needs only to help his team win, and Jackson's numbers certainly mandate his inclusion.

Mickey Mantle ("The Commerce Comet")

Mickey Mantle was the son of an avid baseball fan. When Mantle was born in the mining town of Commerce, Oklahoma, his father named him after his favorite ballplayer, Mickey Cochrane (even though Cochrane's real first name was Gordon and Mickey was a nickname). The young Mantle began playing baseball at a young age and, as he matured, he became known as a good shortstop with great speed and great power, who could hit from both sides of the plate.

Mantle made his Major League debut in 1951 at the age of 19. He suffered a batting slump and launched into temperamental tirades in the clubhouse, so he was sent back down to the minors for more seasoning. He was playing for Kansas City and still slumping (a miserable 0 for 22) when he decided to call his father Elven, better known as Mutt. He decided to tell Mutt he didn't think he wanted to play ball anymore.

Mutt was terminally ill at the time, but rushed to Kansas City and barged into the younger Mantle's room. He began packing his son's suitcase. Mickey asked him what he was doing. "Packing. You're going home," Mutt said. "You're going to work in the mines, that's what we'll do. You can work back down there." Mickey, who was very close to his father, convinced Mutt to let him stay. This was a turning point in the young Mantle's career. He ended the season with a .360 batting average and ascended back to the Majors.

Mantle played most of his career with injuries. A high school football injury had left him with a chronic bone infection in his legs. He had a shoulder operation, a broken foot, and a torn hamstring. Instead of following rehabilitation programs and exercising regularly, Mantle chose to lead "the good life" and party with his teammates off the field. His stated philosophy was "live now." No male member of his family had ever lived past age 40.

Mickey Mantle tied for the American League lead with 11 triples during the 1955 season. But after that he never collected more than six during a campaign and hit an amazingly low number of doubles for a man with his speed.

Despite a series of injuries, Mantle continued to post impressive numbers. In 1956, he hit .353 with 52 home runs and 130 RBI to lead the Majors and win the coveted Triple Crown. Only Rogers Hornsby, Lou Gehrig, and Ted Williams had ever accomplished that feat.

Mantle was generally regarded as having blinding speed (3.1 seconds to first base from the left side) and awesome power. He boasted a career stolen base success rate of 80 percent. He once hit a home run in Washington that was estimated to have traveled an unbelievable 565 feet. He topped that in Yankee stadium by blasting a shot onto the facade of the roof, an estimated 600 feet from home plate. Through 18 seasons in the Majors, Mantle hit 50 or more home runs twice and led the American League in home runs four times. He finished his career with 536 homers. He played in 20 All-Star games and earned the MVP in 1956, 1957, and 1962. Mantle was voted into the Hall of Fame in 1974.

Stan Musial ("The Man")

If ever you need evidence that nice guys can finish first, this is your man. During his career Stan Musial set almost 50 Major League records and was the centerpiece of the championship Cardinal teams of the 1940s and 1950s. Musial was a modest gentleman who was respected by fans and players alike. He simply showed up at the ballpark to do his job–hitting. In fact, he had so much respect around the league that it was the Brooklyn fans who gave him his nickname "The Man."

This son of a Polish immigrant miner turned down a basketball scholarship at University of Pittsburgh to sign as a pitcher/outfielder with the Cardinals in 1938. While playing in the Florida State League in 1940, Musial was 18-5 with Daytona Beach. But that season he permanently injured his throwing arm while making a circus catch in the outfield. His career as a pitcher was over.

Musial used an unusual peekaboo, corkscrew batting stance to win seven batting titles. Batting left-handed, he would curl up his body, and almost seem as though he were looking around a corner. "The one unbreakable rule about hitting is this: a batter hits well with his own particular stance and swing; think twice–or more–before suggesting a change. There is no one correct way to bat, and so of course there is no one correct stance to look for," Musial once said.

Although he was in the World Series his first four full seasons in the Major Leagues, Stan Musial played 17 more years without ever appearing in another Fall Classic.

When Musial came up to the big leagues for his first full season in 1942, his specialties were doubles and triples. The Cardinals won the World Championship in his rookie season. By 1948, he had established himself as a long-ball threat. His lifetime statistics include a .331 batting average, 475 home runs, and 3630 hits. He once hit five home runs in a doubleheader, and during that 1948 season he boasted four games in which he collected five hits.

Dodger manager Leo Durocher was briefing Willie Mays on how to defense the Cardinal hitters before Mays' debut game against the Redbirds. He described the leadoff hitter and the No. 2 hitter, and then he jumped to the cleanup hitter. When Mays asked who was batting third, Durocher said, "The third hitter is Stan Musial. There is no advice I can give you about him."

Cardinal teammate Curt Flood, in his book *The Way It Is,* was describing how he was struggling to learn to hit a curveball. "Musial also helped–mainly by working as hard as he did on his own perfect swing. If this immortal felt the need for frequent extra batting practice, how could I hope to prosper on less effort?"

Musial collected MVP honors three times (1943, 1946, 1948) and finished second in voting four times. He appeared in 24 All-Star games both as a first baseman and as an outfielder. His most famous home run came during the 1955 All-Star game. In the twelfth inning, with the score tied, he stepped to the plate and told catcher Yogi Berra, "I'll get you out of here in a hurry." Then he smashed the first pitch over the wall.

In 1957, as Musial was winding up his career, Brooklyn's Preacher Roe described how to pitch to Musial. "I throw four wide ones, and then I try to pick him off first."

Musial won his last batting title in 1957 at age 36 with a .351 average. In 1962, as a 41-year-old grandfather, he still hit .330—the third best average in the league! He was inducted into the Hall of Fame in 1969.

Willie Mays ("The Say Hey Kid")

At the tender age of 19, Willie Mays was in Minneapolis playing his second year of professional baseball. The Giants sent catcher Hank DeBerry, who had been in the game 30 years, to report on his progress. His report read:

"Sensational. Is the outstanding player on the Minneapolis club and probably in all the minor leagues for that matter. He is now on one of the best hitting streaks imaginable. Hits all pitches and hits to all fields. Hits the ball where it is pitched as good as any player seen in many days. Everything he does is sensational. He has made the most spectacular catches. Runs and throws with the best of them. Naturally, he has some faults, some of which are: charges low-hit balls too much, runs a bit with head down. There have been a few times when his manager needed a rope. When he starts somewhere, he means to get there, hell bent for election. Slides hard, plays hard. He is a sensation and just about as popular with the local fans as he can be—a real celebrity. The Louisville pitchers knocked him down plenty, but it seemed to have no effect on him at all. This player is the best prospect in America. It was a banner year for the Giants when this boy was signed!"

Even after making it to the big leagues, Mays would play stickball with kids in Harlem at night and play baseball with Major Leaguers at the Polo Grounds during the day. His trademarks were making basket catches and losing his hat as he chased after balls. He later admitted that he wore his hat a little small just so that it would fly off.

His sensational ability to make the impossible catch is well documented. In the first game of the 1954 World Series with the score tied and two men on, Vic Wertz launched a

460-foot shot to deep centerfield in the Polo Grounds and Willie Mays made the well-publicized catch.

"As for there being anything difficult about the catch, though, the answer is there wasn't," Mays said. "Any ball you go a long way for is exciting to the fans in the stands, because they're not looking at you when you get your jump on it--they're looking at the hitter. But I'd gotten a good jump, and I had running room, and the ball stayed up for me. I didn't have to pick it off the grass. I didn't have to avoid another fielder, I didn't have to crash the wall. I didn't have to jump in the air, I didn't have to gauge the wind (there was none) or some eccentric thing the ball itself did.

"I doubt there's a day goes by in the big leagues but some outfielder doesn't make a more difficult play than I did on that Wertz ball."

But the throw by Mays carried about 300 feet in the air and was picture-perfect to the infield, a catch and throw that have been recorded as classic Mays.

In the 1959 All Star game, Mays hit a long triple into the deep confines of Forbes Field to win the ball game. Bob Stevens wrote after the game, "The only man who could have caught it, hit it."

Mays collected 11 straight Gold Gloves, set the record for career putouts by an outfielder, set the NL record for total chances, stole 337 bases, and was the first 300/300 man--300 steals and 300 home runs. Twice he hit 50 home runs in a season. He was named MVP in 1954 with a .345 batting average and 41 homers. He was voted MVP again in 1965 when he hit 52 homers (17 in the month of August) to pass the 500 home run mark for his career.

Willie Mays was inducted into the Hall of Fame in 1979.

Willie Mays was the only player to hit 50 or more home runs in a season (51 in 1955) and lead the league in stolen bases the next (40 in 1956). More than a decade and a half later in 1971, he stole 23 bases at age 40.

George Davis

Because George Davis had a reputation as a troublemaker during a troubled period in baseball history, he is probably one of the best ballplayers not in the Hall of Fame. Davis was a star in the National League during a period when the league was ravaged by a divisive power struggle at the top.

Davis broke into baseball as an outfielder with Cleveland, but after two seasons he was traded to New York for future Hall of Famer Buck Ewing. His first four years with the Giants were spent mostly at third base, but by 1897 he had taken over shortstop duties. He served as the Giants' player-manager for part of the 1895 season and then again from mid-1900 to 1901.

He jumped to the White Sox of the American League in 1902 and established himself as a record-setting shortstop. During that 1902 season, he set a new mark for shortstops with a .951 fielding percentage. He collected 600 more hits during his career to set a record for switch hitters that stood until Pete Rose broke it in 1976. Davis still holds the record for most triples (27 in 1893) and the most RBI (134 in 1897) by a switch hitter.

George Davis reached the 2000-hit plateau during the 1902 season and set a record for switch hitters.

But Davis was unhappy with White Sox owner Charles Comiskey's pay structure. During that 1902 season, National League owners were bitterly fighting over who would be appointed president of the league. The American League had appointed Ban Johnson to head the junior circuit and he was taking advantage of the troubled times to establish the American League on equal ground with the National League. The American League was raiding players and gaining credibility, while the National League was feuding and finagling. Davis took advantage of the situation and jumped back to the National League Giants. But peace was eventually restored in the National League. A president was chosen and in 1903 an agreement was reached between the two leagues establishing the American League on equal ground with the National League.

Partly as a result of the truce between the leagues, Davis was "awarded" back to the White Sox in 1903. Davis didn't agree with the decision and decided to sit out the season. John Brush, the newly elected National League president, then sanctioned an illegal scheme devised by the Giants to regain Davis. After four games with the Giants, Davis was slapped with an injunction by the White Sox. The case stayed in court until July 1903 when it was eventually thrown out.

Davis rejoined the Giants in 1904 and played six more seasons in the National League. Previous to the scandal and his one-season stint with the White Sox, Davis never hit below .300 for the Giants. After the scandal, he never hit over .278.

Hugh Jennings ("Ee-Yah")

A colorful and popular player, Jennings was a member of those zany Oriole teams of the 1890s who were as good at circumventing the rules as they were at winning games. He was the captain of that club, and they won the pennant the first three years he played.

Jennings' specialty was getting hit by a pitch. One of the antics of the Orioles during that period was to fake getting hit by a pitch, writhe around on the ground in supposed pain, and pinch themselves to raise a welt. However, Jennings actually was hit in the head and suffered a fractured skull in 1897. Jennings was hit by pitches 49 times in 1896, a record that stood for 75 years.

Oriole teammate John McGraw once described a play that typified his team's shenanigans. "We were on the field and the other team had a runner on first, who started to steal second, but first of all he spiked our first baseman on the foot. Our man retaliated by trying to trip him. He got away, but at second Heinie Reitz tried to block him off while Hughie...covered the bag to take the throw and tag him. The runner evaded Reitz and jumped feet first at Jennings to drive him away from the bag. Jennings dodged the flying spikes and threw himself bodily at the runner, knocking him flat. In the meantime, the batter hit our catcher over the hands with his bat so he couldn't throw, and our catcher trod on the umpire's feet with his spikes and shoved his big mitt in his face so he couldn't see the play."

The umpire, Tim Hurst, said he did the only thing he could do. "I punched Robbie (Wilbert Robinson, the Oriole catcher) in the ribs, called it foul, and sent the runner back."

When Hugh Jennings assumed managerial duties for the Tigers in 1907, he decided to insert a youngster named Ty Cobb into his regular lineup. The Tigers then went from a sixth-place ball club to a first-place pennant contender.

Jennings' career spanned more than 30 years as a player and later as a manager. Even after his physical skills deteriorated later in his career, his leadership and strategic knowledge kept him in the big leagues. After managing in the minors early in the 1900s, Jennings was picked up by the Tigers to be their skipper. During his first three years at the helm for the Tigers, the team won three pennants, but lost each World Series. He became noted for his wild gyrations in the coaching box, cheering on such players as a young Ty Cobb. He would taunt the opposition while in the coaching box and became known for his favorite yell of "Ee-yah," which he claimed was Hawaiian for "Watch out!"

Jennings was named to the Hall of Fame in 1945.

Honus Wagner ("The Flying Dutchman")

Honus Wagner was signed as a 21-year-old shortstop in 1895. He stood 5'11" and weighed 200 pounds, an imposing figure for a shortstop. He was bow-legged and had arms so long that Lefty Gomez once said, "He can tie his shoelaces without bending down."

Wagner played in the minors for two seasons before joining Louisville of the National Association, the beginning of a 21-year career in the Majors. He dominated the National League as a member of the Pittsburgh club in much the same way that Cobb was dominating the American League during this time. Wagner's batting stance has been described as "a man sitting on a bar stool." He used the split-handed grip and swung at everything close. Between 1900 and 1912, he led the league in major offensive categories 38 times with 8 batting championships (in 12 years), 6 slugging championships, 5 stolen base titles, and a .327 career batting average. Voted into the Hall of Fame right after Cobb and right before Ruth, some considered him the greatest player of all time. Quiet, gentle, humble, and very well-liked by other players, Wagner was the direct opposite of Cobb when it came to demeanor and personality.

During his third year in the Majors, a Giant player cracked a home run and Wagner told the player as he was rounding the bases "Nice hit." The player responded by saying, "Go to hell." Wagner said later, "I liked that remark. He was the first Major Leaguer ever to speak to me."

In 1909, Wagner played against Cobb in the World Series. Cobb, sitting on first base, yelled down to him, "Watch out, Krauthead, I'm coming down." As Cobb came barreling into second base, the much bigger Wagner knocked Cobb's teeth loose with the tag.

Some say when he fielded a grounder, he would dig into the ground, scoop up a considerable amount of dirt with the ball, and then let everything go with the throw, thus showering the first baseman with pebbles and dirt. Always willing to tell a tale, Wagner once said a dog ran onto the field during a play and snatched the ball. Wagner claimed he picked up the dog and the ball and threw them both to first for the out.

An original 1909 baseball card of Wagner sold in 1988 for more than $100,000. This card was so valuable because it was distributed as a promotion by a cigarette company. Since he didn't want to encourage kids to smoke, Wagner made the company stop distributing the card after only one printing, making the few cards still in circulation very valuable.

Wagner became a Hall of Famer in 1936.

Remembered as one of the great shortstops of all time, Honus Wagner was still looking for a steady position as he shifted between outfield, third base, and shortstop in 1901 when he was 27 years old.

Mike Schmidt

Mike Schmidt is a perfect example of a great hitter who took a while to develop. Drafted in 1971 out of Ohio State in the second round by the Phillies, Schmidt batted .211 as a shortstop in Double A ball. The next year, in Triple A, he was converted to a third baseman and had a better year—so much better that he was called up to the Phillies for 13 plate appearances. In 1973, he began his first full season and a career that spanned more than 15 years. He became probably the best hitting third baseman of all time, and possibly one of the best fielding third basemen. He had 404 assists in 1974, the most by a National League third sacker, and three years later racked up 396 assists, the second best total. He won nine

Gold Gloves in a row and was voted Most Valuable Player in the National League three times (only Roy Campanella and Stan Musial ever accomplished that feat).

During the 1975 season, power-hitting Mike Schmidt set a Major League record for third basemen by fanning a startling 180 times.

Schmidt's prowess at the plate is in the numbers. He is one of only 14 Major Leaguers to hit 500 home runs or more. He won eight home run crowns and four RBI titles. However, Schmidt did tend to strike out a lot (about three strikeouts for every home run). He had a durable body for baseball, playing in an average of about 147 games each year from 1973 through 1988 and playing in a phenomenal 160 games (in a 162-game season) three times during that time span. Teammate Pete Rose once said, "Just to have his body, I'd trade mine and my wife's and throw in some cash."

Philadelphia was a tough town in which to play. Schmidt once said of the Philadelphia sportswriters, "Philadelphia is the only city in the world where you can experience the thrill of victory and the agony of reading about it the next day."

In 1980, during a sports banquet honoring the world champion Phillies, owner "Ruly" Carpenter said, "What can I say about Mike Schmidt being named MVP for both the National League and the World Series?" Schmidt shouted from the back, "Renegotiate!" The front office of the Phillies must have been listening. Three years later Schmidt hit more than 40 home runs and more than 100 RBI. Despite going 1-20 in the World Series that year, he was awarded a new contract during the off-season–a $2.1 million package that made him the highest paid player in baseball.

George Brett

George Brett came from a family of ballplayers who also included Ken Brett, an older brother who pitched for the Red Sox in the 1967 World Series. Shortly after Brett came up to the Majors, he phoned his father Jack, who thought Ken was the best ballplayer in the family. His dad asked, "Get any hits today?" George said he did not and his father started screaming at him saying "George, your brother's a pitcher and he's outhitting you." (Ken, a pitcher with the Pirates at the time, was involved in a doubleheader that day and had spanked a hit during the first game and a pinch-hit triple during the second game.) When he hung up the phone, George tore it from its mounting, threw it against a wall, and slugged a full-length mirror, shattering it. "Buck Martinez was my roommate then, and poor Buck didn't know what to say," George said.

In his second season, George Brett led the American League with 195 hits, edging out runner-up Rod Carew by a mere three hits.

But Brett soon developed his batting eye and became one of the best hitting third basemen the game has ever known. In 1980, he hovered around a .400 batting average the entire season and finished with a most respectable .390, the highest since Ted Williams in 1941 and within a point of the best average by a third baseman (John McGraw hit .391 in 1899). In 1975, 1976, and 1979, Brett led the American League in both hits and triples during the same season, which only Ty Cobb had done before. He is one of only five players to hit 20 doubles, triples, and home runs in the same season. He won three batting titles, the last in 1990 to become the first player to do so in three decades.

The most famous incident involving Brett was probably the pine tar explosion during a July 1983 game with the Yankees in New York. With one on and two outs in the bottom of the ninth, Brett smacked a Goose Gossage pitch over the right-field fence. Brett had already circled the bases and the Royals were apparently ahead in the game when Billy Martin, the Yankee skipper, complained to umpire Tim McClelland about Brett's bat.

The bat had an excessive amount of the grip-enhancing substance called pine tar on it, Martin said. The rules stipulate that pine tar cannot go up the bat handle more than 18 inches. McClelland, who had conferred with the other umpires, called Brett out for using an illegal bat. Brett went berserk because that meant the game was over and the Yankees had won. During the ensuing argument, Brett was tossed, manager Dick Howser and coach Rocky Colavito were kicked out, and pitcher Gaylord Perry, who had attempted to hide the bat, was also ejected.

American League president Lee MacPhail later overruled the umpires, explaining that the rule on pine tar was merely on the books to keep balls clean and not meant to signify any cheating on the part of the batter. Since the umpires should have merely prevented Brett from using the bat before he batted, the league ruled that the game must be finished and the home run counted. Play was resumed with the Yankees retiring in order and the Royals collecting the win.

Ron Santo

During his 14 seasons with the Chicago Cubs, Ron Santo made his mark as the National League's answer to stellar Brooks Robinson in the American League. Although he lacked the defensive flair of Robinson, Santo was a terror with a bat in his hands. He ranks fourth on the all-time homer list for third basemen behind Mike Schmidt, Eddie Mathews, and Graig Nettles. He had 10 seasons in which he collected 90 or more RBI, with his best effort coming in 1969 when he drove in 129 RBI.

Santo's best offensive season was in 1964 when he hit .313 with 30 homers and 114 RBI. That year he led the league in triples with 13. In 1968, Santo maintained a 28-game hitting streak.

When Ron Santo edged Cardinal Ken Boyer for the 1964 National League Gold Glove at third base, it began a string of five consecutive seasons in which he would collect the award.

Defensively, Santo led National League third basemen in putouts six times, assists seven times, and double plays five times. Only Mike Schmidt handled more chances at third base than Santo.

Santo broke into the Cubs minor league system with teammate Billy Williams. Rogers Hornsby was the hitting instructor for the Cub minor leaguers that season. One day Hornsby gathered his players together to assess their talents. Hornsby sat the young prospects on a row of bleachers and one by one he went down the line berating the players with such comments as, "You better go back to shining shoes because you can't hit." Santo was seated next to Williams and leaned over to his teammate. "If he says that to me, I'm going to cry," whispered Santo. Hornsby came to Williams and said,

"You can hit in the big leagues right now." He moved to Santo and said, "So can you."

Santo played one season with the cross-town White Sox before hanging up his spikes. After his retirement, he opened a successful chain of pizza restaurants in the Chicago area.

Napolean Lajoie ("Nap")

Nap Lajoie was one of the most graceful, consistent, and quick defensive second basemen the game has ever seen. Lajoie was bigger than most infielders of his day (he stood 6'1" and weighed 195 pounds) and, despite playing his career during the dead-ball era, is widely regarded as having plenty of punch in his bat. A right-handed pull hitter, he was feared for his powerful drives down the left-field line. He was so popular among the fans and so respected among his peers that he was instrumental in the launching of the American League and the survival of the Cleveland franchise.

Lajoie began his career in 1896 at age 22 when he joined the Phillies of the National League. His original position was first base, where he played for his first two seasons. In 1897, his first year as an everyday player, Lajoie posted a .363 batting average and led the league in slugging percentage (.578). He moved to second base the following year and led the league in RBI and doubles.

In 1901, the Philadelphia Athletics of the fledgling American League, cross-town rivals of the Phillies, persuaded Lajoie to join their club. Lajoie's defection to the American League provided the instant credibility that Athletics owner Connie Mack and the rest of the league desperately needed. Lajoie tore up the American League that year by leading the league in hits, doubles, home runs, runs scored, and RBI. To top off his season, he posted a .426 batting average that still stands as an American League record.

But the National League was not through with Lajoie. In 1902, the Phillies got a court injunction prohibiting him from playing in the state of Pennsylvania. Using a legal maneuver designed to save the AL, league president Ban Johnson

Nap Lajoie and Harry Bay were featured in the first moving picture ever made of baseball in 1903.

ordered Lajoie to Cleveland, where he instantly revitalized a failing franchise.

In 1903, 1904, and 1910, Lajoie led the American League with averages of .344, .376, and .384. In fact, he hit over .300 in 16 of 21 seasons and ended his career with a lifetime average of .338.

During the 1910 season, Lajoie was locked in a disputed and hotly contested race for the batting championship with Ty Cobb. Lajoie was facing New York's Russ Ford, who wanted to pitch around the second sacker. But in those days, the catcher remained in his crouch rather than raising up for an intentional walk. The pitcher merely threw wide and the catcher would reach out for the pitch. However, his first three times up, Lajoie reached out with one hand and slapped singles to the opposite field. When Nap stepped in for his fourth time up, Ford adjusted the strategy and threw four straight balls behind Lajoie's back.

The award for the batting title in 1910 was a new Chalmers automobile. Lajoie's 8-for-9 day in the final game of the season wasn't enough for the statisticians, as he lost the race to Cobb by .0007. He was given the automobile anyway, despite losing the batting title to the hated Cobb. In 1981, Paul MacFarlane of *The Sporting News* discovered that Cobb got credit for an extra hit that year and Lajoie should have won the title. Commissioner Bowie Kuhn ruled, however, that the records would remain unchanged.

As a player/manager from 1901 to 1909, Lajoie was so popular that his team, the Cleveland Naps, was named after him during his tenure. Lajoie relinquished the reins during the 1909 season because he thought it was hurting his play on the field.

Lajoie was elected to the Hall of Fame in 1937.

Eddie Collins ("Cocky")

In a period when ballplayers were rough and the game was played more with physical ability than with strategy, Eddie Collins was ahead of his time. While attending Columbia University, Collins starred as the captain of the baseball team.

However, perhaps as a testimony of the times, he was barred from playing his senior year because he had played professional baseball under the fictitious name of "Eddie Sullivan." But, atypical of the time, he chose to stay at Columbia to collect his degree and coach the baseball team.

Collins was an extremely heady player. He often planned strategies several plays in advance. He was aggressive and sometimes aloof, but his extreme confidence in his abilities led his teammates and opponents to view him as cocky and arrogant.

In 1917, Eddie Collins collected a salary that was more than three times higher than most of his White Sox teammates, including superstar Joe Jackson.

Offensively, the book on Collins was that he could bunt with the best of them and was an extremely intelligent base runner. His slashing left-handed batting style never won him a batting title (after all, he played during the Ty Cobb era). He was the perfect leadoff or No. 2 hitter because he drew five walks for every strikeout. His 3311 hits is eighth best on the all-time list. Collins finished his career with a .333 lifetime average and 743 stolen bases.

Some of the players against whom Collins played were convinced that he had an unfair advantage on the base paths. These players were sure that his oversized ears acted like sails and, when his ears caught the wind as he rounded the bases, they actually gave him extra speed. Collins is the only player since 1900 to steal six bases in one game–and he did it twice in the span of two weeks in 1912.

He was best known during his 25-year career as a superb second baseman, but perhaps not as graceful as his contemporary, Nap Lajoie. He led all second baseman in fielding average nine times in his career, more than any other second baseman in history. He was the pivot man in the A's $100,000 infield that helped the Philadelphia club win four pennants from 1910 to 1914. That infield consisted of Jack Barry at shortstop, Stuffy McInnis at first base, and Frank Baker at third base. The $100,000 figure, by the way, had nothing to do with how much the players were paid, but instead referred to how much owner Connie Mack could get if he sold the players. Collins later said that this infield was so good because they played as a unit and because they were able to establish good personal relationships on and off the field.

Collins was sold to the Chicago White Stockings in 1915 and starred in the 1917 World Series with a .409 series average. He was also a member of the 1919 White Sox, recorded in history as the famous "1919 Black Sox." Collins was on the "clean" side of that faction-ridden club. He was by far the highest paid player on the team and considered an elitist in the relatively rough world of baseball. Collins was the only member of the club who refused to sharpen his spikes, according to teammate Buck Weaver. "He figures they might come back at him and he'd get hurt playing there in the infield. He was a great guy to look out for himself. If there was a tough gent coming down to second, he'd yell for the shortstop to take the play."

Neither first baseman Chick Gandil (credited with getting the Black Sox scandal underway by approaching a Boston bookmaker with the scheme to throw the World Series) nor shortstop Swede Risberg (also implicated in the scandal) would speak to him. Although he never forgave the eight players implicated in the scandal, Collins still viewed that team as one of the best he played for because of the team's ability to overcome hostility, internal bickering, and downright cheating and still post wins on the board.

Collins became a Hall of Famer in 1939.

Rogers Hornsby ("Rajah")

Rogers Hornsby was quite simply one of best right-handed hitters the game has ever known. He would stand in the far back corner of the batter's box and stride into the pitch. Pitchers would often try to get him low and away, but his ability to move into the pitch frequently countered that strategy with base hits. He had difficulty with the high-and-inside pitch because of his stride, but because umpires respected his batting eye, those pitches were often called balls. Hornsby was known as a line-drive hitter who sprayed the ball to all fields, and his decent speed allowed him to leg out extra-base hits.

Hornsby had the looks of a hero. He was handsome, outspoken, professional, spirited, and motivated. But he was also known for his abrasive personality, and he refused to recognize authority. Extremely self-assured, he reportedly disdained the opinions and feelings of everyone but himself. He was considered by many to be moody, argumentative, blunt, and hypercritical. Some of his contemporaries described him as having "the coldest eyes" they had ever seen. He liked to bet on the horses, but he was never any good at it. He didn't drink or smoke. As has been widely documented, he refused to read (except for box scores in newspapers) or go to movies for fear they would hurt his batting eye.

Rogers Hornsby, known as one of the greatest second basemen ever, broke into the Major Leagues in 1916 as a third baseman and played all of the 1917 season as shortstop.

"Baseball is my life, the only thing I know and can talk about, my only interest," he said. Once, when asked why he didn't play golf like other big leaguers, Hornsby said, "When I hit a ball, I want somebody else to chase it."

Hornsby was a lifetime .358 hitter (second only to Cobb) and hit more than 300 home runs. He was the only right-handed hitter to hit .400 three times, and in 1924 he hit .424. He had a slugging percentage that year of .756, also a record for a right-handed hitter. Hornsby won six consecutive batting titles between 1920 and 1925 and added a seventh in 1928. He led the National League in home runs twice, led in triples twice (with one tie), led in doubles four times, won two Triple Crowns, and was named MVP twice.

Hornsby's batting eye was legendary. In 1927, he was facing Jim "Jumbo" Elliott of the Dodgers. Elliott and catcher Hank DeBerry were arguing with the umpire, Cy Pfirman, over every ball that he called. The count was 3-2 and Elliott threw one down the middle that Hornsby parked over the right-field fence. As Hornsby was making his home run trot around the bases, Pfirman stepped toward the mound and shouted to Elliott, "Mr. Hornsby will let you know when the ball is over the plate."

Hornsby was elected to the Hall of Fame in 1942.

Norm Cash ("Stormin' Norman")

The Chicago Bears of the National Football League were so impressed with Norm Cash as a college player at Sul Ross State in Alpine, Texas, that they drafted him in the 13th round. Cash chose to play baseball instead.

After signing him as an outfielder in 1958, the White Sox converted him to a first baseman during his rookie season. The following year, the Sox dealt Cash to Cleveland in a four-player deal that sent Minnie Minoso to the White Sox for John Romano, Bubba Phillips, and Cash. Cleveland held onto Cash long enough for him to grab a cup of coffee before they traded him in 1960 to Detroit for unknown Steve Demeter. This trade ranked right up there with the Red Sox unloading Babe Ruth to the Yankees. Demeter only had five more Major League at-bats before he retired from baseball.

Known for his outspoken ways, Norm Cash once ridiculed Thurman Munson for his shaggy hairstyle. "Where'd you get that haircut," Cash said, "in a pet shop?"

Cash has a reputation as a one-season flash in the pan. His Hall of Fame League season occurred in 1961, his second year as the Tiger's first sacker. That year Cash hit .361, clubbed 41 homers, and collected 132 RBI. He also led the league in on-base percentage with a .662 mark. Unfortunately for Cash, his career year coincided with the career year for Roger Maris, who broke Babe Ruth's single-season home run mark by hitting 61. Maris won MVP honors despite Cash's exceptional season.

"The only mistake I made in my whole baseball career was hitting .361 that one year," Cash said, "because ever since then people have expected me to keep on doing it."

That being his only "mistake" is a matter of opinion, however. No doubt the fact that the league had just added an expansion team (the Los Angeles Angels) and that Tiger Stadium's shallow right field (as you'll see in Chapter 11, the right-field fence is a relatively short distance for home run hitters) contributed to Cash's success that year. "I owe my success to expansion pitching, a short right-field fence, and my hollow bats," Cash said later in his career.

That reference to "hollow bats" stirred some controversy. Many baseball analysts suspect that some of the Tigers that year were using corked bats. Corking a bat entails boring a hole about a half-inch wide and eight inches deep in the top of the bat, plugging the top two inches of the hole with cork, sawdust, and glue, and then sanding the top so that no one will notice the tampering. Corking bats was and still is illegal. The practice makes the bat much lighter and can add 20 to 50 feet on some line drives.

In any case, 1962 was a miserable year for Cash. He set the kind of record that hitters have nightmares about when his batting average dropped a record 118 points. Throughout the rest of his career he never came within 75 points of hitting as well as he did in 1961 and never again drove in 100 RBI. But his plunge does require some perspective.

Cash had more RBI per official at-bat than his Tiger roommate, Al Kaline, partially because he walked 1043 times in his career. "Prorated at 500 at-bats a year," Cash said after his retirement, "that means that for two years out of the 14 that I played, I never even touched the ball."

When he did touch the ball, he met it with power. Four times he cleared the roof at Tiger Stadium while he was amassing his career total 377 home runs. With his traditional uppercut swing, Cash hit 30 or more homers five times and 20 or more homers 11 times, most in a nine-year span from 1960 to 1969.

Defensively, Cash led the American League in putouts in 1961, fielding average in 1964 and 1967, and assists in 1966 and 1967. Despite the fact that he does not appear in the top ten for games played at first base, Cash is seventh on the all-time list in lifetime assists (1317).

In 1986, a dozen years after his retirement from baseball, Cash fell off a boat, struck his head, and drowned.

Jimmie Foxx ("The Beast")

Foxx was a man of enormous strength who loved to show off his bulging biceps by cutting off the sleeves of his shirts. Lefty Gomez was the victim of that strength one day when Foxx planted one of his pitches in the farthest corner of the third deck in Yankee stadium. "Even his hair has muscles," said Gomez.

Although Foxx was originally signed as a catcher, a fellow by the name of Mickey Cochrane (who was later inducted into the Hall of Fame) beat him out at that position and Foxx moved to first base. For such a big man (six feet tall, 195 pounds of pure muscle), Foxx was exceptionally light on his feet and had a good arm. In fact, he even pitched 10 games and posted a 1.52 ERA.

During the Philadelphia Athletics' dynasty years of 1929-1931, Foxx walloped 100 home runs and drove in 343. In 1932, he launched a serious attempt at breaking Ruth's 60-home run mark for a season, but came up short with only 58 that year. However, his fans noted that he had two home runs taken away by rainouts! Foxx hit 35 or more home runs per season for nine consecutive years.

Although he had won two MVP awards by the time he was 25, Jimmie Foxx was still not considered the top first baseman in the league. Of course, he was playing in the same league with Lou Gehrig.

He collected 169 RBI in that 1932 season and posted a .364 batting average. For his efforts, he was voted MVP and won MVP honors again the following year. During the 1933 season, he won the Triple Crown with 48 home runs, 163 RBI, and a .356 batting average. Foxx thus became the first player in the American League to win the Triple Crown since Ty Cobb in 1909. In 1938, he was voted MVP with 175 RBI and a .349 batting average–thus becoming the first player to win the award three times. His lifetime .609 slugging percentage ranks him behind Ruth, Williams, and Lou Gehrig on the all-time slugging list.

In the 1930 World Series, Foxx hit a home run described by pitcher Burleigh Grimes as "knocking the concrete loose in the center field bleachers." In the 1931 World Series, he hit a home run that impressed a Cardinal bullpen pitcher so much he said, "We were watching that ball for two innings."

Foxx was admitted to the Hall of Fame in 1951.

Lou Gehrig ("The Iron Horse")

As is often the tradition when the rites of spring begin, sportswriters in 1927 were publishing their picks to take it all in the Major Leagues. Many of those sportswriters picked the Philadelphia Athletics to win the 1927 World Series. They weren't even close. The 1927 Yankees won 110 games that year and have become the yardstick by which all great teams are measured.

That was the year Babe Ruth hit 60 home runs, batted .356, and had 164 RBI. But the MVP award that year went to Lou Gehrig, who had 47 homers, 175 RBI, and a .373 batting average. Throughout his career, Gehrig was instrumental in the Yankee dynasty's winning seven pennants. But, of course, the most famous record set by The Iron Horse is the 2130 straight games that he played.

Gehrig's relationship with his mother was well-publicized. His mother would accompany her son to spring training, sometimes on short road trips, or even to the many World Series games in which he starred. His mother underwent surgery before the 1927 World Series and Gehrig almost didn't play. "My place is at my mother's side. She is worth more to me than any ball game, or any World Series that was ever invented," he said. Eventually his mother and his manager reasoned with him to play.

In 1931, Lou Gehrig set a record by hitting three grand-slam homers in a four-day period.

Gehrig was good friends with Ruth until the early thirties when they had a falling out over a family matter. Press accounts portrayed Gehrig as the exact opposite of Ruth, although many suspect that could not have been the case. The two often fished together and barnstormed together during the off-season. The two always expressed sincere admiration for each other's abilities and accomplishments. They would also team up as partners in the bridge games played in the Yankee clubhouse. According to one unnamed source, "They disagree on only one subject, when to take your partner out of a one-no-trump bid."

Throughout his career he admitted, "I'm not a headline guy." He hit a monstrous .545 in the 1928 World Series, but Ruth hit .625. He hit a home run in the 1932 World Series, but Ruth hit his famous "called shot" just ahead of him. Gehrig hit four home runs in a game, but the same day John McGraw retired and stole the headlines.

Gehrig hit the ball hard with topspin, unlike Ruth and Foxx who lifted the ball for greater distance. Ironically, Yankee

Stadium was not a good ballpark for him as a hitter—he actually hit better on the road. Gehrig slapped 23 grand slams (a record still on the books), 73 three-run homers, 166 two-run shots, and 231 home runs with the bases empty (after all, he did follow Ruth in the batting order). His 1.77 RBI-per-home run ratio is the highest among players who have 300 or more round-trippers.

In the 1932 World Series, Gehrig hit three home runs in three games, batted .529, and batted in a four-game record eight runs. He won the Triple Crown in 1934 (.363 average, 49 home runs, 165 RBI).

Gehrig was inducted into the Hall of Fame in 1939.

Willie McCovey ("Stretch")

In the tradition of Jimmie Foxx, Willie McCovey was a frightening sight to opposing pitchers. At 6'4", 198 pounds, Stretch debuted with the Giants in 1959 and in his first game collected two singles and two triples. From the moment he donned the Giants uniform, he was on fire. In his first seven games, he smacked three home runs, collected 9 RBI, and boasted a .467 batting average. He was so hot at the beginning of the year that pitcher Robin Roberts said, "He hit everything I threw." In a subtle display of understatement, pitcher Lew Burdette said, "He hits curves, sliders, and fastballs."

After Willie McCovey joined the Giants in 1959, the San Francisco club faced the dilemma of who to play at first—the hot-hitting Stretch or the hot-hitting Orlando Cepeda (who had 46 homers and 142 RBI in 1961). The Giants solved the problem in 1966 by trading Cepeda to the Cardinals for pitcher Ray Sadecki.

Predictably, McCovey was named Rookie of the Year in 1959 and ended the season with a .354 batting average. Over a 22-year career in the big leagues, McCovey swatted 521 home runs and collected 1555 RBI. He set a National League record with 18 lifetime grand slams and led the league three times in home runs.

During the 1968 through 1970 seasons, McCovey led the league in slugging percentage. He was the RBI champ in 1968 and 1969 and was voted MVP for the 1969 season.

During the seventh game of the 1962 World Series with the Giants down 1-0, McCovey came up in the ninth, facing two outs, the tying and winning runs in scoring position. He hit a searing line drive headed for right field, but the ball was snared by Yankee second baseman Bobby Richardson. During his acceptance speech at the Hall of Fame in 1986, McCovey said, "People ask me how I'd like to be remembered. I tell them I'd like to be remembered as the guy who hit the line drive *over* Bobby Richardson's head."

Carlton Fisk ("Pudge")

A series of injuries early in his career certainly did not bode well for Carlton Fisk. But over his 20-year career, Fisk has proven himself to be one of the most durable catchers in the game. When he broke in with the Boston Red Sox as their everyday catcher in 1972, he clobbered a league-leading 9 triples, 22 home runs, and posted a .293 batting average. It was quite a rookie season that earned him a Gold Glove and a unanimous choice as Rookie of the Year (the first player ever to receive all the votes).

His average dropped to .246 the following year, but he still cranked 26 more home runs. In 1974, he suffered a broken collarbone that sidelined him from the last week in June to the end of the season. During spring training of 1975, Fisk reinjured himself and was unable to play until June, but he hit .331 during the second half of that season to help propel the Red Sox into the World Series.

In 1972, Carlton Fisk became the only American League catcher to lead the circuit in triples.

It was during that 1975 World Series that the entire country saw Pudge in his heroic finest. In the sixth game of the series with the score tied, Fisk got all of a Pat Darcy pitch and sent it sailing toward the left-field foul pole. Fisk started toward first, but used all the body English he could muster to urge the ball fair as it left the park.

Fisk suffered more injuries in 1979, and he only played in about 90 games, mostly as a designated hitter. His last season with the Red Sox was 1980, when he hit .289 and smacked 18 home runs. A clerical blunder on the part of the Red Sox (they failed to have his new contract postmarked on time) enabled Fisk to sign with the White Sox as a free agent for the 1981 season.

At age 37 in 1985, he poked 37 homers, and the following year he reached the 300-homer plateau for his career. In 1988 he broke the record for most games caught in the American

League, a record that he continues to hold today. Fisk's reputation is one of a catcher with an excellent arm who does a fine job of handling a pitching staff. Remarkably, as of this writing, Fisk is still on the White Sox roster, playing catcher, first base, and designated hitter.

Joe Torre ("The Godfather")

Remember when you were playing Little League ball and the manager would always put the catching gear on the biggest, fattest kid on your team? Joe Torre was that kid, but in the Major Leagues rather than Little League.

The Braves put Torre behind the plate because of his propensity to gain and maintain his heavy weight. As a catcher, he wasn't expected to be a fast runner. He had a decent arm and his catching skills were adequate. The real method to this madness, however, was to find a spot in the lineup for Torre's flaming bat. Catchers normally need an occasional day of rest from the demanding duties behind the mask, but in Torre's case that day was usually spent playing first base so the Braves wouldn't miss his bat.

Torre broke in with the Braves as a 20-year-old kid in 1960 late in the season. In his first at-bat against Harvey Haddix, he hit a pinch single. The following year, playing only as a semi-regular, Torre finished second behind Billy Williams as the National League Rookie of the Year.

On opening day in 1965, Joe Torre blasted two home runs to start his season with the Braves. On opening day in 1966, Torre again hit two home runs. Only Eddie Matthews, who also played with the Braves, has ever matched that feat.

By 1963, Torre was playing regularly at catcher and first base. His experience began to show positive results both offensively and defensively. That year he hit .293 with 14 homers. He was voted to the All-Star team for the 1963 through 1967 seasons. In 1964 he led all catchers in fielding and improved his offensive output to a .321 average, 20 homers, and 109 RBI.

Nicknamed The Godfather because of his classic Italian features, Torre continued his surge in 1965 when he hit 27 homers and won the National League Gold Glove award for catchers. The Braves moved from Milwaukee to Atlanta the following season, and The Godfather took full advantage of his new stadium. He hit a career-high 36 homers, batted .315, and roped in 101 RBI. Torre spent most of the 1968 season injured with a broken cheekbone.

In 1969, the Braves traded Torre to the St. Louis Cardinals for Orlando Cepeda. The Cards used Torre primarily at first base to replace Cepeda since they had a fine catcher in Tim McCarver. For each of the next three seasons, Torre collected more than 100 RBI. St. Louis traded McCarver to the Phillies in 1970 and moved Torre back behind the plate. When third baseman Mike Shannon suffered an injury in mid-season, Torre was moved again, this time to third base.

The shuffling between positions didn't affect Torre at the plate. He hit .325 in 1970 and blasted 21 homers. The next year, after an off-season of losing weight, the trim Torre led the National League in total bases (352), hits (230), batting average (.363) and RBI (137) to win the MVP. He led the league in putouts that year, but also tied for the lead in errors by a third baseman.

The Godfather never topped that career year even though he lasted 18 seasons in the Major Leagues. He ended his career with a .297 average, 252 homers, and 1185 RBI.

Roy Campanella ("Campy")

The son of a black mother and an Italian father, Roy Campanella began his professional career when he played with a semi-pro team in his Philadelphia hometown. He played well enough to be signed into the Negro Leagues with the Baltimore Elite Giants at age 15 in 1937. He tried to juggle school and baseball, but finally quit school two years later to play ball full time. In 1939 he became the regular catcher with the Giants.

He soon challenged Josh Gibson as the dominant catcher in the Negro Leagues. He played in All-Star games in 1941, 1944, and 1945. In the fall of 1945, Campanella was catching in an All-Star game against a team of white Major League ballplayers managed by Charlie Dressen. Dressen had orders to meet with Campanella on behalf of the Brooklyn Dodgers of the National League, who later signed him to play Class B ball. That minor league team was run by Buzzie Bavasi and

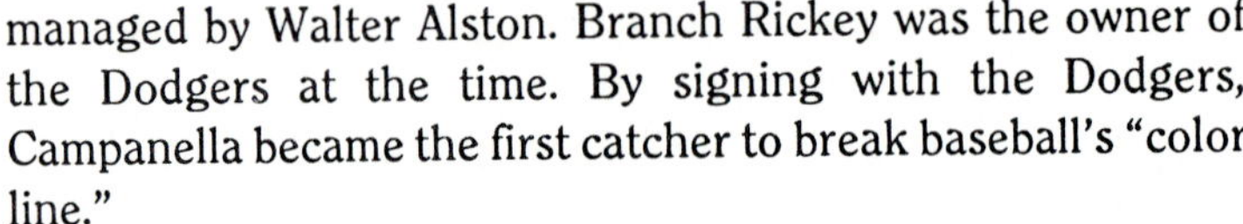

managed by Walter Alston. Branch Rickey was the owner of the Dodgers at the time. By signing with the Dodgers, Campanella became the first catcher to break baseball's "color line."

"They scouted me and were about to sign me. I went into Mr. Rickey's office and sat across the table from him," Campanella described. "He told me he had scouts watching me for months. There was no question I could play. What he couldn't tell was my habits. Did I drink? Did I run around with women? Would I embarrass the club with my conduct? That's what they had to be sure of before they signed any Negro player."

Roy Campanella and Yogi Berra are the only catchers ever to win MVP honors three times.

In 1946, Campanella took MVP honors and in 1947 he was advanced to the Dodgers' International League club. He again won the MVP. In 1948 he was called up to The Show, but Rickey insisted that manager Leo Durocher play Campanella in the outfield. The result was less than successful. Campanella had a sub-par season and was sent back down to the minor league AA club. He played a mere 35 games down in the minors and was hitting .325 when he was called back up to the Dodgers, this time for good.

Campy's rookie year was the only one of his ten seasons in the Major Leagues when he didn't catch more than 100 games. He was obviously an excellent defensive catcher who was known for his ability to handle pitchers. During those ten seasons, the Dodgers won five National League pennants (1949, 1952, 1953, 1955, and 1956) and narrowly missed winning two others. During those five World Series, Campanella caught every inning of every game for the Dodgers. In 1955, the Dodgers beat the cross-town Yankees to become Brooklyn's first World Champions.

When Campanella stepped to the plate, he was a monster. In 1951, he hit .325 with 33 home runs and 108 RBI to win his first National League MVP. That year he edged out Stan Musial in the voting to become the first National League catcher since 1938 to win the honor. In 1953, he collected his second MVP with a .312 average, 41 homers, and 142 RBI.

Campy suffered a chipped bone in his left hand and a damaged nerve during spring training in 1954. He played in 111 games that year and his batting average slipped to .207. Surgery in the off-season corrected the problem and when he returned in 1955, he hit .318, slammed 32 homers, and collected 107 RBI. He was rewarded for his exceptional effort with his third MVP award.

Campanella was permanently injured in an automobile accident in 1958 and forced to retire from baseball. He was voted into the Hall of Fame in 1969.

Johnny Bench

Known for his rifle arm and for his practice of catching with one hand behind his back, some say Johnny Bench was the greatest catcher of all time. Bench might also hold the distinction of being one of the few minor league ballplayers whose club, Peninsula of the Carolina League, retired his number. That honor was given to Bench following his 1966 season in which the 18-year-old pounded 22 home runs in 98 games.

Bench spent most of the next season with Buffalo in the minors but got the call up to the Cincinnati Reds in August of 1967. The next year, the 20-year-old went up to Ted Williams during spring training and asked the Splendid Splinter to autograph a ball for him. Williams wrote, "To a Hall of Famer, for sure."

His first full season, Bench set a record for rookie catchers by playing in 154 games. He also set a record with 40 doubles (the most by a rookie) and ended the season by becoming the first National League catcher to be named Rookie of the Year.

In 1975, Johnny Bench clouted 28 home runs, collected 110 RBI, and hit .283. During the 1975 World Series, he hit a meager .207. In 1976, Bench hit 16 homers, collected 74 RBI, and hit .234. During the 1976 World Series, he hit .533.

Bench played his entire career with Cincinnati's Big Red Machine, a team that won six division titles, four pennants, and two World Series. He batted either fourth or fifth in that impressive lineup and posted some big numbers. In all, he had 11 seasons in which he swatted 20 or more home runs. He won his first MVP award in 1970 when he hit 45 home runs and collected 148 RBI. His second MVP came after an impressive 1972 season in which he hit 40 homers and collected 125

RBI. Those totals were the best in the league, the second time he had taken the home run and RBI jewels of the Triple Crown. His last great offensive season came in 1977 when he hit 31 home runs and had 109 RBI.

Bench was selected to the All-Star team 13 consecutive years. His selection was based as much on his defense as his power hitting. He collected 10 straight Gold Gloves and set career records for putouts and chances. He was also known as a catcher who took control of his pitchers, a trait that he brought with him to the majors and that never left him.

During his rookie season he was catching Jerry Arrigo, who did not have great stuff. "He thought he had a fastball," Bench said. "He was pitching against a hitter I knew he couldn't possibly throw it by. I called for a curve, and he shook it off, a curve again and he shook it off, a curve one more time and he shook it off. He finally threw a fastball outside." To show his disgust, Bench reached out and caught the ball barehanded.

Johnny Bench became a Hall of Famer in 1988.

What To Look For

With the introductions out of the way, you can now associate some personalities with the names of the superstars in the League. You can refer to Table 5-1 to get a sense of the great seasons these guys had. The following is a brief overview of how you can expect each player to perform in the Hall of Fame League. Each player's name is followed by the team and year of his best season.

Babe Ruth (1920 New York Yankees) Without question, Babe Ruth is the greatest player of all time. Even after normalization, his statistics are far above anyone else's in the League. The best left-handed hitter in the League, Ruth has below-average speed and may be a liability on defense. But his numbers at the plate outweigh any deficiencies he may have. He has more power than anyone else, as exemplified by his

.869 slugging percentage and his .514 isolated power percentage. He's great against lefties, but he's an unbelievable hitter against righties. Ruth is a cleanup hitter with no peers.

Ed Delahanty (1896 Philadelphia Phillies) Big Ed boasts good numbers at the plate, but he lacks the home run punch you'd like to see from your outfielders. He has attained his spot among the elite because of his defense and his ability to get on base. Delahanty chews up left-handed pitching, but then again, his numbers against right-handed pitching are also good. Delahanty is one of only two right-handed hitters rated in the top ten outfielders.

In a 1925 game against the St. Louis Browns, Ty Cobb collected six hits in six trips to the plate. Three of those hits were home runs. The next day, he hit two more home runs, thus entering the record books as the only player between 1884 and 1936 to hit five round-trippers in consecutive games.

Ty Cobb (1911 Detroit Tigers) The original burner on the base paths, Cobb most certainly is among the top base stealers in the League. His defense is a bit suspect and he is somewhat weaker against lefties than against righties, but his speed outweighs all else. Cobb is one of the best leadoff hitters in the League.

Tris Speaker (1913 Boston Red Sox) One of the best defensive outfielders in the League, Speaker also offers good speed and an uncanny ability to get on base in the clutch. He has the power to hit doubles and triples. He has trouble hitting left-handed pitching, but has a field day against righties. You would probably have to bat Speaker way down in the lineup against lefties, but he is an excellent No. 2 hitter against the right-handers.

Ted Williams (1941 Boston Red Sox) Williams is one of those players who is just a great hitter. He doesn't have any speed and he has a few problems in the field, but he is a great offensive force. Williams is the second-best left-handed hitter in the League with good power and an exceptional ability to get on base. Williams is the perfect No. 3 hitter.

Joe Jackson (1912 Cleveland Naps) With good speed, solid defense, and good numbers at the plate, Jackson is your basic all-around ballplayer. His normalized batting average of .409 shows he knows how to get on base. He lacks punch at the plate, but he still gets on base for your big hitters and has the speed to steal some bases. Jackson would fit well in the No. 2 spot in your batting order against lefties and No. 3 against righties.

Mickey Mantle (1957 New York Yankees) Mantle is the best switch hitter the Hall of Fame League has to offer. He is a great hitter from both sides of the plate, and his excellent speed will get you some extra bases. He's not a contact hitter, but he does get on base and have good power.

Stan Musial (1948 St. Louis Cardinals) Like many left-handed hitters, Musial seems to struggle a bit against left-handed pitching. He is an excellent hitter, however, with a righty on the mound. He has good power and will hit the ball out of the park. Musial makes a good No. 5 hitter in your order.

Willie Mays, recognized as one of 11 players ever to hit four home runs in a game, is the only player in that group to have ever hit three triples during a game.

Willie Mays (1955 San Francisco Giants) Mays is one of the top three right-handed hitters in the League. He has excellent power with good speed, and he utilizes that speed to give you great defense. He is somewhat weak against right-handed pitchers, but makes up for it when he faces a lefty.

George Davis (1899 New York Giants) Rated as the top shortstop in the League, Davis excels above all others because of his ability to get on base, his good speed, and his exceptional defense. He is a great bunter and a good hit-and-run man. He has a rocket for an arm and exceptional range. The only downside to Davis is that he has no power and will probably bat seventh or eighth.

Hughie Jennings (1896 Baltimore Orioles) Another great defensive player who is excellent at getting on base and advancing base runners, Jennings also lacks power at the plate. He plays good, solid defense and certainly won't hurt your ball club. His great speed will get you many stolen bases throughout the season. Jennings bats in the second spot in the order against left-handed pitching, but must be dropped way down in the order against right-handers.

In 1901, Honus Wagner compiled a .353 batting average, but he was outhit that season by Ed Delahanty who posted a .354 average. Wagner finished fourth in the race for the batting title that year.

Honus Wagner (1905 Pittsburgh Pirates) Like the top two shortstops in the League, Wagner lacks the punch to hit the long ball. But Wagner is probably the best hitting shortstop of the bunch who most certainly will take the extra base and steal a few for you along the way. Wagner makes a good leadoff or No. 2 hitter in your lineup.

Mike Schmidt (1981 Philadelphia Phillies) Schmidt provides excellent power at a position where you like to see a power hitter. He excels far above all other third basemen in the League primarily because of his exceptional power and his exceptional defense. Schmidt is perennially a top pick on Draft Day. Obviously, Schmidt belongs in the meat of the batting order, usually in the cleanup spot against left-handed pitching.

George Brett (1980 Kansas City Royals) Using his good power and great ability to get on base, Brett is the second-best pick for a third baseman. He doesn't have Schmidt's power or Schmidt's defense, but he is a great left-handed hitter who does give you some punch at a power position.

Ron Santo (1966 Chicago Cubs) Santo's overall numbers rank him fifth in the ratings for third basemen, but his defense is what makes him a solid pick. He has no speed and lacks the power you'd like to have at the hot corner, but his defense outshines both of those deficiencies.

Nap Lajoie (1910 Cleveland Naps) If you are the opposition and you have a lefty on the mound, you'd better pitch around Lajoie. He simply eats lefties for lunch. Lajoie is not a power hitter by any means and his fielding is only above-average for the position, but his bat makes him the top-rated second baseman in the League. Lajoie makes a good No. 2 hitter in the batting order.

Eddie Collins (1910 Philadelphia Athletics) Collins commanded a high salary from the A's primarily because he was a great contact hitter with exceptional speed. Only one other second baseman in the League comes close to matching Collins' speed (Joe Morgan). Although he has some trouble hitting left-handed pitching, Collins can still get on base against righties. He has no power. Collins seems to fit in best at the bottom of the batting order, but he could bat second or even lead off.

Rogers Hornsby (1924 St. Louis Cardinals) The best power-hitting second baseman available, Hornsby is awesome against left-handed pitching. He is by no means a defensive gem. In fact, what allows him to be among the top five at his position is his power, which is unusual for a second baseman. Because of his unusual power, Hornsby actually makes a good cleanup hitter.

Norm Cash (1961 Detroit Tigers) If you are looking for a great power hitter against right-handed pitching, this is your man. He can't run and he is only average in the field, but he sure can hit the long ball. He also walks a lot.

Jimmie Foxx hit his 500th career home run in 1940, less than a month before his 33rd birthday. Foxx only played five more seasons before retiring at the end of the 1945 campaign. He ended his career with 534 home runs.

Jimmie Foxx (1933 Philadelphia Athletics) If you are looking for a great power hitter against left-handed pitching, this is your man. He can't run and he is only average in the field, but he sure can hit the long ball. Sound familiar? Foxx is a Norm Cash from the other side of the plate.

Lou Gehrig (1927 New York Yankees) If Babe Ruth were not in the Hall of Fame League, Gehrig would be the most powerful hitter to step in the batter's box. Gehrig does not offer anything spectacular in the field, just awesome power at the plate. He has trouble hitting left-handed pitching, but then lefties are not that common in this League. Gehrig also has better-than-average speed on the base paths.

When Willie McCovey won Rookie of the Year honors in 1959, he became the only player ever to win the award with less than two months of experience at the Major League level.

Willie McCovey (1969 San Francisco Giants) McCovey has about as much power as Gehrig. He is your basic long-ball threat. McCovey's defense is a bit suspect and he has a difficult time hitting left-handed pitching. He will, however, put up some solid home run totals.

Carlton Fisk (1972 Boston Red Sox) No other catcher in the League can compare to Carlton Fisk. He is in a class all by himself. He has good power and is an excellent defensive catcher with an above-average arm. He hits left-handed pitching much better than right-handed. As with most of the catchers, Fisk holds down the sixth or seventh slot in the batting order.

Joe Torre (1966 Atlanta Braves) Torre has good power and defense, but he is a liability on base paths. He'll poke some home runs for you and his arm will keep base runners in check.

Roy Campanella (1951 Brooklyn Dodgers) A carbon copy of Torre, Campanella has a weaker arm and is less valuable defensively than Torre.

Johnny Bench (1972 Cincinnati Reds) Bench is the most powerful hitter among the catchers and loves to go deep. His defense (particularly his arm) suffers significantly in the normalization process.

On Deck

Now that you've met some of the big names in the Hall of Fame League, you can appreciate the vast ability that you have at your disposal. You can see from the normalized and actual statistics in Table 5-1 how great these superstars really were.

But your starting lineup does not consist merely of eight hitters and fielders. If you think some of these guys were characters, wait until you meet some of the pitchers in the League.

Table 5-1.

Actual and Normalized Statistics

		YR	G	AB	R	H	BA	2B	3B	HR	RBI	BB	K	SB	CS	BAT RUNS	STL RUNS	FLD RUNS	TTL PLYR RTG
OUTFIELD																			
RUTH	L	1920	142	458	158	172	.376	36	9	54	137	148	80	14	14				
		AL		498		172	.345	49	9	54		89	77			101	-3	-1	97
DELAHANTY	R	1896	123	499	131	198	.397	44	17	13	126	62	22	37	0				
		NL		522		198	.379	47	17	13		50	22			64	5	19	88
COBB	L	1911	146	591	147	248	.420	47	24	8	127	44	34	83	0				
		AL		606		248	.409	49	24	8		35	34			67	13	7	87
SPEAKER	L	1913	141	520	94	189	.363	35	22	3	71	65	22	46	0				
		AL		497		189	.380	38	22	3		52	21			58	6	22	86
WILLIAMS, T.	L	1941	143	456	135	185	.406	33	3	37	120	145	27	2	4				
		AL		492		185	.376	45	3	37		87	26			88	-1	-4	83
JACKSON, J.	L	1912	152	572	121	226	.395	44	26	3	90	54	29	35	0				
		AL		553		226	.409	46	26	3		43	28			68	4	9	81
MANTLE	S	1957	144	474	121	173	.365	28	6	34	94	146	75	16	3				
		AL		477		173	.363	40	6	34		88	68			83	2	-7	78
MUSIAL	L	1948	155	611	135	230	.376	46	18	39	131	79	34	7	0				
		NL		636		230	.362	49	18	39		63	34			73	-1	5	77
MAYS	R	1955	152	580	123	185	.319	18	13	51	127	79	60	24	4				
		NL		607		185	.305	21	13	51		63	61			53	5	14	72
SS																			
DAVIS	S	1899	108	416	68	140	.337	21	5	1	57	37	18	34	0				
		NL		410		140	.341	23	5	1		30	17			22	5	57	84
JENNINGS	R	1896	130	521	125	209	.401	27	9	0	121	68	11	70	0				
		NL		552		209	.379	30	9	0		54	11			41	9	33	83
WAGNER	R	1905	147	548	114	199	.363	32	14	6	101	54	49	57	0				
		NL		517		199	.385	34	14	6		43	46			53	8	18	79
3B																			
SCHMIDT	R	1981	102	354	78	112	.316	19	2	31	91	73	71	12	4				
		NL		359		112	.312	22	2	31		58	69			63	1	31	95
BRETT	L	1980	117	449	87	175	.390	33	9	24	118	58	22	15	6				
		AL		457		175	.383	35	9	24		46	22			74	1	4	79
SANTO	R	1966	155	561	93	175	.312	21	8	30	94	95	78	4	5				
		NL		545		175	.321	29	8	30		57	72			46	-2	25	69
2B																			
LAJOIE	R	1910	159	591	145	227	.384	51	7	4	125	60	26	27	0				
		AL		523		227	.434	54	7	4		48	23			72	2	22	96
COLLINS, E.	L	1910	153	583	81	188	.322	16	15	3	81	49	41	81	0				
		AL		518		188	.363	18	15	3		39	36			35	13	31	79
HORNSBY	R	1924	143	536	121	227	.424	43	14	25	94	89	32	5	12				
		NL		570		227	.398	47	14	25		71	33			81	-5	-8	68

Table 5-1.

Actual and Normalized Statistics (continued)

		YR	G	AB	R	H	BA	2B	3B	HR	RBI	BB	K	SB	CS	BAT RUNS	STL RUNS	FLD RUNS	TTL PLYR RTG
1B																			
CASH	L	1961	159	535	119	193	.361	22	8	41	132	124	85	11	5				
		AL		541		193	.357	32	8	41		74	79			75	0	5	80
FOXX	R	1933	149	573	125	204	.356	37	9	48	163	96	93	2	2				
		AL		588		204	.347	45	9	48		58	90			72	-1	5	76
GEHRIG	L	1927	155	584	149	218	.373	52	18	47	175	109	84	10	0				
		AL		633		218	.344	61	18	47		65	85			76	3	-6	73
MCCOVEY	L	1969	149	491	101	157	.320	26	2	45	126	121	66	0	0				
		NL		484		157	.324	36	2	45		73	60			71	0	-5	66
C																			
FISK	R	1972	131	457	74	134	.293	28	9	22	61	52	83	5	2				
		AL		429		134	.312	30	9	22		42	77			44	0	19	63
TORRE	R	1966	148	546	83	172	.315	20	3	36	101	60	61	0	4				
		NL		543		172	.317	23	3	36		48	59			42	-2	12	52
CAMPENELLA	R	1951	143	505	90	164	.325	33	1	33	108	53	51	1	2				
		NL		518		164	.317	35	1	33		42	51			43	-1	8	50
BENCH	R	1972	147	538	87	145	.270	22	2	40	125	100	84	6	6				
		NL		500		145	.290	30	2	40		60	74			46	-2	4	48

Table 5-2.

Statistics Against Right-Handed and Left-Handed Pitching

					VS LEFT										VS RIGHT									
	SL %	OB %	ISO PWR	OTS %	AB	H	2B	3B	HR	BB	K	SL %	OB %	BAT RNS	AB	H	2B	3B	HR	BB	K	SL %	OB %	BAT RNS
OUTFIELD																								
RUTH	.869	.463	.514	.402	135	44	14	3	15	25	20	.807	.431	94	310	114	35	6	39	64	51	.895	.476	118
DELAHANTY	.608	.434	.229	.264	157	62	15	5	4	16	7	.631	.451	72	365	136	32	12	9	34	15	.599	.426	61
COBB	.609	.441	.199	.269	182	70	14	7	2	9	10	.571	.414	53	424	178	35	17	6	26	24	.625	.453	72
SPEAKER	.563	.439	.183	.247	150	53	11	6	1	15	6	.527	.412	45	347	136	27	16	2	37	15	.579	.451	63
WILLIAMS, T.	.706	.470	.330	.332	147	52	13	1	10	22	7	.660	.438	73	345	133	32	2	27	65	19	.725	.483	94
JACKSON, J.	.603	.451	.194	.272	166	64	13	7	1	11	8	.566	.424	55	387	162	33	19	2	32	20	.618	.463	73
MANTLE	.686	.462	.324	.317	145	54	13	2	11	30	21	.717	.480	92	332	119	27	4	23	58	47	.673	.454	79
MUSIAL	.680	.419	.318	.285	192	65	14	5	11	17	10	.635	.392	59	444	165	35	13	28	46	24	.699	.431	79
MAYS	.635	.370	.330	.235	183	58	7	4	16	20	19	.661	.384	61	424	127	14	9	35	43	42	.623	.364	49
SS																								
DAVIS	.428	.386	.087	.165	123	42	7	2	0	12	5	.431	.400	26	287	98	16	3	1	18	12	.427	.380	20
JENNINGS	.465	.434	.087	.202	167	64	9	3	0	21	3	.473	.452	47	385	145	21	6	0	33	8	.462	.426	38
WAGNER	.540	.432	.155	.233	155	61	11	4	2	16	14	.555	.450	60	362	138	23	10	4	27	32	.534	.424	49
3B																								
SCHMIDT	.644	.408	.332	.262	110	35	7	1	10	20	22	.673	.423	71	249	77	15	1	21	38	47	.631	.401	59
BRETT	.657	.439	.275	.289	140	49	10	3	7	15	6	.614	.413	60	317	126	25	6	17	31	16	.677	.451	80
SANTO	.569	.385	.248	.219	160	54	9	2	9	17	22	.588	.401	53	385	121	20	6	21	40	50	.561	.379	43
2B																								
LAJOIE	.586	.482	.152	.282	155	70	17	2	1	16	7	.606	.503	81	368	157	37	5	3	32	16	.578	.473	69
COLLINS, E.	.473	.408	.110	.193	155	53	5	4	1	10	10	.445	.382	24	363	135	13	11	2	29	26	.485	.418	40
HORNSBY	.661	.465	.263	.307	171	71	15	4	8	23	10	.690	.485	90	399	156	32	10	17	48	23	.649	.456	76
1B																								
CASH	.674	.434	.317	.293	163	54	9	2	12	21	22	.632	.408	61	378	139	23	6	29	53	57	.692	.445	80
FOXX	.699	.406	.352	.284	176	64	14	3	15	18	28	.733	.423	82	412	140	31	6	33	40	62	.685	.398	68
GEHRIG	.721	.405	.376	.292	188	61	17	5	13	17	24	.676	.380	62	445	157	44	13	34	48	61	.740	.416	82
MCCOVEY	.686	.413	.362	.283	148	44	10	1	13	22	17	.642	.388	58	336	113	26	1	32	51	43	.706	.424	77
C																								
FISK	.579	.374	.266	.216	131	42	9	3	7	14	24	.595	.386	50	298	92	21	6	15	28	53	.571	.368	42
TORRE	.568	.372	.251	.212	162	53	7	1	11	16	18	.586	.388	49	381	119	16	2	25	32	41	.560	.366	39
CAMPENELLA	.580	.368	.263	.213	154	51	11	0	10	13	16	.597	.383	50	364	113	24	1	23	29	35	.572	.361	40
BENCH	.599	.366	.309	.219	148	45	9	1	12	18	23	.622	.380	53	352	100	21	1	28	42	51	.589	.360	43

HOF - 19
NEW YORK
CHRISTY MATHEWSON
NEW YORK GIANTS – PITCHER
1904
ALL TIME LEADER
SMOKY JOE WOOD
MOST CONSECUTIVE VICTORIES, A.L. – 16
ALL TIME LEADER
W
WALTER JOHNSON
MOST SHUTOUTS, CAREER – 110
1929

CHAPTER 6

The Pitchers

"Nobody likes to hear it, because it's dull. But the reason you win or lose is darn near always the same...pitching."

–Earl Weaver

Throughout the history of the game, baseball has struggled to balance pitching and hitting. After all, the essence of the game is the classic confrontation of pitcher versus hitter. Baseball seasons are described as "hitters' years," "pitchers' years," "live-ball eras," and "dead-ball eras." Rules committees have struggled for 125 years to attain an even balance between pitching and hitting. Following a "year of the pitcher," rules invariably have been changed to shift the balance toward hitting. Following a "year of the hitter," rules invariably have been changed to shift the balance toward pitching.

Early in its history, baseball was dominated by pitchers. In 1889, a rule was introduced making the pitcher face the batter and not raise either foot unless he was delivering the ball from the pitcher's "box" to the batter. He was also required to hold the ball in front of him in plain view of the umpire. In 1893, the "box" was eliminated and the pitcher's "plate," now known as the *pitching rubber,* was introduced. The pitcher was required to take one step to deliver a pitch while keeping one foot in contact with the "plate" as he delivered the ball. That same year, the pitching distance was increased to the present-day distance of 60 feet 6 inches. As a result, 1894 saw the greatest offensive explosion in baseball history. By 1902, the rules required the pitcher to deliver his pitch within 20 seconds or be called for a balk.

In 1903, the present-day rule was implemented stating that the pitcher's "mound" could be no more than 15 inches higher than the baselines and home plate. Until 1920, the pitcher could use whatever he wanted to enhance his grip on the ball. That year, however, the rulemakers banned pitchers from applying any foreign substances to the ball. The substitution of clean white balls for dirty brown balls ushered in the offensive explosion of the 1920s and the 1930s known as the "live-ball era." By 1950, the pitcher could only assume one of two recognized positions before he pitched (the windup and the set).

With the introduction of the expanded strike zone in 1963, home run totals in the Major Leagues revealed that 274 fewer round-trippers were hit than in 1962. The new rule contributed to a significant 10 percent decrease in home run totals between the two seasons.

Rules pertaining to the strike zone have been changed four times in this century. Obviously, a shrinking strike zone benefits the hitter, and an expanding strike zone benefits the pitcher. From 1887 to 1949, the strike zone was from the shoulders to the knees. From 1950 to 1962, the zone was shrunk to span the armpits to the top of the knees. The strike zone was increased in 1963 to include the top of the shoulders to the knees. Pitchers such as Sandy Koufax and Bob Gibson began to overpower hitters. In 1969, the rulemakers reverted back to a smaller strike zone from the armpits to the top of the knees. Today's strike zone, first introduced in 1988, extends from about "mid-torso" to the top of the knees. Figure 6-1 shows the fluctuations in the strike zone through the years.

Casey Stengel, Hall of Fame manager of the New York Yankees and other teams, is credited with saying, "Good pitching always stops good hitting, and vice versa." Casey's oxymoron frames the basic question you face in assembling a winning team—do you want good pitching or good hitting? Which is more important to a ball club is a question that has been debated throughout the history of baseball.

Many baseball people subscribe to the theory that pitching is the most important aspect of the game. They point out that teams with great pitching have won pennants more often than teams with great hitting. The great teams of the past noted for their hitting (for example, the 1927 Yankees, a team by which all great teams are measured) also had several good pitchers in their rotations. Teams such as the 1930 Philadelphia Phillies (who had eight .300 hitters in their lineup but

Figure 6-1.

The fluctuating strike zone

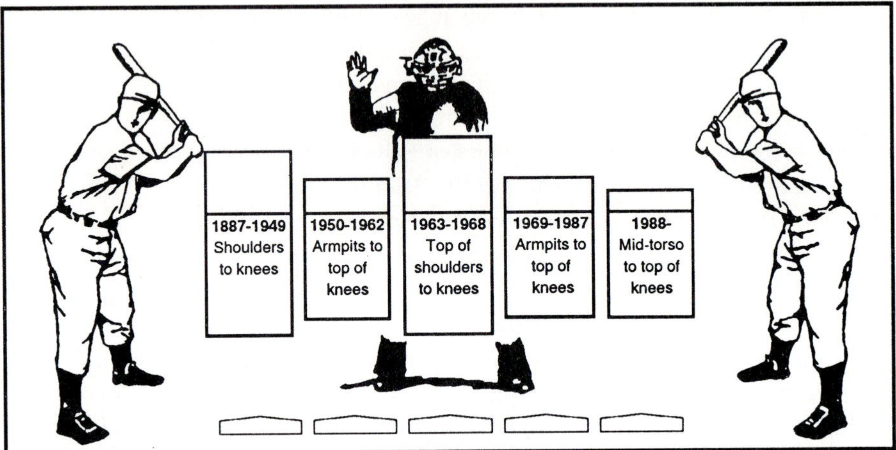

finished eighth) and the 1947 Giants (who broke several home run records only to finish fourth) had great hitting, but lacked prowess on the mound. Conversely, teams like the Dodgers of the 1960s had very little offensive punch, but had superb pitching that won them several pennants.

Walter Alston, Hall of Fame manager of the Dodgers, once said, "When you get consistently good pitching, you keep the score low, and you have a chance in every game. You can try to use all the ways there are to score a run, and benefit from any error or lucky break. You're never out of the game. But if your own pitching gives up a lot of runs, there will be lots of times when you're out of business early, where the only way to get back is with a lot of slugging of your own. So it's pretty hard to be lucky when your pitching is bad."

Modern pitching staffs are comprised of three components: starters, middle relievers, and closers. Starting pitchers of today bear no resemblance to the greats of the past such as Jack Taylor of the Cardinals (who from 1898 to 1906 started 273 games and finished all but 3) or Joe Oeschger (who in 1926 pitched all 26 innings of a 1-1 tie). Before the turn of the century, a relief pitcher was merely a fielder who exchanged positions with the starting pitcher. In fact, until the 1940s, relief pitchers were viewed as players who were inexperienced or not considered good enough to make the starting rotation.

In today's game, excellent pitchers are held out of the starting rotation to fill the role of closer. Closers generally pitch in late innings when your team is ahead in order to "close out" the win. As a result, good baseball teams win more than 95 percent of the time they take a lead into the eighth inning.

The Value of Starting Pitchers

The pitcher is the man on the field who initiates the game. Theoretically, he dictates the action according to his whims and wishes. He pitches the ball how he wants and, hopefully, where he wants. In essence, hitting is a reaction to what the pitcher does. The hitting team can win a game with one home run, one act in its rawest form, but a team in the field must get 27 outs to win the game. The pitcher's role is to get those 27 outs.

In order for a starting pitcher to be successful, he must rely on his defensive fielders. Because no one has ever struck out all of the hitters in a game, the pitcher must do the next best thing–prevent the hitter from making solid contact with the ball.

Generally, a pitcher must have the control to throw strikes when he needs to and the control to pinpoint pitches just off the plate in order to tempt the hitter. The pitcher also must be able to keep the batter from timing the pitches and teeing off on what is served. Having good "stuff" means that a pitcher has a variety of pitches he can rely on to keep the hitter off balance. A pitcher who lacks control must have an outstanding fastball in order to be successful.

Earl Weaver is credited with being one of the first managers to keep extensive information on the strengths and weaknesses of his players and those of his opponents. Weaver would consult "the book" on these players in order to make strategic decisions throughout the game.

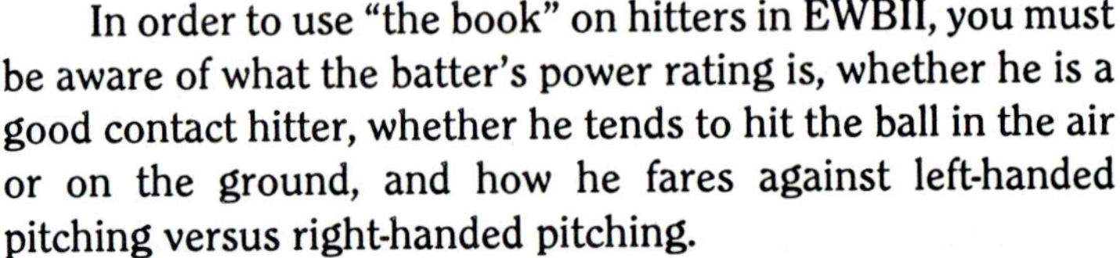

In order to use "the book" on hitters in EWBII, you must be aware of what the batter's power rating is, whether he is a good contact hitter, whether he tends to hit the ball in the air or on the ground, and how he fares against left-handed pitching versus right-handed pitching.

Right/left matchups are the most important strategic moves a manager makes. When considering whether to use a right-handed pitcher or a left-handed pitcher against a hitter or against an opposing lineup, the manager must keep a couple of factors in mind.

The Detroit Tigers set a Major League record by going 39 consecutive seasons before the club got a no-hit performance by one of its pitchers. The streak came to an end in 1912 in the second game of a doubleheader when George Mullin no-hit the St. Louis Browns.

Right-handed hitters are more successful against left-handed pitchers and vice versa. The two major reasons for this are sight and spin. For a right-handed hitter, a delivery from a lefty is coming from the first-base side of the mound, and not from behind the hitter's back. The hitter thus requires less turning of his head to pick up the pitch than is required to get a right-hander's pitch in his field of vision. A curveball from a lefty thrown to a right-handed batter tends to curve toward the batter. The ball appears to move more toward the hitter because it is coming from the opposite direction.

Unlike pitchers of yesteryear who delivered the ball underhand, pitchers of modern-day baseball throw overhand. The underhanded motion is more fluent and less strenuous than the overhanded pitching motion (just ask the pitcher on your softball team), which strains the joints and muscles. Throwing 100 to 150 pitches a game is extremely hard on the body. As a result, pitchers must take rest periods in order to perform at the peak of their abilities. Starting pitchers usually work on three days of rest (although in recent years some managers have gone to four days).

The pitching motion, although hard on the body, can be a weapon for the pitcher if it is used effectively. Pitchers at the turn of the century would have a whole repertoire of deliveries to keep the hitters guessing. The modern tendency is to use the same delivery with different pitches so that a hitter cannot tell what pitch is coming merely by the way it is delivered.

The arsenal of modern-day pitchers consists of eight basic pitches. The *fastball* must not only be delivered with speed, it must also come at the hitter with some movement. The *curveball* is sometimes called a "bender" because of its change of direction. A *change-up* is an off-speed pitch that is usually slower than a fastball or curve. A *slider* is a cross between a fastball and a curve that looks like a fastball, but at the last second veers to one side. The *screwball* is in essence a reverse curveball. It is most popular with lefties because when thrown left-handed, it breaks away from a right-handed hitter. The *knuckleball* is a pitch with no spin. Its floating motion makes its destination unpredictable, even to the pitcher and the catcher. A *sinker* is a special kind of fastball that has more horizontal break. The *split-fingered fastball,* or *forkball,* dubbed the "pitch of the 1990s," is in this category because it comes in like a fastball and drops dramatically at the last second. Good pitchers generally have at least three of these pitches at their disposal.

Knuckleballer Dutch Leonard no-hit the St. Louis Browns in 1916 the day after he was knocked out of a game in the first inning.

As a manager, you must be aware of the effect of your ballpark on your pitching staff. For example, Yankee Stadium is a notorious left-handed hitter's park because of the short right field porch. Left-handed pitchers often see success when pitching in Yankee Stadium. Conversely, Fenway Park has a short left field porch and is a notorious right-handed hitter's park. Left-handed pitchers thus have far less success in Fenway than in other parks.

Starting pitchers of today accept the fact that their managers are looking for seven strong innings before calling on the bullpen. Gaylord Perry, who won the 1978 Cy Young Award as a starter, completed only five of his 37 starts that year. Unlike in the early years of baseball, starters can rely on the bullpen to bail them out of tough situations or to come in when the game is getting out of hand. Today's teams carry usually ten pitchers, and five members of that pitching staff are relievers.

The Value of the Bullpen

In baseball, hitting is based on rhythm, and pitching is based on disruption of that rhythm. Relief pitching is used to break up the rhythm of hitting. Right-handers are brought in to face right-handed hitters, curveballers replace fireballers, or submariners replace pitchers with traditional overhand deliveries.

Starting pitchers rely on the location and selection of their pitches to keep hitters off-balance. By the late innings of a ball game, a starter may run out of "tricks," allowing the hitters to catch up to him. In the late innings, a relief pitcher is tougher on a hitter than a starter because the hitter has seen just about all a starter has to offer. A reliever has the upper hand because the batter is allowed to see so few pitches in order to make the necessary adjustments. That is why relievers are sometimes called in to face only one batter.

An ongoing debate in baseball is which role (starter or reliever) is most important to a ball club. After he lost the Cy Young balloting to Tom Seaver in 1973, Mike Marshall said, "Seaver won 19 games and I won 14 and saved 31 more... Who do you feel is more valuable to your club, Seaver or me? You have a good starter, he wins a game. What does he do for the next four? He sits around and watches.... But here is a relief pitcher who can pitch his nine innings in three or four of these games and can help you win three or four."

Control is important for a relief pitcher. A starter can issue two walks per outing and be considered a control artist. A reliever who issues two walks per outing is considered expendable. A relief pitcher must throw strikes because the tying or winning runs are often on base, and retiring the batter is of prime importance. A starter has a margin for error in that he can give up a run or two early and still win. A reliever has little or no margin for error.

Before the 1950s, relief pitchers were stigmatized as not being good enough to start. Starters occasionally appeared in relief roles, but this was viewed mainly as just getting work in between starting assignments. In the early years of the game, pitchers who could strike out hitters were usually made into starters. The relief pitcher who could get the critical strikeout at a critical point in the game was rare.

Before Ryne Duren came into the spotlight in the 1950s, relievers were expected to throw ground balls to get outs. A manager would view his reliever as a fifth infielder, increasing the chance of getting out of an inning late in the game. In the past 20 or 30 years, fireballing strikeout artists have taken over the role of top relievers, often with an "out" pitch they rely on when they need a strikeout. With the advent of artificial surfaces, the strikeout has become increasingly important because routine ground balls often scoot through for base hits.

In recent years, managers have placed great importance on their bullpens. Sparky Anderson, during his reign as manager of the Cincinnati Reds, was called Captain Hook for his propensity to go to the bullpen. In 1970, Anderson's Big Red Machine took the pennant with starters completing only 32 games. In 1972, Anderson's starting pitchers recorded only 25 complete games and in 1975 only 22 complete games while winning pennants.

Not since the advent of the live-ball era has a trend affected the game so much. The emergence of the relief pitcher has been gradual. Figure 6-2 shows how the percentage of complete games by starting pitchers has declined through the decades while the percentage of saves by relief pitchers has been on the rise.

Saves were not an official statistic until 1969 when the rule stipulated that a reliever could be credited with a save if

Figure 6-2.

The emergence of relief pitching

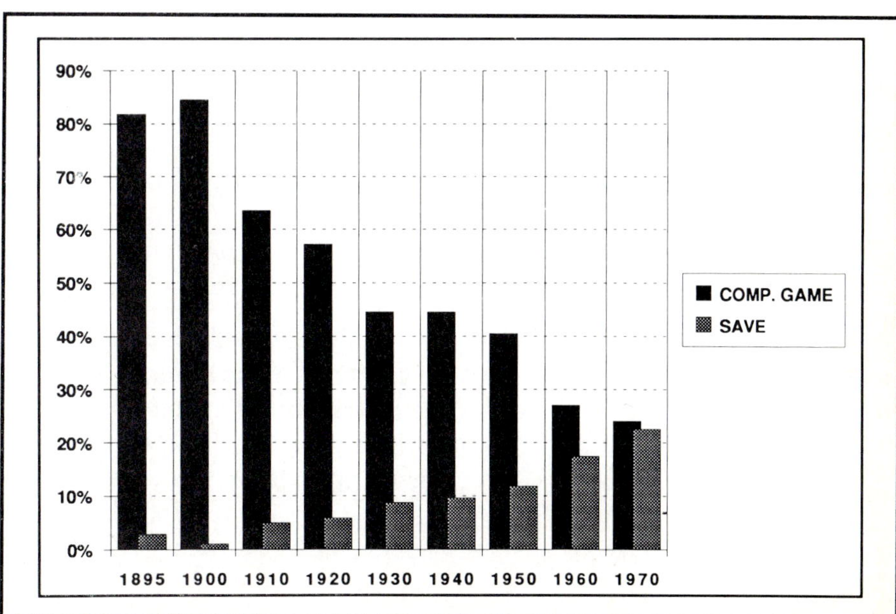

he came in and protected any lead. In 1973, the rules were tightened and in 1975 they were liberalized. Today, a save generally is credited when the reliever finishes a team win by protecting a lead of three runs or less for one inning or more, faces the potential tying run (whether that run is on base, at bat, or on deck), or pitches effectively for three innings regardless of the score.

Just how much work a reliever can endure is a subject of debate. Mike Marshall pitched in 106 games and appeared in 208 innings for the Dodgers in 1974, but by 1977 he was out of baseball. Since the turn of the century, baseball analysts have been saying that relievers were overworked when they appeared in 30 games, then 40 games, then 50, 60, 70, 80, and even 90. The answer to the riddle of how much to work a reliever is not clear because no one really knows the physical limits of the human body when throwing a few innings every day. Relievers, who rely on sinkers to get outs, are even more effective when they are tired (they claim their ball has more bite than when they are "too strong").

With the importance of your pitching staff in perspective, you are ready to meet some of the heroes of the hill in the Hall of Fame League. Be prepared to meet some real characters like the hitters you met in Chapter 5. An unwritten axiom of baseball is that it takes a unique sort of individual to be a pitcher, and it takes a unique sort of pitcher to be a reliever. And if the reliever is left-handed, anything can happen.

Heroes of the Hill

As with the hitters, the men you are about to meet come from different eras in the history of baseball. Because these players are representing different periods of history, you should note how the game has changed, and how the role of the pitcher has changed, throughout the course of history. These trends might be more evident in Table 6-1, located at the end of this chapter, which provides the pertinent actual (top line) and normalized (bottom line) statistics on each player. Chapter 4,

"The Statistics," gives a brief explanation of what each statistic means. Table 6-2, also located at the end of this chapter, shows how these pitchers fare against right-handed hitting and left-handed hitting.

The pitchers you are about to meet and their representative seasons are as follows.

Starters Joe Wood (1912), Walter Johnson (1913), Christy Mathewson (1909), Wes Ferrell (1935), Bob Lemon (1948), Charles Bender (1910), Ed Walsh (1910), Lefty Grove (1931), Ron Guidry (1978), Grover Cleveland Alexander (1915), Carl Hubbell (1933), Addie Joss (1908)

Relievers Dennis Eckersley (1990), Bruce Sutter (1977), Tug McGraw (1980), Rich Gossage (1977), Dan Quisenberry (1983), Rollie Fingers (1981), Hoyt Wilhelm (1954)

Joe Wood ("Smoky Joe")

Joe Wood's blazing fastball was legendary. Some say he may have had the best fastball in baseball history, perhaps even better than his contemporary Walter Johnson. Big Train was asked one time about the comparison. "Can I throw harder than Smoky Joe Wood? Listen, my friend, there's no man alive can throw harder than Smoky Joe Wood," Johnson said.

At the young age of 22, Wood began the 1912 season seeking to improve the 23-17 year he had the previous season. He spent the year locked up in a race with Johnson to set the record for most consecutive wins. At one point in the season, Wood had won 13 straight and was setting his sights on Johnson's record of 16 straight set earlier in the year. At his home stadium of Fenway Park, Wood faced Johnson in a head-to-head matchup. Wood won the game 1-0 and went on to get two more straight victories before finally losing. He had tied Johnson's mark. In all, the two great pitchers faced each other 27 times throughout their careers and Wood came out on top 11 times.

That 1912 season was a career year for Wood. He had a 34-5 season mark and led the league with 35 complete games and 10 shutouts. He even batted .290 for the season. In a World Series that included a tie in Game 2, he won the first and fourth meetings with complete-game performances, lost the seventh game, and came back in relief to beat Christy Mathewson in the eighth game for the coveted World Championship.

The Red Sox may have overworked Joe Wood during the final phase of the 1912 season, even though they won the pennant easily. After the 1912 season, Wood never again performed for a full season.

The number 13 proved unlucky for Smoky Joe. While fielding a ground ball in the spring of 1913, he slipped on some wet grass and broke his right thumb. Although he was able to resume his pitching when the cast was removed, he did so in pain and without the same velocity. By 1915 he was still competitive—so competitive that he led the league with a 15-5 record and a 1.49 ERA. But the pain was so unbearable that at age 26, Smoky Joe decided to retire.

Like many great athletes, Wood couldn't stand life without baseball. In 1917 he persuaded the Cleveland Indians to give him another shot. He only pitched in five games that season. The next year, he gave up pitching and tried his hand at the outfield and at second base. In 119 games, he hit .296 and displayed some power. During one game at the cavernous Polo Grounds, he tied the game with a home run in the seventh inning and won the game with another dinger in the 19th. Smoky Joe finished his career in 1922 after playing in 142 games, hitting a respectable .297 with 8 homers and 92 RBI.

Walter Johnson ("Big Train")

After growing up in Humboldt, Kansas, Walter Johnson played semi-pro baseball in the Northwest as a teenager before signing with the Washington Senators at age 19. One of the few men in the history of the game to never play minor league ball, Johnson never played on another team during his 21 years in the Major Leagues.

A tall man with unusually long arms, Big Train had a whipping, easy sidearm motion. His biggest fear was that he would hurt someone with his blazing fastball, a fact that was well-known by other ballplayers. Ty Cobb would often take advantage of this fear by deliberately crowding the plate when he faced Johnson. There was nothing fancy about Walter

Johnson as a pitcher. He just had a fastball that no one could hit. New York outfielder Birdie Cree once said the only way to hit Walter Johnson's fastball was to swing as the pitcher's arm began to descend.

Walter Johnson pitched seven Opening Day shutouts during his career with the Senators. Of the 14 Opening Day contests in which he started, he won 9 of them.

Johnson was blessed with amazing strength in his arm and outstanding stamina. His remarkable ability to pitch with little rest was best illustrated during a two-week stretch in his second season in September 1908. He started on a Friday by shutting out New York 3-0 and allowed only five hits in the game. The next day, he pitched and shut out the Highlanders on three hits. Baseball was not allowed on Sunday back then, so during Monday's doubleheader, his manager again gave him the nod. He responded with a two-hit shutout of New York. Finally he took three days off. After his brief rest, he came out to beat the A's 3-2, and the very next day he beat the A's 5-4. Again he rested for two days. He returned to the mound to pitch three shutout innings in relief against the White Sox, and then the next day he finally lost to Hall of Fame pitcher Rube Waddell in 10 innings (2-1). The winning run in his only loss during this span was scored on a pop bunt that no one could field. During this two-week period, Johnson pitched 58 innings, allowed eight runs, won five games, and saved one.

Once when Washington was playing Cleveland, Ray Chapman was the batter facing Johnson. Big Train quickly brought the count to two strikes and Chapman headed for the dugout. Umpire Billy Evans reminded Chapman that he still had one strike and Chapman replied, "You can have it. It wouldn't do me any good." Evans called Chapman out.

Clyde Milan roomed with Johnson for 14 years. "He not only had the greatest arm of all time, but the finest disposition you could imagine. He had some sort of phobia about young fellows breaking into baseball. He'd never embarrass them. If we had a comfortable lead, he'd always lay in nice fat ones for rookies and let them hit it. Once a youngster got four hits off Walter, and when the fellow came up for the fifth time, Walter didn't even try to get even. Just the opposite–he tossed the ball up to him nice and easy, so the kid could get five for five.

When the youngster popped up, I think Walter was more disappointed than the hitter."

One of the tragedies of baseball is that Johnson played on a really bad team. The Senators finished in the second division 10 of the 21 seasons that Johnson was in the Majors. Not until his 18th year with the Senators did the club give him a chance to appear in the World Series. Despite the fact that he was almost 34 years old and had collected 23 wins that season, had led the league in ERA, in strikeouts, and in shutouts, Johnson was extremely nervous about the Series. He lost the first game and the fifth game. In the seventh game, he came in to pitch relief. He held New York for four innings and the Senators finally won the deciding game of the World Series in the 12th inning. This was the only time Walter Johnson would appear in the World Series.

Over the span of his career, Johnson earned 417 wins (second to Cy Young in the record books), threw 110 shutouts (an all-time record), and had a career ERA of 2.17. He won more than 30 games in two seasons and won more than 20 games in 10 other seasons. Johnson's phenomenal control is reflected in the fact that he had only one season in which he walked more than 100 batters. In the 1912 season, Johnson won 16 straight games without a loss and in 1913 he boasted a 36-7 record with a 1.09 ERA. As a reliever, he was 40-30 with 34 saves during his career.

Walter Johnson was one of the first five players elected to the Hall of Fame in 1936.

Christy Mathewson ("Matty")

Meet the ideal All-American boy, the perfect role model, the kind of person every mom and dad wants their child to be. The son of wealthy parents in Factoryville, Pennsylvania, Mathewson was a field goal kicker on the football team in addition to playing baseball at Bucknell University in nearby Lewiston. He was elected class president, a member of the glee club, and a member of the literary society. He was a handsome man with a mild demeanor and a good education, and he was a superb all-around athlete. What more could you ask for?

Matty broke into the Major Leagues with the Giants in 1900 and was a 20-game winner his rookie season. He defied the traditional "sophomore jinx" by winning 30 games his second year with the club. For the years 1903 to 1905, Mathewson collected 30 wins, 33 wins, and 31 wins. But in 1908, he topped all of those seasons by winning an amazing 38 games.

Connie Mack, Hall of Fame manager for the Philadelphia Athletics, said, "With [Walter] Johnson, it was brute force. With Mathewson, it was knowledge and judgment, perfect control and form." That famous control referred to by Mack was responsible for Matty's 391 innings pitched, 259 strikeouts, and 42 walks in 1908. In 1913, he averaged only 0.6 walks per nine innings pitched. As Johnny Evers said, "He could throw a ball into a tin cup at pitching range." Matty was the epitome of a control pitcher.

Christy Mathewson and Joe "Iron Man" McGinnity combined for 68 victories in 1904 to set a modern-day record for two pitchers on the same team. Mathewson won 33 games and McGinnity won 25.

His most famous pitch was called a "fadeaway," a pitch that is known today as a screwball. The right-hander would throw the fadeaway with an unnatural twist of the arm, so he only used it about a dozen times in a game. On the average, he would throw between 75 and 80 pitches during each outing. He once won a game by throwing only 67 pitches.

Mordecai "Three-Finger" Brown described Mathewson's entrance before a game as "lordly." "He'd always wait until about 10 minutes before game time, then he'd come from the clubhouse across the field in a long linen duster like auto drivers wore in those days, and at every step the crowd would yell louder and louder."

Mathewson won five pennants with the Giants. In the 1905 World Series, he pitched three shutouts in six days and gave up only 14 hits and one walk.

While serving in the Army during World War I, Mathewson was exposed to poison gas. He died of tuberculosis at age 45.

Christy Mathewson was one of the first five men elected to the Hall of Fame in 1936.

Wes Ferrell

During the Depression of the early thirties, Wes Ferrell, who had won 20 or more games the previous four seasons, was forced to take a $7000 cut in pay. "Even then I was still driving a better car than the club owner," Ferrell said.

Ferrell was a wild man on the mound and off the mound. During those four seasons, his walk totals were higher than his strikeout totals. Ferrell was viewed by manager Roger Peckinpaugh as having a bad attitude. Despite Ferrell's spectacular record over the previous four seasons, Peckinpaugh chose Mel Harder as his Opening Day pitcher for 1932. Ferrell and his manager were engaged in a heated argument during one game in which Peckinpaugh tried to pull the right-hander. Ferrell was eventually fined for refusing to leave the mound. He finished that 1932 season with 23 wins.

When Wes Ferrell pitched a no-hitter in 1931 against the Browns, the game's only questionable call came after his own brother hit a smash that appeared headed for a base hit to left. Wes Ferrell's shortstop snared the ball, but couldn't get Rick Ferrell at first. The play was ruled an error.

Peckinpaugh's perception was based in part on Ferrell's fierce competitive nature. Teammate Bill Werber said, "I've seen him, after being removed from a ball game, hit himself in the jaws with both fists and nearly knock himself out,...jump in the air and crunch the face out of an expensive watch,...tear card deck after card deck to pieces because he wasn't getting good hands. He hated to lose at anything. He was a very determined competitor, the kind you like to have on your side." Ferrell was also known for his love of astrology, often guiding his actions by the actions of the stars.

An excellent hitter as pitchers go, Ferrell posted a .280 lifetime batting average. He hit nine homers in 1931 and 38 over the course of his career. "I didn't see any big deal in being a good hitter as well as a good pitcher. A lot of guys could do it if they tried." On July 19, 1933, Wes and Rick Ferrell, who was a catcher, became the first brothers to hit homers in the same game, while playing on opposite teams. After they finished their careers, the younger brother, Wes, actually had more career home runs than his older brother, Rick.

In 1935, Ferrell experienced arm problems and had used all the patience manager Peckinpaugh had to offer, so the Indians dealt him to the Red Sox, where he joined his brother. He was forced to switch from being a fireballer to a curveball artist with off-speed stuff, but he had his finest year leading the American League with 25 victories, 31 complete games, and 322 innings pitched. And he also hit .347.

Ferrell was elected to the Hall of Fame in 1984.

Bob Lemon ("Lem")

Bob Lemon broke in with the Indians in 1941 as a light-hitting third baseman. He had an erratic arm and his throws always seemed to sink away from the first sacker.

Lemon served in the Navy for three years during World War II and returned after military duty to join the Indians as a 26-year-old pitching prospect. Four years after his return, he became a 20-game winner as the No. 2 starter in the rotation behind Bob Feller. The Indians took the 1948 pennant. Not only did Lemon toss a no-hitter against the Tigers during the season, he collected two wins against the Braves in the World Series.

Lem posted the most total innings in the American League four times and had the most complete games five times. He had six seasons in which he collected 20 or more wins. During the period from 1948 to 1956, he averaged 21 victories per season. The only year during that stretch that he didn't win at least 20 was in 1951 when he collected only 17 victories.

With the likes of Early Wynn, Feller, Mike Garcia, and Herb Score, Lemon was the mainstay of a pitching staff that won an unbelievable 111 games in 1954. During that campaign, Lemon led the staff with a 23-7 record.

In 1978, Bob Lemon assumed the skipper's post with the Yankees when they were 10 1/2 games out of first and guided them to a last-day tie for first with Boston and a playoff victory. It was Lemon's only first-place finish in his eight years as a Major League manager.

Lemon's best pitch was a sinker that hitters would beat into the ground. He was always known for a touch of wildness (just as he was during his infielder days), as is reflected in the fact that he walked 1251 and struck out 1277 in his career. He also had a winning percentage as a pitcher of .618 with a lifetime record of 207-128.

Lem was a good hitter for a pitcher. He sometimes filled in as a pinch hitter and had 31 hits in 109 plate appearances in that role. In 1949, he hit 7 home runs, which ranks second behind Wes Ferrell's record 9, and hit a total of 37 dingers during his career, also second to Ferrell's 38.

Bob Lemon was elected to the Hall of Fame in 1976.

Charles Bender ("Chief")

The son of a German father and a Chippewa Indian mother, Charles Bender left the White Earth Indian reservation in Minnesota at age 8 to attend a federally funded Episcopalian school in Philadelphia. Bender was a good student and, after leaving school at age 13, he returned to the reservation. He lasted on the reservation only two months before leaving to attend Carlisle Indian School, also Jim Thorpe's alma mater. While attending Carlisle, Bender started playing baseball, and when he graduated at age 19, he signed with the Athletics in 1903.

Injuries played an important role in the big right-hander's career. In the postseason of 1905, the Athletics announced that Bender would start in Connie Mack's World Series pitching rotation because of an injury to Rube Waddell. The club said Waddell was injured while playfully wrestling with a teammate, but suspicions arose that gamblers had gotten to Waddell, even though nothing was proven. In 1910, Eddie Plank was injured and so Mack pitched only Bender and Jack Coombs in the five-game World Series that the Athletics won four games to one. In 1913, Mack promised to pay Bender's $2500 mortgage if The Chief would pitch out of turn instead of the injured Coombs. Bender won Coombs' start and also his own.

Charles Bender was not only a good starting pitcher, he led the American League with 13 saves in the 1913 campaign.

The Chief used a high leg kick and an overhand delivery. His favorite pitch was the "talcum ball," which he rubbed with talcum powder to smooth out the surface. The pitch was an effective sinker.

Some say Bender would not have been as effective had he not been on the Athletics because he had a tender arm and the team had pitching depth. Bender only won 20 games twice in his 16-year career, but four times his ERA was under 2.00.

Bender was an excellent athlete who played several games as an infielder and several as an outfielder. He appeared as a pinch hitter 29 times in his career. He was also known as an excellent sign stealer who would coach the bases in between starts.

Chief Bender was elected to the Hall of Fame in 1953.

Ed Walsh ("Big Ed")

Sam Crawford, a lifetime .309 hitter with the Reds, once said of Ed Walsh's spitball, "I think the ball disintegrated on the way to the plate and the catcher put it back together again; I swear, when it went past the plate it was just the spit that went by."

During the latter part of the 19th century, many pitches were developed that are familiar to fans of today. Candy Cummings was the first to use the curveball, Ed Nolan came up with the overhand curve, Fred Nichols and Tommy Bond introduced the sinker, Charles Sweeney developed the screwball, Tim Keefe perfected the change-up later popularized by Amos Rusie, and Elmer Strickett began using moisture on the ball, commonly known as the spitball. Pitchers dominated years from 1902 to 1919 primarily because of the variety of their repertoires.

Walsh was a mule train driver in the Philadelphia coal mines when he was 11 years old. In 1904, at age 24, he joined the White Sox. Although the spitballing Strickett was never effective, he did teach the pitch to his roommate Walsh. Before Strickett taught him the new pitch, Walsh had only a straight fastball to serve the hitters. It took the big right-hander two seasons to master control of the spitter, but by the middle of the 1906 season he won seven games during a White Sox 19-game winning streak (four of those victories were shutouts). Walsh won two World Series games that year as the Sox upset the favored Cubs.

"When I loaded up the spitter, I kept the glove in front of my mouth so I could bluff the pitch. I didn't throw the spitter on every pitch. I managed two or three to every hitter. The other times I relied on my fastball, which I threw with the same motion. I'd grip the ball with the fingers close together and the thumb underneath. I let the ball slip from under my wet fingertips. Learning the release is the trick," Walsh said.

Big Ed said that his spitter had four different breaks. "I could break the ball down and away, straight down, down and in, and up. To get the rise, I threw underhand, but the other three pitches were thrown with the same motion as my fast one," he said.

Big Ed Walsh walked with a distinctive swagger. Writer Charles Dryden described Walsh as "the only man who could strut while standing still."

Jack Chesbro used the now-illegal spitter and won 41 games in 1904. But a wild pitch by Chesbro allowed the winning run to score for Boston and he lost the American League pennant on the last day of the season. Walsh also used the spitter to win 40 for the Chicago White Sox in 1908. During that season, he actually collected two complete-game victories during a doubleheader. Amazingly, during those two games he only walked one batter. He won more than 45 percent of the White Sox victories that year and appeared 17 times in relief. But he, too, lost the pennant on the last day of the season.

Walsh was a durable pitcher who in 1907 had 422 innings pitched with 37 complete games and a 1.60 ERA to lead the American League in those two categories. For the 1907 and 1908 seasons, he pitched a whopping 866 innings.

In 1910, Walsh led the American League with a 1.26 ERA. He was also a 20-game loser as the White Sox batted just .211 as a team. He followed that season with 27 victories in 1911 and 1912.

He was elected to the Hall of Fame in 1946.

Robert Grove ("Lefty")

Lefty Grove is generally regarded as the best left-hander ever to take the mound. Unfortunately, the flamethrowing Grove had a fiery temper to match his unhittable fastball.

Unlike many of today's fireballing hurlers who rely on the movement of their fastball to beguile hitters, Grove's bread-and-butter pitch didn't move much at all, except that it came at the hitter with a velocity matching Walter Johnson's best pitch. He led the AL in strikeouts for seven consecutive seasons, victories four times, ERA nine times, and winning percentage five times. But in his wake, Grove also left torn uniforms, dented water buckets, damaged lockers, and alienated teammates.

Grove broke in with Jack Dunn's Baltimore Orioles of the International League in 1920. Dunn was a shrewd businessman who knew the value of his personnel. He refused to sell Grove to a Major League club until he could get the right price, a price that increased every year. After four years, Grove had won 108 games and had yet to make an appearance in the Major Leagues. Connie Mack finally persuaded Dunn to sell Grove to the Athletics in 1925 for a record $100,600 (the previous record was set by the Red Sox who had paid a flat $100,000 for a pitcher named Babe Ruth). Finally, at age 25, Lefty Grove made it to the Show.

Grove's rookie season gained him the reputation as a wild man—literally. He did lead the league in strikeouts his innaugural season with 116, but he also had more than 130 walks. He was extremely disagreeable after a loss and would often throw clubhouse tantrums. He was careful to punch lockers with his right hand, however, and his philosophy on kicking water buckets was simply, "Always be sure the bucket is empty."

It was a couple of years before Lefty hit his stride. By 1926, he began posting the numbers that heralded him as an upcoming star. That season he led the league in ERA and strikeouts. Then for the next seven seasons, he began leading the Athletics to dominance in the American League. From 1929 through 1931, the A's won four pennants. Grove amassed a 31-4 record in 1931 and won the MVP. During that 1931 season, Lefty was trying for a record-breaking 17th consecutive victory, but the Athletics couldn't score a run. After the game's only hit, a substitute outfielder misjudged a line drive and the winning run crossed home plate. After he retired, Grove admitted he could have forgiven the substitute if only he could remember his name. But the person he could not forgive was star outfielder Al Simmons, who missed the game that day to keep a doctor's appointment.

Although Robert Moses Grove is in the record books as a 300-game winner as a starter, few people realize that he actually racked up 55 saves as a reliever during his 17-year career. Grove also started 616 games and completed 298 of those contests.

By 1933, "Groves" (Mack's nickname for Lefty because that was how his name would appear in the boxscores while pitching for Baltimore) led the league with 24 wins. But the country was gripped by the Depression and crowd attendance was dropping dramatically in Philadelphia. Mack became strapped for cash and sold Grove to the Red Sox for $125,000.

Grove's first year with Boston was a struggle. Plagued with a sore arm, he finished the year with an 8-8 mark. As Mack said, "Groves was a thrower until we sold him to Boston and he hurt his arm. Then he learned to pitch." No longer able to serve up unhittable fastballs, Grove learned to be a "curves and control" pitcher.

Grove returned to form with his new style in 1935 when he won his final 20-game season, and followed that with two more 17-win years. In 1941, Lefty Grove became the sixth modern pitcher to win 300 games. His lifetime record was 300-141.

Lefty also holds a dubious batting record. His 593 strikeouts are the most ever recorded by a pitcher. Despite his lack of batting prowess, Grove's pitching was good enough to get him inducted into the Hall of Fame in 1947.

Ron Guidry ("Louisiana Lightnin'")

The Yankees were known during the 1970s as a team that would acquire pitchers through trades and free agency. A strong left-hander from the swamps of Louisiana, Guidry had trouble finding a regular spot in the Yankee rotation until 1977 at the age of 26. At 5'11", some said the 160-pounder was too small to pitch effectively in the Major Leagues. That year Guidry was 16-7 and came up with his famous slider. He led the Majors in victories from 1977 through 1987 with 168 wins. Known as a great athlete, Louisiana Lightnin' won five straight Gold Glove awards (1982 through 1986) and even played the outfield a couple of times.

Guidry's best season was in 1978 when he led the American League in wins (25), winning percentage (25-3 for .893), and ERA (1.74), and pitched nine shutouts. He pitched 273 innings that season and allowed only 187 hits. He struck out 248 and walked only 72 batters. In a game against the California Angels, he struck out 18 and called the performance "perhaps my greatest single thrill." He won the Cy Young award in 1978 and probably would have taken MVP had Boston's Jim Rice not put together a career year.

Off the field, Ron Guidry fashioned himself a musician—a drummer, to be precise. In fact, he even joined the Beach Boys for a post-game concert one year at Yankee Stadium.

In late July, the Yankees were 10 1/2 games behind the first-place Red Sox. Miraculously, the Yanks closed that deficit and by the last day of the season they were tied. Guidry, who was pitching on short rest, got the nod for the playoff game. Going into the seventh inning, the Red Sox were leading 2-0 when shortstop Bucky Dent came up to face Boston's Mike Torrez. Dent blasted a shot into the screen over the Green Monster in left field to give the Yankees a 3-2 lead. The Yanks went on to win the game 5-4. In the postseason, Guidry racked up two more wins.

Although Guidry never again had a year like 1978, he did manage to put together a 21-9 record in 1983 and a 22-6 record in 1985. Over the course of his 11-year career, Guidry posted 170 victories to become the fourth-best all-time winning pitcher for the Yankees.

Grover Cleveland Alexander ("Pete")

A shy, freckled-faced kid from Nebraska, Grover Cleveland Alexander signed a big league contract for a whopping $750 with the Philadelphia Phillies in 1911. His first year he won 28 games, a record for rookie pitchers, and from 1915 to 1917 he won 31, 33, and 30 games. One season during his 20-year career (1916) he had 16 shutouts, despite the fact that his Phillies were playing home games in the notorious hitter's park, Baker Bowl. A short right field porch (272 feet) in Baker Bowl was described as being so close that a first baseman going back for a popup had to be careful not to bump into the right fielder.

Alexander's repertoire featured a good fastball, a better curve, and a fadeaway he would use as an out pitch. He used a short, easy, graceful tossing motion, but had tremendous control. Pete had a minimal windup, a short stride, and a three-quarter overhand delivery. The book on him said he had no change-up to speak of, but used varying speeds for his fastball and curve. He was famous for keeping the ball low and outside to hitters.

Pete's appearance might have been the opposite of Christy Mathewson's. He had a shambling walk and his uniform never seemed to fit. His hat always looked as though it were a size too small.

Alexander's stint in the Army during World War I cost him a year and a half of Major League baseball. But the stint may have been more costly than just lost time. A shell burst near his ear at one point and during a training drill accident, he was exposed to poison gas. Pete was an epileptic who suffered seizures in the dugout, but never on the mound. As the years passed, he became an alcoholic.

Although Grover Cleveland Alexander belongs to an elite group of Major League pitchers who won 300 or more games in their careers, he distinguished himself among that group as one of the few pitchers never to throw a no-hitter.

In 1926, Alexander was playing for the Cardinals, who were facing the Yankees in the Fall Classic. The Yankees that year featured Babe Ruth and Lou Gehrig. Player-manager Rogers Hornsby had pitched Alexander for nine innings in Game 6 to collect a win. The next day, during Game 7, Alexander had assumed that he was finished for the Series. But in the sixth inning, Hornsby brought in the 39-year-old right-hander with St. Louis leading 3-2, bases loaded, two out, and the dangerous hitter Tony Lazzeri at the plate.

When Alexander came in, Hornsby, standing on the mound, asked him how he felt. "Okay," Alexander said, "but no warm-up pitches. That would be the giveaway." Hornsby asked him how he wanted to pitch to Lazzeri. "I'm giving him a fastball well inside on the first pitch," he said. "You can't do that," Hornsby said, since Lazzeri was a dead fastball hitter. "Yes I can. If I get it far enough inside, he'll foul it. Then I'll have a strike on him. Then I'll give him curves on the outside that he won't touch," Alexander said. As predicted, Lazzeri jumped all over the fastball and hit it a ton–foul. Alexander then struck out Lazzeri on two sharp-breaking curves to end the inning. After the game, a reporter asked Alexander how he felt after striking out Lazzeri. Alexander said, "Go ask Lazzeri how he felt."

Pete chalked up 190 wins during his seven years with the Phillies and added another 183 while pitching for the Cubs and Cardinals. His 373 career total is third best of all time. Over his 20-year career, he had three 30-win seasons, six 20-win seasons, and 90 career shutouts (a mark that is second only to Walter Johnson in the record books).

The final years of Alexander's life were spent in alcoholic misery. He was elected to the Hall of Fame in 1938.

Carl Hubbell ("King Carl")

King Carl was signed to a minor league contract while he was working in the oil fields of his native Oklahoma. While pitching for Oklahoma City in the Western League, he perfected his famous screwball. The Detroit Tigers purchased Hubbell from Oklahoma City, but Tiger manager Ty Cobb refused to allow the young pitcher to throw "that thing" during spring training and Hubbell failed to make the Major League club. He was outrighted to Beaumont in the Texas League in 1928, where a Giants scout saw him and convinced John McGraw to acquire him. Unlike Cobb, McGraw encouraged the young left-hander to utilize his best pitch, and utilize it he did.

Hubbell became known as a screwball artist. Because he threw the pitch so much (a screwball requires a clockwise snap of the wrist for a leftie), King Carl's left arm became so twisted by the end of his career that the palm of the hand actually faced outward.

In his rookie year with the Giants in 1928, Hubbell went 10-6. Over the next 15 seasons, he established himself as the top pitcher in the National League. By 1933, the first year he won MVP, he had five straight winning seasons to his credit, winning 18 games in two of those years. Hubbell considered an 18-inning shutout in 1933 to be his best game ever, a game in which he walked not one batter. For the season, he pitched 10 shutouts and boasted a 23-12 record with an ERA of 1.66.

Hubbell followed that performance with a 21-12 record in 1934. That season he led the league with a stingy 2.30 ERA and made his mark in baseball history at the Polo Grounds in July during the annual All-Star game. Locked in a pitching matchup with crosstown rival Lefty Gomez, Hubbell showed what his famous screwball could do to a hitter. With the baseball world as his witness, Hubbell fanned in succession Babe Ruth (on five pitches including a screwball for a called third strike), Lou Gehrig (on four pitches), Jimmie Foxx (on three screwballs), and in the next inning, Al Simmons and Joe Cronin. Bill Dickey managed a sharp single and Gomez stepped to the plate. Gomez looked at catcher Gabby Hartnett and said, "You are now looking at a man whose batting average is .104. What the hell am I doing up here?" Hubbell struck out Gomez to establish an All-Star record of six strikeouts. As the inning ended, second baseman Frankie Frisch of the Cardinals said, "I could play second base 15 more years behind that guy. He doesn't need any help. He does it all by himself."

Carl Hubbell pitched more shutouts in 1933 than the entire pitching staffs of seven of the eight American League clubs that year.

In 1935, Hubbell went 21-12, and the following year he led the Giants to a pennant with a 26-6 season. He won his second MVP in 1936 and also began an amazing streak. In July of that year, he had a 10-6 record. He then won 16 straight games through the end of the season. He won eight more consecutive games to begin the 1937 season for a total of 24 straight victories. By winning 22 games in 1938, he completed his fifth straight 20-game winning season and led the Giants to yet another pennant.

During the final six seasons in the Major Leagues, Hubbell became a spot starter. His only losing season came in 1940 when he ended the year with an 11-12 record. His career totals were 253-154.

King Carl was elected to the Hall of Fame in 1947.

Adrian Joss ("Addie")

Baseball history is blemished with many tragedies, such as the untimely death of Ed Delahanty and the tragic alcoholism of Grover Cleveland Alexander. Unfortunately, the story of Adrian Joss is among them.

Addie Joss was a tall man at 6'3" with long arms and a pitching delivery only he could muster. Using an exaggerated pinwheel motion, Joss earned the nickname "The Human

Hairpin." He would pivot away from the hitter before the pitch, and then he would come in sidearm with a pitch that many batters swore dipped, leveled off, and dipped again. As unusual as his style may have been, no one could argue with the results. Joss was the hardest pitcher in baseball history to reach base against, allowing just 8.7 runners and only 1.4 walks per nine innings pitched during his nine-year Major League career.

An exhibition game played to benefit the widow of Addie Joss in 1911 was actually the first modern-day Major League All-Star game, although the first official All-Star game was not played until 1933 in Chicago for the city's Century of Progress Exposition.

During his second season in the minors with Toledo of the Western Association, Joss was a 25-game winner. He made his Major League debut in 1902 and struck out four of the first six men he faced. He finished the day with a one-hitter. A few days later, he just missed a no-hitter when with two outs in the ninth, an error opened the door and two singles followed. That season he led the American League with five shutouts and ended the year with a 17-13 mark for the fifth-place Cleveland ballclub. The next year, Cleveland climbed to third place behind Addie's solid 18-13 season. From 1905 through 1908, Joss won at least 20 victories each season. He tied Chicago's Doc White for the AL lead in victories in 1907 when he won his career-high 27.

Addie Joss enjoyed his best season in 1908 when Cleveland was battling Big Ed Walsh's White Sox and Ty Cobb's Tigers for the pennant. Walsh was a 40-game winner in early October and Joss was having another fine season (he had won seven of his club's first 11 games). The two went head-to-head in one of the most memorable pitching matchups in Major League history. Big Ed tossed a four-hitter that day, struck out 15, and allowed only one run. However, Joss was not to be denied. He topped that performance with a perfect game, winning 1-0. Cleveland ultimately finished the season a half game behind the Tigers for the pennant, but Joss was 24-11 with a 1.16 ERA on the year. Two years later, Joss no-hit the White Sox again, but he injured his arm that season and finished the year with a 5-5 mark.

Joss was a workhorse who finished 234 of the 260 games he started. Addie and Big Ed were constantly battling on the field and finished their careers ranking first and second in lifetime ERA (Joss had a 1.88 ERA and Walsh had a 1.82 ERA). The two were good friends who enjoyed barbershop singing. Often they would harmonize on the sidelines before a game.

Addie Joss' love of the game of baseball contributed to his untimely death. During spring training in April 1911, he pushed himself to regain his old form after he had missed most of the 1910 season because of injury. He wouldn't admit to anyone that he was ill. Cleveland was in Chattanooga for an exhibition game when Joss fainted and was hospitalized. He apologized to his teammates for what he called his "baby trick." Eleven days later he died of tubercular meningitis. His teammates threatened to boycott opening day when the league refused to give them a day of mourning. Eventually Cleveland postponed their season opener with Detroit that year so that the team could attend funeral services in Toledo.

The career of Addie Joss lasted but nine years. Under eligibility rules for the Hall of Fame, a player must complete 10 full seasons. But in the case of Addie Joss, the Veteran's Committee waived the eligibility requirement and elected him to the Hall of Fame in 1978.

Dennis Eckersley ("The Eck")

When the Red Sox traded Dennis Eckersley to the Cubs in 1984, they received in return Bill Buckner and Mike Brimley.

Dennis Eckersley broke into the Major Leagues in 1975 as a flamethrowing right-hander for the Cleveland Indians. He was a cocky 20-year-old starting pitcher with long hair and an explosive fastball. In 1976 he struck out 200 batters, and in 1977 he pitched a no-hitter against the California Angels. Eckersley made the All-Star team three times as an Indian (where he played for three seasons), won 20 games with the Red Sox (where he pitched for about six seasons), and pitched in the post-season for the first time while with the Cubs.

Eckersley was traded to the Oakland A's in 1987 and converted to a reliever. That year he fanned 113 batters in 116 innings. Eckersley made the conversion from glamorous starter to blue-collar fireman grudgingly at first. But between 1988 and 1990, he averaged 40 saves a year. In 1988, he saved all four Oakland wins in the American League Championship Series. He followed that post-season performance by winning three ALCS games in 1989 against Toronto. During the 1990 campaign, Eckersley appeared in 63 games and recorded a phenomenal 48 saves. He also posted an incredible 0.61 ERA and walked only 4 batters all year!

The Eck is quick to spread accolades among his teammates. He has suggested that the A's were the first ballclub to be based on pitching and defense because of their ballpark. "My success is based on the team's success, maybe more than anybody on the team because of the way I've been used," he said.

Bruce Sutter

Best known for his split-fingered fastball and his curve, Bruce Sutter was regarded as unhittable during his sophomore season in 1977. One hitter described the split-finger as coming in like a fastball and winding up like a dead fish. Hitters consistently swung over the ball and missed completely.

During that 1977 season, Sutter's Cubs were sitting in first place all of June and all of July. By mid-July, Sutter had recorded 24 saves. But the right-hander suffered a knot behind his right shoulder and did not record a save for the next five weeks. When he came back in the first week of September, he fanned six Montreal Expos in succession, three of them with nine pitches. Despite being injured for five weeks, Sutter's season totals for 1977 were 62 games, 31 saves, 7 wins, an ERA of 1.35, and 129 strikeouts in 107 innings.

The 1979 Cy Young winner, Bruce Sutter racked up a Major League-leading 37 saves during that campaign.

The following year, Sutter put together a great first half. He pitched in 34 games, had 5 wins, 3 losses, 14 saves, and a 1.77 ERA before the All-Star break. He was the winning pitcher in the All-Star game with 1 2/3 innings of hitless relief. But he began to falter during the second half of the season. He recorded only 13 more saves, 3 wins, 7 losses, and an ERA of 5.02. Some analysts feared the end of his career. But the problem turned out to be in his motion rather than his arm.

Sutter was traded to St. Louis in 1981, and in 1982 he gathered 36 saves on the way to a Cardinal World Championship. In 1984, he had a career high 45 saves to lead the National League as its top reliever for the fifth time.

Frank McGraw ("Tug")

Although McGraw is known mostly for his wild-man antics on the mound, few people realize that Tug was the barometer for the 1973 Miracle Mets, and fewer still realize that it was he who coined the Mets' famous rallying cry that year, "Ya gotta believe."

The Mets cut half a dozen games off of their 12 1/2 game deficit that year to climb within 6 1/2 of first place by the end of August. McGraw was slumping with an 0-6 record at that point, but regained his form to surge the Mets into first place by the end of September. During the last month of the season, McGraw racked up 11 saves and four victories. He finished the season with 25 saves.

As a bullpen ace in 1969, Frank McGraw was a member of the New York Mets, who won the National League pennant that year without leading the league in any major category except wins (100). McGraw's best seasons came with pennants as he posted his best numbers with the 1969 Mets, the 1973 Mets, and the 1980 Phillies.

"Some days you tame the tiger," McGraw once said, "and some days the tiger has you for lunch." With that typical reliever mentality, McGraw would thrill the crowd by walking off the mound, slapping his gloved right hand against his thigh, and screaming at no one in particular. His mother must have known when McGraw was a baby that her son had the unique mental capacity to become a bullpen ace. She gave him the nickname "Tug" because he would tug when she breast-fed him.

Serving as the main man out of the bullpen for nine seasons with the Mets, McGraw's best numbers came during the 1972 season. That year he was 11-4 with 27 saves and a 1.70 ERA. He worked the final two innings of the All-Star game that year and got the win after giving up only one hit and striking out four.

McGraw spent 10 seasons with the Phillies after leaving the Mets in 1975. His best season with the Phillies was in 1980 when he collected three World Series saves and five League Championship Series saves. McGraw had 180 lifetime saves.

Rich Gossage ("Goose")

Goose Gossage was a heat-throwing right-hander who only pitched in 28 minor league games before being called up to the Show. As a starter in the minor leagues, his record was 18-2 with an ERA of 1.83. Gossage broke in with the White Sox at age 20 to be half of the youngest relief pair ever in the

Major Leagues (the other half was Terry Forster, a lefty). In 1973 he posted a 7-0 record in relief, but in 1973 was sent back down to the minors because of a 0-4 start with an ERA of 7.43

While in the minors, Gossage rediscovered his fastball. Back up to the Sox under manager Chuck Tanner's tutelage, he posted a 4-6 record with only 1 save in 1974. In 1975, Gossage won Fireman of the Year with 26 saves and 1 win. In 142 innings, he struck out 130 and allowed only 99 hits as he learned to stay away from a mediocre curveball and stick with nothing but heat.

When the White Sox traded Goose Gossage and Terry Forster to the Pirates in the winter of 1976, they received in return Richie Zisk and Silvio Martinez.

In 1976, Paul Richards took over the managerial duties in Chicago and tried to convert the Goose into a starter. The experiment failed miserably as Gossage stumbled his way to a 9-17 record. He was traded in December of that year.

Gossage arrived in Pittsburgh at the ripe old age of 26 to rejoin former manager Tanner. That season he chalked up 11 relief wins and 26 saves with an ERA of 1.62. For every nine innings he pitched that year, Goose fanned more than 10 and allowed only about 5 hits.

The following year, 1977, the Pirates signed Kent Tekulve (who was destined to be a great right-handed reliever for Pittsburgh) and Gossage played out his option. He signed for megabucks with the Yankees in 1978.

Despite a sluggish start, he ended that season by winning his second Fireman of the Year award and was instrumental in the Yankees' overcoming a 14-game deficit to take the pennant. His numbers for 1978 were 27 saves and 10 victories.

Dan Quisenberry ("The Quiz")

Dan Quisenberry patterned his trademark underhanded delivery after star reliever Kent Tekulve of the Pirates. When The Quiz first came up to the Major Leagues, his only pitch was a sinker. When he would finish a game, his catcher, John Wathan, would say, "Way to mix 'em up," and Quisenberry would reply, "Way to call 'em."

For the period 1980-1985, Quisenberry led the American League in saves five out of six years. In all, he won Fireman of the Year honors four times. His best year was 1983 when he posted 45 saves (fourth best in history). Known for his impeccable control, Quisenberry allowed more than 15 walks in a campaign only three times in his 10-year career. This accomplishment seems even more incredible when you consider the fact that he pitched in more than 125 innings five times.

Dan Quisenberry pitched a grueling 194 innings his senior year at La Verne College and developed a sore arm. To alleviate the problem, he began throwing with a submarine motion.

In addition to his odd, underhanded delivery, the Quiz was also noted for an off-the-wall sense of humor. Some of his most notable quotations include,

* "They found a delivery in my flaw."
* "I have seen the future and it is much like the present, only longer."
* "It really helps to be stupid if you're a relief pitcher. You can't be thinking about too many things. You can't be on the mound worrying about a 35-inning streak where you haven't given up a double to a left-handed batter or something. Relief pitchers have to get into a zone of their own. I just hope I'm stupid enough."
* "A manager uses a relief pitcher like a six-shooter. He fires until it's empty and then takes the gun and throws it at the villain."

When he won Fireman of the Year in 1982, Quisenberry said, "I want to thank all the pitchers who couldn't go nine innings, and Manager Dick Howser, who wouldn't let them."

Roland Fingers ("Rollie")

Through his 17-year Major League career, Rollie Fingers compiled more saves (341) than any other relief pitcher the game has ever seen. He was known for his durability and his control. He never pitched for more than two innings at a time so that he could maintain his strength. His main pitches were a sinker and a slider, which he complemented later in his career with an effective forkball.

The tall (6'4"), lanky right-hander with the trademark handlebar mustache actually began his career as a starter with the Oakland Athletics. For each of the 1969, 1970, and 1971 seasons, Fingers broke spring training as a starting pitcher but ended the year as a reliever. Fingers quickly became the main man in the bullpen for the A's as they rolled to five division titles, three pennants, and three World Championships through the early and mid 1970s.

After becoming a full-time reliever in 1971, Fingers won 11 games in relief and saved 21. In 1972, he collected another 22 saves with a 1.92 ERA and led the American League in game appearances (76) in 1974. He was named MVP of the 1974 World Series after he won one game and saved two. In World Series competition, Fingers saved a total of six games, which is still a Major League record.

During the 1973 season, Roland Fingers notched a 1.91 ERA on the season and a phenomenal 0.66 ERA in the World Series.

The A's owner, Charlie Finley, was both colorful and despised throughout the league. He would sign players for specialty duties (such as the designated pinch runner Allen "Panamanian Express" Lewis who once tried to score from second base via the pitcher's mound), introduced orange baseballs and color-coded bases, and pioneered colored uniforms. His mistreatment of his players and managers was well known and well documented. The A's won the pennant in 1975, but were swept in the World Series by the Red Sox. In the summer of the following year, Finley, who was faced with the prospect of losing Fingers to free agency, tried to sell the right-hander to Boston for $1 million. Commissioner Bowie Kuhn voided the sale "in the best interest of baseball."

Finley's fear of free agency proved to be correct. In 1977, Fingers signed with San Diego and led the National League that year in appearances with 78 and in saves with 35. Despite losing 13 games in relief in 1978, he still collected 37 saves that year. By 1979 he was slumping and collected just 13 saves with a 4.50 ERA. But that was the year he developed his forkball and his effectiveness returned.

In 1980, Fingers saved 23 games and won 11 in relief. At age 34, Fingers was considered over the hill by the Padres and he was part of an 11-player trade with the Brewers in Milwaukee. Fingers blossomed with his new club in the familiar confines of the American League. He led the league with 28 saves and a 1.04 ERA in 1981 while he led the Brewers to their first post-season competition. That year he figured prominently in more than half of the Brew Crew's victories and was rewarded with both the MVP and Cy Young awards.

An arm injury during the 1982 season caused him to sit out the entire 1983 season. He returned to action in 1984 and at age 38 he collected 23 saves and posted a scant 1.96 ERA. He retired at the end of the 1985 season after suffering the year with a 5.04 ERA.

Rollie Fingers was inducted into the Hall of Fame in January of 1992.

Hoyt Wilhelm ("Snacks")

Hoyt Wilhelm was one of baseball's first superstar relief pitchers. He appeared in more games (1070) than any other pitcher in history. He set records for relief wins (123), games pitched in relief (1018), games finished by a pitcher (651), and innings pitched in relief (1870). As a knuckleball artist, he pitched for 21 years in the Major Leagues. He displayed not only longevity in the big leagues, but also perseverance, as he was given his unconditional release nine separate times.

Wilhelm began experimenting with the knuckleball while pitching for his North Carolina high school. He had read an article about Dutch Leonard, one of the game's first knuckleball artists, and decided the flutterball was the pitch for him. Wilhelm signed a minor league contract after high school and played one season before going into the Armed Services during World War II. As an infantryman, he received the Purple Heart after being wounded during the Battle of the Bulge.

When he returned from the war, he resumed his professional baseball career. He was a 20-game winner for two minor league seasons. The Giants were pleased with his pitching and signed him in 1948 to play in their farm system. He spent four more years in the minors before he was finally called up to the

Major Leagues in 1952. The Giants decided they would try their 29-year-old rookie as a relief pitcher. The experiment was successful. Wilhelm led the league in winning percentage (.833), ERA (2.43), and game appearances in relief (71). He also set a record with 15 wins in relief.

Wilhelm pitched for the Giants for five seasons, but his last two seasons were unspectacular. In 1955, he did not record a save and his ERA ballooned to 3.93. In 1956, he appeared in 64 games for the Giants, but his ERA was 3.83. The Giants traded him in 1957 to St. Louis, who then sold him to Cleveland.

Wilhelm had logged 363 consecutive appearances through the years as a relief pitcher when, in 1958, Indians manager Bobby Bragan decided to insert him into the starting rotation. Snacks made six starts for the Indians and had one complete game, but amassed a dismal 2-7 record. The Indians waived him and he was picked up by the Orioles.

In his first trip to the plate, Hoyt Wilhelm hit a home run. He never hit another in the next 20 years. In his second trip to the plate, he hit a triple. He never hit another. His lifetime batting average was .088.

In his ninth Major League start in 1958, he collected his first victory as a starter when he pitched a no-hitter for the Orioles against the Yankees. His opponent, Don Larsen, pitched a one-hitter through six, but Oriole catcher Gus Triandos homered off Yankee reliever Bobby Shantz for the 1-0 victory. The no-no was Wilhelm's only victory that season for the Orioles. Manager Paul Richards stuck with Wilhelm in the starting rotation the next season and, after winning his first nine starts, Wilhelm finished with a 15-11 mark. He posted the American League's best ERA (2.19) in the 1969 campaign. Wilhelm stuck exclusively with his knuckler, which hitters couldn't hit and catchers couldn't catch. Even armed with oversized catcher's mitts, five of his receivers throughout his career set records for the most passed balls in an inning.

By 1960, the Orioles were enjoying the emergence of young starting pitchers, and so the 37-year-old Wilhelm was moved back to the bullpen. He was traded to the White Sox before the beginning of the 1963 season. He had an ERA below 2.00 in each season from 1964 to 1968 with 77 saves. In 1964, at age 41, he notched 41 saves for the Sox with an ERA of

1.99. In 1967, he posted his career-best ERA of 1.31. At the age of 45, he appeared in 72 games for the White Sox in 1968. During his six seasons with the White Sox, he worked in a total of 361 games.

Although the Royals acquired Wilhelm in the 1968 expansion draft, they traded him to the Angels. In September of 1969, the Angels dealt him to the Atlanta Braves. He posted a 2-0 mark with two saves for the Braves that season as Atlanta marched to the National League West division title. The following season he led the Braves in games pitched and in saves before they dealt him to the Cubs.

In 1985, Hoyt Wilhelm became the first relief pitcher inducted into the Hall of Fame. He was the first pitcher inducted who had fewer than 150 wins.

What To Look For

You've now met 20 of the top pitchers in the Hall of Fame League. You can refer to Table 6-1 and Table 6-2 to get a sense of the great seasons these hurlers had. If you would rather not scan through statistics, the following is a brief overview of how you can expect each player to perform in this league. Each player's name is followed by the team and year of his best season.

Joe Wood (1912 Boston Red Sox) Smokey Joe is the premier pitcher in the Hall of Fame League. He boasts excellent velocity on his pitches and excellent control. His strikeout numbers will always be in the top dozen for the League. Wood does not give up the long ball very often.

Walter Johnson (1913 Washington Senators) Big Train has impeccable control of his pitches and, of course, throws with blazing speed. Batters facing him suffer an anemic collective batting average of less than .150. If they do hit it, however, it will probably go a long way, as Johnson is prone to giving up the home run. However, he trims his opponents' on-base percentage to less than .200.

Christy Mathewson (1909 New York Giants) Mathewson does not throw with the velocity of either Wood or Johnson, but he has better control. His mastery of his pitches cuts down on the long balls he gives up. Opposing hitters can get to him, but with a solid defense he is definitely an ace.

Walter Johnson was a 20-game winner in 1925, but that season he also became the only 20-game winner to hit over .400 when he posted a .433 batting average for the campaign.

Wes Ferrell (1935 Boston Red Sox) Ferrell is the type of pitcher who does not have blazing speed on his fastball and does not impress you with his control, but he is a winner on the mound. He is an excellent hitter for a pitcher.

Bob Lemon (1948 Cleveland Indians) Lemon can be wild at times, as his control rating is very low. His ERA hovers around the 2.00 level, and he does walk a lot of batters. Like Ferrell, he is a good hitter.

Charles Bender (1910 Philadelphia Athletics) The Chief is a control pitcher whose velocity is above average. He doesn't give up the long ball that often, and his normalized ERA is respectable.

Ed Walsh (1910 Chicago White Sox) Big Ed is a steady rock on the mound. He has good velocity and great control on his pitches. He's a workhorse who can get you into the late innings.

Lefty Grove (1931 Philadelphia Athletics) Grove's most notable asset is his control, which is excellent. He has above-average velocity and will give you between 250 and 300 innings over the course of a season.

Ron Guidry (1978 New York Yankees) Lightnin' is an appropriate nickname for a pitcher who throws as hard as

Guidry. He has good control of his pitches. This is probably the best flamethrowing lefty available for a starting rotation.

Grover Cleveland Alexander (1915 Philadelphia Phillies) A control pitcher by reputation, Pete does have some good pop on his fastball. He doesn't tire easily and might give you more than 250 innings.

Carl Hubbell is the only Hall of Fame player to live more than 40 years after his induction.

Carl Hubbell (1933 New York Giants) Whereas Guidry is your best bet for a flamethrowing lefty, Hubbel is your best bet for a left-handed control pitcher. Walks are few and far between for King Carl, and his ERA shows how tough it is to score against him.

Addie Joss (1908 Cleveland Indians) Strictly a control pitcher who has no real velocity to speak of, Joss does not tire easily, and his total innings for the year will surprise you.

Dennis Eckersley (1990 Oakland Athletics) The incredible 1990 statistics for Eck make him your best pick for a closer. He not only has excellent control, but he has amazing heat to go with it. He does not even know the meaning of the word "walk."

Bruce Sutter (1977 Chicago Cubs) True closers are hard to find in the Hall of Fame League, but along with Eckersley, Sutter is a natural for the position. He's only good for a couple of innings per game, so use him wisely.

Tug McGraw (1980 Philadelphia Phillies) McGraw has good control and better heat. His ERA may seem a bit high, but he has a rubber arm and can pitch with little rest.

Rich Gossage (1977 Pittsburgh Pirates) Gossage is nothing but pure heat. Hitters know it and managers know it. No matter who knows what's coming from this guy, he's still tough to hit.

Dan Quisenberry (1983 Kansas City Royals) Quisenberry's submarine delivery poses little strain on his arm. He'll give you a lot of innings and show excellent control in almost every one.

Rollie Fingers (1981 Milwaukee Brewers) Fingers has one of the best blends of control and velocity you can find for a reliever. If you don't get one of the top two superstar relievers, Fingers is a solid pick.

Hoyt Wilhelm (1954 New York Giants) Wilhelm's knuckleball doesn't have any stuff on it, but then a knuckleball is supposed to float. He doesn't give up many long balls and his ERA is most respectable.

A Break in the Action

You have now met enough hitting, fielding, and pitching superstars to field one of the greatest teams ever assembled. As a manager, however, you must keep your eye on the little things that win baseball games. What happens when this finely tuned machine you call your team needs some extra spark? The answer lies in the men you have on your bench, the men you turn to in clutch situations.

Table 6-1.

Actual and Normalized Pitcher Statistics

		YR	W	L	TG	GS	CG	IP	H	HR	BB	K	ERA	ER	PIT RNS	BAT RNS	FLD RNS	TTL PLYR RTNG
STARTERS																		
R	WOOD	1912	34	5	43	38	35	344	267	2	82	258	1.91	73				
		AL						243					1.94	52	69	9	2	80
R	JOHNSON	1913	36	7	48	36	29	346	232	9	38	243	1.14	44				
		AL						261					1.96	57	69	9	0	78
R	MATHEWSON	1909	25	6	37	33	26	275	192	2	36	149	1.15	35				
		NL						237					2.04	54	66	8	2	76
R	FERRELL	1935	25	14	41	38	31	322	336	16	108	110	3.52	126				
		AL						236					2.30	60	58	16	1	75
R	LEMON	1948	20	14	43	37	20	294	231	12	129	147	2.82	92				
		AL						239					2.23	59	60	12	3	75
R	BENDER	1910	23	5	30	25	25	250	182	1	47	155	1.58	44				
		AL						203					2.13	48	64	9	1	74
R	WALSH	1910	18	20	45	36	33	370	242	4	61	258	1.26	52				
		AL						249					2.01	56	67	4	3	74
L	GROVE	1931	31	4	41	30	27	289	249	10	62	175	2.06	66				
		AL						252					1.79	50	74	-2	-1	71
L	GUIDRY	1978	25	3	35	35	16	274	187	13	72	248	1.74	53				
		AL						250					1.92	53	70	0	1	71
R	ALEXANDER	1915	31	10	49	42	36	376	253	3	64	241	1.22	51				
		NL						248					1.98	54	68	0	2	70
L	HUBBELL	1933	23	12	45	33	22	309	256	6	47	156	1.66	57				
		NL						248					2.04	56	66	1	3	70
R	JOSS	1908	24	11	42	35	29	325	232	2	30	130	1.16	42				
		AL						248					2.05	56	66	2	1	69

		YR	W	L	TG	GS	SV	IP	H	HR	BB	K	ERA	ER	PIT RNS	BAT RNS	FLD RNS	TTL PLYR RTNG
RELIEVERS																		
R	ECKERSLEY	1990	4	2	63	0	48	73	41	2	4	73	0.61	5				
		AL						73					1.69	14	77	0	-3	74
R	SUTTER	1977	7	3	62	0	31	107	69	5	23	129	1.35	16				
		NL						110					1.86	23	72	0	1	73
L	MCGRAW	1980	5	4	57	0	20	92	62	3	23	75	1.47	15				
		NL						91					1.89	19	71	0	0	71
R	GOSSAGE	1977	11	9	72	0	26	133	78	9	49	151	1.62	24				
		NL						136					2.04	31	66	2	-1	67
R	QUISENBERRY	1983	5	3	69	0	45	139	118	6	11	48	1.94	30				
		AL						145					2.08	34	65	0	1	66
R	FINGERS	1981	6	3	47	0	28	78	55	3	13	61	1.04	9				
		AL						82					2.10	19	65	0	0	65
R	WILHELM	1954	12	4	57	0	7	111	77	5	52	64	2.11	26				
		NL						119					2.02	27	67	-5	1	63

Table 6-2.

Pitchers Versus Right-Handed and Left-Handed Hitting

	OVERALL		VS. LEFT							VS. RIGHT						
	OPP BA	OPP OB%	AB	H	HR	BB	K	OPP BA	OPP OB%	AB	H	HR	BB	K	OPP BA	OPP OB%
STARTERS																
WOOD	.133	.180	405	55	3	24	84	.136	.184	436	57	3	25	98	.130	.177
JOHNSON	.100	.123	419	43	13	11	85	.103	.126	451	44	14	12	98	.098	.121
MATHEWSON	.144	.174	401	60	4	15	59	.150	.180	430	60	5	15	69	.140	.169
FERRELL	.160	.212	407	67	5	28	37	.165	.218	436	68	5	28	44	.156	.207
LEMON	.144	.220	404	60	4	40	56	.149	.225	434	61	5	41	64	.141	.215
BENDER	.155	.198	348	56	2	19	58	.161	.204	373	56	3	19	68	.150	.191
WALSH	.130	.169	415	56	7	20	81	.135	.175	444	56	8	20	93	.126	.164
GROVE	.142	.178	263	36	3	11	47	.137	.172	618	89	6	28	106	.144	.181
GUIDRY	.153	.204	264	39	2	17	70	.148	.199	621	96	5	40	156	.155	.206
ALEXANDER	.148	.186	421	64	3	20	74	.152	.190	452	65	4	21	85	.144	.182
HUBBELL	.179	.207	270	47	2	9	39	.174	.201	636	115	5	23	86	.181	.209
JOSS	.154	.175	424	67	5	11	46	.158	.179	455	68	6	12	53	.149	.171
RELIEVERS																
ECKERSLEY	.127	.138	121	16	1	1	34	.132	.139	130	16	1	2	39	.123	.136
SUTTER	.132	.175	183	25	1	10	62	.137	.181	197	25	2	10	71	.127	.169
MCGRAW	.147	.197	96	14	1	6	23	.146	.196	224	33	2	14	51	.147	.197
GOSSAGE	.124	.197	225	29	3	21	71	.129	.203	241	29	3	21	83	.120	.191
QUISENBERRY	.173	.187	254	45	2	4	23	.177	.190	272	46	2	5	27	.169	.184
FINGERS	.169	.199	143	25	1	5	30	.175	.203	153	25	1	6	34	.163	.195
WILHELM	.146	.227	201	30	1	22	32	.149	.233	217	31	2	22	37	.143	.222

HOF - 1986
ERNIE LOMBARDI
CINCINNATI REDS – CATCHER
MEL OTT
NEW YORK GIANTS – OUTFIELD
1928
HOF - 1980
CHUCK KLEIN
PHILADELPHIA PHILLIES – OUTFIELD
1938

CHAPTER 7

The Bench

"Ted Williams is the man who always said that hitting a baseball was the toughest thing in sports. And I'm a disciple who says that hitting a baseball when you're coming off the bench, bottom of the ninth, against somebody throwing heat or split-fingered magic, is the toughest part of the toughest thing. But it's better than lifting things."

–Jay Johnstone, *Temporary Insanity*

Don't get too comfortable behind that desk. As any successful manager will tell you, games are not won from behind a desk. Now that you've met the stars that will be in the starting lineups for the clubs in your league, it's time to familiarize yourself with the spot where your real work will be done–the dugout.

Walking down the runway, you can almost feel the butterflies start to flutter in your stomach, even though no game is taking place and no fans are in the stands. Don't worry, runways are designed to whet your competitive appetite as you make your way to the dugout.

You'll notice a lot of spike scars in the pine slab that is the lower part of the bench. That's because veteran ballplayers never sit with their feet on the floor of the dugout, but rather sit up on that shelf behind the padded back of the bench with their feet resting on the area where you will normally be sitting. That is the reason *riding the bench* often results in splinters lodging in the seat of your pants.

It is here on the bench where most of your managerial decisions will be made. While your team is in the field, you'll be joined by a group of ballplayers not in the starting lineup. These players are not just there to keep you company while your club is on the field. They will have important roles to play as the game unfolds. As a manager, your job will be to determine when those roles will be called on.

These are your platoon players, your bench strength. The term "platoon players" refers to players who excel at some aspects of the game, but are not good enough overall to break into the starting lineup every day. These players share playing time with other players (*platooning*), depending on whether your opponent is starting a right-handed pitcher or a left-handed pitcher. These guys and others are not your "bench strength" because of their prowess at lifting weights, but rather because they come off the bench to inject strength into your lineup at critical points in the game.

Platooning has not always been a part of baseball. In fact, when it actually did start is something of a mystery.

A Brief History Lesson

Before the turn of the century, Major League ball clubs carried only 11 men on their rosters–eight regular players, two pitchers, and a substitute. Back then, pitchers were delivering their stuff underhand and could pitch every other day.

Switch hitting, which by definition implies recognition of the advantages of lefty versus righty pitcher/batter combinations, has been around since the beginning of the game. Bob Ferguson was the first professional player to use the switch-hitting technique in 1871. By 1889, other players were beginning to emerge as successful switch hitters. That year, Tommy Tucker established himself as the Major League's first outstanding switch hitter when he won the batting title for the American Association with a .372 average.

Although platooning existed in the early 1900s, it was rare. Some historians claim that platooning began as early as 1908. Others point out that the Detroit ball club began platooning catchers Boss Schmidt and John Warner as early as 1906. In 1914, manager George Stallings took his Boston Braves from last place in mid-July to the pennant by using all of the players on his roster. He was widely acclaimed for platooning his outfielders throughout the season to keep them rested and to gain the upper hand on his opposition. In 1920, manager Tris Speaker of Cleveland platooned his outfielders and his first baseman throughout the season and into the World Series.

By 1930, platooning had fallen into disfavor among Major League managers. But in 1949, manager Casey Stengel revived the strategy with the Yankees, perhaps because during his playing career Stengel himself enjoyed success as a platoon player.

Appropriately enough for Earl Weaver Baseball II players, it was Earl Weaver himself who took platooning to a new level of sophistication while he managed the Baltimore Orioles. In 1968, Weaver began keeping statistics on pitcher/batter and lefty/righty matchups so that he could scientifically apply the art of platooning. Weaver's tactics launched a new age for platooning systems in the Major Leagues.

The Modern Roster

Today's Major League teams carry a roster of 25 players. By position, this roster usually consists of ten pitchers, six or seven infielders, five or six outfielders, and two or three catchers.

Managers usually carry ten pitchers on their roster so that they can use four or five starters, three middle relievers (who are able to pitch more than two innings in a game), and two closers (a left-hander and a right-hander). This constitutes the pitching staff that was discussed in Chapter 6.

Traditionally, infielders are known for their defensive prowess. If the situation dictates that an infielder be lifted late in the game for a pinch hitter, the manager wants to be sure he can insert a substitute who is as defensively sound as the starting infielder.

Outfielders, on the other hand, are traditionally the sluggers on the ball club. The defensive aspect of the outfield should not be overlooked, however. If you must pinch hit for one of your sluggers in a tight situation, you may want to have a defensive specialist to send to the field in the next half inning.

At the turn of the century, the term "in a pinch" was used to refer to tight situations in a ball game, similar to the term "clutch" that is used today. Thus, substitute hitters who came into the game in these situations were referred to as "pinch hitters."

Catching is a thankless, physically demanding position. Most managers carry at least two catchers because of the risk of injury to a starter. Some catchers are better defensively than they are at bat, and you may be forced to pinch hit for your starter late in the game. Carrying three catchers on your squad provides extra insurance against injury to both the starter and a substitute, a rare occurrence but certainly possible.

Setting up a platoon system is a good way to get the most out of your team. Throughout the history of baseball, managers have watched other managers and paid close attention to what strategies and styles spelled success on the diamond. Copying another manager's system is not against the rules. No one can argue with Earl Weaver's success as a manager and, in fact, many Major League ball clubs today have computerized Weaver's concepts. You'll learn more about successful managers and their strategies in Chapter 12 and become familiar with Weaver's strategies in Chapter 13.

Although you'll pencil in nine starters for every ball game, you'll have 16 more at your disposal. The pitchers' roles have already been discussed. The others are pine timers, guys you'll sit next to on this bench throughout the course of the game, guys you should know as well as the starting nine on the field.

As Casey Stengel once said, "The secret to managing is to keep the guys who hate you away from the guys who are undecided." You'll be spending a considerable amount of time with your platoon players here on the bench. It's important that you get to know them so that you know who to keep away from whom, and who to use when.

Prime Time Pine Timers

"Riding the pine" or "pine time" is baseball jargon for sitting on the bench. Making their way down the runway about now are some of the best pine timers in the EWBII Hall of Fame League, men who played every day back when they were "just" Major League stars. If you can get some of these players on your squad, you'll open up a whole new world of managerial strategies.

The players you are about to meet are collected from the following three categories (each player's representative year follows his name):

Infielders Luke Appling (1936), Robin Yount (1982), Al Rosen (1953), Paul Molitor (1987)

Outfielders Rocky Colavito (1958), Hank Aaron (1962), Mel Ott (1929)

Catchers Roger Bresnahan (1906), Ernie Lombardi (1938)

Table 7-1, located at the end of this chapter, shows the actual and normalized statistics for each player. Table 7-2, also located at the end of this chapter, shows their performances against left-handed and right-handed pitching (for complete records on the Hall of Fame League, see Appendixes A and B). For information about their fielding records, see Appendix C.

Luke Appling ("Old Aches and Pains")

Some say Luke Appling led the league every year in hypochondria. Appling overcame sore ankles, pinkeye, constant flu bugs, a sore back that never healed, sore throats, chills, vertigo, an actual broken finger, and a fractured leg to become one of the most productively hitting shortstops in Major League history. He played 20 years on a mediocre White Sox team and usually led the team in game appearances every season. Only Luis Aparicio, who eventually took over shortstop duties from Appling, played more American League games at shortstop than Old Aches and Pains.

The Sox never played in a World Series with Appling on the squad. His popularity among true Sox fans was displayed in 1969 when a poll honored him as the greatest living White Sox player. Ironically, Appling was almost a Cub. After playing two years at Oglethorpe University, he signed a pro contract with the Atlanta Crackers of the Southern Association. He was actually sold to the Cubs late in the 1930 season, but a cash transaction brought him to the White Sox and the confines of Comiskey Park.

When he first came up to the Major Leagues, Appling was less than dazzling defensively. He always displayed a powerful arm, but his throws were often inaccurate and wild. For some reason, he had trouble fielding even routine ground balls. For four years Appling struggled in the field at a position where defense is the name of the game.

At age 42, Luke Appling set a record by playing 141 games at shortstop in 1949. That season he batted .301, scored 82 times, and collected 7 stolen bases.

Jimmy Dykes became the manager of the White Sox in 1934 and made Appling his pet project. He worked incessantly with the young infielder, constantly instilling confidence and providing needed defensive practice. It was about this time that Appling also discovered that he lacked the necessary power to drive the ball out of spacious Comiskey Park. He adjusted his batting style and stance, and soon he gained the reputation as the best hitter in the business at fouling off pitches.

Batting in the leadoff spot, Appling would work a pitcher until he got a pitch he could drive. Legends abound with the number of pitches he could foul off in succession. He is credited with fouling off 12 straight into the stands when the stingy White Sox front office refused to give him a dozen souvenir balls for friends. Another legend says he fouled off 14 straight when the front office turned down his request for two game passes. And yet another legend says he fouled off 19 straight just trying to wear out the pitcher.

Appling's career season came in 1936 when he won the AL batting title with a .388 average. That was the first time a White Sox player had ever won a batting title. That year he put together a 27-game hitting streak and went seven-for-seven over a three-game span. He won his second batting title in 1943 with a .328 average.

Appling's defense improved with age. Despite the fact that he led the league six times in errors for American League shortstops, he finished his career with seven seasons of leading the league in assists.

Over the span of his career, Appling batted higher than .300 fifteen times, scored more than 1000 runs, batted in more than 1000 runs, and walked more than 1300 times.

Appling was elected to the Hall of Fame in 1964.

Robin Yount

Widely acclaimed as a shoe-in for Hall of Fame induction when he retires, Robin Yount broke in with the Milwaukee Brewers as an 18-year-old shortstop in 1974. He held the starting job primarily because of his glove for his first six years in the league. He didn't start showing his offensive prowess at the plate until 1978, a year he overcame an ankle injury to finish the season with a respectable .293 average.

Over the next two seasons, Yount underwent extensive weight training to strengthen his body. The results were undeniably better power numbers at the plate. In 1980 he led the Major Leagues with 49 doubles and 82 extra-base hits. That season he became the first shortstop in 15 years to finish the campaign with more than 300 total bases.

Robin Yount used the 1982 and 1983 seasons to prove he could hit for extra bases. In 1982 he hit 46 doubles to tie for the league lead. In 1983, he cranked 10 triples.

In 1982, he was still improving his power hitting. He was voted MVP by a landslide after slugging 29 homers, posting a .331 batting average, collecting 114 RBI, and having the best slugging average in the American League (.578). He also set a record with 367 total bases.

That was the year the Brew Crew made their first appearance in World Series competition. Yount was responsible for the post-season success when he hit two home runs off Oriole hurler Jim Palmer on the final day of the season to clinch the pennant. Although the Brewers eventually lost the Series to the Cardinals, Yount batted .414 and set a record with two four-hit games. He finished the 1982 World Series with 12 hits in 29 at-bats.

Shoulder surgery at the end of the 1984 season forced Yount to abandon shortstop for center field. He lost a significant amount of his power because of the injury, but in 1989 he bounced back with a .318 batting average and 103 RBI to grab his second MVP award. He was the first player to win the MVP at two different positions.

Al Rosen ("Flip")

Rosen joined the Cleveland Indians in 1947, but his glove was so bad that he couldn't displace Ken Keltner as the regular third baseman. A tough, hard-nosed player with plenty of power, Rosen actually broke his nose 11 times as an amateur boxer. He acquired his nickname of Flip while pitching softball on the sandlots of Miami.

From 1947 to 1949, Rosen appeared in only 35 games for Cleveland. In 1950 he showed his muscle and clobbered 37 homers to set an American League record for rookies that stood until 1987. He also improved his defense enough that year to lead the league in assists.

Al Rosen started maturing as a ballplayer in 1952. That year he led the American League with 105 RBI, 297 total bases, and 178 runs produced.

Three years later, Rosen's bat exploded. He led the American League in 1953 with 43 homers and 145 RBI. He lost the batting title on the last day of that season to Mickey Vernon despite his own impressive .336 average. Flip's numbers that year earned him his only MVP.

He was off to a good start in 1954 when he suffered a broken finger. Even after it healed, the injury permanently impaired Rosen's grip on the bat. Despite the fact that his batting numbers dropped significantly, he did lead the Indians to an American League record 111 victories and the pennant that year. From 1950 to 1954, when he retired at age 32, Rosen averaged .298 with 31 homers and 114 RBI.

Paul Molitor ("The Ignitor")

When Robin Yount suffered his ankle injury in 1978, the Brewers brought in the right-handed-hitting Paul Molitor to replace Yount at shortstop and to fill in occasionally at second base. Three years later, Molitor was moved to center field and

Paul Molitor set a Milwaukee Brewers team record by scoring 136 runs in 1982.

later, following surgery to repair torn left ankle ligaments, to right field.

In 1982, the Brew Crew moved Molitor again to third base. During the season he led the American League in hitting with a .302 average. That was the year the Brewers played in the World Series, and Molitor made history by getting five hits during a 10-0 trouncing of the Cardinals in Game One of the Series.

Molitor suffered a severe elbow injury in 1984 that required surgery. He bounced back in 1985 and was voted Milwaukee Comeback Player of the Year.

The 1987 season began with Molitor missing 44 games because of injury. Again he came back and put together a 39-game hitting streak, the most consecutive games since Joe DiMaggio's 56-game hitting streak in 1941. That year he finished second in the league with a .353 batting average, but led the league with 114 runs scored and 41 doubles.

Since 1982, Molitor has primarily been used as a third baseman. But in recent years the Brew Crew has used him almost exclusively as a designated hitter in an effort to protect him from injury.

Rocco Colavito ("Rocky")

So popular was Rocky Colavito in Cleveland that even when he suffered a batting slump, some sportswriters would say, "Don't knock the Rock." In 1976 Cleveland fans voted the Bronx muscle man the most memorable personality in Indians history.

Colavito made it to the big leagues in 1955, but only for a quick cup of coffee before he was sent back down to the minors for more seasoning. In July of the following year, he was called up to the Majors and started his amazing string of 11 straight seasons of hitting more than 20 homers a year, averaging 32 per campaign. Manager Joe Gordon convinced the Rock to cut down his powerful swing to add more power. The result was that Colavito was the among the five youngest players to hit the 300-home run mark when he hit the magic number at age 31.

The 1958 season was the year that Colavito racked up some career numbers. He hit .303 with 41 home runs and 113 RBI. He followed that performance in 1959 with 42 homers to tie Harmon Killebrew for the league title. He was the first Indian to have back-to-back 40-homer seasons. He hit the ball so well in the 1958 season that he hit four home runs in consecutive at-bats during a game at Baltimore.

For some still unexplained reason, the Cleveland front office decided in 1960 to trade the power-hitting Colavito to Detroit for singles-hitting Harvey Kuenn. Rocky spent a year adjusting to his new ball club, but by 1961 he was back on track. That year he had his greatest season, hitting .290 with 45 homers and 140 RBI.

The Rock lacked speed, but his excellent fielding skills and rocket arm made him one of the best right fielders in the game. From 1964 to 1966, he played in 234 consecutive games without committing an error. He led the league in assists only once, but that was primarily because no one would run on his gun.

While playing for the Yankees in 1968, Rocky Colavito actually appeared as a relief pitcher during a tight game. By getting the victory, Colavito became the first nonpitcher ever to be credited with a win.

Hank Aaron ("Hammer")

Known throughout the baseball world as the man who broke Babe Ruth's career home run record, Hank Aaron was a quiet, unassuming superstar who probably would not be recognized on the street. To this day, Aaron claims to have never seen any of his 755 home runs. Instead, he kept his head down until he reached first base because he said "looking at the ball go over the fence isn't going to help."

Pitchers in the National League feared Aaron's long ball abilities. Claude Osteen, a pitcher for the Dodgers during the mid-1960s and early 1970s, said, "Slapping a rattlesnake across the face with the back of your hand is safer than trying to fool Hank Aaron."

Aaron tied Babe Ruth's record in the first game of the April 1974 season. Balls that were served to 40-year-old Hammerin' Hank were specially marked so that they could be verified under a fluorescent light as being "The Ball." He tied the record on his first swing of the season. Then he sat out a

The year was 1963, and Hank Aaron was putting on a clinic at the plate. That season Aaron led the majors in runs (121), RBI (130), total bases (370), slugging percentage (.586), and runs produced (207). Just for good measure, he tied Willie McCovey for the home run crown with 44.

few games to make sure that he would break Ruth's record of 714 at his home stadium in Atlanta.

Al Downing of the Dodgers threw Aaron a 1-0 fastball that he smashed into the Braves bullpen in left field. Tom House, a relief pitcher, caught the ball and ran it in to Aaron. "What made it all worthwhile was what I saw when I ran in with the ball holding it in my gloved hand, running really fast–in fact, my teammates joked afterwards that it was the fastest I'd run in a couple of years–really just wanting to get rid of it, to put it in Henry's hand. In that great crowd around home plate I found him looking over his mother's shoulder, hugging her to him, and suddenly I saw what many people have never been able to see in him–deep emotion...I looked and he had tears hanging on his lids. I could hardly believe it. 'Hammer, here it is,' I said. I put the ball in his hand. He said, 'Thanks kid,' and touched me on the shoulder. I kept staring at him. And it was then that it was brought home to me what this home run meant, not only to him, but to all of us."

Aaron led the league four times in home runs, four times in RBI, three times in runs scored, twice in hits, and twice in batting average. The Braves won the world championship in 1957 and Aaron was named league MVP. He hit 40 home runs or better eight times over a 23-year career, the last time at age 39. For those who enjoy numbers, just running out his home runs Aaron covered a distance of 51 miles.

Hank Aaron was inducted into the Hall of Fame in 1982.

Mel Ott ("Master Melvin")

As a 16-year-old, Mel Ott was playing semi-pro baseball near his home in Gretna, Louisiana, when the wealthy owner of the Patterson Braves spotted his talent. Harry Williams took a liking to the young kid, and during a stop in New York on his way back from Europe in August of 1925, he met with Giants manager John McGraw and told him about the young talent. After the meeting, Williams sent a postcard to Ott that read simply, "Report to McGraw at the Polo Grounds for a tryout September 1." Ott thought the postcard was a hoax devised by his teammates and ignored the directive. When Williams returned from his trip and found Ott still catching for the Patterson club, he bought him a train ticket and dragged him to the station.

McGraw liked what he saw and decided to keep Ott with the Giants. Efforts by minor league manager Casey Stengel to convince McGraw to send Ott to the minors for some seasoning failed. McGraw wanted Ott at his side in the Major Leagues, literally. Ott spent the next two seasons planted next to McGraw on the bench, learning his trade from the master. McGraw admitted he didn't want the young Ott to even sit with any of the veterans on the club.

Seventeen-year-old Mel Ott became the youngest player in the National League to get a pinch hit when he reached base safely in 1926.

Those first two years Ott was used primarily as a pinch hitter. During his orientation period he learned how to play right field, center field, third base, and second base. He led the National League in pinch-hit appearances with 46 in 1927.

Standing but 5'9" and weighing 160 to 170 pounds, Ott was a bit small for a ballplayer. The left-hander used a distinct high leg kick to begin his batting motion, partially in an effort to compensate for his lack of size and strength. Ott would lift his front foot high with his weight perfectly balanced on the fulcrum of his bat handle at his belt to propel his body momentum into pitches and start his swooping uppercut swing. The motion also enabled him to golf high fly balls into the short left field upper confines of the Polo Grounds 256 feet away. His unorthodox batting stance was often the subject of friendly needling by his teammates. Even McGraw expressed concern. But Ott answered all his critics with undeniable results. McGraw finally conceded, "Just keep swinging that way, son."

For 22 seasons Ott terrorized opposing pitchers whom he affectionately referred to as "cousins." By the time he celebrated his 19th birthday, Ott was a regular in the Giants lineup. In 1929, he had his best offensive season with 42 home runs and 151 RBI. He led the league in walks that season for the first of six times. Ten times Ott collected more than 100 walks in a season. He tied for the home run crown in 1932, 1934, and 1937, but had sole possession of the homer title in

1936, 1938, and 1942. Over the course of his career, Ott hit 511 dingers, batted .304, and set National League records for runs (1859), RBI (1860), and walks (1708).

One particular group of "cousins" who feared Ott was the Philadelphia pitching staff in 1929. The Phillies pitchers walked Ott four times when he came to bat on the final day of the season. The fifth time he stepped into the batter's box, the bases were loaded. Rather than give Ott a chance to tie Phillie teammate Chuck Klein for the homer title, the Philadelphia pitcher intentionally walked Master Melvin. This day was but one of four times in Ott's career that he drew five walks in a single game.

McGraw had the foresight to convert the teenaged Ott to an outfielder to preserve his young legs as long as possible. The decision was wise, for after two decades with the Giants, Ott was forced to retire as a player in 1947 because of chronic leg problems. The Giants' front office could see the end of his playing days approaching and hired him as a player-manager in 1942. As is sometimes the case with managing, the frustration of his team's poor playing often resulted in uncharacteristic outbursts of temper. In 1946, he became the first manager ever to be thrown out of both games of a doubleheader.

Ott retired from baseball after the 1948 season. He was elected to the Hall of Fame in 1951.

Roger Bresnahan ("The Duke of Tralee")

A fireplug of a player, Bresnahan stood 5'9" tall and weighed 200 pounds. He was a compact man whose concentration on the game bordered on ferocious. His Irish temper often showed itself in his taunting of teammates who were not giving their best effort, taunting of opponents, and taunting of umpires, which often resulted in one of his many ejections or suspensions. But he could play any position on the field and introduced many equipment innovations for catchers that are the norm today.

Bresnahan was originally signed as a pitcher by Washington. In his debut as an 18-year-old right-hander, Bresnahan shut out the Browns 3-0. He wound up that rookie season by winning four games for the Senators, who released him the following spring when they could not agree on how much he should be paid. He played the next two seasons in the minors for the Cubs organization.

John McGraw, who became a close friend of Bresnahan's, got him on the Orioles in 1901. After two unsuccessful starts, the Orioles began playing him at second base, third base, the outfield, and catcher. At midseason, McGraw jumped ship for the American League Giants and Bresnahan followed him. It was in 1905 while with the Giants that Bresnahan began full-time duties as a catcher.

Using the thick-handled bottle bat popular during that era, Bresnahan posted his best season in 1903 when he hit .350, had 42 extra-base hits, and captured 34 stolen bases. He was surprisingly fast for a catcher and often batted first or second in the lineup.

After playing 139 games as catcher for the Giants in 1908, Roger Bresnahan never again was a full-time Major League ballplayer.

After suffering head injuries from a beaning in 1905, Bresnahan began experimenting with a leather helmet manufactured by the Reach Company. It resembled half a football helmet designed to cover the left side of a right-handed hitter's head and the right side of a left-handed hitter's head. The idea never really caught on at the time. Two years later, Bresnahan became the first catcher to openly wear shin guards. Although some infielders in the Negro Leagues reportedly had worn them and a few players supposedly wore them under their socks, Bresnahan was the first to openly wear them in 1907. The innovation brought jeers from the fans and from his opponents. Some historians say that he borrowed the idea from the game of cricket.

Bresnahan caught Christy Mathewson and Joe McGinnity while playing with the Giants from 1902 to 1908. He is the only catcher to have been the receiver for four World Series shutouts (three of those were by Mathewson) in 1905. He also batted .313 in that Series.

The lore of the day said that Bresnahan was born in Tralee, Ireland, and thus was nicknamed The Duke of Tralee. He was actually born (and died) in Toledo, Ohio.

Bresnahan was selected to be in the Hall of Fame in 1945.

Ernie Lombardi ("Schnozz")

Using an interlocked grip on the league's heaviest bat in the 1930s and 1940s, Ernie Lombardi was the first catcher ever to win two batting titles. He was so slow afoot that infielders would play in the shallow outfield and still be able to throw him out at first base. Some said he had to hit .400 to hit .300 because he never got any "leg hits."

Lombardi used his muscular body to power legendary line drives. He was known for his easy manner and his banana nose, but his defensive skills were somewhat suspect. Because he had feet of lead, whenever a pitch got just a few feet away from him it was a sure passed ball. No one ever questioned his durability, however.

After he broke into the minors with Oakland of the Pacific Coast League at 18 years of age, Lombardi had three seasons in which he caught 120, 164, and 146 games. During those seasons he hit .377, .366, and .370. The Dodgers bought his contract in 1931 and traded him to Cincinnati the following season in a six-player deal.

While in a Reds uniform, Lombardi caught more than 100 games for ten straight seasons and hit .300 in seven of those years. When he won his first batting title in 1938 with a .342 average, 19 homers, and 95 runs, he was voted National League MVP. He also caught Johnny Vander Meer's consecutive no-hitters that year.

During the 1938 season, Ernie Lombardi grounded into a National League record 30 double plays.

He was one of the main reasons the Reds won pennants in 1939 and 1940. Unfortunately, he is probably most remembered for a play in the fourth and final game of the 1939 World Series against New York. The Yankees had runners on first and third with the score tied in the tenth. Joe DiMaggio ripped a single to score the go-ahead run. The right fielder misplayed the ball and Charlie Keller, the runner on first, came screaming around third and headed for the plate. He collided with

Lombardi and hit Schnozz where the chest protector didn't protect. Lombardi lay on the ground in agony as DiMaggio rounded the bases and scored. The newspapers unfairly labeled the play as "Lombardi's Swoon."

In 1942, Schnozz was sold to the Braves, where he won his second batting title with a .330 average.

Partially because of the 1939 World Series collision, voters for the Hall of Fame failed to recognize Lombardi until 1986, nine years after his death.

What To Look For

As with the everyday players on your roster, your bench players have their strengths and their weaknesses. The following is a brief overview of what to look for from the bench players you just met. Each player's name is followed by the team and year of his best season.

Luke Appling (1936 Chicago White Sox) Luke Appling is a steady performer whose main contribution is as a defensive replacement in late innings. Although he is weak against both right-handers and left-handers, he does show a bit of improvement when facing the lefties.

Robin Yount (1982 Milwaukee Brewers) Yount has enough pop in his bat to be a good pinch hitter, especially against left-handed pitching. Defensively he could use some improvement, especially when it comes to arm strength.

Al Rosen (1953 Cleveland Indians) An excellent pinch hitter against left-handed pitching, Rosen displays significant power in his stroke. His .627 slugging percentage against the lefties makes him an excellent choice when you need a big shot.

Paul Molitor (1987 Milwaukee Brewers) The Ignitor is a good contact hitter who would be good to get something going when your team seems stymied at a critical point in the game. He is a good bunter and a good hit-and-run man.

Rocky Colavito (1958 Cleveland Indians) The consummate power hitter, Colavito makes a good right-handed pinch hitter who handles lefties very well.

Hank Aaron (1962 Milwaukee Braves) 1962 was one of Hammerin' Hank's most productive years for the long ball. There's no doubt that he would give you a chance at the long ball coming off the bench.

Mel Ott hit more home runs in one park than any other player in history. During his 22 seasons with the Giants, he smacked 323 of his career 511 homers while playing at home in the Polo Grounds.

Mel Ott (1929 New York Giants) Ott's numbers at the plate are not that impressive until you inspect his power. He packs some punch and will not hurt you as a defensive replacement in the outfield.

Roger Bresnahan (1906 New York Giants) Bresnahan has good speed for a catcher, but he lacks power and his arm is only average.

Ernie Lombardi (1938 Cincinnati Reds) An adequate pinch hitter against the lefties, Lombardi will certainly hit the ball hard. As you have read, he has to hit the ball hard because he has absolutely no speed.

Time To Choose Up Sides

You have now met enough ballplayers to fill out two excellent rosters. But the Earl Weaver Hall of Fame League contains enough players to fill out the rosters for ten teams. As you progress through subsequent chapters, you'll become familiar with 100 more ballplayers, enough to choose up sides for several teams in your league. You'll learn how to draft your teams, how to set up the league, how to enter necessary data into EWBII, and how to take advantage of the many customizing features of the game.

Table 7-1.

Actual and Normalized Statistics for Platoon Players

		YR	G	AB	R	H	BA	2B	3B	HR	RBI	BB	K	SB	CS	BAT RUNS	STL RUNS	FLD RUNS	TTL PLYR RTG
SS/2B																			
APPLING	R	1936	138	526	111	204	.388	31	7	6	128	85	25	10	6				
		AL		597		204	.342	35	7	6		68	27			32	-1	17	48
YOUNT	R	1982	156	635	129	210	.331	46	12	29	114	54	63	14	3				
		AL		633		210	.332	48	12	29		43	62			46	2	-3	45
3B/1B																			
ROSEN	R	1953	155	599	115	201	.336	27	5	43	145	85	48	8	7				
		AL		612		201	.328	31	5	43		68	48			54	-2	0	52
MOLITOR	R	1987	118	465	114	164	.353	41	5	16	75	69	67	45	10				
		AL		490		164	.335	44	5	16		55	68			45	9	-5	49
OUTFIELD																			
COLAVITO	R	1958	143	489	80	148	.303	26	3	41	113	84	89	0	2				
		AL		488		148	.303	30	3	41		67	86			56	-1	6	61
AARON	R	1962	156	592	127	191	.323	28	6	45	128	66	73	15	7				
		NL		613		191	.312	31	6	45		53	74			46	0	13	59
OTT	L	1929	150	545	138	179	.328	37	2	42	151	113	38	6					
		NL		605		179	.296	47	2	42		68	39			44	-1	15	58
C																			
BRESNAHAN	R	1906	124	405	58	114	.281	22	4	0	46	81	36	25					
		NL		354		114	.322	25	4	0		65	31			32	3	-1	34
LOMBARDI	R	1938	129	489	60	167	.342	30	1	19	95	40	14	0					
		NL		495		167	.337	32	1	19		32	14			36	-3	-3	30

Table 7-2.

Platoon Player Performance Against Left-Handed and Right-Handed Pitching

					VS LEFT										VS RIGHT									
	SL %	OB %	ISO PWR	OTS %	AB	H	2B	3B	HR	BB	K	SL %	OB %	BAT RNS	AB	H	2B	3B	HR	BB	K	SL %	OB %	BAT RNS
SS/2B																								
APPLING	.453	.409	.112	.185	179	62	10	2	2	25	8	.458	.426	38	418	142	25	5	4	43	19	.451	.401	30
YOUNT	.583	.374	.252	.218	191	65	15	4	9	15	19	.602	.388	52	442	145	33	8	20	28	43	.575	.368	43
3B/1B																								
ROSEN	.606	.396	.277	.240	185	63	10	2	13	22	15	.627	.411	61	427	138	21	3	30	46	33	.596	.389	51
MOLITOR	.543	.402	.208	.218	151	51	14	2	5	21	21	.556	.419	52	339	113	30	3	11	34	47	.537	.394	42
OUTFIELD																								
COLAVITO	.628	.387	.325	.243	147	46	9	1	13	22	27	.653	.402	63	341	102	21	2	28	45	59	.617	.381	52
AARON	.602	.366	.290	.220	184	59	10	2	14	18	23	.625	.381	54	429	132	21	4	31	35	51	.592	.360	43
OTT	.588	.367	.292	.216	184	50	13	1	12	21	11	.549	.346	33	421	129	34	1	30	47	28	.605	.376	49
C																								
BRESNAHAN	.416	.427	.094	.178	106	34	8	1	0	24	9	.415	.446	37	248	80	17	3	0	41	22	.417	.419	30
LOMBARDI	.521	.378	.183	.197	148	51	10	0	6	12	4	.534	.394	42	347	116	22	1	13	20	10	.515	.371	33

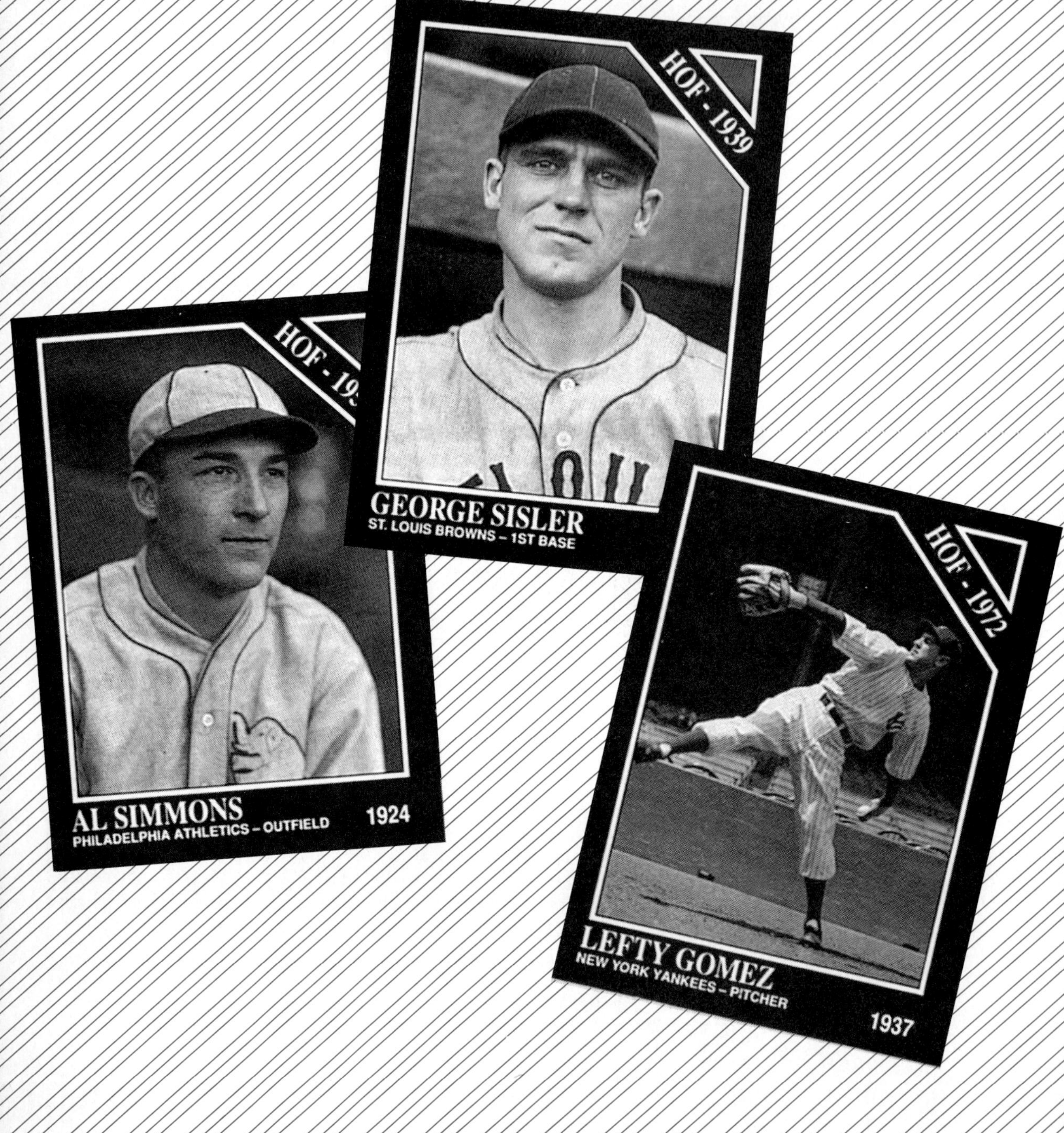

HOF - 1939
GEORGE SISLER
ST. LOUIS BROWNS – 1ST BASE
AL SIMMONS
PHILADELPHIA ATHLETICS – OUTFIELD
1924
HOF - 1972
LEFTY GOMEZ
NEW YORK YANKEES – PITCHER
1937

CHAPTER 8

The Scouting Report

"When I broke into baseball, each club had two scouts—one west of the Mississippi and the other east of the Mississippi. Now the Dodgers have a scout who works the west side of Wilshire Boulevard and another who works the east side."

—Fresco Thompson, former Vice President of the Los Angeles Dodgers

Managing can take a lot out of you. Even though you feel a little weary and your eyes are a bit bleary, your work is still not complete. You've now met more than 50 of the best players in the Earl Weaver Hall of Fame League. But what about the other 250 players? You're probably pretty tired of conducting interviews and reading statistics to familiarize yourself with the stars who make up the player pool.

In order to be an effective manager, you must at least be familiar with all the players in the league. In real life, this information is gathered and reported by scouts. Major League ball clubs usually employ a staff of more than two dozen scouts. These scouts canvass geographical regions across the country looking for raw talent, or watch minor league teams and report on the development of players. Scouts also watch other Major League teams to get "the book" on the competition.

In the early days of baseball, gathering "the book" on another team was done primarily in preparation for playing in the World Series. Through the years, the practice was expanded to watching teams throughout the season, game by game, for two primary purposes: to evaluate talent for possible trades and to size up the competition. Obviously, your franchise runs on a much tighter budget than a Major League ball club does, and you cannot afford to hire two dozen scouts to gather player information for you. Since the Earl Weaver Hall of Fame League does not develop "raw talent" and does not use a minor league system per se, compiling a "book" on other teams and players is the only real scouting to be done.

Major League scouts are extremely important to the success or failure of their teams. Teams today spend inordinate sums of money and inordinate amounts of time scouting other teams, looking for that extra edge that might provide a win sometime during the season. The scouts in the field fill their notebooks with comments about players. Baseball's storyteller, Joe Garagiola, once quoted Dave Philley, a former outfielder turned scout. Garagiola said Philley would use the notation "K.P." in his notes. When Garagiola asked Philley what that meant, Philley said, "Kain't Play."

On the final two days of the 1938 season, Hank Greenburg needed two home runs to break Ruth's single season mark. The first day he failed to hit one out of spacious League Park in Cleveland. The second day he failed to homer off Bob Feller, who fanned 18 Tigers.

Obviously, in the course of watching a player perform, a scout cannot record flowing prose about every player or team. Sometimes scouts use jargon. You can imagine the shorthand and vernacular a scout might use.

For instance, "good stick" means the player is a good hitter. A "contact hitter" is one who consistently gets the ball in play and seldom strikes out. "Packs a punch" means a player hits with power, and a player's ability to "go deep" means he can hit the long ball. A "good eye" means the hitter usually swings at strikes and lets balls go by; an indication of this ability is that he walks a lot. A "burner" or a player with "good speed" means a good base runner. "No legs" means he lacks any speed on the base paths. A "good glove man" means the player is defensively solid. Having a "rocket" or a "cannon" refers to a player with a strong–and usually accurate–throwing arm.

For pitchers, you might run across the description of a "good control man." This means he has solid mastery of all his pitches and throws strikes. A "fireballer" with "heat" refers to a pitcher who throws a fastball more than 90 miles per hour.

On the final day of the 1904 season, Jack Chesbro of the Yankees threw a spitball past his catcher in the ninth inning, allowing the winning run to score for Boston. The victory erased New York's half-game lead and gave the pennant to the Red Sox.

If he gives up the "long ball," the pitcher is prone to serving up home runs.

When scouts return from a trip, they prepare long flowing reports for their bosses (such as the excerpt about Willie Mays in Chapter 5, "The Hitters"). These reports could take you almost as long to read as it would to interview the players themselves. Rather than spending the better part of the next few weeks interviewing all the players in the league, you can use the information presented in this chapter to familiarize yourself with the strengths and weaknesses of most of the remaining players. You'll notice that "the book" on these players is presented just as the scouts recorded it in their notebooks, complete with jargon. This enables you to get the feel for what the scouts saw as they actually watched the players perform.

The scouting report presented here groups the players by position. Pertinent biographical data immediately following the player's name tells you from which side of the plate the player hits, with which arm the pitcher throws, and the year and league in which he played. Following a brief description of each player's abilities is a table that shows important statistical information about the player's best year. You'll want to use this information when you pick your team on Draft Day (see Chapter 9), when you put together your starting lineups and starting rotation, and when you're considering a trade with another team. The order of presentation within position groups is based on the total player rating (TPR), with the players showing the highest TPR presented first. For a complete listing of all player ratings, as well as all other statistical information on the players, see Appendixes A through F.

What to look for in your players can only come as a result of your own opinions and your own judgments. Branch Rickey once said that the five basic skills necessary to be a successful baseball player are to run, throw, field, hit, and hit with power. If you keep those tenets in mind as you scout around to fill your roster, you'll probably end up with a winner. As Garagiola once said, "It's pitching, hitting, and defense that wins. Any two can win. All three make you unbeatable."

Scouting reports are subjective, and scouts merely express their opinions about the players. It is possible that "the book" on a player may not hold true for a given season, but then, it is more likely that over the course of time the scouts will be telling it like it is.

Hitters and Position Players

A few of the players presented in this section will be picked up in later rounds of the draft to fill out rosters as everyday players. Most of these players, however, are role players. Included here are platoon players who only face one kind of pitching and pinch hitters who can hit one kind of pitching but lack the numbers to be in the lineup in a starting role. Also included in this section are defensive specialists who are inserted into a game in the late innings to protect a lead.

During his first three years in professional baseball, Bucky Walters was a third baseman. His impressive .376 batting average in the Pacific Coast League in 1933 caught the attention of the Boston Red Sox.

The table following the scouting notes shows important summary statistics that give you an idea of a player's strengths and weaknesses. Slugging percentages (SL%) and on-base percentages (OB%) are shown for a hitter facing a left-handed pitcher (VS L) and a right-handed pitcher (VS R). The next six columns show statistics used in EWBII to rate skill levels of the players at various aspects of the game. The columns show ratings for power hitting (PWR), hit-and-run prowess (H/R), bunting (BNT), running speed (RN), defensive range (RG), and throwing strength (AR). For a more detailed discussion of what each of these EWBII ratings mean, see Chapter 4, "The Statistics."

Outfielders

Keep in mind that outfielders are traditionally the best hitters on your squad. If you are carrying outfield defensive specialists, remember that these players will be seeing action in a minimal number of innings. By the same token, if you are carrying outfielders who can hit but lack some defensive prowess, they can provide needed pinch-hitting strength in critical situations.

Jimmy Sheckard (L, 1903, NL)

Lacks power, but has blazing speed. Handles the bat well (good bunter and good hit-and-run man). Rates near the top for defense. Could be a good leadoff or No. 2 hitter. If not, bat him low in the order.

SL% VS L	OB% VS L	SL% VS R	OB% VS R	PWR	H/R	BNT	RN	RG	AR
.465	.385	.509	.424	4	9	8	10	10	9

Rickey Henderson (R, 1990, AL)

A burner on the base paths. Good eye at the plate. Walks a lot and steals even more. Hits with more power against left-handed pitching. One of best leadoff hitters in the game, Rickey holds baseball all-time records both for career stolen bases and for leading off a game with a home run. In 1990, Henderson led the American League with 118 runs scored, 65 stolen bases, and an on-base percentage of .440.

SL% VS L	OB% VS L	SL% VS R	OB% VS R	PWR	H/R	BNT	RN	RG	AR
.639	.427	.604	.402	8	8	7	10	5	5

Cy Seymour (L, 1905, NL)

Average defensive player. Good extra-base hitter against right-handed pitching. Significantly weaker against lefties. Strictly a platooner who should only see right-handed pitchers. Has the punch to come off the bench against righties and can be a good pinch hitter.

SL% VS L	OB% VS L	SL% VS R	OB% VS R	PWR	H/R	BNT	RN	RG	AR
.562	.416	.617	.455	5	7	7	7	5	5

Sam Thompson (L, 1895, NL)

Excellent hitter against right-handed pitching, mediocre against lefties. Platoon player who should only be in lineup against right-handers. Performs well in No. 3 slot in the order. Good man for hitting doubles. Average defensive outfielder.

SL% VS L	OB% VS L	SL% VS R	OB% VS R	PWR	H/R	BNT	RN	RG	AR
.579	.371	.634	.406	7	7	7	7	6	6

Fred Clarke (L, 1897, NL)

Excellent hit-and-run man with blazing speed. Good bunter, but lacks any power. Overall, good at getting on base. Platoon player to see only righties, and then would make good leadoff hitter.

SL% VS L	OB% VS L	SL% VS R	OB% VS R	PWR	H/R	BNT	RN	RG	AR
.516	.413	.567	.453	4	10	9	10	5	5

Chuck Klein (L, 1930, NL)

Runs like he's carrying a baby grand piano. Very slow. Great glove man. Great power against righties and mediocre power against lefties. Bat him low in the order because of lack of speed.

SL% VS L	OB% VS L	SL% VS R	OB% VS R	PWR	H/R	BNT	RN	RG	AR
.544	.339	.595	.369	7	3	4	3	9	10

Joe DiMaggio (R, 1939, AL)

Big stick against lefties, gets a lot of extra-base hits. Excellent fielder who makes few errors. Better-than-average power and speed. Solid hitter for middle of order (No. 4 or No. 5 spot). Not a star in the field, but won't really hurt you. Holds baseball's all-time record for hits in most consecutive games.

SL% VS L	OB% VS L	SL% VS R	OB% VS R	PWR	H/R	BNT	RN	RG	AR
.660	.425	.624	.401	8	4	5	4	5	5

Andre Dawson (R, 1981, NL)

Great glove, good speed, above-average at the plate. Goes deep more against lefties and legs out extra-base hits. Fits in well in lower third of batting order.

SL% VS L	OB% VS L	SL% VS R	OB% VS R	PWR	H/R	BNT	RN	RG	AR
.598	.375	.571	.355	7	6	6	8	7	7

Carl Yastrzemski (L, 1968, AL)

No speed on base paths. Great glove and decent power. Likes right-handed pitching better than lefties. Platoon him to see only right-handers and you have a good stick for your No. 5 hitter.

SL% VS L	OB% VS L	SL% VS R	OB% VS R	PWR	H/R	BNT	RN	RG	AR
.538	.395	.594	.434	7	3	3	4	6	6

Pedro Guerrero (R, 1985, NL)

Choo-choos like a freight train on the base paths and could use some work in the outfield. Hits with good power and loves to go deep. Good man to put in the heart of batting order (No. 5 or No. 6).

SL% VS L	OB% VS L	SL% VS R	OB% VS R	PWR	H/R	BNT	RN	RG	AR
.631	.432	.596	.408	8	3	3	4	5	5

Joe Kelley (R, 1896, NL)

Solid hit-and-run man. Exceptional speed and exceptional bunter. Weak defensively. If you can sacrifice the defensive, good man for leadoff or No. 2 spot.

SL% VS L	OB% VS L	SL% VS R	OB% VS R	PWR	H/R	BNT	RN	RG	AR
.561	.431	.539	.410	5	9	10	10	5	4

Reggie Jackson (L, 1969, AL)

In a nutshell, he's a stick, a big stick against right-handers. Tremendous power but couldn't lay one down if it were thrown underhanded. Average fielder with average arm. Classic cleanup hitter against righties. Don't play him against lefties. Good pick to come off bench as pinch hitter.

SL% VS L	OB% VS L	SL% VS R	OB% VS R	PWR	H/R	BNT	RN	RG	AR
.632	.357	.692	.388	10	3	1	5	4	5

Harry Heilmann (R, 1923, AL)

Strictly a platoon player against lefties. Weak arm, weak range in outfield. Above-average power numbers and fits in well as a cleanup hitter against southpaw pitching. Lousy speed, not much better glove.

SL% VS L	OB% VS L	SL% VS R	OB% VS R	PWR	H/R	BNT	RN	RG	AR
.629	.460	.595	.434	6	4	5	4	4	3

Frank Robinson (R, 1966, AL)

Scary how powerfully he hits southpaws. In top five hitters of League for power against the lefties. No legs, not good contact man, but never pitch lefty against him. Also a stick against righties. Good man for heart of order.

SL% VS L	OB% VS L	SL% VS R	OB% VS R	PWR	H/R	BNT	RN	RG	AR
.707	.425	.663	.400	10	2	2	3	3	3

Al Kaline (R, 1967, AL)

Decent power and average fielder. Not good contact man but can go deep for you, especially against the southpaw.

SL% VS L	OB% VS L	SL% VS R	OB% VS R	PWR	H/R	BNT	RN	RG	AR
.606	.436	.576	.409	7	3	4	4	5	5

Elmer Smith (L, 1896, NL)

Sign of the times. Good contact hitter with little power. Above-average range and arm in field. Solid numbers against right-handers, but shouldn't face lefties. Have to bat him low in the order. Defensive pick.

SL% VS L	OB% VS L	SL% VS R	OB% VS R	PWR	H/R	BNT	RN	RG	AR
.479	.405	.525	.441	4	7	8	7	6	6

Willie Stargell (L, 1973, NL)

Powerful left-handed hitter who'd make a solid platooner. Doesn't run well and plays field better than some. Known mostly for long ball against the righties. A good pinch hitter to face right-handers. Could hit in heart of order when platooned.

SL% VS L	OB% VS L	SL% VS R	OB% VS R	PWR	H/R	BNT	RN	RG	AR
.621	.359	.684	.392	10	2	1	3	4	4

Al Simmons (R, 1930, AL)

Good power, mediocre glove man. Makes good contact and favors lefties far more than righties. Bat him cleanup against a lefty, but drop him to No. 6 hitter against righties.

SL% VS L	OB% VS L	SL% VS R	OB% VS R	PWR	H/R	BNT	RN	RG	AR
.663	.389	.627	.367	8	5	5	6	5	4

Willie Keeler (L, 1897, NL)

They don't call him "Wee Willie" for nothing. No power, but a terror on the base paths. Great speed, great hit-and-run man, great bunter. Good pick for making things happen. Put him in against right-handers and you have a good No. 2 hitter.

SL% VS L	OB% VS L	SL% VS R	OB% VS R	PWR	H/R	BNT	RN	RG	AR
.506	.416	.555	.458	3	10	10	10	3	4

Elmer Flick (L, 1900, NL)

Strictly platoon player to see only right-handed pitching. Solid contact man from a time when power wasn't important. Fits in well as No. 2 hitter against the righties. Above-average defensive ballplayer.

SL% VS L	OB% VS L	SL% VS R	OB% VS R	PWR	H/R	BNT	RN	RG	AR
.516	.390	.566	.428	5	7	7	8	5	6

Sherry Magee (R, 1910, NL)

Good No. 3 hitter against lefties, but keep him out of lineup against right-handers. Excellent speed, but lacks any range or any arm in the field. Very good hit-and-run man with mediocre power.

SL% VS L	OB% VS L	SL% VS R	OB% VS R	PWR	H/R	BNT	RN	RG	AR
.600	.453	.570	.427	6	9	8	10	3	2

Goose Goslin (L, 1928, AL)

Above-average hitter who plays solid "D" in the field. Not a big stick by any means, just good all-around player. Platoon him to see only right-handed pitching.

SL% VS L	OB% VS L	SL% VS R	OB% VS R	PWR	H/R	BNT	RN	RG	AR
.540	.377	.595	.412	6	6	6	6	5	4

Cesar Cedeno (R, 1973, NL)

Blazing speed and excellent hit-and-run man. Good defensively with good arm and good range. Not much power for an outfielder. Platoon to see only lefties and could fit into the No. 6 or No. 7 slot.

SL% VS L	OB% VS L	SL% VS R	OB% VS R	PWR	H/R	BNT	RN	RG	AR
.571	.381	.544	.361	6	8	6	10	6	6

Mike Donlin (L, 1903, NL)

Good speed, good range, decent arm. Lacks any substantial power. Because of lack of power, not a good man to play in a power position every day. Defensive sub in late innings.

SL% VS L	OB% VS L	SL% VS R	OB% VS R	PWR	H/R	BNT	RN	RG	AR
.483	.374	.528	.411	4	6	7	7	7	6

Sam Crawford (L, 1903, AL)

Good late-round pick in draft. Good contact hitter, good bunter, good range, decent arm. Lacks any power or would go higher in draft. Would make good defensive sub or decent backup to starter.

SL% VS L	OB% VS L	SL% VS R	OB% VS R	PWR	H/R	BNT	RN	RG	AR
.507	.368	.554	.403	5	7	7	7	6	7

Roberto Clemente (R, 1969, NL)

Decent power at plate and great arm in outfield. Won't hurt your ball club. Good all-around player. Could use more punch in bat. Most effective as platoon player who hits fifth against lefties. Good pinch hitter against southpaws.

SL% VS L	OB% VS L	SL% VS R	OB% VS R	PWR	H/R	BNT	RN	RG	AR
.580	.425	.556	.401	6	4	4	5	3	8

George Foster (R, 1977, NL)

Could hurt you on the base paths. Solid defensively with good power at the plate. Hits lefties better than righties and would have to be platooned. Could be a good stick to pinch hit when need long ball.

SL% VS L	OB% VS L	SL% VS R	OB% VS R	PWR	H/R	BNT	RN	RG	AR
.673	.371	.602	.353	9	2	2	3	6	6

Ralph Kiner (R, 1947, NL)

Needs an oxygen mask coming into second base and runs like a shotputter in the 100-yard dash. Great power against the lefties, and above-average in the field. Another platoon player. Would bat him fifth or use as pinch hitter against left-handed pitching.

SL% VS L	OB% VS L	SL% VS R	OB% VS R	PWR	H/R	BNT	RN	RG	AR
.650	.378	.614	.357	9	2	2	3	5	6

Joe Medwick (R, 1937, NL)

Another bumbler on the base paths who can barely catch the ball. Strong suit is good power numbers against the southpaws. Most certainly a platoon pick or a good pinch hitter when you need the long ball with a lefty on the mound.

SL% VS L	OB% VS L	SL% VS R	OB% VS R	PWR	H/R	BNT	RN	RG	AR
.646	.410	.612	.385	7	3	4	3	4	4

Ken Williams (L, 1923, AL)

Good left-handed platoon player with decent power against right-handers. Solid range and decent arm. Don't expect him to steal, and you'd probably need a pinch runner in a tight situation.

SL% VS L	OB% VS L	SL% VS R	OB% VS R	PWR	H/R	BNT	RN	RG	AR
.542	.366	.592	.401	7	3	4	3	6	6

Tony Gwynn (L, 1987, NL)

In top ten contact hitters in the League. Great bunter with great speed. No power, so would have to hit him second in batting order. Might be good pinch hitter to get on base when you need more than one run. Setup man for power hitter.

SL% VS L	OB% VS L	SL% VS R	OB% VS R	PWR	H/R	BNT	RN	RG	AR
.467	.394	.512	.430	4	8	8	9	5	4

Jim Wynn (R, 1965, NL)

Has some of the best range in the outfield since Ty Cobb. Above-average power numbers, but nothing spectacular. Defensive pick all the way. Could bat low in the order, but only against left-handers. If you want him in there, either platoon him or use in late innings.

SL% VS L	OB% VS L	SL% VS R	OB% VS R	PWR	H/R	BNT	RN	RG	AR
.525	.392	.508	.369	6	7	5	10	6	5

Tim Raines (S, 1985, NL)

Base stealer deluxe. Switch hitters are hard to find in this League, and this is a good one. Could use some work on defense, and does not have any power. Has the speed to be an effective pinch runner.

SL% VS L	OB% VS L	SL% VS R	OB% VS R	PWR	H/R	BNT	RN	RG	AR
.506	.416	.493	.394	4	8	9	10	4	5

Dave Parker (L, 1977, NL)

One of best defensive outfielders available. Excellent range and cannon for an arm. Has average power and absolutely no legs left. So weak against lefties that you would most certainly have to platoon him. Serves well as pinch hitter in the late innings.

SL% VS L	OB% VS L	SL% VS R	OB% VS R	PWR	H/R	BNT	RN	RG	AR
.482	.346	.528	.378	5	2	2	3	9	9

Billy Hamilton (L, 1895, NL)

Another one of those turn-of-the-century contact hitters who specialize in getting on base and stealing the opponent blind. Lacks defensive skills. Would have to be platooned against right-handers only.

SL% VS L	OB% VS L	SL% VS R	OB% VS R	PWR	H/R	BNT	RN	RG	AR
.460	.408	.504	.446	3	9	10	10	3	3

Minnie Minoso (R, 1954, AL)

Above-average across the board. Put him out there and he can't hurt you in the field or at the plate. Nothing spectacular. Would make a good sub in case your starter goes down with an injury.

SL% VS L	OB% VS L	SL% VS R	OB% VS R	PWR	H/R	BNT	RN	RG	AR
.555	.400	.533	.381	6	5	5	6	6	6

Fred Lynn (L, 1979, AL)

Good power against the righties and that's about it. Nothing on the base paths and don't expect him to ever lay one down. Wouldn't rely on him for any hit-and-run plays.

SL% VS L	OB% VS L	SL% VS R	OB% VS R	PWR	H/R	BNT	RN	RG	AR
.568	.364	.623	.396	8	2	2	3	4	4

Paul Waner (L, 1936, NL)

No speed and not a hit-and-run man. Above-average in the field with decent range and a decent arm. Works best as defensive sub, but could be a good backup to your starters in the outfield.

SL% VS L	OB% VS L	SL% VS R	OB% VS R	PWR	H/R	BNT	RN	RG	AR
.480	.395	.524	.430	4	3	5	3	5	6

Pete Rose (S, 1969, NL)

Don't expect much more than solid defense. Below-average hitter from both sides of the plate with no legs. Sub him in the late innings for defensive purposes.

SL% VS L	OB% VS L	SL% VS R	OB% VS R	PWR	H/R	BNT	RN	RG	AR
.538	.438	.520	.410	5	3	4	3	5	6

Rusty Staub (L, 1969, NL)

Good left-handed power hitter, but must have a right-handed power hitter to complement him. Would use only as platooner or as a pinch hitter. Can't run a lick. If he gets on base, will need a pinch runner.

SL% VS L	OB% VS L	SL% VS R	OB% VS R	PWR	H/R	BNT	RN	RG	AR
.532	.370	.582	.401	7	2	3	3	5	5

Dave Winfield (R, 1979, NL)

Good right-handed power hitter, but must have a left-handed power hitter to complement him. Sound familiar? Can run a lick, but that's about it. Platoon with someone like Staub or use as defensive sub. Can provide pinch-hitting power.

SL% VS L	OB% VS L	SL% VS R	OB% VS R	PWR	H/R	BNT	RN	RG	AR
.574	.391	.550	.368	7	3	4	4	6	5

Bobby Murcer (L, 1972, AL)

No speed, and not that good defensively. Does poke with power against right-handers. Platoon player all the way. Fits in best as basic pinch hitter against right-handed pitching.

SL% VS L	OB% VS L	SL% VS R	OB% VS R	PWR	H/R	BNT	RN	RG	AR
.557	.357	.613	.390	8	2	3	3	4	5

Hack Wilson (R, 1930, NL)

Excellent power, but no speed and not a good contact hitter. When he hits it, it either goes out or is caught for an out. Probably want to platoon. Pinch hit him in late innings when you need long ball.

SL% VS L	OB% VS L	SL% VS R	OB% VS R	PWR	H/R	BNT	RN	RG	AR
.647	.372	.610	.352	9	2	2	3	5	4

Utility Middle Infielders

Players found in this category usually are excellent defensively or are predominantly better hitters against one type of pitcher. The advantage to these players is that they can play either shortstop or second base, which you may find beneficial in the event your starter goes down with an injury.

Ray Chapman (R, 1917, AL)

Good contact hitter with great speed. Solid defensive fielder who is good at getting on base against lefties. Good defensive sub for late innings. Probably pinch hit for him when he gets to bat.

SL% VS L	OB% VS L	SL% VS R	OB% VS R	PWR	H/R	BNT	RN	RG	AR
.423	.378	.421	.358	3	7	7	9	6	6

Ozzie Smith (S, 1984, NL)

One of the top two defensive middle infielders available. Pick for defense or for contact hitting. Good bunter with great speed. Hits evenly from both sides of the plate, which isn't much.

SL% VS L	OB% VS L	SL% VS R	OB% VS R	PWR	H/R	BNT	RN	RG	AR
.348	.354	.357	.334	2	7	7	9	7	7

Ernie Banks (R, 1959, NL)

That rare middle infielder with great power numbers. Falls off in the contact hitting department. Higher on-base numbers against lefties, but packs punch against both right-handers and left-handers. Would platoon to face only lefties and bat in No. 6 spot. Good pinch hitter to face southpaws.

SL% VS L	OB% VS L	SL% VS R	OB% VS R	PWR	H/R	BNT	RN	RG	AR
.603	.363	.572	.343	8	2	2	3	4	5

Utility First and Third Basemen

Remember that first base and third base are usually power-hitting positions, and most of the guys in this category fit the bill. These are usually one-sided hitters who require platooning, but the fact that they can play two positions certainly outweighs the bad qualities they may possess. Some of these guys are actually defensive picks who do not rate highly for their power numbers at a power position.

Jimmy Williams (R, 1899, NL)

Good hit-and-run man and good bunter. Has mediocre power. Not good man to play at power position. Does get on base a lot. Not bad defensively. Would make good backup for a starter.

SL% VS L	OB% VS L	SL% VS R	OB% VS R	PWR	H/R	BNT	RN	RG	AR
.551	.418	.531	.396	5	6	7	7	5	4

Eddie Mathews (L, 1954, NL)

Great power hitter, but does not hit for average. Not much speed afoot and subpar as a defensive pick. Platoon to face only righties and he can hit sixth. Use as pinch hitter when need power shot.

SL% VS L	OB% VS L	SL% VS R	OB% VS R	PWR	H/R	BNT	RN	RG	AR
.568	.348	.621	.378	9	4	3	5	4	4

Graig Nettles (L, 1971, AL)

Excellent range with a rocket arm. Mediocre power at the plate and no speed to speak of. Hard to find one better defensively. Use in late innings to protect a lead.

SL% VS L	OB% VS L	SL% VS R	OB% VS R	PWR	H/R	BNT	RN	RG	AR
.416	.316	.454	.344	5	2	3	3	9	9

Shortstops

Overall ratings for shortstops in the Hall of Fame League suffer a dramatic dropoff after you get past the top three. If you don't get one of the top three shortstops, who are outstanding players, you're looking at a crop of talent that certainly cannot boast the all-around numbers attributed to the top three (see Chapter 5). Still, shortstop is a key defensive position on your team, and what makes the top three players stand out so far above the rest is the offensive punch they provide. The remaining players in the shortstop pool do have a little something they can bring to the party, however.

Bill Dahlen (R, 1896, NL)

Exceptional hitter against left-handed pitching. Exceptional speed with a better-than-average arm. Mediocre power and could cover a bit more ground, but defensively sound overall. Could bat No. 2 against the lefties, but drop him down to lower third of order against the righties.

SL% VS L	OB% VS L	SL% VS R	OB% VS R	PWR	H/R	BNT	RN	RG	AR
.529	.402	.512	.380	5	9	8	10	6	6

Cal Ripken (R, 1984, AL)

Would have trouble beating a tortoise in a footrace. Average power and does not hit right-handers nearly as well as lefties. Makes a good No. 6 or No. 7 hitter with lefty on the mound. Has a great arm and good range at the position.

SL% VS L	OB% VS L	SL% VS R	OB% VS R	PWR	H/R	BNT	RN	RG	AR
.538	.382	.518	.360	6	2	3	3	7	7

Dick Bartell (R, 1937, NL)

No burner on base paths, can't hit-and-run, and has trouble with the bunt. Great range and a decent arm. Bat him eighth and hope either he or the pitcher can advance runners.

SL% VS L	OB% VS L	SL% VS R	OB% VS R	PWR	H/R	BNT	RN	RG	AR
.477	.359	.467	.339	4	3	4	3	8	7

Lou Boudreau (R, 1948, AL)

Your basic, everyday ballplayer who's not spectacular at anything but steady at everything. Dramatic difference in getting on base against lefties and righties. Probably want to use as a backup.

SL% VS L	OB% VS L	SL% VS R	OB% VS R	PWR	H/R	BNT	RN	RG	AR
.545	.422	.524	.396	5	3	5	3	5	4

Bobby Wallace (R, 1901, NL)

No power, but above-average bunter with above-average range and decent arm. No speed. Has to bat in lower third of order, probably in No. 7 or No. 8 slot.

SL% VS L	OB% VS L	SL% VS R	OB% VS R	PWR	H/R	BNT	RN	RG	AR
.491	.379	.479	.358	4	5	6	6	6	7

Arky Vaughn (L, 1938, NL)

No speed, no power, only average contact hitter. If you get stuck with him at shortstop, might want to take hard look at platooning. Use only against right-handers and bat in No. 7 or even No. 8 spot in order.

SL% VS L	OB% VS L	SL% VS R	OB% VS R	PWR	H/R	BNT	RN	RG	AR
.437	.374	.478	.405	4	4	5	4	6	5

Third Basemen

Traditionally a power-hitting position, this League features two players (George Brett and Mike Schmidt) who not only are superstar hitters, but they can also field with the best of them (see Chapter 5). Unfortunately, when you examine the ratings past those two, the quality starts to drop dramatically at this position. You'll pay big bucks in the draft (see Chapter 9, "Draft Day") for those top two superstars, and then it will be a while before third basemen are drafted.

John McGraw (R, 1899, NL)

Not a power hitter by any stretch of the imagination. Because of his era, can make contact with the best of them. Great at bunting, hit-and-run plays, and runs well. Below-average range for a third baseman. Could be a good leadoff or No. 2 hitter.

SL% VS L	OB% VS L	SL% VS R	OB% VS R	PWR	H/R	BNT	RN	RG	AR
.491	.518	.482	.488	2	9	10	9	4	5

Art Devlin (R, 1906, NL)

This guy has wheels and is an excellent fielder. Makes good contact but has absolutely no power. Bat him low in the order and could get something going in later innings.

SL% VS L	OB% VS L	SL% VS R	OB% VS R	PWR	H/R	BNT	RN	RG	AR
.455	.435	.448	.411	3	8	8	9	8	7

Harlond Clift (R, 1937, AL)

Best arm of the bunch and great range for position. Not much pop in bat, which is a shame, since he's not a contact hitter either. No speed. Would have to bat in No. 7 or No. 8 spot.

SL% VS L	OB% VS L	SL% VS R	OB% VS R	PWR	H/R	BNT	RN	RG	AR
.532	.359	.516	.342	6	3	3	4	9	10

Frank Baker (L, 1912, AL)

Don't be fooled by nickname of "Home Run" (he got the moniker the previous season when he hit key World Series homers). Only average power, but good man to use against right-handers. Don't play him against the lefties. Solid No. 2 hitter.

SL% VS L	OB% VS L	SL% VS R	OB% VS R	PWR	H/R	BNT	RN	RG	AR
.527	.376	.577	.411	6	8	7	9	5	5

Wade Boggs (L, 1987, AL)

More of an offensive pick than defensive. Has decent power but has trouble hitting the left-handers. Platoon him and bat him third against right-handers. If you don't have a complement to insert against lefties, use him as a pinch hitter.

SL% VS L	OB% VS L	SL% VS R	OB% VS R	PWR	H/R	BNT	RN	RG	AR
.549	.391	.605	.430	6	3	4	3	4	4

Harmon Killebrew (R, 1969, AL)

Best long-ball hitter among all third basemen. Can't run and is a defensive liability, but has tremendous power. Can't play against right-handed pitching. The perfect pinch-hitting long-ball threat with southpaw on the mound.

SL% VS L	OB% VS L	SL% VS R	OB% VS R	PWR	H/R	BNT	RN	RG	AR
.648	.397	.612	.377	9	3	2	4	3	2

Second Basemen

As is the case with the shortstops, second basemen in this League who can hit a ton and can provide slick fielding are at a premium. However, the differences between the superstars at this position and your solid, everyday players is not nearly as drastic as it is at shortstop. Remember that your middle infielders are probably your two most important defensive positions.

Cupid Childs (L, 1896, NL)

One of top five best fielders in the group. No punch in his bat, and only mediocre bunter. Numbers against lefties and righties not that different. Defensive pick all the way. If he's not used as defensive sub or as a backup, bat him eighth.

SL% VS L	OB% VS L	SL% VS R	OB% VS R	PWR	H/R	BNT	RN	RG	AR
.409	.377	.445	.411	2	5	7	6	8	9

Frankie Frisch (S, 1927, NL)

No power, but good contact man. Great range and rocket arm. Third best defensive second baseman. Gets good marks for being a switch hitter and has good speed. Bat him eighth to get on base for late-inning rallies.

SL% VS L	OB% VS L	SL% VS R	OB% VS R	PWR	H/R	BNT	RN	RG	AR
.451	.365	.445	.345	3	7	8	8	8	9

Jackie Robinson (R, 1951, NL)

Solid all-around player who can play every day. Numbers don't stand out in any one category. Above average in all categories and doesn't matter who he faces. Does seem to hit lefties a little better than righties. Bat him sixth against lefties and seventh against right-handers.

SL% VS L	OB% VS L	SL% VS R	OB% VS R	PWR	H/R	BNT	RN	RG	AR
.539	.418	.520	.393	5	5	6	6	6	5

Joe Morgan (L, 1975, NL)

One of the best speedsters among second basemen. Will steal some bases. Mediocre power but good hit-and-run man. Could bat leadoff or second against right-handers. May have to be platooned against southpaws, or else bat him in the lower third of the order.

SL% VS L	OB% VS L	SL% VS R	OB% VS R	PWR	H/R	BNT	RN	RG	AR
.500	.394	.547	.432	6	9	7	10	4	5

Bobby Grich (R, 1983, AL)

Not much power, but good range. Defensive pick. Could be everyday player. Slow as molasses, but fields almost as smooth. Must bat seventh or eighth to be effective at plate.

SL% VS L	OB% VS L	SL% VS R	OB% VS R	PWR	H/R	BNT	RN	RG	AR
.491	.415	.480	.392	5	1	2	2	6	7

Miller Huggins (S, 1905, NL)

Switch hitter with no power. Can put the bat on the ball. Platoon him to face only right-handers and bat him in No. 7 spot. Great arm, one of the best guns in the group.

SL% VS L	OB% VS L	SL% VS R	OB% VS R	PWR	H/R	BNT	RN	RG	AR
.376	.394	.383	.374	2	5	6	6	7	8

Glenn Hubbard (R, 1985, NL)

By far best defensive player in group. Brings nothing else to the party but exceptional defense. Purely defensive pick, but good one. Use as defensive sub or backup to starter.

SL% VS L	OB% VS L	SL% VS R	OB% VS R	PWR	H/R	BNT	RN	RG	AR
.308	.315	.324	.298	2	2	2	3	9	10

First Basemen

Outside of the outfield, this position provides most of the power in your lineup. When comparing players to the likes of Cash, Foxx, Gehrig, and McCovey, you may find apples and oranges on your scouting report. You can find a couple of sleepers in the group of first basemen, but overall, most of these guys are platoon players who can only hit one type of pitching really well. Defensively, the group as a whole fields only average when compared to, say, shortstops or second basemen. But remember that first base is a position in which you insert a hitter (preferably a power hitter) into your lineup.

George Sisler (L, 1920, AL)

Mediocre power, but good contact hitter. Does have best range and arm of the group. Can bat second against righties, but drop him down to seventh or eighth against lefties.

SL% VS L	OB% VS L	SL% VS R	OB% VS R	PWR	H/R	BNT	RN	RG	AR
.539	.374	.589	.411	6	7	7	7	7	7

Richie Allen (R, 1972, AL)

Great power with average speed. Definitely can go deep and likes to do it against the lefties. Possible platoon player, although won't hurt you if he's in there every day. Would use as cleanup hitter against lefties. Good all-around pinch-hitting prospect.

SL% VS L	OB% VS L	SL% VS R	OB% VS R	PWR	H/R	BNT	RN	RG	AR
.690	.422	.649	.395	9	4	2	6	3	3

Hank Greenburg (R, 1938, AL)

Exceptional power. Big stick who swings for fences against the lefties. Weaker against right-handed pitching, but not a liability. Bat him in No. 5 slot against the lefties and drop him down against a rightie. Good pinch hitter, or backup to starter. Average glove man.

SL% VS L	OB% VS L	SL% VS R	OB% VS R	PWR	H/R	BNT	RN	RG	AR
.654	.369	.619	.351	10	2	2	3	5	6

Eddie Murray (S, 1984, AL)

Good pick if first four first basemen in League have been taken. Solid power from both sides of plate with solid defense in field. Will start for a lot of clubs, but most effective as pinch hitter or backup player.

SL% VS L	OB% VS L	SL% VS R	OB% VS R	PWR	H/R	BNT	RN	RG	AR
.561	.404	.537	.380	6	3	3	4	5	6

Bobby Allison (R, 1964, AL)

Good power hitter against lefties, and won't hurt you in the field. Strictly a platoon player who should see only lefties. Good pinch hitter coming off bench in late innings when you need a good pop.

SL% VS L	OB% VS L	SL% VS R	OB% VS R	PWR	H/R	BNT	RN	RG	AR
.608	.381	.577	.363	8	3	2	5	4	5

Ted Kluszewski (L, 1954, NL)

Monster at plate who hits only for power and only against right-handed pitching. Could be a liability in the field. Would make good back-up or great pinch hitter for isolated power in tight situation.

SL% VS L	OB% VS L	SL% VS R	OB% VS R	PWR	H/R	BNT	RN	RG	AR
.555	.343	.610	.370	8	3	3	3	3	4

Catchers

Catchers in the Hall of Fame League are all good. The problem here is that you have Carlton Fisk and then all the rest of the catchers. The ratings for Fisk against both righties and lefties are far and away much better than all other catchers. Unfortunately, Earl Weaver Baseball has no provision for measuring how well a catcher handles pitchers, which is the strong suit for many of the players at this position. Since you cannot measure that attribute in a catcher, you might consider looking at the catcher's power and his arm. Catchers are notoriously slow runners, as is the case with most of the receivers in this League.

Gary Carter (R, 1982, NL)

Great arm and above-average power. Does favor the lefties significantly more than righties. Can hold down No. 7 spot in order against lefties, but drop him down to No. 8 against the righties.

SL% VS L	OB% VS L	SL% VS R	OB% VS R	PWR	H/R	BNT	RN	RG	AR
.527	.378	.508	.356	6	2	2	2	6	7

Bill Freehan (R, 1964, AL)

No power, but a good arm. Not a player in lineup for any offense, but does provide a solid defender against base path burners. Must hit at low end of the order, preferably in No. 8 spot.

SL% VS L	OB% VS L	SL% VS R	OB% VS R	PWR	H/R	BNT	RN	RG	AR
.490	.361	.479	.344	5	4	4	5	7	7

Mickey Cochrane (L, 1933, AL)

Decent power for a catcher, but a weaker-than-average arm. Can't run at all, and his range leaves something to be desired. Is a left-handed bat, which is a plus. Should be platooned and played only against right-handers. Bat him sixth.

SL% VS L	OB% VS L	SL% VS R	OB% VS R	PWR	H/R	BNT	RN	RG	AR
.504	.385	.555	.424	6	3	4	3	4	4

Thurmon Munson (R, 1973, AL)

Sub-par power, but good arm. Has good range for catcher. Would work well with wild pitchers and cut down on pass balls. Can't even run to the refrigerator and back. In fact, runs like he's carrying the refrigerator with him. Platoon so he sees only lefties.

SL% VS L	OB% VS L	SL% VS R	OB% VS R	PWR	H/R	BNT	RN	RG	AR
.510	.367	.496	.348	5	2	3	3	7	7

Gabby Hartnett (R, 1928, NL)

Good gun and decent range. Probably will cut down on pass balls and throw out most of the runners trying to steal. Decent power. Platoon to face only southpaws, and bat him seventh.

SL% VS L	OB% VS L	SL% VS R	OB% VS R	PWR	H/R	BNT	RN	RG	AR
.521	.384	.503	.364	6	2	3	3	6	6

Ted Simmons (S, 1973, NL)

No power, but good arm and great range. Solid defensive pick for a receiver. Switch hitter who hits righties and lefties the same, which is just average and not spectacular.

SL% VS L	OB% VS L	SL% VS R	OB% VS R	PWR	H/R	BNT	RN	RG	AR
.464	.388	.456	.366	4	3	4	3	6	7

Pitchers

One characteristic of the Hall of Fame League, as with the real-life Major Leagues, is that quality left-handed pitching is at a premium. Lefties counter left-handed sluggers like Babe Ruth and Ted Williams (if you can counter those guys) and keep the likes of Ty Cobb off the bases (as much as possible).

You need at least four starters in the Hall of Fame League and at least five relievers to round out your pitching rotation.

As with the hitters and position players, a table follows each scouting report. Again, this table shows important summary statistics that give you an idea of a player's strengths and weaknesses. The earned run average (ERA) is the normalized number for the pitcher. The EWBII ratings that follow the ERA show the pitcher's speed (S), control (C), fatigue (F), bunting ability (B), and skill at holding runners on base (HO). Refer to Chapter 4, "The Statistics," for a more detailed explanation of EWBII ratings. The last four columns indicate how the pitcher performed against left-handed hitters (VS L) and right-handed hitters (VS R). These figures represent the hitter's batting average (OPP BA) and the hitter's on-base percentage (OPP OB%).

Starters

You'll notice that many of the top starting pitchers in the League come from the era around the turn of the century. You'll recall that era as being the time when few runs were being scored and pitchers were dominating baseball. Little wonder that even after normalizing statistics from their representative seasons these pitchers would settle in at the top of the League.

Doc White (L, 1906, AL)

Excellent control pitcher. Mediocre stuff. Excellent ERA and is a lefty, so gets extra credit. Will end up as a No. 1 starter on someone's club. Others available who are better aces, but he won't hurt you.

ERA	S	C	F	B	HO	OPP BA VS L	OPP OB% VS L	OPP BA VS R	OPP OB% VS R
2.00	4	9	6	5	5	.143	.179	.151	.188

Nig Cuppy (R, 1896, NL)

Excellent control man who gets a batter out, not always striking him out. Very low ERA. Will go into late innings. Solid No. 2 starter for your rotation who fares better against right-handed hitters.

ERA	S	C	F	B	HO	OPP BA VS L	OPP OB% VS L	OPP BA VS R	OPP OB% VS R
1.97	3	9	8	5	5	.145	.180	.138	.170

Bucky Walters (R, 1939, NL)

Will go a lot of innings and have a lot of complete games. In the upper echelon of right-handed starters. Will strike out a lot, even though not a fireballer, but also walks a lot. Not bad at the plate. No. 1 starter all the way.

ERA	S	C	F	B	HO	OPP BA VS L	OPP OB% VS L	OPP BA VS R	OPP OB% VS R
2.19	4	5	8	7	5	.148	.209	.140	.200

Kid Nichols (R, 1897, NL)

Excellent control, but not much heat. Gets a lot of complete games because of good stamina. Excellent ERA makes him a good pick as a No. 2 starter in rotation.

ERA	S	C	F	B	HO	OPP BA VS L	OPP OB% VS L	OPP BA VS R	OPP OB% VS R
1.88	4	10	8	4	4	.130	.160	.123	.154

Warren Spahn (L, 1953, NL)

Live fastball, good control, will last until you get in middle-reliever range. Fields position okay. One of the top three lefties in League. Works best as No. 2 starter in rotation.

ERA	S	C	F	B	HO	OPP BA VS L	OPP OB% VS L	OPP BA VS R	OPP OB% VS R
2.00	6	7	7	5	5	.158	.203	.163	.209

Ted Lyons (R, 1939, AL)

Excellent control with a very good walks-to-strikeout ratio. ERA within acceptable limits. Can probably get you to a short reliever. Significantly better pitcher against right-handed hitters.

ERA	S	C	F	B	HO	OPP BA VS L	OPP OB% VS L	OPP BA VS R	OPP OB% VS R
2.04	4	10	6	5	3	.155	.182	.146	.172

Amos Rusie (R, 1897, NL)

Excellent ERA. Great control and a finisher, unless he gets in rare trouble. A workhorse on the mound from an era when pitchers lasted forever. Use as No. 2 man.

ERA	S	C	F	B	HO	OPP BA VS L	OPP OB% VS L	OPP BA VS R	OPP OB% VS R
1.94	4	8	8	4	5	.139	.183	.130	.173

Lefty Gomez (L, 1937, AL)

Will get you to late innings, and has above-average stuff. Not a great fielder by any means. Seems to fit in well as a No. 2 starter. Pitches equally well against lefties or righties. Is a solid pick.

ERA	S	C	F	B	HO	OPP BA VS L	OPP OB% VS L	OPP BA VS R	OPP OB% VS R
1.82	7	6	7	3	3	.136	.190	.144	.199

Jack Chesbro (R, 1904, AL)

Great control, but biggest asset is he never gets tired. A complete game starter all the way. Relies on off-speed stuff (which would be a spitter if it were still legal).

ERA	S	C	F	B	HO	OPP BA VS L	OPP OB% VS L	OPP BA VS R	OPP OB% VS R
2.07	5	8	9	5	5	.149	.192	.141	.184

Bob Feller (R, 1939, AL)

The classic fireballer whose fastball is in the class of Walter Johnson. Probably won't go more than seven. ERA a bit high for a No. 1 man, but would nicely fill out anybody's staff. Probably best as No. 3 starter.

ERA	S	C	F	B	HO	OPP BA VS L	OPP OB% VS L	OPP BA VS R	OPP OB% VS R
2.06	8	3	7	5	4	.133	.215	.126	.206

Burleigh Grimes (R, 1920, NL)

Great control pitcher who strikes out many more than he walks. Probably won't need much more than a closer for help. Does much better against right-handed hitters.

ERA	S	C	F	B	HO	OPP BA VS L	OPP OB% VS L	OPP BA VS R	OPP OB% VS R
2.27	4	8	7	6	5	.171	.213	.162	.201

Vic Willis (R, 1899, NL)

Goes a lot of innings mostly with off-speed pitches. Excellent ERA numbers indicate he's a pesky type of pitcher. Difficult to figure out if you're a hitter.

ERA	S	C	F	B	HO	OPP BA VS L	OPP OB% VS L	OPP BA VS R	OPP OB% VS R
1.86	4	5	8	3	4	.117	.182	.109	.170

Jack Taylor (R, 1902, NL)

ERA is a bit bothersome, which indicates he does give up some hits. Has excellent control and stamina. Probably good enough for a No. 2 or No. 3 man in rotation.

ERA	S	C	F	B	HO	OPP BA VS L	OPP OB% VS L	OPP BA VS R	OPP OB% VS R
2.12	3	10	8	5	5	.166	.193	.158	.183

Camilo Pasqual (R, 1959, AL)

Fireballer with average control. ERA higher than most of top dogs. Strikes out more than twice the number he walks. Don't rely on him to be the ace of your staff.

ERA	S	C	F	B	HO	OPP BA VS L	OPP OB% VS L	OPP BA VS R	OPP OB% VS R
2.26	8	6	6	6	6	.175	.229	.164	.215

Relievers

This is a position that is tough to scout. These guys live in a world all their own, and you don't know where they are when you call on them to pitch. Still, there's a considerable amount of talent among the relievers, primarily in the role of closer. Middle relief specialists are tough to come by, and sometimes your pitching staff will consist of a sixth or seventh starter who can relieve a lot of innings when your starter gets in trouble. If you have the luxury of open spots on your pitching staff, consider getting a right-handed and a left-handed closer. The better balance you have between right-handers and left-handers in your relief corps, the more flexibility you will have during a game.

Tom Burgmeier (L, 1980, AL)

Classic closer good for maximum two innings per outing. Excellent control man who mixes heat and off-speed stuff. Best lefty closer in the League.

ERA	S	C	F	B	HO	OPP BA VS L	OPP OB% VS L	OPP BA VS R	OPP OB% VS R
1.69	5	9	1	4	7	.171	.205	.178	.212

Willie Hernandez (L, 1984, AL)

A closer who goes out day after day after day. Great live fastball with good control. Does give up the long ball, especially to right-handed hitters. Willie Hernandez won the Cy Young award and the MVP in the American League as he grabbed 32 saves in his first 32 save opportunities.

ERA	S	C	F	B	HO	OPP BA VS L	OPP OB% VS L	OPP BA VS R	OPP OB% VS R
1.88	8	7	2	4	3	.144	.194	.149	.200

Don Mossi (L, 1954, AL)

Classic starter/reliever who can go the distance. Would make a good swing man in rotation or good middle reliever. Relies on off-speed stuff to keep hitters guessing. Boasts an excellent ERA.

ERA	S	C	F	B	HO	OPP BA VS L	OPP OB% VS L	OPP BA VS R	OPP OB% VS R
1.90	6	3	2	4	3	.118	.204	.128	.211

Ted Abernathy (R, 1967, NL)

Great closer who throws dynamite heat. Right-handers have a real tough time against him. Keep an eye on him. Can be wild at times. Could hurt you if not pitching well.

ERA	S	C	F	B	HO	OPP BA VS L	OPP OB% VS L	OPP BA VS R	OPP OB% VS R
1.92	8	3	2	2	6	.142	.220	.137	.214

John Hiller (L, 1973, AL)

A strong left-handed middle reliever with a blazing fastball that he has trouble controlling at times. Doesn't give up a lot of runs, but is prone to giving up long ball.

ERA	S	C	F	B	HO	OPP BA VS L	OPP OB% VS L	OPP BA VS R	OPP OB% VS R
1.97	10	6	2	4	4	.144	.199	.151	.207

Sid Monge (L, 1979, AL)

Middle reliever with a good fastball and little control. Walks a lot of hitters and gives up a lot of home runs. More effective against left-handed hitters.

ERA	S	C	F	B	HO	OPP BA VS L	OPP OB% VS L	OPP BA VS R	OPP OB% VS R
2.00	8	3	2	4	4	.135	.216	.138	.219

Jim Kern (R, 1979, AL)

Excellent fastball artist with acceptable control. Walks a lot of hitters, especially lefties. Probably want to use in short relief situations.

ERA	S	C	F	B	HO	OPP BA VS L	OPP OB% VS L	OPP BA VS R	OPP OB% VS R
2.00	10	4	2	4	3	.138	.212	.132	.204

Lindy McDaniel (R, 1960, NL)

Middle reliever who can spot-start. Good swing man for any staff. Has heat and can spot it where he wants to. Fares a little better against the right-handed hitters, but nothing significant.

ERA	S	C	F	B	HO	OPP BA VS L	OPP OB% VS L	OPP BA VS R	OPP OB% VS R
2.15	9	8	2	4	5	.159	.200	.148	.187

Ron Perranoski (L, 1969, AL)

Mediocre stuff and lacks control. When he's on his game, he'll get the outs in the middle innings for you. Manages to not give up the big hit, but can be prone to putting men on.

ERA	S	C	F	B	HO	OPP BA VS L	OPP OB% VS L	OPP BA VS R	OPP OB% VS R
2.00	5	3	2	3	5	.150	.229	.160	.239

Ellis Kinder (R, 1953, AL)

Decent middle reliever, although better in short relief. No heat and only mediocre control. Use only in spot situations and preferably against right-handed hitters.

ERA	S	C	F	B	HO	OPP BA VS L	OPP OB% VS L	OPP BA VS R	OPP OB% VS R
2.30	4	6	2	6	4	.151	.211	.141	.198

Transforming Your Information

You now have the look of a baseball manager armed with a considerable amount of information. The more you know, the more you need to know. Now you need to know how to use all of the information you've accumulated over the past few chapters and how to transform that information into a winning ball club.

HOF - 1975
EARL AVERILL
CLEVELAND INDIANS – OUTFIELD
LEFTY GROVE
PHILADELPHIA ATHLETICS – PITCHER
1925
HOF - 1962
BOB FELLER
CLEVELAND INDIANS – PITCHER
1938

Draft Day

"What makes you or breaks you is the ability to choose from among the in-betweens those boys who will go on to make good."

–Branch Rickey

Congratulations! You have been promoted to the combined position of general manager and owner. Of course, you'll still be serving as the on-field general of this club. In addition to your normal duties as the manager, you'll now assume the responsibilities of wheeling and dealing for your ball club. Now that you are familiar with the player pool and know something about what it takes to put together a winning club, it's time you learned about your front-office responsibilities.

As a general manager, you must translate your newfound knowledge about the player pool into a team philosophy. You must know how to construct a ball club so that all the vital roles of your team are filled with the best available talent, and you must know how much to pay for that talent. When all of your preparations are complete, you'll represent your team on Draft Day.

Most participants in the Hall of Fame League agree that Draft Day is as much fun as the World Series. The draft lasts several hours and progresses in a way that no one can predict. Every Draft Day has a unique character and flavor. Draft Day is a special occasion for the Hall of Fame League. You and the other League owners get to vote on who are the best players of all time. It is an experience best described as fun in its purest form.

The draft is your first real taste of league competition. The structure is basically that of an auction. You sit down across the table from the other owners and bid play money for players. The highest bidder gets the player. That sounds simple enough. But the real fun begins when the players you covet are purchased by other teams. You must be able to adapt to ever-changing conditions and to make key decisions quickly. You must be aware of what other teams are doing, as well as what you can do to come away with the best team money can buy.

Before you can cash in on the fun, you still have some work to do. Previous chapters familiarized you with more than half the players in the Hall of Fame League. By now you should know the superstars and how to evaluate the extraordinary talent that makes up the player pool. Just a little more homework and you'll be ready for Draft Day.

The Player Puzzle

Knowing how to put together winning combinations of 25 players from a player pool of 300 is the key to a successful draft. As you have learned, ball clubs are comprised of hitting, fielding, and pitching. The players you choose determine your strengths and weaknesses in these three areas. The relative importance you place on these three aspects of your club determines the character of your team. You begin by taking a step back from all the individuals and their statistics. It's time to take a look at the whole picture.

Offense

As discussed briefly in Chapter 8, "The Scouting Report," the offensive role of a hitter is often determined by his spot in the batting order. You should be familiar with the primary role of each spot in the batting order in order to find a player to fit that role.

Think of your batting order in three segments: the top of the order, the meat of the order, and the bottom of the order. Because your lineup will bat around, on the average, about four times a game, the top of your order (the first three spots) will account for more than a fourth of your total at-bats during a game. The meat of your order (the second three spots), which should consist of hitters who are good at knocking in runs, will bat slightly less often. The bottom of the order (the last three spots), usually hitters with less skill at the plate, come to the plate least frequently.

No. 1 (Leadoff)

Traditionally, your leadoff hitter is a player with speed who is good at getting on base. Power is a luxury in the leadoff spot, found in special players like Rickey Henderson or Ty Cobb. The leadoff hitter is important not just because he is your team's first batter of the game. After all, you can only be assured that he will lead off an inning once (the first inning) during the whole game. That first at-bat is important, however, because it sets the offensive tone for your team. If he gets on, you have increased your chances of creating a run. As a matter of fact, the first batter in any inning is important for that very reason.

You may think that the mathematical probabilities of going through the nine-man batting order in varying multiples of three, four, or five batters or more would decrease the chances of a No. 1 hitter leading off any inning except the first. But keep in mind that the pitcher, who is invariably the worst hitter in your lineup and almost always placed in the No. 9 slot, will make the third out of an inning more often than a mathematical distribution would indicate.

Your best bets for a leadoff hitter are Ty Cobb, Rickey Henderson, Joe Kelley, Honus Wagner, or John McGraw.

No. 2

The best batter for this spot is one who can direct hits to right field (thereby hitting behind the leadoff hitter at first base), who bunts well, rarely strikes out, and who can reliably execute the hit-and-run play. The No. 2 batter is responsible for advancing the leadoff hitter, but he must also be a hitter with a good on-base average. After all, if the leadoff hitter fails to get on, the No. 2 hitter must set the table for the meat of the order. Many managers like to use a left-handed batter in this spot, especially against right-handed pitching.

Good picks for a No. 2 hitter include Willie Keeler, Hughie Jennings, Tris Speaker, Nap Lajoie, or Joe Jackson.

No. 3

You want the best hitter on your team to bat in the No. 3 spot for two reasons. If either or both the No. 1 and No. 2 hitters get on base, you want your No. 3 man to advance the runners and hopefully score a run. If neither the No. 1 nor No. 2 hitters reach base safely, you want your best hitter at the plate to keep the inning alive. Since your top two spots in the order are your best hitters at getting on base, the No. 3 hitter should be the best at knocking in runs. This guy should hit for a high average and with power.

Good picks for this slot would be Ted Williams, Stan Musial, George Brett, Cy Seymour, and Norm Cash.

The Meat (Nos. 4, 5, 6)

The meat of your order should consist of your big RBI men with home run power. The cleanup hitter (No. 4) should be the best long-ball slugger on the club. The No. 5 and No. 6 spots should have the power to drive in runners. The No. 4 and No. 5 batting spots usually see the most RBI opportunities over the course of the season. Of these three spots, the No. 6 generally has the least power.

With the abundance of good power hitters in the League, suggesting a few names for the meat of your order might be stating the obvious. Babe Ruth, Ted Williams, Mickey Mantle, Stan Musial, Joe DiMaggio, Mike Schmidt, George Brett, Jimmie Foxx, Lou Gehrig, and Willie McCovey are all great picks.

The Bottom (Nos. 7, 8, 9)

Usually, the remainder of your batting order is filled with players who are in the lineup for reasons other than their hitting. You'll probably want the best hitter of this group to bat in the No. 7 spot. Sometimes a player with speed is placed in the No. 8 position so that he can try to steal a base and set up an opportunity to pinch hit for the pitchers. As mentioned, pitchers always bat in the No. 9 spot, unless you are playing in a league that uses the designated hitter rule.

Defense

By comparing the roles of the defensive positions on the field with the talent available at those positions, you begin to see how your starting lineup could look. You can also begin to formulate where you might need platoon players for offensive purposes or to solidify your lineup defensively. The other part of team defense, pitching, is discussed later in this chapter.

Outfield

A third of the hitters in the player pool are outfielders. Obviously, this position has a lot of depth. Because of the large number of outfielders, you can often defer making decisions about what to look for from this position until your optimum team philosophy emerges.

The best hitters in the League are outfielders. This is traditionally one of the three positions where you find power hitters. (The other two are first base and third base.) This league has many power hitters who can play every day. This group also contains some excellent platoon players who boast impressive power against one kind of pitching, but aren't quite good enough to start against the other kind of pitching. The best examples of that probably would be Reggie Jackson and Willie Stargell, who hit a ton against the right-handers, but can be a liability with a southpaw on the mound.

Of all the defensive positions, you probably have the most flexibility with the outfield. Superstars are abundant, but expensive (you'll learn about pricing later in this chapter). Platoon players are abundant and significantly cheaper, but you'll need two of them to equal one everyday player.

The meat of your order comes from either the outfield or the other two power positions. If you are able to fill any of the No. 4, 5, and 6 spots with sluggers from other positions, it will be easier to put platoon combinations that have some punch from the remaining outfielders, first basemen, or third basemen. This is one of the keys to your team having better-than-average hitting.

The Corners (First Base, Third Base)

These are the other two power positions. Third basemen were once prized for their defense, but in the modern game, defensive skill for your cornerman is not as important as his power performance.

Some of the best sluggers in the Hall of Fame League are first basemen. The top half dozen first basemen (Norm Cash, Jimmie Foxx, Lou Gehrig, George Sisler, Willie McCovey, and Richie Allen) are great power hitters, but once those guys are taken, you could be looking at a defensive pick or a strict platooner.

Third base has three truly great offensive players in Mike Schmidt, George Brett, and John McGraw. But there is a definite gap between the quality of these three and the rest of the group. If you do not get one of the top picks (and they will be expensive), forget about drafting a third baseman until the later rounds.

The Middle (Shortstop, Second Base)

The great middle infielders are some of the most coveted players in the Hall of Fame League. These are your most skilled defensive players, which is important since most of the plays during a game are made up the middle. Players combining a solid defense and good offense at this position are rare. As a result, there are gaps between top performers and everyone else at both positions.

At shortstop, the top three players look similar, but there is a subtle difference. George Davis is the top-rated shortstop because he is so good defensively that his numbers vault him to the top. Hughie Jennings and Honus Wagner are in the top three because they are sound defensively, but they are also great leadoff hitters. Neither is as good defensively as Davis, but their offensive numbers get them rated in the top three. After the top three shortstops, the overall quality drops dramatically. If you cannot land one of these three, you're looking at defensive role players or platooners.

The dropoff in quality for second basemen doesn't really occur until the first six players are taken. However, first-rated Nap Lajoie's TPR is about 20 points higher than second-rated Eddie Collins, so Lajoie sits alone at the top of the heap. After Collins, the next four players are grouped fairly tightly, but none approaches his overall quality.

Landing top-quality infielders is one of the keys to establishing a pitching/fielding, defensive team philosophy. Defense up the middle is critical to this approach, and getting some hitting at the same time helps, since much of your budget must be spent on pitching.

Catcher

This is a difficult position to evaluate. Catchers in EWBII are not rated for how well they handle pitchers or how well they call a game, which is a big part of a catcher's job. Consequently, you are left with such measurements as arm (significant for throwing out potential base stealers), range (significant for cutting down passed balls and wild pitches), and batting skills. Because of the great speed in the player pool, a catcher in the Hall of Fame League must be good defensively. Some of the catchers have isolated power. Carlton Fisk stands out as the best pick of the bunch, but after he goes you can probably get a player almost as good. Left-handed hitting catchers with whom you can platoon are rare.

Pitching

As discussed in Chapter 6, "The Pitchers," the makeup of your pitching staff depends on your team philosophy. You must have at least a nine-man pitching staff, and some teams prefer to carry ten pitchers. Your staff can include six starters and three relievers, or five starters, three relievers, and one swing man. How many pitchers you carry depends on the quality of your starters and whether you plan on a four- or five-man rotation.

Left-handed pitchers are scarce in the League (as in the Major Leagues). If you want a quality left-handed pitcher, be prepared to pay big money.

Of the 90 starting pitchers in the player pool, less than a third of them can be considered quality starters. Of these, less than 10 qualify as the ace of a pitching staff, the guy who would hold down your No. 1 spot in the rotation. The dropoff in TPR for the top starting pitchers in the League and the top No. 2 starters is about 10 points. The difference in ratings between the highest rated No. 2 starter and the lowest rated No. 4 starter is only a half dozen TPR points.

In other words, aces are hard to come by, and after they are gone, the pitchers all rate closely together. This means that if you are trying to build a stellar pitching staff, you must be prepared to draft from within the top dozen pitchers available in the player pool. These include Joe Wood, Walter Johnson, Christy Mathewson, Wes Ferrell, Bob Lemon, Doc White, Bucky Walters, Chief Bender, Ed Walsh, Kid Nichols, Nig Cuppy, Warren Spahn, and Ted Lyons.

Quality left-handed pitching in the Hall of Fame League is a rare commodity that can command a high price on Draft Day.

Only a couple of relievers (Dennis Eckersley and Bruce Sutter) stand out above all the rest. For the most part, relievers should be picked according to how you want to round out your pitching staff. At best, relievers only pitch half as many innings as starters. No good general manager would attempt to build a pitching staff around a relief corps even if his starting pitching is so bad that his relievers will be seeing a disproportionate number of innings. Often, bringing in a relief pitcher means your team is behind.

Never get caught without a closer. A closer can be a decisive factor in the close games that separate good teams. The Hall of Fame League only has a few pitchers who fit that role exceptionally well. You should also try to get a good middle reliever to use on days when your starter gets knocked out early.

Keep an eye on how the draft progresses. Sometimes owners begin panicking, and all the quality pitching is drafted in a span of a few rounds. If that panic occurs early in the draft, the prices of pitchers will remain relatively high. Nonetheless, you are well advised not to ignore pitching altogether. The player pool has 26 hitters who hit 40 or more homers a season. Pitching prices often hold steady (and high) through the first ten rounds of the draft.

Pricing

Now that you are familiar with what it takes to put together a winning club, you must need a system that assigns a dollar value to each player you want on your team. You may not have to worry about long-term contracts, gate attractions, or even superstar egos. But you also do not have an endless supply of money.

Each franchise in the League begins with $400 in play money. This, in effect, is the Hall of Fame League salary cap. On Draft Day, you bid for players of your choice, thus spending the $400 in the most expeditious way you can.

The Oakland Athletics boasted the highest payroll ever in the Major Leagues in 1991. Coincidentally, the total payroll amount was close to $40 million. That number provides a convenient way to translate the "play money" spent in the Hall of Fame League into hard cold cash. By multiplying the owner's $400 by 100,000, you now have a figure comparable to what a Major League team pays its players in today's dollars. Using that multiple, you can translate what prices are paid during the draft into a real-life salary for all of the players in the Hall of Fame League.

When you look at the play money in terms of equivalent millions of dollars of real money, you realize that you must be careful not to waste your $400 on lesser talent. Because you have a limited supply of money, it helps to have a feeling for the relative value of each player in order to know when the bidding is getting too high. Ideally, you should assign a dollar value to the top 50 or 75 players.

Since you want the most talent for your money, it helps to pick up some players at a discount. If you get caught up in a bidding war for a player, you must be careful not to overpay. Overpaying for too many players results in a team without depth, a team with weaknesses that your opponents most certainly will take advantage of. Be cautious about paying more than a player is worth. At some price, you should allow the franchise owners who are bidding against you to purchase the player. Eventually, after your opponents overspend for enough players, you'll be able to pick up players at bargain prices.

Simple mathematics tells you that to draft a 25-man roster, you can spend an average of $16 per player. You might think that $16 would be what you would pay for an average player. However, in the Hall of Fame League, the stars are the difference between winning and losing. As a result, you will be forced to pay $50 or more for real talent and less than $5 for most of your average players.

Branch Rickey's most quoted saying was, "Luck is the residue of design."

As with any economic system, the forces of supply and demand determine the price of your players. Owners must pay what the market commands. Because of this, you must determine how much you are willing to pay for certain players and how you will fill out your roster with less valuable players.

One of the best ways to determine what you might pay for a player is to keep track of the winning bids for that player from season to season. But what happens if you are a new owner, or if your league is too young to have such a history? In those cases, you need a pricing system.

Under the Cost of Players (COP) system (explained in the next section), Babe Ruth, the greatest baseball player of all time, is being paid a record $7.7 million—the highest salary ever! If Ted Williams could actually collect the $6 million he's being paid in the Hall of Fame League or Mickey Mantle actually cashed in his $5.8 million check, maybe they'd still be around today. The top infielders in the league are not exactly underpaid. Hughie Jennings, one of the best shortstops ever to wear a glove, is pulling in a cool $4.7 million. Nap Lajoie is raking in $6.5 million for playing second base and Mike

Schmidt, of course, is being paid a handsome $5.8 million for holding down the hot corner.

This all is not too far-fetched. The two top-paid players in the Major Leagues in 1991 (Bobby Bonilla and José Canseco) command between $4 million and $5 million a year. So far, these guys haven't put up the numbers to reach the upper echelon of the Hall of Fame League. It only makes sense that Babe Ruth would make much more money.

When you extrapolate the Hall of Fame prices into real dollars for pitchers, you see that the top 40 starters are all paid more than $1 million a year. The difference between the top performers and the worst performers in that group of 40 pitchers is extreme. Smoky Joe Wood and Walter Johnson are the highest paid pitchers at $6.8 million each, with Christy Mathewson close behind at $6.7 million. Starting pitchers command almost as much money as the top position players in the League.

None of the relief pitchers top the $2 million mark and, in fact, less than a dozen even clear $1 million. Of the relievers, Bruce Sutter is the highest paid at $1.9 million, with Jesse Orosco hot on his heels with $1.8 million.

The Cost of Players (COP) System

Paying whatever it takes to get the ballplayers you want is a haphazard approach to spending a limited supply of money, an approach that seldom produces a winning team. The other owners in the League can capitalize on your stubbornness and force you to pay far more than each player is worth. Any free agent in Major League baseball today will tell you that market value is just the price a particular owner was willing to pay.

Although a player's price is determined by competitive bidding, you must have a starting point. The Cost of Players (COP) system determines an approximate price for players. Your goal, therefore, is to pay less than the COP price while forcing your fellow franchise owners to pay at least that much and preferably more.

The first step of the COP system is to recognize that a player provides value to a team in one of three ways: hitting, fielding, and pitching. One of baseball's unique features is that, although it is known as a team game, each baseball play involves only one or two players at a time. It is a team game made up of sequential performances by individuals. A player's contribution to winning consists of making a finite number of plays (or events) involving one or more of the three basic skills.

The following four factors determine the events in which a player is involved and how well a player performs relative to the rest of the League:

* The number of plate appearances depends on a hitter's spot in the batting order. Platoon players have fewer plate appearances because they don't play every day. Because there are more right-handed pitchers than left-handed pitchers, left-handed platoon players bat more often than right-handed platoon players.

The COP system establishes a mathematically derived base price for a player. In effect, this is the player's assessed value in the draft.

* The number of plays in which a fielder is involved depends on what position he plays. Many of the plays on the baseball field are made up the middle, so middle infielders invariably see more chances. Again, a platooner's expected chances are less than those of an everyday player.
* The number of innings a pitcher is on the mound is proportional to the spot he holds in the pitching rotation. As an example, if you have a four-man starting rotation, each starter sees about 300 innings. With that rotation, your two main relievers get about 100 to 150 innings of work in a season. The other members of your staff will see less than 100 innings each.
* The total player rating (TPR) determines how far above or below average a player will perform. Remember that the TPR is the sum of the linear weights stats of batting runs, stealing runs, fielding runs, and pitching runs (see Chapter 4, "The Statistics," for a complete discussion of linear weights). If you calculate the average TPR for the player pool in the Hall of Fame League, and compare it

with a particular player's TPR to that league average, you can produce the player's Relative TPR.

Based on these assumptions, the COP system assigns a percentage to a player that reflects the number of plays (events) in which he will be involved, divided by the total number of plays (events) the team will have in a season. That percentage is then multiplied by his Relative TPR, and that product is multiplied by the amount of money in the draft to establish a price. Another way to describe the COP system is that it simply determines how involved the player is in the game and how good he is relative to the other players.

Remember that your initial stake in the draft is $400. As each round passes and you begin picking up players, that amount decreases. It is difficult to predict how much that decrease will be from pick to pick, but you can get a sense of how much money you will be spending for your top picks. As the draft progresses, each owner has less and less money to spend, and the price of each player invariably decreases.

MSRP

The COP system is only a starting point. If, during the early stages of the draft, an owner pays $60 for a player you valued at $50, does this mean that your system is completely inaccurate? How much is that player really worth? Your calculated $50 is based on statistical information, but the $60 price paid is what the market said the player was worth. How do you account for the differences in market price and the COP price? An easy way to account for such differences is to use the Manager's Suggested Retail Price (MSRP).

Tables 9-1 and 9-2, located at the end of this chapter, show the COP price for each hitter (or position player) and pitcher, respectively, in the Hall of Fame League. The tables also include the price paid for each player drafted for a 1991 Northern California league. To incorporate historical market prices into the dollar amount assigned to the players, the COP price has been averaged with the 1991 price to provide the

MSRP. For the pitchers listed in Table 9-2, the ROT column indicates the projected spot in the pitching rotation.

You'll notice that two columns of prices appear after the MSRP. The Real Dollars column shows how much each player might be making in real money based on the results of the 1991 draft. The Claiming Bid column reflects a price at which a player can be claimed with no competitive bidding from other owners. Claiming Bids are part of the ground rules of the draft.

Ground Rules

At the beginning of the draft, the Commissioner outlines the timetable for the coming season. Trading deadlines are set, as are dates by which managers must submit their pitching rotations. Deadlines are set for building team stadiums (see Chapter 11, "Building the Perfect Ballpark") and for establishing managerial strategy profiles (see Chapter 12, "Molding the Perfect Manager"). Proposed changes are discussed with the owners, and votes are taken to determine if any of these proposals will take effect.

With the new business out of the way, ground rules are set for Draft Day activities. First, a draft order is established. This is the order in which owners will be allowed to introduce players for bidding. One effective way to establish the draft order is to draw slips of paper out of a hat. Written on each piece of paper is a number. The owner with the number 1 gets to start by introducing bidding on a player of his choice. Then the owner who picks 2 introduces another player, and so on. Another method is to draw from a deck of cards. The owner who draws the highest card is first to introduce a player, then the owner with the next highest card introduces, and so on.

The draft order works around in sequence and returns to the first owner in reverse sequence. As an example, for an eight-team league, the draft order would be 1 through 8 for the first round and 8 through 1 for the second round, 1 through 8 for the third round, and so on. Owners who draft first and last will be introducing two consecutive players from the second round on.

Three owners must be designated to track the progress of the draft for the League front office. One owner must keep track of what players are selected and by whom. This information is necessary for the front office to align players on their new teams, as described in Chapter 10, "The Commissioner's Tools." An efficient method for tracking the draft picks and their prices is to use preprinted forms that contain the names of the players in alphabetical order, as shown in Figure 9-1. Use one form for hitters and one form for pitchers. Two owners must track how much money is spent by each team, round by round, to ensure that no one exceeds the $400 limit. Two owners are necessary for this so that the "auditing" function can be incorporated in the draft.

On Draft Day, owners spend their allotted $400 on players by bidding against each other, with the highest bidder gaining rights to the player.

To begin the draft, an owner introduces a player's name and his position. The owner who introduces the player has the choice of submitting an opening bid for the player or claiming the player at the established claiming price. After the player is introduced with an opening bid, the other owners are called on, generally in the draft order selected earlier. Each owner may increase the bid for the player or bow out of the process. The bidding continues until one owner has made a bid and all other owners have bowed out. The owner who bids the highest price gets the player, and the amount of the bid is subtracted from that team's total funds.

If the claiming price is bid when introducing the player, the owner purchases the player for the claiming price and no bidding takes place. This may sound like an easy way to pick up players. However, the claiming price is actually about 1.5 times higher than the calculated COP price. If you want to claim a player at the claiming price, you'll be paying top dollar. On the other hand, there is no risk that you will be outbid for the player.

Figure 9-1.

Tracking sheet for the Hall of Fame League's draft picks

NAME	POS	Team	$	NAME	POS	Team	$
AARON	789			CAREY	789		
ALLEN	3			CARTER	2		
ALLISON	3			CASH	3		
APARICIO	64			CEDENO	789		
APPLING	64			CEPEDA	3		
ASHBURN	789			CHANCE	3		
AVERILL	789			CHAPMAN	64		
BAILEY	2			CHILDS	4		
BAKER	5			CLARK,J	789		
BANCROFT	64			CLARKE	789		
BANKS	64			CLEMENTE	789		
BARFIELD	789			CLIFT	5		
BARTELL	6			COBB	789		
BELL	5			COCHRANE	2		
BENCH	2			COLAVITO	789		
BERRA	2			COLLINS,E	4		
BOGGS	5			COLLINS,J	53		
BOTTOMLEY	3			CRAWFORD	789		
BOUDREAU	6			CRONIN	6		
BOYER,K.	53			DAHLEN	6		
BRADLEY	5			DAVIS,G	6		
BRESNAHAN	2			DAWSON	789		
BRETT	5			DECINCES	5		
BROCK	789			DELAHANTY	789		
BURGESS	2			DEVLIN	5		
CAMILLI	3			DICKEY	2		
CAMPENELLA	2			DIMAGGIO	789		
CAREW	4			DOERR	4		

Drafting Tools

No matter how much homework you've done and no matter how prepared you think you are, Draft Day can be an overwhelming experience. You must be able to adapt and to make decisions quickly.

The key to success is good organization. Organize the information you think will be needed in order to make quick decisions. You should know something about all the players in the pool. You should know what positions have depth, how players are grouped according to skill level, and where there are gaps between the skill levels of players. You must also know which players you want on your team and how much you are willing to pay to get them. This means you must have a team philosophy in mind.

No one can draft a team comprised solely of superstars. The salary cap prevents this from happening and ensures an even distribution of talent in the League. Therefore, you must identify which superstars will anchor a team fitting your philosophy. Remember that while you were reviewing the available talent, you formulated a philosophy about what kind of team you wanted. You decided whether you wanted a strong hitting team with adequate pitching, a strong pitching team with adequate hitting, or whatever.

Construct depth charts of players who fit your philosophy, complete with the prices you are willing to pay. One depth chart should be based on possible batting orders (No. 1 through No. 8 hitters) and one should be based on the defensive positions. Construct a separate chart for your top 30 pitching picks. These depth charts are the blueprint of your team.

As the draft progresses and the owners gobble up players, cross them off your depth charts. By keeping track of what players you want and who is taken during the draft, you can decide when you should pay the big bucks for a player and when you should shop for bargains.

Prior to the draft, the League office distributes statistical breakdowns of players in the League. These breakdowns invariably contain more information than you can remember during the heat of the draft. Depth charts are handy tools to have with you on Draft Day because they are a condensed version of that information.

Figure 9-2 shows a sample of a depth chart for the shortstop position. By breaking down the player pool and organizing separate lists based on positions and batting order, you now have a reference tool that allows you to stay on top of the draft as it progresses. You might want to put these lists in a binder with separator tabs indicating positions. This allows you to refer quickly to see how a player might fit your team when he is introduced to the bidding.

Organization of information allows you to quickly adjust to the ever-changing environment of player availability on Draft Day.

As the player pool shrinks and the available talent dwindles, you must be able to identify your needs quickly and efficiently. To keep track of who you have drafted and how they fit into your team structure, use a form such as the one shown in Figure 9-3. This form shows how your draft is progressing by giving you a list of the players you have drafted, in what order you drafted them, and how much you paid. You also can track how much money you have spent. Figure 9-4 shows another form that you can use. This form guides you through the construction of a batting order against right-handed and left-handed pitching, shows you what defensive positions must be filled, and tracks the construction of your pitching staff.

Merely keeping track of how your team is shaping up and ignoring how the other teams in the League are shaping up is an isolationist approach to the draft that is seldom effective. A more successful approach is to track the other teams as they are assembled.

By using a grid such as the one shown in Figure 9-5, you can see how the other teams in the League are filling out. This grid allows you to see what needs have been filled by the other teams and where voids exist. By knowing what the other teams must draft, you can adapt to bidding situations for players because you know how badly another team needs an individual player. This tool also helps you gauge how much another owner is willing to pay for individual players. This information

Figure 9-2.

Condensed player information

	NAME	$	OVERALL OBS	OVERALL SL %	OVERALL OB %	OVERALL ISO PWR	OVERALL SR	OVERALL FR	OVERALL BR	TPR	P	H	B	R	RG	AR	VS LEFT SL %	VS LEFT OB %	VS LEFT OBS	VS LEFT BR	VS LEFT SR	TPR	VS RIGHT SL %	VS RIGHT OB %	VS RIGHT OBS	VS RIGHT BR	VS RIGHT SR	TPR
S	DAVIS,G	43	.810	.419	.391	.082	5	57	23	**85**	2	6	8	7	9	10	410	407	816	23	6	**86**	422	385	807	23	5	**85**
R	JENNINGS	47	.895	.454	.441	.080	9	33	42	**85**	2	9	10	9	7	7	448	459	907	47	9	**89**	456	433	889	35	9	**77**
R	WAGNER	45	.969	.530	.439	.149	8	18	55	**81**	4	9	8	10	6	5	532	457	989	62	9	**88**	530	431	961	48	8	**74**
R	DAHLEN	34	.899	.504	.395	.183	8	24	39	**71**	5	9	8	10	6	7	502	411	913	48	9	**81**	504	388	892	35	8	**67**
R	RIPKEN,C	31	.886	.511	.374	.206	0	35	35	**69**	6	2	3	3	7	8	511	389	900	45	0	**80**	512	368	880	33	0	**67**
R	BARTELL	21	.812	.462	.351	.160	-2	42	20	**59**	4	2	4	2	8	7	456	364	821	30	-2	**69**	464	345	808	19	-2	**59**
R	BOUDREAU	19	.923	.498	.425	.166	0	10	46	**55**	4	3	5	3	5	5	496	442	938	53	0	**62**	498	418	916	40	0	**49**
R	WALLACE	19	.845	.478	.367	.135	1	27	26	**54**	3	5	6	6	6	7	474	382	856	37	1	**64**	479	361	840	25	1	**53**
L	VAUGHN	11	.861	.463	.398	.145	0	19	33	**51**	4	4	5	4	6	5	414	374	788	24	0	**42**	484	409	892	35	0	**54**
R	CRONIN	17	.838	.460	.378	.150	-1	24	27	**50**	4	3	5	4	6	7	454	393	848	35	-1	**59**	462	371	833	24	-1	**47**
R	HARRAH	1	.859	.456	.403	.164	2	13	34	**49**	4	4	4	5	5	6	450	419	869	39	2	**55**	458	396	854	28	2	**43**
R	TINKER	1	.774	.434	.339	.138	5	29	12	**46**	4	7	7	8	7	6	427	352	779	22	5	**56**	438	334	771	12	5	**46**
		24	**.864**	**.472**	**.392**	**.147**	**3**	**28**	**32**	**63**	**4**	**5**	**6**	**6**	**7**	**7**	**465**	**404**	**869**	**39**	**3**	**69**	**476**	**387**	**862**	**30**	**3**	**60**

Figure 9-3.

Worksheet for draft picks and prices

TEAM:

PLAYER	POS	$ PD
1		
2		
3		
4		
5		
6		
7		
8		
9		
10		
11		
12		
13		
14		
15		
16		
17		
18		
19		
20		
21		
22		
23		
24		
25		

Figure 9-4.

Worksheet for batting order and roster

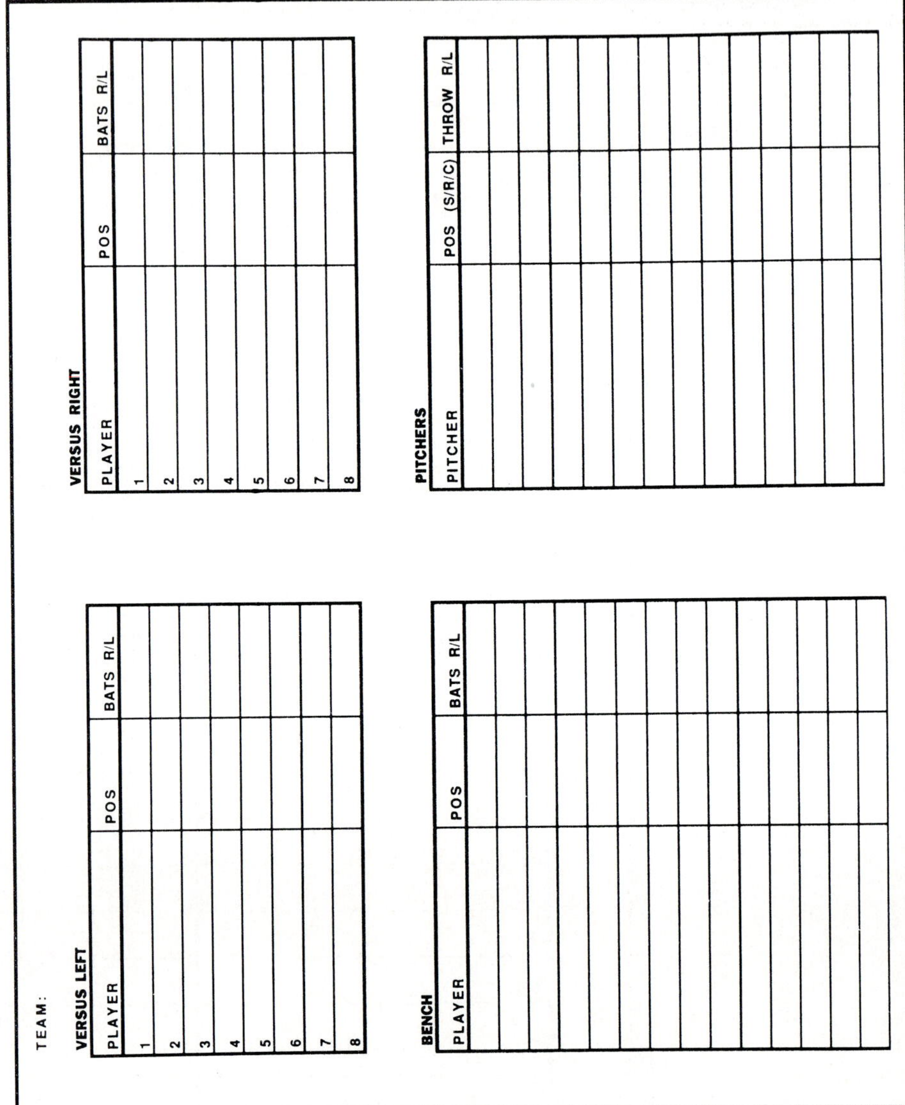

TEAM:

VERSUS LEFT

PLAYER	POS	BATS R/L
1		
2		
3		
4		
5		
6		
7		
8		

VERSUS RIGHT

PLAYER	POS	BATS R/L
1		
2		
3		
4		
5		
6		
7		
8		

BENCH

PLAYER	POS	BATS R/L

PITCHERS

PITCHER	POS (S/R/C)	THROW R/L

Figure 9-5.

Worksheet for tracking draft picks of all teams

	C	1B	2B	3B	SS	OF	SP	RP
WH								
TN								
RL								
RD								
MD								
KS								
RG								
MS								

aids you in spending your money wisely. As the draft progresses, clubs will desperately need position players and begin bidding against each other for a few remaining good players. This drives up prices and sometimes forces owners to spend their money inefficiently.

Remember that the market value of players at the beginning of the draft is different from the market value at the end of the draft. Think of the draft as consisting of three phases. Phase 1 is usually when the highest prices are paid for players because everyone has $400 with which to work. Phase 2 is when prices begin to level off. Phase 3 is when several teams are out of money.

Phase 3 is when you can pick up bargain players. How you spend your money, of course, determines how soon you run out. It is dangerous to run out of money too soon. Every roster must contain 25 players. Even without money, you must fill that 25-player roster. If you run out of money, you no longer participate in the bidding process. You must wait for all the other teams to spend their money before you can pick up players to fill your roster. Only after all teams have spent their $400 will you be able to select any players. When all teams have spent their funds, owners then claim players from the remaining pool at a $0 value.

Draft Strategies

To avoid spending all your money in the first two phases of the draft and waiting around while the rest of the League runs out of money, you must employ a draft strategy. Several strategies have been tried in the Hall of Fame League. Some of these have proven to be quite successful, while others have proven embarrassing. Because of the ever-changing conditions in the draft, you may want to have a couple of different strategies in mind before the draft begins so that you can adapt to current conditions as the draft progresses.

The Bidding Strategy

This strategy is the most conventional way to approach the draft. You simply define the players you want by how much you are willing to pay. You only bid up to the amount you feel is a fair value. If you are able to pick up a player at less than that maximum price, you save yourself money. The risk with this strategy is that if you are outbid for enough key players, you can fail to assemble enough talent to field a winning team.

The Claiming-Price Strategy

To employ this approach, you try to find the bargains among the claiming prices set by the League. Rather than participating in the bidding process, you wait for your turn to introduce players and use the opportunity to claim quality players at low prices. This way you save your money so that you can outbid other teams in the later rounds.

This strategy is based on filling out your bench first and selecting your starting lineup last. It works especially well if you can find quality players with low claiming prices. Using this approach often means that by the 10th round of the draft you will have selected more players for your roster than any other team and will also have the most money left.

A variation of this strategy is to use the claiming price to be sure you get the superstars you want to anchor your team. Claiming superstar players is expensive, but it also prevents other owners from outbidding you. During the 1991 draft of the Northern California Hall of Fame League, all owners claimed players on their first-round selections. You cannot use claiming prices to select a team of superstars, however. If you use the claiming price strategy for selecting only superstars, you will also spend all your money quickly and have to wait out all but the final phase of the draft before you can complete your roster. You will end up with a lousy team featuring some big-name players.

The Giveaway or Stealing Strategy

To employ this strategy, you introduce players at extremely low prices and hope that all the other owners either pass on the player or that the bidding price stays lower than the market value of the player. In other words, you are trying to pick up quality players at bargain prices. You know what players are available at bargain prices, and after you have introduced the player at a below-bargain price, you hope you can save money and pick up a quality player.

This is a risky strategy that counts on the other owners being willing to give away quality talent at low prices. It is also called the Stealing Strategy because in effect you are trying to steal talent without really paying a fair price.

The Depth Chart (Gap Method) Strategy

While researching the player pool prior to the draft, you should identify positions where players are closely grouped together by skill level. In effect, you have identified a depth chart of the League. At a few positions in the League, a gap exists between top-quality players and the next tier of players. By ensuring that you draft from the top tier at these positions, you ensure that there will be a similar gap between the skill level of your team and the skill level of other teams. The theory behind this strategy is that you want to incrementally widen the gap between your team and other teams so that you have the best overall team in the League.

The Lefty-Pitching Strategy

By drafting an all left-handed or predominantly left-handed pitching staff, you skew the distribution of a rare commodity in the League. Left-handed pitching offsets some of the devastating effects of the League's superstar power hitters, such as Babe Ruth and Lou Gehrig. If you can also obtain quality left-handed hitting, it will be hard for the other teams to stop your team.

If you use the Lefty-Pitching strategy, you can build a ballpark with a short right field and a cavernous left field. This strategy results in a team built around a pitching staff with a mediocre supply of position players and hitters. Using this strategy produces some interesting scenarios for the season. Your team will certainly have a big advantage at home, where you play 81 games. The problem with this strategy is that it is extremely hard to implement.

The Sucker Strategy

This is a strategy of introducing players that you have no interest in having on your team. In theory, you want to force other owners to spend their money early in the draft for players you do not want. Be careful of this strategy. You can introduce a player and offer a low bid, but drop out immediately. Some owners try this strategy and exploit the bidding process in an attempt to drive up prices for players they don't want. If you become involved in a bidding war, you must know exactly how much another owner is willing to pay so that his bid will always top yours. Watch out–you may end up drafting a player you don't need and spending more money than you can afford.

The Freeze-Out Strategy

If you sit back and wait for everyone to spend their money on the high-priced players, you will be able to save all your funds while the rest of the owners spend theirs. With this strategy, you hoard your bankroll until the other owners have little or no money remaining. You then use your funds to dominate the bidding for remaining players. A player might be worth $40, but if no other owner has more than $20 left, the player is yours for $21. In the latter stages of the draft, you can effectively use the Sucker strategy to force an owner to spend all his remaining funds to pick up a marginal player.

This strategy may not be an efficient use of time or money. By taking a low-key approach to spending money on players, you may find that the other owners in effect freeze you out of drafting quality players. The result can be a team comprised solely of mediocre or even lesser talent.

The Stockpile Strategy

By drafting more players at a position than you really need, you actually keep other teams from putting together a well-rounded roster. This strategy is especially effective when used in conjunction with the Depth Chart strategy. By preventing other teams from drafting successfully at any position, you force teams to use mediocre players in starting roles because quality talent is no longer available. If you are an owner who enjoys making trades, this stockpile can become extremely valuable when the draft concludes.

Trading

Every league should have an owner who enjoys the trading process. One Hall of Fame League has an owner nicknamed Trader Mike. He derives almost as much pleasure from making deals as he does from drafting his team. Trader Mike enjoys putting together packages, phoning fellow owners, proposing trades, and moving players. Without people like this in the League, owners who are not successful in the draft are stuck with a team they don't really like. Managing a team you are not happy with destroys the basic purpose of being involved in the Hall of Fame League—having fun.

Within minutes after the conclusion of the 1991 draft, Trader Mike announced that he had made his first deal of the year. He had traded his outfielder Ed Delahanty straight up for outfielder Willie Stargell. Every league should have a Trader Mike. He adds a behind-the-scenes facet to the game that makes owning and managing a team even more enjoyable.

Trading players is an art. It requires a certain amount of character in a team owner. A good trader must be able to identify the needs of his own team and the needs of other teams in the League. He must be able to put together a deal that will satisfy his own needs without sacrificing too much. He must be able to convince another team owner that he can offer something valuable in order to get want he wants. A good trade is a win/win situation for both teams.

The history of Major League baseball is sprinkled with characters like Trader Mike. Trades such as the Delahanty-for-Stargell deal are known as *challenge trades.* You are trading an outfielder for an outfielder, a power hitter for a power hitter, and you are challenging the other team to achieve better results than you can because of the trade. These trades are rare in the history of baseball, primarily because of their risky nature. But baseball history is full of multiplayer swaps, some of which were unbelievably bad.

In the winter of 1900, the Cincinnati Reds decided they were giving up on a minor league pitcher who had compiled an 0-3 record in his only stint in the Major Leagues. They decided to trade the minor leaguer to the New York Giants for future Hall of Famer Amos Rusie. This sounds like a lopsided trade in favor of the Reds. But Rusie was in the twilight of his career and had already won 243 games. He finished his career with 245 total victories. The minor leaguer was Christy Mathewson, who played in the Majors for 17 years and won 343 games, 100 more games than Rusie had won at the time of the trade. A bad trade? Yes, but not in favor of the Reds.

One of Branch Rickey's baseball tenets was "Trade a player a year too early rather than a year too late."

An example of a team unable to identify its own needs came in the spring of 1927. The Senators decided to trade Buddy Myer to the Red Sox straight up for Topper Rigney. Myer played in 133 games for Boston that year and finished the season with a .288 batting average. He appeared in 147 games in 1928 and hit an impressive .313. Rigney, on the other hand, played 45 games for the Senators in 1927 and then retired from baseball. By the end of the 1928 season, the Senators were beckoning the services of Myer and traded five players to the Red Sox to get him back. No Hall of Fame players were involved in either of these deals, but the example shows how bad trading can be costly to a ball club.

In Chapter 5, "The Hitters," and Chapter 7, "The Bench," you read about the exploits of another team apparently unclear on the finer points of trading ballplayers. In the spring of 1960, the Cleveland Indians traded Norm Cash—for a player who only had five more total at-bats in his career—and Rocky Colavito, a proven slugger—for a singles hitter named Harvey Kuenn—to the Detroit Tigers, all within a one-week period.

In the winter of 1971, the New York Mets traded future Hall of Famer Nolan Ryan and three other players to the

California Angels for Jim Fregosi. Ryan won 138 games during his eight-year stay with the Angels and has since crossed the magical 300-win career mark. Fregosi, on the other hand, only played 146 games and never hit over .240 for the Mets.

The moral of these stories is that if you're going to deal with the likes of Trader Mike, you better know what you are getting and what you are giving up. Otherwise, you may end up on the short end of a deal and actually hurt your team more than you help.

A League Is Born

When the dust settles from Draft Day and the flurries of trading activity calm down, a new Hall of Fame League is born. Players have been chosen and the money has all been spent. Teams have been refined and the talent has been aligned. The time has come for another season to unfold.

In order to get your season underway, you must first use the Commissioner's Disk II Utility in the EWBII game to put everything in order, to set up your season, and to get your league ready to play.

Table 9-1.

Prices for Hitters and Position Players, Sorted by Highest to Lowest Real Dollars by Position

	NAME	COP $	1991 $	MSRP $	REAL $ (X1000)	CLAIM $
OUTFIELD						
L	RUTH	67	86	77	$7,700	104
L	COBB	49	77	63	$6,300	76
L	WILLIAMS,T	47	73	60	$6,000	73
S	MANTLE	42	75	58	$5,800	65
R	DELAHANTY	49	61	55	$5,500	76
L	JACKSON,J	42	47	44	$4,400	65
L	SPEAKER	46	41	43	$4,300	71
R	HENDERSON	43	41	42	$4,200	67
L	MUSIAL	37	47	42	$4,200	57
R	MAYS	34	46	40	$4,000	53
R	DIMAGGIO	32	37	35	$3,500	50
L	JACKSON,R	18	37	28	$2,800	28
L	SHECKARD	36	15	26	$2,600	56
R	ROBINSON,F	27	14	21	$2,100	42
L	THOMPSON	23	16	20	$2,000	36
R	SIMMONS,A	24	14	19	$1,900	37
R	GUERRERO	27	9	18	$1,800	42
L	KLEIN	28	6	17	$1,700	43
L	STARGELL	15	20	17	$1,700	23
L	SEYMOUR	23	4	14	$1,400	36
R	DAWSON	26	3	14	$1,400	40
R	KELLEY	28	1	14	$1,400	43
R	HEILMANN	11	18	14	$1,400	17
R	COLAVITO	10	17	14	$1,400	16
L	CLARKE	22	4	13	$1,300	34
R	KALINE	24	3	13	$1,300	37
L	YASTRZEMSKI	18	6	12	$1,200	28
L	FLICK	15	3	9	$900	23
L	KEELER	15	1	8	$800	23
L	GOSLIN	14	1	8	$800	22
L	SMITH,E	13	2	7	$700	20
L	OTT	13	2	7	$700	20
R	MAGEE,S	9	2	6	$600	14
R	AARON	9	2	6	$600	14
R	MEDWICK	9	3	6	$600	14
R	CEDENO	9	1	5	$500	14
R	FOSTER	9	1	5	$500	14
R	CLEMENTE	8	1	4	$400	12
R	KINER	8	1	4	$400	12
R	WYNN	7	1	4	$400	11
R	WILSON,H	7	1	4	$400	11
L	DONLIN	1	1	1	$100	1
L	CRAWFORD	1	1	1	$100	1
L	WILLIAMS,K	1	1	1	$100	1
L	GWYNN	1	1	1	$100	1
S	RAINES	1	1	1	$100	1

Table 9-1.

Prices for Hitters and Position Players, Sorted by Highest to Lowest Real Dollars by Position (continued)

	NAME	COP $	1991 $	MSRP $	REAL $ (X1000)	CLAIM $
L	PARKER	1	1	1	$100	1
L	HAMILTON	1	1	1	$100	1
L	LYNN	1	1	1	$100	1
R	MINOSO	1	1	1	$100	1
S	ROSE	1	2	1	$100	1
L	WANER,P	1	1	1	$100	1
L	STAUB	1	1	1	$100	1
R	WINFIELD	1	1	1	$100	1
L	MURCER	1	1	1	$100	1
S	CAREY	1	1	1	$100	1
R	JOHNSON	1	1	1	$100	1
R	BARFIELD	1	1	1	$100	1
L	WHEAT	1	1	1	$100	1
R	LEZCANO	1	1	1	$100	1
R	RICE	1	1	1	$100	1
R	CLARK,J	1	1	1	$100	1
L	POWELL	1	2	1	$100	1
L	ASHBURN	1	1	1	$100	1
R	KELLER	1	1	1	$100	1
L	WILLIAMS,B	1	1	1	$100	1
L	SNIDER	1	1	1	$100	1
R	HAFEY	1	1	1	$100	1
L	AVERILL	1	1	1	$100	1
L	SLAUGHTER	1	1	1	$100	1
L	BROCK	1	1	1	$100	1
UTILITY INFIELD						
R	YOUNT	6	1	3	$300	9
R	BANKS	6	1	3	$300	9
R	APPLING	1	1	1	$100	1
R	CHAPMAN	1	1	1	$100	1
R	PECKINPAUGH	1	1	1	$100	1
R	FREGOSI	1	1	1	$100	1
S	SMITH,O	1	1	1	$100	1
R	JACKSON,T	1	1	1	$100	1
L	SEWELL	1	1	1	$100	1
R	MARANVILLE	1	1	1	$100	1
S	BANCROFT	1	1	1	$100	1
R	APARICIO	1	1	1	$100	1
R	ROSEN	8	4	6	$600	12
L	MATHEWS	11	2	6	$600	17
R	WILLIAMS,J	1	1	1	$100	1
R	MOLITOR	1	1	1	$100	1
R	MELTON	1	2	1	$100	1
R	ZIMMERMAN	1	1	1	$100	1
L	NETTLES	1	2	1	$100	1
R	COLLINS,J	1	1	1	$100	1
R	ROBINSON,B	1	2	1	$100	1

Table 9-1.

Prices for Hitters and Position Players, Sorted by Highest to Lowest Real Dollars by Position (continued)

	NAME	COP $	1991 $	MSRP $	REAL $ (X1000)	CLAIM $
R	GROH	1	1	1	$100	1
R	BOYER	1	1	1	$100	1
L	EVANS	1	1	1	$100	1
SHORTSTOP						
R	JENNINGS	45	48	47	$4,700	70
R	WAGNER	44	42	43	$4,300	68
S	DAVIS,G	42	36	39	$3,900	65
R	DAHLEN	33	7	20	$2,000	51
R	RIPKEN,C	30	7	19	$1,900	47
R	BARTELL	20	7	14	$1,400	31
R	BOUDREAU	19	4	11	$1,100	29
R	WALLACE	18	1	10	$1,000	28
R	CRONIN	16	1	9	$900	25
L	VAUGHN	11	2	6	$600	17
R	HARRAH	1	1	1	$100	1
R	TINKER	1	1	1	$100	1
THIRD BASE						
R	SCHMIDT	54	61	58	$5,800	84
L	BRETT	42	48	45	$4,500	65
R	MCGRAW	34	25	30	$3,000	53
R	SANTO	28	6	17	$1,700	43
R	DEVLIN	26	4	15	$1,500	40
R	CLIFT	22	1	11	$1,100	34
R	DECINCES	18	1	10	$1,000	28
L	BAKER	16	2	9	$900	25
L	BOGGS	14	2	8	$800	22
R	BRADLEY	8	2	5	$500	12
R	BELL	7	1	4	$400	11
R	KILLEBREW	1	2	1	$100	1
SECOND BASE						
R	LAJOIE	58	71	65	$6,500	90
R	HORNSBY	35	45	40	$4,000	54
L	COLLINS,E	37	33	35	$3,500	57
L	MORGAN	28	17	22	$2,200	43
R	ROBINSON,J	26	10	18	$1,800	40
L	CHILDS	31	4	17	$1,700	48
S	FRISCH	27	7	17	$1,700	42
R	GRICH	20	10	15	$1,500	31
R	SANDBERG	8	13	10	$1,000	12
L	CAREW	12	1	7	$700	19
S	HUGGINS	9	1	5	$500	14
L	GEHRINGER	1	1	1	$100	1
S	SCHOENDIENST	1	1	1	$100	1
R	DOERR	1	1	1	$100	1
R	HERMAN	1	1	1	$100	1
R	HUBBARD	1	2	1	$100	1
R	MAZEROSKI	1	1	1	$100	1
L	EVERS	1	1	1	$100	1

Table 9-1.

Prices for Hitters and Position Players, Sorted by Highest to Lowest Real Dollars by Position (continued)

	NAME	COP $	1991 $	MSRP $	REAL $ (X1000)	CLAIM $
FIRST BASE						
L	CASH	41	65	53	$5,300	64
R	FOXX	38	60	49	$4,900	59
L	GEHRIG	37	58	47	$4,700	57
L	MCCOVEY	29	46	38	$3,800	45
R	ALLEN	24	31	27	$2,700	37
R	GREENBURG	18	29	24	$2,400	28
L	SISLER	25	6	16	$1,600	39
L	FOURNIER	12	14	13	$1,300	19
L	CAMILLI	11	2	6	$600	17
L	TERRY	10	1	6	$600	16
R	ALLISON	6	1	3	$300	9
R	CHANCE	5	1	3	$300	8
R	CEPEDA	6	1	3	$300	9
L	TENNEY	1	1	1	$100	1
L	HERNANDEZ	1	2	1	$100	1
S	MURRAY	1	1	1	$100	1
L	MIZE	1	2	1	$100	1
L	MATTINGLY	1	1	1	$100	1
L	KLUSZEWSKI	1	1	1	$100	1
R	YORK	1	1	1	$100	1
L	BOTTOMLEY	1	1	1	$100	1
CATCHER						
R	FISK	21	26	24	$2,400	33
R	TORRE	16	7	12	$1,200	25
R	CAMPENELLA	15	5	10	$1,000	23
R	CARTER	13	8	10	$1,000	20
R	BENCH	14	6	10	$1,000	22
R	FREEHAN	12	4	8	$800	19
L	COCHRANE	9	2	6	$600	14
L	BAILEY	8	1	4	$400	12
L	BERRA	7	1	4	$400	11
R	MCFARLAND	5	1	3	$300	8
R	MUNSON	5	1	3	$300	8
R	HARTNETT	5	1	3	$300	8
R	HOWARD,E	5	1	3	$300	8
L	MCCARVER	6	1	3	$300	9
S	SIMMONS,T	1	2	1	$100	1
L	PORTER	1	2	1	$100	1
R	ROMANO	1	1	1	$100	1
L	DICKEY	1	1	1	$100	1
L	BURGESS	1	1	1	$100	1
R	BRESNAHAN	1	1	1	$100	1
R	LOMBARDI	1	1	1	$100	1
R	FERRELL	1	1	1	$100	1

Table 9-2.

Prices for Pitchers, Sorted by Highest to Lowest Real Dollars for Starters and Relievers

NAME	ROT	COP $	1991 $	MSRP $	REAL $ (X1000)	CLAIM $
STARTERS						
WOOD	1	56	80	68	$6,800	87
JOHNSON	1	48	88	68	$6,800	74
MATHEWSON	1	53	81	67	$6,700	82
LEMON	1	50	62	56	$5,600	78
ALEXANDER	2	40	71	56	$5,600	59
HUBBELL	2	39	69	54	$5,400	57
WALSH	1	49	54	52	$5,200	76
WHITE	1	45	59	52	$5,200	68
WALTERS	1	46	56	51	$5,100	70
BENDER	1	44	56	50	$5,000	65
CUPPY	2	41	56	49	$4,900	60
NICHOLS	2	36	59	48	$4,800	51
RUSIE	2	37	51	44	$4,400	51
FERRELL	2	42	42	42	$4,200	64
GOMEZ	4	26	57	42	$4,200	36
SPAHN	2	38	43	41	$4,100	54
WILLIS	3	30	51	41	$4,100	39
GROVE	3	30	51	41	$4,100	39
LYONS	3	33	40	37	$3,700	47
GRIMES	2	33	39	36	$3,600	48
GRIFFITH	4	24	46	35	$3,500	8
LUQUE	4	25	41	33	$3,300	36
MAYS	2	38	21	30	$3,000	54
YOUNG	4	23	21	22	$2,200	8
PASCUAL	2	35	7	21	$2,100	50
JOSS	3	31	10	21	$2,100	40
GUIDRY	3	35	4	20	$2,000	48
BRECHEEN	3	29	7	18	$1,800	37
NEWHOUSER	3	28	8	18	$1,800	37
CHESBRO	3	32	1	17	$1,700	45
TAYLOR	3	31	1	16	$1,600	43
KOUFAX	4	22	10	16	$1,600	1
WADDELL	4	23	9	16	$1,600	1
FELLER	3	29	1	15	$1,500	37
PETERS	4	25	1	13	$1,300	34
NEWCOMBE	4	24	1	13	$1,300	8
HUTCHINSON	4	24	1	13	$1,300	8
BRIDGES	4	23	2	13	$1,300	8
TUDOR	4	23	1	12	$1,200	1
ALLEN	7	5	9	7	$700	1
BROWN	7	5	6	6	$600	1
LEE	7	5	1	3	$300	1
SHANTZ	7	5	1	3	$300	1
RUFFING	7	5	1	3	$300	1
PARNELL	7	5	1	3	$300	1
LOPAT	7	5	1	3	$300	1

Table 9-2.

Prices for Pitchers, Sorted by Highest to Lowest Real Dollars for Starters and Relievers (continued)

NAME	ROT	COP $	1991 $	MSRP $	REAL $ (X1000)	CLAIM $
PASSEAU	7	5	1	3	$300	1
CARLTON		0	2	1	$100	1
LEONARD,D		0	2	1	$100	1
DAVIS		0	1	1	$100	1
RYAN		0	1	1	$100	1
MCGINNITY		0	1	1	$100	1
RUCKER		0	1	1	$100	1
SHOCKER		0	1	1	$100	1
DRYSDALE		0	1	1	$100	1
HORLEN		0	1	1	$100	1
FORD,W		0	1	1	$100	1
MCDOWELL		0	1	1	$100	1
ANTONELLI		0	1	1	$100	1
SCOTT		0	1	1	$100	1
RICHARD		0	1	1	$100	1
REUSCHEL		0	1	1	$100	1
PERRY,G		0	1	1	$100	1
DEAN		0	1	1	$100	1
HARDER		0	1	1	$100	1
LEIBRANDT		0	1	1	$100	1
CICOTTE		0	1	1	$100	17
WYNN		0	2	1	$100	16
GARVER		0	1	1	$100	14
FABER		0	2	1	$100	16
VANCE		0	1	1	$100	16
STIEB		0	1	1	$100	14
TROUT		0	1	1	$100	14
SEAVER		0	1	1	$100	14
LEEVER		0	2	1	$100	11
REULBACH		0	1	1	$100	11
DOWNING		0	1	1	$100	11
COOPER,W		0	1	1	$100	11
PIERCE		0	1	1	$100	9
MALONEY		0	1	1	$100	1
COOMBS		0	1	1	$100	1
GIBSON		0	1	1	$100	1
BLACKWELL		0	1	1	$100	1
POLLET		0	1	1	$100	1
TANANA		0	1	1	$100	1
MCNALLY		0	1	1	$100	1
WARNEKE		0	1	1	$100	1
CANDELARIA		0	1	1	$100	1
JOHN		0	1	1	$100	1
BUNNING		0	1	1	$100	1

Table 9-2.

Prices for Pitchers, Sorted by Highest to Lowest Real Dollars for Starters and Relievers (continued)

NAME	ROT	COP $	1991 $	MSRP $	REAL $ (X1000)	CLAIM $
RELIEVERS						
SUTTER	5	10	27	19	$1,900	59
OROSCO	5	10	26	18	$1,800	56
ABERNATHY	5	9	23	16	$1,600	47
MCGRAW	5	9	21	15	$1,500	45
ECKERSLY	5	9	18	14	$1,400	36
HERNANDEZ	5	9	18	14	$1,400	36
BURGMEIER	5	10	16	13	$1,300	62
HILLER	6	7	12	10	$1,000	1
MONGE	6	7	12	10	$1,000	1
QUISENBERRY	6	7	9	8	$800	8
MOSSI	6	7	9	8	$800	1
LINZY	5	11	1	6	$600	71
MCDANIEL	6	7	1	4	$400	8
KINDER	6	7	1	4	$400	8
GOSSAGE	6	7	1	4	$400	1
PERRANOSKI	6	6	2	4	$400	1
KERN		0	2	1	$100	1
SCURRY		0	2	1	$100	1
RIGHETTI		0	2	1	$100	1
REGAN		0	2	1	$100	1
HRABOSKEY		0	2	1	$100	1
SMITH		0	2	1	$100	1
FINGERS		0	1	1	$100	1
MURPHY		0	1	1	$100	1
WILHELM		0	1	1	$100	11
TEKULVE		0	1	1	$100	11
LAVELLE		0	1	1	$100	11
GARBER		0	1	1	$100	1
MARSHALL		0	1	1	$100	1
GRANT		0	1	1	$100	1

HOF - 19
RED FABER
CHICAGO WHITE SOX – PITCHER
1922
HOF - 1982
TRAVIS JACKSON
NEW YORK GIANTS – SHORTSTOP
HOF - 1981
JOHNNY MIZE
ST. LOUIS CARDINALS – 1ST BASE
1936

CHAPTER 10

The Commissioner's Tools

"There are a lot of people who know me who can't understand for the life of them why I would go to work on something as unserious as baseball. If they only knew."

—Bart Giamatti, former Commissioner of Major League Baseball

During your brief stint as a general manager, you have learned that one of the most important components of your ball club is organization. You have learned to organize the available data on players in the League and to use that data to organize a philosophy for your team. You have also learned to organize your tools and strategies for Draft Day to put together a winning ball club.

Organization is also the key to a successful league. With the proper organizational tools available to the people running your league, you and your fellow league members will realize the full enjoyment of the Hall of Fame League.

As discussed in Chapter 2, "Playing the Game," you can enhance the EWBII game by purchasing separately the Commissioner II utilities program. This program allows you to manipulate statistics for players in the League, set up the alignment of teams in your league, move players from team to team, set up a schedule for your league, and print various statistical reports.

You can play the Hall of Fame League without purchasing the Commissioner II program, but in order to do so you must have a copy of the League on disk. Without the Commissioner II program, you can play games with teams as they are established on your disk copy of the League. However, you will not be able to manipulate the statistics or move players from team to team without the Commissioner II program.

To play in the Hall of Fame League and realize its maximum potential, you should purchase a copy of the Commissioner II program. With this program, you can use all the information in this book to create the League according to the whims and wishes of all the franchise owners in your league.

Chapter 2 discussed the installation of the Commissioner II program and briefly described the major utilities offered on the disk. This chapter and the next two chapters discuss in more detail how to use these utilities to set up your league. Most of the utilities are covered here. Chapter 11, "Building the Perfect Ballpark," discusses in detail the editing of ballparks and Chapter 12, "Molding the Perfect Manager," discusses the editing of managers.

You may notice that some of the utilities offered in the Commissioner II program are similar to utilities accessed through the Main Menu of EWBII. In particular, the Lineup and Roster features in EWBII are expanded with some of the editing utilities in the Commissioner II program.

As discussed in Chapter 2, you invoke the Commissioner II program from the Advanced Features menu of EWBII. To start the Commissioner II program from DOS, change directories to the EWB20 subdirectory that contains the Commissioner II program. Type **EWB2 C** at the DOS prompt to bypass the EWBII program and enter the Commissioner II program directly.

Main Menu

When you enter the Commissioner II program, the main menu consists of four major categories of utilities to be used in conjunction with the Earl Weaver Baseball II game, as shown in Figure 10-1. These categories are Editing, League Management, Statistics, and Accumulated Stats. Several utilities that are useful when setting up the Hall of Fame League are contained within each category.

Notice that a designation for the current league appears at the top of the screen. This designation is important not only

Figure 10-1.

The main menu of the Commissioner's Disk II program

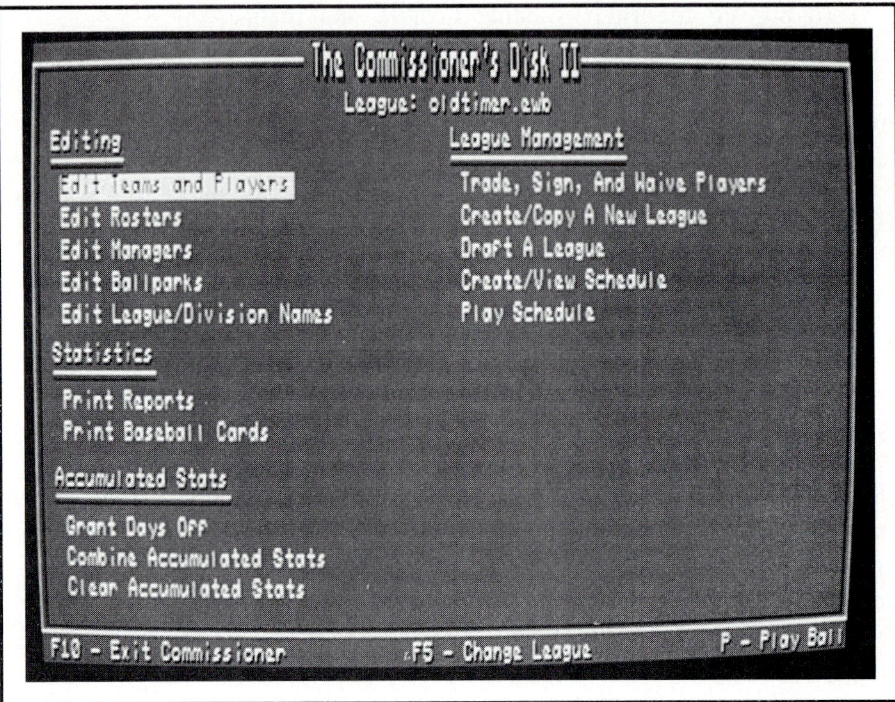

to be sure the changes you are making affect the correct league, but also because EWBII remembers the last league that was active during a Commissioner II session. If you last worked on a league located on a floppy disk, Commissioner II automatically searches the floppy disk for the current league when you enter the program. You should always activate a league on your hard disk before ending a Commissioner II session. Otherwise, if you do not have a floppy disk inserted in the drive, the program crashes.

If you worked on a league from a floppy disk during your last session with the Commissioner II program, be sure the disk is inserted in the drive before rebooting the program.

At the bottom of the screen are three options. The F10 key is used throughout the Commissioner II program to quit most utilities. The F5 key is used from the main menu and from most of the utility menus to change leagues. If you press F5, a menu appears asking you to tell the program where to find the new league. Enter the path and filename information, and the new league becomes the current league. Pressing P tells EWBII to begin playing a game.

To select a utility from the main menu, move the cursor highlight to the desired utility with the arrow keys and press ENTER.

Editing

The Editing utilities are your primary tools for customizing teams and players in the Hall of Fame League. With these utilities, you edit statistics and settings for teams, rosters, ballparks, managers, and the League in general. Because the utility for editing ballparks is discussed in detail in Chapter 11 and the utility for editing managers is discussed in detail in Chapter 12, those utilities are not covered here.

Edit Teams and Players

You can customize your team in EWBII by selecting this utility from the main menu. This option on the main menu may be somewhat misleading because you are actually editing teams in the League and the players on those teams. The Edit Rosters utility, which actually allows you to manipulate the roster of your team, is discussed in the next section.

Editing Team Stats

When you select the Edit Teams and Players option, a screen appears showing a team name and a list of players on that team. The cursor highlight begins on the team currently available for editing. If you want to select another team, press F6. A Select Teams screen appears showing all of the teams in the current league. To select a new team, move the cursor highlight to that team and press ENTER. You can bypass the Select Teams screen by pressing F3 to activate the next team in the list of teams in the league or pressing F4 to activate the previous team in the list of teams in the league. If you want to select a team from another league, you must press F5 to change leagues and then follow the procedures just discussed.

To edit statistics for the current team, press F1 (Edit Stats). The cursor highlight moves from the left side of the screen (where the team and players are listed) to the right side of the screen where the editing options are located. To edit one of the options, highlight that option and begin typing.

For the Team Name option, you can accept the name of the team currently recorded for the active league or type in a new name. New names can be up to ten characters long. To accept the current name or the new name, press ENTER to move to the next option. To change a team's historical won/lost record, you highlight the number in either the Won column or the Lost column. Each column is edited separately and can contain a number with up to three digits (255 is the maximum number). When you have typed in the correct number (or to accept the default number), press ENTER. The procedure for editing a team's accumulated won/lost record is the same.

Use the Edit Teams and Players utility to edit statistics for players in the League.

By moving to the Team Color option, you can customize the color of your team for game animation by selecting blue, dark blue, burnt orange, orange, brown, black, or green. You use this option to tell the EWBII program what color to use for the graphic display of your team's uniforms.

The next two options set the name of your home ballpark and which computer manager will be running your team (see Chapter 11 and Chapter 12 for more information about customizing these features).

The Designated Hitter Rule option is a toggle that turns the DH rule on and off for the current team. The last option on this screen sets the two-letter abbreviation used by EWBII to refer to your team. The abbreviation is used in the filename when box scores from a game are saved to disk.

The Salary and Number Of Reserves options cannot be edited.

To return to the team name and list of players on the left side of the screen, press F1 (Go To List). If you want to add a team, press F2. A Create Team In menu appears and asks you where to locate the new team you are creating. To delete a team, press F7. A Delete Team menu appears and offers you options for erasing team information and all player information for that team, erasing team information and making all players on that team free agents, and for cancelling the Delete Team request.

When you have finished editing a team's statistics, press F10 to return to the main menu.

Editing Player Stats

This utility is probably the most important aspect of the Commissioner II program. Through this utility you customize the statistics for not only the players on your team, but also all the players in the League. Statistics for the players are used by EWBII to make the players realistically perform in game situations.

To edit a player's statistics, use the arrow keys to move the cursor highlight to the player's name. The right portion of the screen displays the selected player's historical statistics and accumulated statistics, as shown in Figure 10-2. The Hall of Fame League uses normalized historical statistics for the player's best season (his Hall of Fame League season). Note that this data is normalized for the League. See Chapter 4, "The Statistics," for a detailed discussion of normalized statistics. The appendixes list the normalized historical statistics for each player in the Hall of Fame League. A player's *accumulated statistics* reflect how he has done in games played with EWBII.

To edit a player's statistics, press F1 (Edit Stats). The top portion of the editing screen contains biographical data about the player. Listed here are the player's last name, his first name, how he bats or pitches (right, left, or switch), his primary defensive position (Pos1), his secondary defensive position (Pos2), his skin color (Skin) for proper graphic representation of the player during game animations, his playing status, the year of the player's representative season, an identification number (Id #), and the player's salary. The Skin field also includes a coding for whether the pitcher is involved in a league that uses the designated hitter rule.

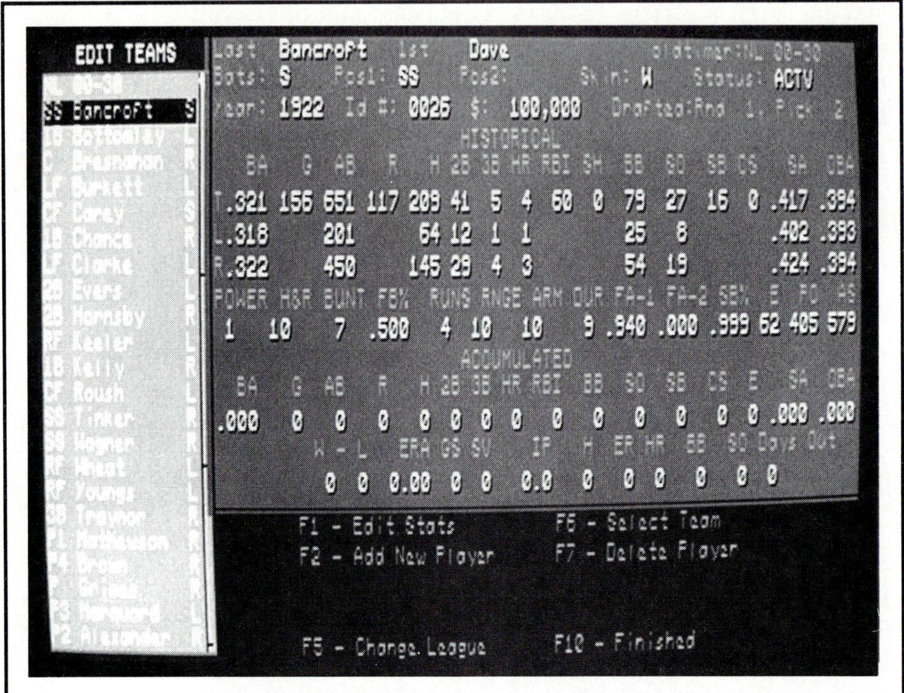

Figure 10-2.

Data input for editing players' statistics

The Status option shows whether the selected player is active (ACTV), a reserve player (RESV), on the disabled list (DL), in the low minor leagues (FARM), in the high minor leagues (AAA), in the medium-level minor leagues (AA), or a free agent (FREE). This option may not be modified. The status of a player is determined by his position on the team roster and whether he is injured. The status of players is discussed in more detail in the Edit Rosters section of this chapter.

Id # shows a number that is used by EWBII to locate an individual player. Although you may change a player's ID number, this practice is strongly discouraged. This ID number is used in the utilities for copying teams and players. If you change this number, the Commissioner II program cannot find the player.

The historical statistics for the hitters and position players include batting average (BA), games (G), at-bats (AB), runs (R), hits (H), doubles (2B), triples (3B), home runs (HR), runs batted in (RBI), sacrifice hits (SH), bases on balls (BB), strikeouts (SO), stolen bases (SB), caught stealing (CS), slugging average (SA), and on-base average (OBA). The batting average (BA) category is not accessible because it is calculated automatically by EWBII. The tables in Appendix B use the abbreviations OB% and SL% to denote on-base average and slugging average.

EWBII ratings for players in the Hall of Fame League are calculated mathematically and not generated by using the Auto Rate feature of the Edit Teams and Players utility.

The historical statistics for pitchers include won-lost record (W - L), earned run average (ERA), games appeared in (G), games started (GS), complete games (CG), saves (SV), innings pitched (IP), opponents' batting average (BA), opponents' at-bats (AB), opponents' hits (H), earned runs given up (ER), home runs given up (HR), walks (BB), strikeouts (SO), and number of batters hit by a pitch (HB). A special section of the pitcher's statistics shows how he does at the plate. These statistics include his batting average (BA), at-bats (AB), hits (H), home runs (HR), and sacrifice hits (SH). Again, the batting average statistic is not accessible because it is calculated automatically by EWBII.

Notice that for each of the statistical categories, numbers appear for the player overall, versus right, and versus left. As discussed in Chapter 4, the numbers versus right and versus left are especially significant for platoon players.

The ratings used by EWBII to denote skill level appear beneath the historical statistics for hitters and position players. These ratings for nonpitchers include power (POWER), hit and run (H&R), bunt (BUNT), fly ball percentage (the percentage of times the hitter places the ball in the air, denoted by FB%), running (RUNS), range at his defensive position (RNGE), the strength of his arm (ARM), the durability of the player (DUR), fielding average for his primary position (FA-1) and his secondary position (FA-2), stolen base percentage (SB%), errors (E), putouts (PO), and assists (AS).

For the pitchers, the EWBII ratings include speed (SPEED), control (CONTROL), fatigue (FATIGUE), fly-ball percentage (FB%), bunting (BUNT), holding runners on base (HOLD), durability (DUR), fielding average (FA), and balks (BK). Pitchers' batting stats include batting average (BA), at-bats (AB), hits (H), home runs, (HR), and sacrifice hits (SH).

The EWBII program can automatically set ratings for a player based on his available statistics. To automatically rate the player, press F9 (Auto Rate Player). However, for the Hall of Fame League, all ratings have been mathematically calculated and may not agree with the EWBII automatic ratings. The ratings appearing in the appendixes should be used for players in the Hall of Fame League, and the Auto Rate feature should not be used.

The accumulated statistics show how a player has performed in games played with EWBII.

To return to the list of players, press F1 (Go To List). To change players, move the cursor highlight to the player's name and the statistics screen changes to reflect the current player. To add a player to a team, press F2. A message appears in the upper-left corner of the screen telling you the player is being added to the reserves of the current team. You then have a fresh statistics screen in which to enter the player's data. To view statistics for the previous player, press F3. To view statistics for the next player, press F4. To clear all the statistics for a player, press F7. To restore the statistics, press F8. When you have finished editing player statistics, press F10 to return to the main menu.

Edit Rosters

This utility is similar to the Roster Screen feature of the EWBII game discussed in Chapter 2. The options for this utility allow you to set the starting lineup for a selected team and to designate which players are on the active roster (the ACTV status). As with the other utilities on the main menu, you activate this utility by moving the cursor highlight to Edit Rosters and pressing ENTER.

The Roster screen shows ROSTER in the upper-left corner of the screen, the name of the team in the upper-right corner, the team's batting order, players on the bench, and pitchers. Toward the bottom of the screen on the left side is the Display Stats Type box. This box displays four options for which statistics you want displayed on this screen (total historical, total accumulated, versus left historical, and versus right historical).

To view the previous team in the league, press F3. To view the next team in the league, press F4. To change to another league, press F5.

When adjusting a batting order, always be sure that you have a player in every defensive position.

For the hitters and position players, this screen shows the defensive position of the player, the player's name, how he bats (right, left, or switch), his batting average, his home run total, his on-base average, and his EWBII ratings for power and for speed. For pitchers, the screen displays the spot in the pitching rotation, how the pitcher throws (right or left), his earned run average, his total number of strikeouts, walks given up (BB), homers given up, and his EWBII fatigue rating.

To view all of the statistics for a player, highlight his name and press SPACEBAR. A screen appears displaying the statistical information described previously in the "Editing Player Stats" section. To deactivate this screen, press SPACEBAR again.

To change the batting order for the selected team, move the cursor highlight to the name of the player you want to reposition and press ENTER. Move the cursor highlight to the name of another player you want to reposition and press ENTER. The two players are then switched in the batting order.

To move a player from the bench into the starting lineup, move the cursor highlight to his name and press ENTER. Move the cursor highlight to the batting order section of the screen and position it on the name of the player to be replaced. Press ENTER, and the bench player is inserted into the lineup to replace the starter. When you are moving players from the bench into the starting lineup, always be sure that you have a player in every defensive position.

Although you can change the defensive position of a player in your lineup, this change does not affect his defensive designation for a primary position and secondary position. In other words, you can insert an outfielder to play first base for a game, but his primary position will remain outfield. Changing a player's defensive position only affects where he will play in the game. To change a starter's defensive position, highlight his name and press LEFT ARROW to move the cursor to his defensive position. Press ENTER, and a box appears showing all defensive positions. Move the cursor to the desired defensive position and press ENTER.

A player can be in a game out of position, but his primary and secondary positions are not changed in his statistical record.

As explained in Chapter 2, you designate a pitcher's spot in the rotation by highlighting his name and pressing a key combination from ALT-1 through ALT-6. See Chapter 2 for more details on setting your starting rotation.

To view all the players on a team's roster, including all of the reserve players (RESV status), press R. To move a player from the active roster to the reserve roster, move the cursor highlight to his name and press ENTER. Move the cursor highlight to the name of the reserve player you want to activate in his place, and press ENTER again or press ESC to cancel.

You may come up with a lineup that works best against left-handed pitching and one that works best against right-handed pitching. By setting your lineup accordingly, you can save that lineup by pressing G. The option also allows you to load a particular lineup and to change that lineup.

When you have finished editing your team roster, press F10 to return to the main menu.

Edit League/Division Names

When you select this utility from the main menu, the Edit League/Division Names screen appears. The screen shows the current league (designated by L1 and L2) and the divisions within that league (designated by D1 and D2). Listed under each division are the names of each team in the division.

To change a name, move the cursor highlight to that name and press ENTER. You then type in the new name, which may be up to nine characters in length. When you want to save the new name, press F9. To clear a name, highlight the name and press ALT-C. To clear all the names on the list, press ALT-A.

To choose a manager for the highlighted team, press F1. Use this option when you are assigning managers to new teams or to teams that were created with versions of the game previous to EWBII.

When you have finished editing league or division names, press F10 to return to the main menu.

League Management

In addition to the Editing utilities, the League Management utilities are very important to the operation of the Hall of Fame League. Included in this group of utilities are functions for manipulating player movement between teams, establishing new leagues, drafting players for a league, and setting up a schedule for your league.

Trade, Sign, And Waive Players

By selecting this utility from the main menu, you can trade players between teams, waive players (cut them from your squad and allow another team to sign them as free agents), assign players to reserve status, copy players (referred to as *cloning*), or sign free agents. The opening screen, shown in Figure 10-3, has two boxes on the left that display the two teams involved in the player movement. The right of the screen displays the functions that determine the player movement between the two teams.

The roster boxes on the left show the player's defensive position, his name, and how he bats (right or left). To scroll through the list of teams in the current league, press F3 to select the previous team in the list and F4 to select the next team in the list. If you want to change leagues, press F5. You may also press F6 to invoke the Select Teams screen for choosing a specific team. If you are looking for a specific player, press ALT-F.

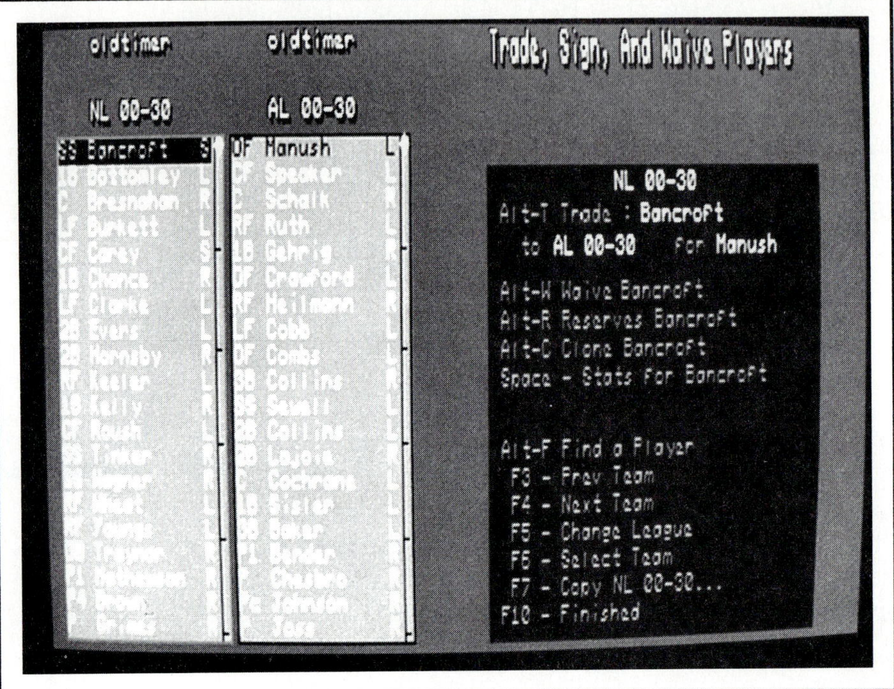

Figure 10-3.

Opening screen for the Trade, Sign, And Waive Players utility

The roster box on the left represents the team that is working the deal (that is, the team that is offering a trade, waiving a selected player, signing reserves, or cloning a selected player). The roster box on the right is the team with whom the deal is being made.

To trade a player, highlight his name. Press RIGHT ARROW to move to the roster box on the right and highlight the name of the other player involved in the trade. If you want to view the statistics for selected players, press SPACEBAR.

On the right side of the screen is a dialog box that summarizes the proposed deal. For example, if you selected Bancroft from NL00-30 in the left roster box and Manush from AL00-30 in the right roster box, the summary reads "Bancroft to AL00-30 for Manush." To consummate the trade, press ALT-T.

To waive a player and make him eligible to be signed by another team, highlight his name in the roster box and press ALT-W. To assign a player to reserve status, highlight his name and press ALT-R. You can still trade or waive a player after he has been assigned reserve status.

You can only have 25 players with an active status on your roster. All other players must have a reserve status.

Activating a player from a reserve status may require other roster moves. Remember that you have a 25-player limit for your active roster. If you want to activate a player from the reserve roster, you must make room for him by either waiving a player or designating someone on the active roster for reserve status. To activate a player, highlight his name and press ALT-A.

To clone (or copy) a player, highlight his name and press ALT-C. Use this option to assign a player to several teams. The cloned player is assigned to the reserve roster until you move him with one of the other options.

You can copy entire teams by pressing F7. This function places a copy of the current team into another league or division without affecting the original team. After you press F7, a Copy *YourTeamName* menu appears. Highlight the league and division to which you want to copy the team and press ENTER. At the top of the menu you see the name of the team to be copied and the destination for the copy. Use the F5 function to change leagues if necessary. You can only copy teams to leagues and divisions that have vacant team slots.

Free agents are players who have been waived (or cut) from a team roster. You can view the free agents released by a team through the roster boxes. To sign a free agent, highlight his name in the free agent section of the roster box. In the other roster box, activate the team to sign the free agent. Press ALT-S and the free agent is assigned to the reserve roster of the new team, unless room is available on the active roster.

When you have finished trading, waiving, and signing players, press F10 to return to the main menu.

Create/Copy A New League

This utility enables you to create a new league or to copy an existing league. These functions can be most useful when you are first establishing a new league for EWBII.

The opening screen for this utility displays the current league at the top and offers you two choices: F7 (Create New League Now) and F8 (Duplicate Current League). As is the case with most utilities in the Commissioner II program, the F5 key allows you to change leagues.

If you press F7 to create a new league, the program asks for a path in which to create new files. After you select a path, the computer begins creating the necessary files for the league. In order to view this league, you must have files with an .EWB, .FRM, and .MGR extension in the same path or subdirectory of the new league. If one of these files is missing, you can't view the new league.

To duplicate the current league, press F8. You will be asked for the path of the duplicate league. Enter the correct path and the program duplicates the current league.

When you have finished creating a new league or copying an existing league, press F10 to return to the main menu.

Draft A League

The drafting utility for the Commissioner II program is not used in the Hall of Fame League. The brief description that follows explains how this utility works so that you can use it for another league.

Before you begin a draft, be sure the current league contains the players to be drafted. When you select the Draft A League utility from the main menu, the Draft Setup screen in Figure 10-4 is shown, which is divided into four segments.

The upper-left part of the screen contains the options for conducting the draft. Here you select whether you want the draft order to remain the same for each round, reverse each round, or continue in random order.

The teams from which players will be selected are displayed in the bottom-left part of your screen in the Players In Pool box. To delete teams from the list, press F6 (Select Players In Pool). The Select Teams screen appears, and you highlight

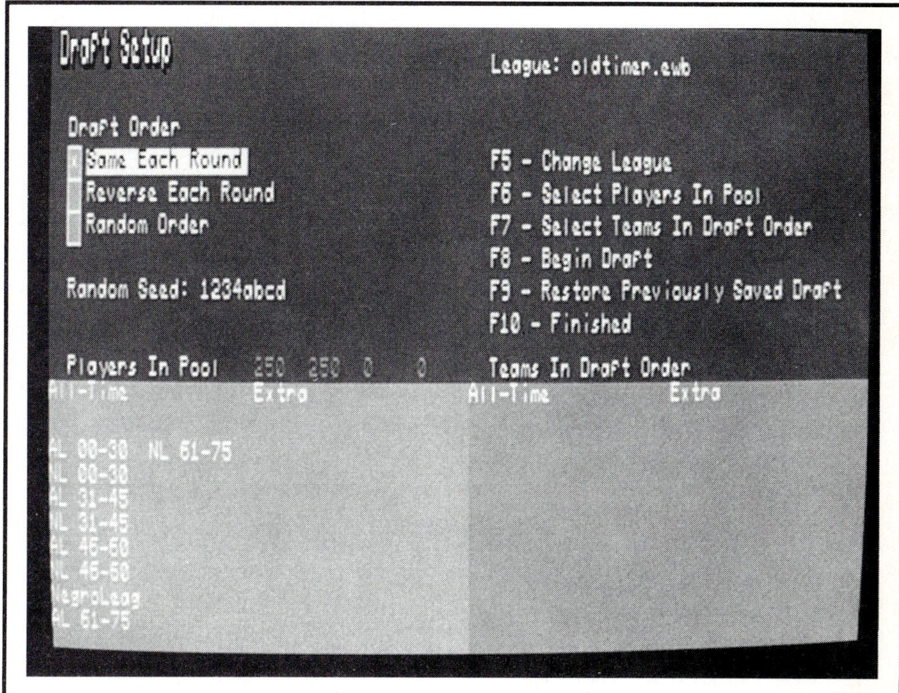

Figure 10-4.

The Draft Setup screen

those teams you want to remain in the player pool. Any teams you do not select in this manner are removed from the draft. When you have finished selecting teams, press F10 to return to the Draft Setup screen or press ESC to cancel. Those teams that you have selected are now displayed in the Players In Pool box.

The lower-right portion of the screen contains the Teams In Draft Order box. The teams that will draft players are displayed in this box. To select the order in which teams will draft players, press F7 (Select Teams In Draft Order). The Select Teams screen appears. Highlight the teams in the order they will draft and press F1. As you highlight each team and press F1, a number appears next to each team name to indicate the draft order. When the order has been established, press F10 to return to the Draft Setup screen or press ESC to cancel.

The Players In Pool box on the bottom-left part of your screen now displays the teams supplying players in the draft. Teams In Draft Order now displays teams participating in the draft, with a number indicating their sequence in the draft order. To begin the draft, press F8 (Begin Draft). A dialog box appears in the upper-left of the screen indicating how many empty slots are available for players. Click on the READY box or press ESC to cancel.

Drafting teams for the Hall of Fame League is not done using the Draft A League utility.

You now see the Draft screen. At the top of the screen is a status report indicating the round, the pick in the round, which team had the last pick, and which team has the next pick. The box in the center of the screen is the drafting box. At the top of this box is the name of the team that is currently picking a player, the name of the player up for selection, his ID number, his position, his status, and his salary. At the bottom of this box is an option for showing a player's statistics. If this option has been selected, the player's stats are displayed on the left side of the box.

To scroll to the previous player in the list, press F3. To scroll to the next player, press F4. To draft the player, press F1. If you decide to cut a player that you have drafted, scroll to his name and press F5. A player can only be cut from a team that has drafted him. To sign a player as a free agent, press F6. Signing a free agent simulates teams trading draft picks.

The right side of the Draft screen contains several options. At the bottom of those options are your choices for having reports displayed on the screen, sent to the printer, or saved to a disk file. At the top of the options are several choices for printing reports. You may choose to print a draft report on all the players in the selected league or just the available players in the league. You can also print a team roster by choosing a team through the Select Teams screen. You can choose to print a report on the number of players in the draft who have been selected (the Roster Size option) or the order in which teams choose players in each round (the Draft Order option). Figure 10-5 shows a sample report.

Figure 10-5.

A sample draft report

SHAFER Team Roster

R/ P	Name		Pos	BA	G	AB	R	H	HR	SB
1/ 1	Willie	Mays	LF	.307	157	585	118	180	50	24
3/ 1	Bobby	Murcer	RF	.323	123	633	83	205	40	11
4/ 1	Johnny	Bench	C	.296	158	581	97	172	46	6
5/ 1	Ken	Boyer	IF	.294	130	469	81	138	26	8
6/ 1	Rogers	Hornsby	2B	.385	138	586	133	226	9	12
7/ 1	Ty	Cobb	RF	.404	146	531	147	215	7	83
11/ 1	Eric	Davis	OF	.286	108	461	88	132	30	50
12/ 1	Dave	Parker	OF	.329	161	598	109	197	19	17
13/ 1	Gabby	Hartnett	C	.289	141	421	84	122	15	3
14/ 1	Darryl	Strawberry	RF	.287	150	594	102	171	46	29
15/ 1	Bobby	Grich	IF	.289	143	626	80	181	17	14
16/ 1	George	Davis	SS	.338	108	402	68	136	1	34
18/FA	Miller	Huggins	2B	.288	149	461	117	133	1	27
19/FA	Doug	Decinces	3B	.295	116	555	70	164	29	7
19/FA	Rudy	York	1B	.277	155	518	90	144	32	5
19/ 1	Reggie	Jackson	LF	.302	161	569	112	172	51	13

R/ P	Name		Pos	ERA	W-	L	SV	IP	BA	BB	SO
2/ 1	Dave	Righetti	P	1.99	8	8	46	131.0	.176	31	102
8/ 1	Wes	Ferrell	P	3.05	25	14	0	238.1	.212	61	81
9/ 1	Hoyt	Wilhelm	P	1.27	8	3	12	92.0	.163	30	79
10/ 1	Nig	Cuppy	P	2.60	25	14	0	245.1	.216	38	59

Remaining Picks

Pick 1 in each Round

The Print By Position option determines what players are included in the print options just described. When you select this option, a box appears offering you the choices of including all players in your report, all fielders, all catchers, all first basemen, all second basemen, all third basemen, all shortstops, all infielders, all left fielders, all right fielders, all center fielders, all outfielders, all pitchers, all starting pitchers, all relief pitchers, or all designated hitters.

The last options on the right side of the screen allow you to skip a team's turn in the draft and go to the next team in the draft order by pressing ALT-S. If you press ALT-U, you can undo the pick of the previous team in the draft.

When you have finished with your draft, press F8 (Save Current Draft) or F9 (Make A League). To exit the Draft screen and return to the main menu, press F10.

Create/View Schedule

This utility establishes a schedule for your league based on the criteria you set. First you establish the total number of games each team will play during the season. You then set the maximum number of games two teams will play in each series.

The lower-left portion of the opening Create Schedule screen displays the teams for which you are scheduling a season. To change the teams in this box, press F6 and the Select Teams screen appears. Highlight the teams you want to include in your season and press ENTER. A division must have more than one team to be included in the schedule. To schedule inter-divisional play, each division must contain an equal number of teams. Press F10 to return to the Create Schedule screen. To save a schedule, press F9. To load a previously saved schedule, press F4.

To view a schedule, you first select a destination (the screen, printer, or disk file). You have two groups of options for printing (or viewing) a schedule. For All Teams or for One Team, you can view a schedule of the games only, of the games and scores, and of the record against opponents. Figure 10-6 shows a sample schedule.

Play Schedule

You must create a schedule in order to play a season through the Commissioner II program.

To use this utility, you must create and save a schedule with the Create/View Schedule utility. The Play Schedule screen displays in the lower-left corner the teams that have been scheduled to play. In the upper-left corner of the screen are the game days and teams for the first day of the season and the last day of the season. This information is provided so that you can be sure your schedule has been properly set.

To automatically accumulate statistics or to save box scores from games played, select either of the options below the schedule status information. To designate a team to be a user team, press F6. The User Teams screen appears, and you highlight those teams that you want to be run by a user. This option allows you to play or manage a user team throughout a schedule.

In the upper-right portion of the Play Schedule screen are two groups of options. The Computer Games options allow

Figure 10-6.

A sample schedule

SCHEDULE: 1

Day	NELSON	DIVEL-R	LYNCH	GOLDST	HUFF	SHAFER	DIVEL-M	SHIER
1	LYNCH	GOLDST	@NELSON	@DIVEL-R	DIVEL-M	SHIER	@HUFF	@SHAFER
2	LYNCH	GOLDST	@NELSON	@DIVEL-R	DIVEL-M	SHIER	@HUFF	@SHAFER
3	LYNCH	GOLDST	@NELSON	@DIVEL-R	DIVEL-M	SHIER	@HUFF	@SHAFER
4	LYNCH	GOLDST	@NELSON	@DIVEL-R	DIVEL-M	SHIER	@HUFF	@SHAFER
5	GOLDST	@DIVEL-M	SHAFER	@NELSON	SHIER	@LYNCH	DIVEL-R	@HUFF
6	GOLDST	@DIVEL-M	SHAFER	@NELSON	SHIER	@LYNCH	DIVEL-R	@HUFF
7	GOLDST	@DIVEL-M	SHAFER	@NELSON	SHIER	@LYNCH	DIVEL-R	@HUFF
8	GOLDST	@DIVEL-M	SHAFER	@NELSON	SHIER	@LYNCH	DIVEL-R	@HUFF
9	HUFF	SHAFER	@DIVEL-M	@SHIER	@NELSON	@DIVEL-R	LYNCH	GOLDST
10	HUFF	SHAFER	@DIVEL-M	@SHIER	@NELSON	@DIVEL-R	LYNCH	GOLDST
11	HUFF	SHAFER	@DIVEL-M	@SHIER	@NELSON	@DIVEL-R	LYNCH	GOLDST
12	HUFF	SHAFER	@DIVEL-M	@SHIER	@NELSON	@DIVEL-R	LYNCH	GOLDST
13	@SHAFER	HUFF	@SHIER	DIVEL-M	@DIVEL-R	NELSON	@GOLDST	LYNCH
14	@SHAFER	HUFF	@SHIER	DIVEL-M	@DIVEL-R	NELSON	@GOLDST	LYNCH
15	@SHAFER	HUFF	@SHIER	DIVEL-M	@DIVEL-R	NELSON	@GOLDST	LYNCH
16	@SHAFER	HUFF	@SHIER	DIVEL-M	@DIVEL-R	NELSON	@GOLDST	LYNCH
17	DIVEL-M	SHIER	@HUFF	@SHAFER	LYNCH	GOLDST	@NELSON	@DIVEL-R
18	DIVEL-M	SHIER	@HUFF	@SHAFER	LYNCH	GOLDST	@NELSON	@DIVEL-R
19	DIVEL-M	SHIER	@HUFF	@SHAFER	LYNCH	GOLDST	@NELSON	@DIVEL-R
20	DIVEL-M	SHIER	@HUFF	@SHAFER	LYNCH	GOLDST	@NELSON	@DIVEL-R
21	@GOLDST	DIVEL-M	@SHAFER	NELSON	@SHIER	LYNCH	@DIVEL-R	HUFF
22	@GOLDST	DIVEL-M	@SHAFER	NELSON	@SHIER	LYNCH	@DIVEL-R	HUFF
23	@GOLDST	DIVEL-M	@SHAFER	NELSON	@SHIER	LYNCH	@DIVEL-R	HUFF
24	@GOLDST	DIVEL-M	@SHAFER	NELSON	@SHIER	LYNCH	@DIVEL-R	HUFF
25	SHIER	@LYNCH	DIVEL-R	@HUFF	GOLDST	@DIVEL-M	SHAFER	@NELSON
26	SHIER	@LYNCH	DIVEL-R	@HUFF	GOLDST	@DIVEL-M	SHAFER	@NELSON
27	SHIER	@LYNCH	DIVEL-R	@HUFF	GOLDST	@DIVEL-M	SHAFER	@NELSON
28	SHIER	@LYNCH	DIVEL-R	@HUFF	GOLDST	@DIVEL-M	SHAFER	@NELSON
29	@LYNCH	@GOLDST	NELSON	DIVEL-R	@DIVEL-M	@SHIER	HUFF	SHAFER
30	@LYNCH	@GOLDST	NELSON	DIVEL-R	@DIVEL-M	@SHIER	HUFF	SHAFER
31	@LYNCH	@GOLDST	NELSON	DIVEL-R	@DIVEL-M	@SHIER	HUFF	SHAFER
32	@LYNCH	@GOLDST	NELSON	DIVEL-R	@DIVEL-M	@SHIER	HUFF	SHAFER
33	@DIVEL-R	NELSON	@GOLDST	LYNCH	@SHAFER	HUFF	@SHIER	DIVEL-M
34	@DIVEL-R	NELSON	@GOLDST	LYNCH	@SHAFER	HUFF	@SHIER	DIVEL-M
35	@DIVEL-R	NELSON	@GOLDST	LYNCH	@SHAFER	HUFF	@SHIER	DIVEL-M
36	@DIVEL-R	NELSON	@GOLDST	LYNCH	@SHAFER	HUFF	@SHIER	DIVEL-M
37	@DIVEL-M	@SHIER	HUFF	SHAFER	@LYNCH	@GOLDST	NELSON	DIVEL-R
38	@DIVEL-M	@SHIER	HUFF	SHAFER	@LYNCH	@GOLDST	NELSON	DIVEL-R
39	@DIVEL-M	@SHIER	HUFF	SHAFER	@LYNCH	@GOLDST	NELSON	DIVEL-R
40	@DIVEL-M	@SHIER	HUFF	SHAFER	@LYNCH	@GOLDST	NELSON	DIVEL-R
41	@HUFF	@SHAFER	DIVEL-M	SHIER	NELSON	DIVEL-R	@LYNCH	@GOLDST
42	@HUFF	@SHAFER	DIVEL-M	SHIER	NELSON	DIVEL-R	@LYNCH	@GOLDST
43	@HUFF	@SHAFER	DIVEL-M	SHIER	NELSON	DIVEL-R	@LYNCH	@GOLDST
44	@HUFF	@SHAFER	DIVEL-M	SHIER	NELSON	DIVEL-R	@LYNCH	@GOLDST
45	@SHIER	LYNCH	@DIVEL-R	HUFF	@GOLDST	DIVEL-M	@SHAFER	NELSON
46	@SHIER	LYNCH	@DIVEL-R	HUFF	@GOLDST	DIVEL-M	@SHAFER	NELSON
47	@SHIER	LYNCH	@DIVEL-R	HUFF	@GOLDST	DIVEL-M	@SHAFER	NELSON
48	@SHIER	LYNCH	@DIVEL-R	HUFF	@GOLDST	DIVEL-M	@SHAFER	NELSON
49	DIVEL-R	@NELSON	GOLDST	@LYNCH	SHAFER	@HUFF	SHIER	@DIVEL-M
50	DIVEL-R	@NELSON	GOLDST	@LYNCH	SHAFER	@HUFF	SHIER	@DIVEL-M

you to set the mode in which you want your games to be played (see Chapter 2 for a complete description of game modes). The User Games options allow you to set the mode for games requiring user interface (Chapter 2 contains a complete description of the user modes).

To establish game settings for the schedule, press F1. The Schedule Settings screen appears and offers you several options. The Designated Hitter Settings are used to establish when the designated hitter is to be used in games. The Eligibility Settings are used to establish if starting pitchers can be used as relievers, if injuries can occur to players, if injured players are eligible to play in games, and whether resting pitchers can pitch on their days off. The Starters Settings establish how many starters are included in a team's pitching rotation (0 to 9) and the maximum number of rest days starters can have (0 to 9). If you want a starting pitcher's number of rest days to be based on the number of innings he pitched, highlight the Innings Pitched option and press ENTER. If you want a starter's number of rest days to be based on the type of pitcher he is, highlight the Type of Pitcher option and press ENTER. When you have finished establishing your schedule settings, press F1 to return to the Play Schedule screen.

To begin playing a schedule, press P. To exit the Play Schedule screen and return to the main menu, press F10.

Statistics

The Statistics utilities are used to print a variety of reports and "baseball cards" of your favorite players. You can customize the reports to include a variety of statistics. Although the utilities are titled Print Reports and Print Baseball Cards, you can view the reports and the cards on the screen or you can save them to a disk file. *If you use this utility for printing, be sure your printer is connected to your computer and turned on.* If you attempt to print from the Commissioner II program and your printer is not ready, you receive an error message at the top of your screen, and the program crashes.

Print Reports

This utility generates reports based on selected criteria for individual categories. When you select this utility from the main menu, the Print Reports screen appears. Notice that the screen is divided into four major sections.

The lower-left portion of the screen, Teams In Sort, displays the teams used to generate your report. To select specific teams, press F6. The Select Teams screen appears and you see all teams in the current league listed with boxes to the left of their names. Move the cursor highlight to the desired team or teams and press ENTER. The box to the left of the name shows an X for the selected teams. When you have finished making your selections, press F10. The Print Reports screen now displays the selected teams in the lower-left portion of the screen.

If you want to generate a report on a team in another league, press F5 to change leagues.

By generating statistical reports on players in the Hall of Fame League, you can see who the league leaders are in a variety of categories.

The upper-left portion of the Print Reports screen contains options and criteria for creating your report. The first option sets which players to include in the report. Your choices here are active players, reserves, free agents, or a combination of all three. The next option determines where to send the report. You can display the report on your screen, send the report to your printer, or send the report to a disk file. You can only choose one of these display options.

Several options set the criteria for your report. The first criterion establishes how you want the statistics sorted. You may choose to sort by all players on the selected teams, by a specific position (catcher, first base, second base, third base, shortstop, left fielder, right fielder, center fielder), by general position (infielders or outfielders), by all pitchers, by starting pitchers, by relievers, or by designated hitters.

Next you establish how you want to sort the data. Your choices here are from highest to lowest or from lowest to highest. Your next criterion is whether you want to sort the data based on individual statistics or by team statistics.

The STATS=0 option is a toggle (press ENTER) between Included and Not Included. This option indicates whether to include a statistic that equals a zero value. You then establish by which defensive position the program should consider players. Your two options here are sorting based on a player's primary position and sorting based on a player's secondary position. The Extra Cols option determines what other statistics are displayed with the chosen statistic. Your choices here are to include no other statistics other than the one you have chosen for your report (None), all available statistics (Total Stats), a combination of your chosen statistic and other available statistics (Splits/Comp), or your chosen statistic with EWBII ratings (Ratings).

The List Length option determines how long you want your report to be. You can choose to have only one player in your report or as many as 999. The Min At Bats option allows you to narrow down the number of players eligible to be in your report by establishing the minimum number of at-bats a player must have to be included in the report. Similarly, the Min Innings option establishes the minimum number of innings necessary for a pitcher to be included. Either number can be as high as 999.

The right-hand portion of the screen contains the Select Stat to Display box. This is the area where you select a specific category about which you want your report generated. You have 13 major categories to choose from, with multiple statistics in each category. Those categories and the statistics included in each are as follows.

Team Stats Historical team standings, accumulated team standings, historical team totals, accumulated team totals, historical rosters, accumulated rosters, ratings rosters.

Batters' Hist. Total Batting average, at-bats, runs, hits, doubles, triples, home runs, RBI, walks, strikeouts, stolen bases, caught stealing, sacrifice hits, plate appearances, on base average, slugging average, fly/groundball ratio, fielding average, fielding average 2, errors, putouts, assists, caught stealing %.

Batters' Hist. vs. Left Batting average, at-bats, hits, doubles, triples, home runs, walks, strikeouts, plate appearances, on base average, slugging average.

Batters' Hist. vs. Right Batting average, at-bats, hits, doubles, triples, home runs, walks, strikeouts, plate appearances, on base average, slugging average.

Pitchers' Hist. Total ERA, wins, losses, saves, games started, complete games, innings pitched, batting average, at-bats, hits, earned runs, home runs, walks, strikeouts, fly/groundball ratio, balks, hit batsman, fielding average.

Pitchers' Hist. vs. Left Batting average, at-bats, hits, home runs, walks, strikeouts.

Statistical reports including historical or accumulated data can be generated for teams, batters, and pitchers.

Pitchers' Hist. vs. Right Batting average, at-bats, hits, home runs, walks, strikeouts.

Pitchers as Batters Batting average, at-bats, hits, home runs, sacrifice hits.

Batters' Accum. Batting average, at-bats, runs, hits, doubles, triples, home runs, RBI, walks, strikeouts, stolen bases, caught stealing, errors, plate appearances, on base average, slugging average.

Pitchers' Accum. ERA, wins, losses, saves, games started, innings pitched, hits, earned runs, home runs, walks, strikeouts.

Batters' Ratings Power, speed, range, arm, bunting, hit and run, durability.

Pitchers' Ratings Fatigue, velocity, control, bunting, holding baserunners, durability.

Miscellaneous Games, accumulated games, days out, player ID, salary.

Figure 10-7 shows a sample report on home run leaders for a league.

When you have finished creating your reports, press F10 to return to the main menu.

Print Baseball Cards

Don't get too excited about this utility. Obviously, photos of players are not available in EWBII and, consequently, when you select this option you are really only printing encapsulated statistics on the players, similar to what you find on the back of baseball cards. To get the fancy photographs and graphics that appear on the front of baseball cards, you'll have to buy the real thing.

Figure 10-7.

A sample league report sorted by top home run hitters

```
Sort By: Home Runs/All Players/Primary /AB > 300
Rank Name           Team
  1. Mitchell, K.    HUFF          52
  2. Jackson, R.     DIVEL-M       51
  3. Mays, W.        SHAFER        50
  4. Greenberg, H.   GOLDST        50
  5. Foster, G.      GOLDST        50
  6. Ruth, B.        SHIER         49
  7. Kiner, R.       DIVEL-M       48
  8. Foxx, J.        SHIER         47
  9. Killebrew, H.   LYNCH         47
 10. Stargell, W.    NELSON        47
 11. Strawberry, D.  DIVEL-M       46
 12. Bench, J.       SHAFER        46
 13. Gentile, J.     HUFF          45
 14. Banks, E.       DIVEL-R       45
 15. McCovey, W.     DIVEL-R       44
 16. Canseco, J.     LYNCH         43
 17. Colavito, R.    DIVEL-R       43
 18. Rosen, A.       NELSON        43
 19. Gehrig, L.      NELSON        42
 20. Mathews, E.     NELSON        41
```

When you choose Print Baseball Cards from the main menu, the screen display shows a team and its players in a box on the left side of the screen. The box is flashing to indicate that this is the current team. To move from the flashing box and change settings for printing the baseball cards, press F1 (Edit Settings).

The first option for this utility is to select which team or teams you want the cards printed for. Your choices are the current team, all teams, or selected teams. Use the F3 key to scroll to the previous team in the list of teams in the current league or the F4 key to scroll to the next team. To change leagues, use the F5 key.

If you press F6, the Select Teams screen appears. Select your team or teams by highlighting the name and pressing ENTER. When you have finished making your selections, press F10 or press ESC to cancel.

The next option sets the paper supply for your printer. You may select continuous feed or single sheet. The Display option enables you to direct the output of the baseball cards to the screen, printer, or disk file. The Paper Size option tells the Commissioner II program what size of paper you are using in your printer. Your choices are (in inches) 3 x 5, 4 x 6, and 8.5 x 11 (3 per page).

To print the baseball cards, press F7. Figures 10-8a and 10-8b show two samples of the printed baseball cards. The card in Figure 10-8a was generated by using the Printer option. The card in Figure 10-8b is a sample that was saved to a disk file and touched up with a desktop publishing program.

When you have finished creating your reports, make sure you have activated the team box on the left side of the screen and press F10 to return to the main menu.

Accumulated Stats

The Accumulated Stats utility allows you to manipulate statistics for players and teams in your league. Also included with this utility is an option for determining rest periods for players.

Figure 10-8a.

Sample baseball card generated using the Printer option

```
Johnny Bench          SHAFER      1972  C   3B
Bats: R                \B

           BA    G   AB   R    H   2b  3b HR RBI
         .296   158 581   97 172  25   2 46 148

           SH   BB   SO   SB  CS   SA    OBA
            0  104   92    6   6  .583  .402

         POWER H&R  BUNT  RUNS  RANGE  ARM  FA-1  FA-2
         8       2    2     2      5     5  .989  .913

          BA    AB   H   2b  3b  HR  BB   SO    SA   OBA
  VsL:  .296   581  172  25   2  46104    92   .583  .402
  VsR:  .000     0    0   0   0   0   0    0   .000  .000
```

Grant Days Off

This utility grants days off to a team, a few selected teams, or all the teams in a league. To set the criteria for granting days off, press F1 to access the utility options.

The Current Team option establishes the team displayed on the left of the screen. The All Teams option grants days off to all teams in the current league. The Selected Teams option invokes the Select Teams screen where you highlight a team name and press ENTER to select it. The Days Off option allows you to enter a number from 0 to 9 for the number of days off to grant the selected team or teams.

To scroll through the list of teams in the current league, press F3 to access the previous team and F4 to access the next team in the list. To change leagues, press F5. To clear all previous settings, press F8.

After you have established which team or teams are affected, and after you have set the correct number of days off to be granted, press F7 (Grant Days Off Now). When you have finished granting days off, press F10 to return to the main menu.

Figure 10-8b.

A sample baseball card after saving the card to a disk file and touching it up with a desktop publishing program

Johnny Bench		SHAFER		1972	C	3B
Bats: R	\B					

BA	G	AB	R	H	2b	3b	HR	RBI
.296	158	581	97	172	25	2	46	148

SH	BB	SO	SB	CS	SA	OBA
0	104	92	6	6	.583	.402

POWER	H&R	BUNT	RUNS
8	2	2	2
RANGE	ARM	FA-1	FA-2
5	5	.989	.913

	BA	AB	H	2b	3b	HR	BB
VsL:	.296	581	172	25	2	46	104
VsR:	.000	0	0	0	0	0	0

	SO	SA	OBA
VsL:	92	.583	.402
VsR:	.000	.000	0

Combine Accumulated Stats

Use this utility to combine the accumulated statistics for players with identical ID numbers in different leagues, to combine the won/loss records of teams that exist in more than one league, or to combine newly downloaded statistics for a player with his existing stats. Chapter 2 describes in detail the downloading feature of the Commissioner II program.

The Combine Player Stats option adds the accumulated statistics of players in a league file to accumulated statistics of those same players in another league file. This option is useful when you are playing several leagues with the same players and you want to see how they are performing overall. This option does not affect players who are not playing in both leagues. Because this accumulation is based on a player's ID number, you should not change player's ID numbers.

To invoke this option, highlight the option on the menu and press ENTER. Select the Add team listed option and enter the team name. Select the To team listed option and enter the team name. If you want to change leagues to select a different team, press F5 (Change ADD League) or F6 (Change TO League).

The Combine Won/Loss option works in the same fashion but combines the overall records of the selected teams in both leagues.

To combine the statistics or won/loss records, press F7. When you have finished combining statistics, press F10 to return to the main menu.

Clear Accumulated Stats

This utility clears all accumulated statistics for a team, a few selected teams, or all the teams in a division or league. You can clear player statistics, won/lost records for a team, or both. Clearing these statistics erases them permanently. Be careful when using this option.

Once you have selected this utility from the main menu, you see a screen that displays the current league at the top. To change the current league, press F5.

Once you have loaded the correct league, you establish which teams you want to clear the accumulated statistics for. First you select all teams in the league or a few teams in the league. Next you establish whether you want to clear player statistics, won/lost records for the selected team or teams, or both. After you have established which teams are to be affected, press F7 (Clear Stats Now).

When you have finished clearing accumulated statistics, press F10 to return to the main menu.

Fun Time

The utilities you have worked with so far in the Commissioner II program have been organizational in nature. You've learned how to enter data for your league, how to align the teams for your league, and how to schedule your league. Now it's time to come up with a place to play by creating your very own ballpark. It's time to have some creative fun.

HOF - 1947
MICKEY COCHRANE
PHILADELPHIA ATHLETICS – CATCHER
HANK GREENBERG
DETROIT TIGERS – OUTFIELD
1940
HOF - 1968
GOOSE GOSLIN
WASHINGTON SENATORS – OUTFIELD
1922

CHAPTER 11

Building the Perfect Ballpark

"Several rules of stadium building should be carved on every owner's forehead. Old, if properly refurbished, is always better than new. Smaller is better than bigger. Open is better than closed. Near beats far...Inside should look as good as outside. Domed stadiums are criminal."

–Thomas Boswell, in his book *How Life Imitates the World Series*

The beauty of baseball is that it can be played anywhere–vacant lots, public streets, playgrounds, parking lots, even on a computer. The ballparks where Major League baseball games were played are filled with the lore, the legends, and even the ghosts of seasons past.

The game has become more sophisticated over the past century, and so have the fields on which the game is played. As discussed in Chapter 1, baseball in the 1800s was often played in a pasture with "natural boundaries" such as rows of trees marking fair territory. As the game gained popularity, entrepreneurs eager to make money from ticket sales began staging ball games in a more structured environment. In the mid-1800s, "parks" lasted less than half a dozen years. Owners would buy or lease land and construct wooden fences and bench bleachers to accommodate the crowds. Players would often help construct the fields.

Baseball before the turn of the century was a transient sport. Clubs would play in a city only as long as fans would come to games. When the crowds started dwindling, the clubs moved on. Because of this, parks were not constructed to be permanent facilities. Fires would often destroy the wooden bleachers. If a team lost its home field because of a fire, a new facility was quickly constructed, sometimes while the team was on a road trip.

By the early 1900s, owners began to settle into cities and franchises settled into more permanent ballparks. New construction materials, particularly concrete and steel, replaced wooden structures. As the Major Leagues began to support themselves, newly found financial security and the desire to increase attendance revenues resulted in the construction of massive structures that became known as *stadiums.*

New York was the site of the first "stadium" in baseball history with the opening of Yankee Stadium in 1923. No other stadium in the history of baseball successfully matched the grandeur of Yankee Stadium. Several owners tried, but the results were poor imitations.

Just as baseball is a symbol of society, a ballpark is the icon of a team. No two ballparks are alike. With individual character and many times with individual playing conditions, each ballpark adds a unique stamp to a community and a team that is never exactly duplicated. A ballpark affects the host community as much as it affects the home team.

Legendary Effects

Since the turn of the century, baseball team owners have realized that, to be a financial success, a team must put the fans in the stands. The owners do their part to keep attendance high by providing facilities with easy access and comfort for the fans. The team does its part by winning ball games. The storied parks of the past reflect this teamwork.

Sometimes, as was the case with Fenway Park in Boston, businesses would move in around the site of a new ballpark, even before construction was finished. Other times, as was the case with Shibe Park in Philadelphia, the new structures doomed surrounding neighborhoods that deteriorated rapidly after the construction of the massive stadiums. Crosley Field in Cincinnati was first constructed on a plot of land surrounded by vacant lots. Over the years, the area became industrialized so much that in its final seasons, Crosley was surrounded by factories. In the case of Ebbets Field in Brooklyn, the entire city fell in love with the stadium and the team.

When it was first constructed, Ebbets Field was not located in the heart of Brooklyn. It was located between upper-class Bedford and suburban Flatbush. But through the years, the city grew up around the ballpark. The appeal of Ebbets Field was that it was accessible to 90 percent of the Brooklyn population through mass transportation. Using the El, a trolley, or subway, more than 4 million people were within 45 minutes of the ballpark.

During the 1991 season, less than a third of the teams in Major League baseball played their home games on artificial surfaces. Of the 12 National League teams, however, 6 clubs hosted games on the turf. Of the 14 American League teams, only 3 played on artificial surfaces at home.

As far back as the 1890s, owners realized the importance of convenience to the fans. F.D. Robinson, owner of the 1890 Cleveland Spiders, chose a site for his stadium that could be serviced by his own streetcar company. Robinson made sure that the public transportation could deliver patrons no more than 20 feet from the gates of League Park.

A trip to the ballpark has always been fun. Promotions to attract fans have become increasingly popular. But the appeal of the game itself has always been the main attraction, even for those who could not afford the price of admission. Around the turn of the century, visiting teams would ride in a parade like a circus through town to announce their arrival to take on the home team.

At Cleveland's League Park, kids would congregate outside the stadium and wait for home runs to clear the right field wall. If they got the ball, they could turn it in for free admission to the park. On August 11, 1929, Jack Geiser was chasing balls and got Babe Ruth's 500th career home run. He turned in the ball and received $20 from the Babe, an autographed ball, and a chance to sit next to Ruth in the Yankee dugout.

Those who did not want to wait for home run balls found perches around League Park from which to view the game. One popular spot was the fire escape at nearby Dunham School. But the view there was limited. Other more daring freeloaders would scale to the top of the Andrews Storage building.

Probably the best example of watching a game and not paying the admission price still occurs at Fenway Park. Residents across the street from the stadium can actually watch the game from their apartments or from rooftops.

In 1908, the Giants were hosting the Cubs for a one-game playoff at the Polo Grounds to determine the National League pennant winner. Because advance ticket sales had not been instituted back then, a quarter of a million people showed up the day of the game looking for a seat. One fan put a wooden plank between the nearby El platform and the fence surrounding the park so fans could walk into the park for free. The New York *Evening Telegram* reported, "From the pressbox, the skyline everywhere was human heads. They were located on the grandstand, roofs, fences, 'L' structures, electric light poles and in the distance on smokestacks, chimneys, advertising signs, and coping of apartment houses."

As you'll see later in this chapter, groundskeepers at the storied parks of the past often would doctor the field to benefit the home team. Such tricks were not illegal, but they certainly affected the way games were played.

Your Stadium and Your Team

You may not be able to shuttle fans into your stadium via mass transportation, and you certainly won't have to worry about fans watching games for free. As an EWBII owner, you are not subjected to the financial roller coaster of fan attendance and gate revenues. But you do have an obligation to your team to provide the best facility possible to maximize the skills of the players on your team.

If your team has a strong pitching staff, you'll want to play in a pitcher's park. If your lineup is stacked with power hitters, you'll want the short porches of a hitter's park. If you boast blazing team speed, perhaps you'll want a fast Astroturf on which to play your games. In other words, the character of your team should be reflected in the stadium in which your team plays its home games. After all, half your games will be played in the friendly confines of home.

The EWBII program allows you to customize your stadium so that you can maximize your team's performance. In order to design the perfect stadium, you must be aware of which individual characteristics of a ballpark are going to impact the performance of your team. To understand these characteristics, you must first understand how to utilize the Edit Ballparks utility included with the Commissioner II program. Once you understand the utility, you must then become familiar with the ballparks included in EWBII and their unique characters. After all, these ballparks will provide the "blueprints" from which you will construct the perfect stadium.

The Edit Ballparks Utility

To view or edit a ballpark, select Edit Ballparks from the main menu of the Commissioner II program. The Edit Parks screen, shown in Figure 11-1, displays a list of available ballparks and individual statistical characteristics. To select a stadium for viewing or editing, highlight the name of the stadium in the box on the left side of the screen. The right side of the screen shows a full range of characteristics pertaining to each ballpark. As you scroll through the list of ballparks, notice that the data on the right side of the screen is updated to reflect the current ballpark.

This data determines the conditions under which games will be played at a particular ballpark. The data can be considered in the following four major groups:

Groundwork This group of data includes the name of the park, the playing field surface (grass or artificial turf), and whether this is an indoor or outdoor stadium.

Figure 11-1.

Opening screen for the Edit Ballparks utility

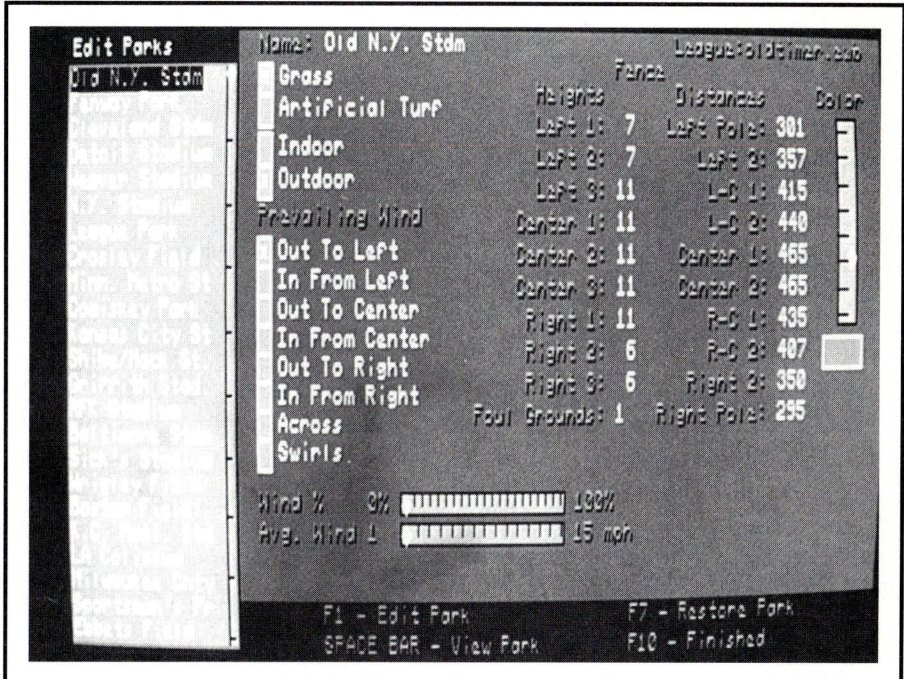

Winds This group of data pertains only to outdoor stadiums. The Prevailing Wind characteristic determines the direction of any prevailing winds in the park (out to left, in from left, out to center, in from center, out to right, in from right, across, or swirls). The Wind % setting determines the percentage of time that the wind blows. The Avg. Wind characteristic determines the maximum velocity of the prevailing wind (from 0 m.p.h. to 15 m.p.h.).

Fences The statistics in this group set the heights for fences at nine checkpoints along the outfield wall (three points each in left field, center field, and right field). The distances from home plate to eight outfield spots and from home to the foul poles are recorded in the next column. Finally, the size of the foul grounds is determined by a number from 1 to 27.

Color This setting determines the prevailing color of the stadium and of its fixtures for graphic display of games.

To view a selected ballpark, press SPACEBAR. Different camera views are available to change the angle from which you view the park. Chapter 2 provides a complete discussion on the use of the EWBII Camera feature. To alter the camera view, press any number from 1 through 9. To zoom in, press = and to zoom out, press -. The ALT-M key combination moves the camera down and the ALT-I key combination moves the camera up. In order to get a new focus, press ALT and a number key from 1 through 9. Press ESC to return to the Edit screen.

To edit a selected ballpark, press F1. The highlight moves out of the ballpark list to the criteria. When you edit a ballpark, the name and characteristics of the original park are overwritten. For this reason, you should never edit ballparks on your original disks. Otherwise, you will lose the historical parks that come with the EWBII game. To edit one of the characteristics, highlight the characteristic and press ENTER. For the surface selection, indoor versus outdoor, or prevailing wind, selecting the option places an X in the box of your choice. For the Wind % and Avg. Wind characteristics, press the LEFT ARROW and RIGHT ARROW keys to place the wind speed indicator where you want it. To change the color, press the UP ARROW and DOWN ARROW keys to select the color of your choice. For the other characteristics, you must enter a number.

If you want to restore a park to its original condition, press F7. This restores an edited ballpark only if you have not already saved any changes. To return to the ballpark list, press F1. To return to the main menu, press F10.

The program may slightly adjust some of the wall heights and distances after you have entered and saved the changes.

The Ballparks

In order to understand the full effect a stadium can have on the performance of a team, you should become familiar with existing stadiums and their unique characteristics. The EWBII program provides 30 stadiums from the past and present to use as a guide when designing your home park. Included here are brief histories on 20 of those ballparks. Notice the trends that evolved through the history of the game and how the construction of these parks affected the games played there.

Yankee Stadium, New York, New York

In 1921, the Yankee ownership decided to move their club and establish an identity separate from the Giants, with whom they had been sharing the Polo Grounds. They selected a ten-acre parcel in the West Bronx, a particularly favorable site because it was across the Harlem River from the Polo Grounds. In 1923, the Yankees moved into their new home.

The stadium was designed in the mold of the Yale Bowl, with dimensions that favored the strong left-handed hitting of the Yankee teams of the 1920s. A short right field porch was designed to accommodate the power of Babe Ruth and Lou Gehrig. Ruth hit a game-winning homer the first contest played in the new confines.

During the 1923 season, the angle between the bleachers and the right field foul pole was asymmetrical and caused tricky bounces for balls hit here. The angle was eliminated the following season by moving home plate 13 feet closer to the fences, thus decreasing the distance to the left-center field wall from 500 feet to 490 feet. Because of the immense distance to the left-center field wall, this area of the outfield has been dubbed "Death Valley." A total of 20 inside-the-park home runs were hit during the first season. Underneath second base was a brick-lined vault 15 feet deep that housed electrical, telephone, and telegraph connections used during boxing events at the stadium.

At the beginning of the 1927 season, Ruth had publicly proclaimed that he preferred hitting at the Polo Grounds. By the end of the 1927 season, Ruth had clobbered 60 home runs and decided that he liked Yankee Stadium after all. In 1928, the grandstands were extended beyond the left field foul pole. Triple decking was added past the right field foul pole in 1937 and 1938. A ten-foot chicken-wire fence was used at one time to separate the field from the right field bleacher section affectionately referred to as Ruthville.

By the mid-1970s, Old Yankee Stadium was in need of repair. The stadium was refurbished at a cost of $100 million, three times the cost of building Royals Stadium in Kansas City.

OLD YANKEE STADIUM
HOME TO: YANKEES–AL (1923-1973)
SURFACE: Bluegrass
WIND: Prevailing out to left
FENCES:

HEIGHTS		DISTANCES	
Left 1	7	Left Pole	301
Left 2	7	Left 2	357
Left 3	11	Left-Center 1	415
Center 1	11	Left-Center 2	440
Center 2	11	Center 1	465
Center 3	11	Center 2	465
Right 1	11	Rt-Center 1	435
Right 2	6	Rt-Center 2	402
Right 3	6	Right 2	350
		Right Pole	295
Foul Grnd	1		

NEW YANKEE STADIUM
HOME TO: YANKEES–AL (1974-Present)
SURFACE: Bluegrass
WIND: Prevailing out to left
FENCES:

HEIGHTS		DISTANCES	
Left 1	8	Left Pole	312
Left 2	7	Left 2	386
Left 3	7	Left-Center 1	400
Center 1	7	Left-Center 2	430
Center 2	7	Center 1	421
Center 3	7	Center 2	416
Right 1	9	Rt-Center 1	384
Right 2	10	Rt-Center 2	352
Right 3	10	Right 2	309
		Right Pole	309
Foul Grnd	7		

Fenway Park, Boston, Massachusetts

This legendary park is named Fenway because it is located in a marshy area of Boston known as the Fens. A classic hitter's park, Fenway is most difficult on left-handed pitchers. The outfield has 17 different facets and barriers. Left field has no foul territory because the grandstands butt up against the foul line. If a ball is hit hard past the third baseman, the runner should be aware that the ball might ricochet off the wall back to the shortstop. The right field foul pole is much closer to home plate than the left field pole. Within ten feet of the left field pole, however, the fence bows out from almost 370 feet in the left field power alley and, in fact, reaches an impressive 420 feet in left-center field where the flagpole rests. Only six players (Hank Greenberg, Jimmie Foxx, Moose Skowron, Carl Yastrzemski, Bobby Mitchell, and Jim Rice) have hit homers just to the right of that flagpole.

Fenway Park was the site of the only World Series played in two American League parks. The Braves won the National League pennant in 1914 and played their World Series games at Fenway (home to the American League Red Sox) because the seating capacity was greater at Fenway than at old South End Park.

The huge 37-foot wall in left field, known as the Green Monster, was once covered with so many advertisements that it had very little green coloring. The famous screen atop the Green Monster was installed in 1936 to catch homers and help save windows in buildings on the street below. In 1947, the advertisements were removed and the wall was painted green. In front of the Green Monster is an incline known as Duffy's Cliff. Inclines were used in the ballparks to warn outfielders of the wall before warning tracks were installed. From 1912 to 1933, the incline extended from the left field foul pole to the flagpole in center. The incline was named for Red Sox left fielder Duffy Lewis, who was the master at playing the cliff. In 1934 a warning track was installed and the incline was greatly reduced, but not completely eliminated.

In an effort to help Ted Williams hit more home runs to right in 1940, the Red Sox added the right field bullpens (called Williamsburg), thus reducing the distance to the fence by 25 feet. No ball has ever been hit over the right field roof at Fenway.

The wind in the park usually helps the hitters. After a new pressbox was built in the late 1980s, the wind began to swirl. Foul balls are often pushed back into fair territory by the wind.

HOME TO: RED SOX–AL (1912-Present)
SURFACE: Bluegrass
WIND: Prevailing out to left averaging 12 m.p.h.
FENCES:

HEIGHTS		DISTANCES	
Left 1	37	Left Pole	312
Left 2	12	Left 2	365
Left 3	6	Left-Center 1	420
Center 1	7	Left-Center 2	394
Center 2	8	Center 1	414
Center 3	8	Center 2	379
Right 1	8	Rt-Center 1	338
Right 2	4	Rt-Center 2	323
Right 3	8	Right 2	302
		Right Pole	302
Foul Grnd	3		

Municipal Stadium, Cleveland, Ohio

This was the first municipally owned stadium in the Major Leagues. The stadium was constructed on the shores of Lake Erie on the site of an old landfill. The fill for this area was mostly crushed automobiles and tires. Years after it was opened, the outfield began sagging because of the poor quality of landfill used. Sometimes referred to as the "Mistake by the Lake," Municipal Stadium was originally part of an urban renewal plan that also included a shopping mall to be constructed on a pier in the lake. The stadium was built, but the mall was never completed.

The teepees that appear beyond the center field wall were constructed in 1946. Prior to the 1947 season, an incline existed in front of the center field wall. But the incline was not as necessary here as in other parks. Only Mickey Mantle, Rocky Colavito, and Frank Howard ever came close to parking a shot in the center field bleachers. Their blasts traveled 460-plus feet, but fell short of the fence. Inner fences were installed in 1947 to cut down on the home run distance, make the fences more symmetrical, and eliminate the incline in center field. Municipal Stadium is a classic pitcher's park.

HOME TO: INDIANS–AL (1939-Present)
SURFACE: Bluegrass
WIND: Prevailing out to left averaging 15 m.p.h.
FENCES:

HEIGHTS		**DISTANCES**	
Left 1	9	Left Pole	319
Left 2	9	Left 2	342
Left 3	8	Left-Center 1	376
Center 1	8	Left-Center 2	399
Center 2	8	Center 1	399
Center 3	9	Center 2	385
Right 1	9	Rt-Center 1	342
Right 2	9	Rt-Center 2	319
Right 3	9	Right 2	319
		Right Pole	319
Foul Grnd	4		

Detroit Stadium, Detroit, Michigan

The site for Detroit Stadium (sometimes called Tiger Stadium) was originally a cobblestone hay market. Construction workers failed to put enough fill over the cobblestones when preparing the site, and the stones would poke through the stadium surface every now and then.

This stadium features the only double-decked outfield bleachers in the Major Leagues. The second deck in right field overhangs the playing field by about ten feet. Because this area on the playing field is shielded from stadium lights, a row of spotlights is mounted under the overhang to illuminate the right field warning track.

A spot in front of home plate, once called Cobb's Lake, is where groundskeepers would soak the area with water before games to slow down Ty Cobb's bunts. The scoreboard was located in dead center field until 1961. During that season, Norm Cash, Al Kaline, and Charlie Maxwell complained that it hindered the batter's view of the ball. The Tigers solved the problem by moving the scoreboard to its present position on the left field fence.

The field orientation benefits right-handed pitchers. Because home plate and the batter's boxes are oriented toward right-center rather than straight out to the mound, right-handed pitchers tend to get more outside-corner strike calls.

A sign above the Visitors' clubhouse door at Detroit Tiger Stadium reads "Visitors' Clubhouse—No Visitors Allowed."

Nonetheless, this has always been known as a hitter's park. The 1987 Tigers hit more home runs than any other team except the 1961 Yankees.

HOME TO: TIGERS–AL (1912-Present)
SURFACE: Bluegrass
WIND: Prevailing out to left blowing more than half the time at an average speed of 12 m.p.h.
FENCES:

HEIGHTS		DISTANCES	
Left 1	9	Left Pole	339
Left 2	9	Left 2	439
Left 3	9	Left-Center 1	439
Center 1	9	Left-Center 2	325
Center 2	9	Center 1	325
Center 3	9	Center 2	325
Right 1	9	Rt-Center 1	325
Right 2	9	Rt-Center 2	325
Right 3	9	Right 2	325
		Right Pole	325
Foul Grnd	1		

League Park, Cleveland, Ohio

League Park featured a Fenway-in-reverse configuration. The center field wall was originally 460 feet from home plate, but stands were constructed in 1920 to cut that distance down to about 420 feet. The right field foul pole, however, was less than 300 feet away.

Steel beams protruded from the surface of the right field fence, causing strange bounces for balls hit off the wall. Originally, the right field wall was constructed of wood (which tended to deaden line drives), but a new wall was constructed of concrete, 20 feet high with a 20-foot screen on top. When balls hit the concrete, they would bounce back toward the infield. When balls hit the screen, they would either bounce straight off, lose all momentum and fall at the base of the wall, or stick in the screen for a ground-rule double.

Stands were constructed along the foul lines to cut down on the foul territory. Along the right field line where the home dugout was located, the seats were positioned far enough back from the field to provide a full view of the action from the dugout. A bullpen was added down in the left field corner. With the seats along the left field line protruding farther than the seats on the opposite side of the field, the bullpen was actually tucked in behind the grandstands. A left fielder chasing fair balls down the line into the bullpen area had to throw over the stands to get the ball back to the infield.

Between 1933 and 1947, the Indians held the unique distinction of playing their home games at two different parks. On weekdays, the Indians preferred the smaller seating capacity of League Park. On Sundays and holidays, the team would play games at the roomier Municipal Stadium.

The list of tenants for League Park illustrates the trouble the city of Cleveland experienced in naming their Major League ball club.

HOME TO: BRONCOS–AL (1901); BLUES–AL (1902-1904); NAPS–AL (1905-1911); MOLLY McGUIRES–AL (1912-1914); INDIANS–AL (1915-1947)
SURFACE: Grass
WIND: Prevailing out to left
FENCES:

HEIGHTS		DISTANCES	
Left 1	4	Left Pole	355
Left 2	4	Left 2	374
Left 3	8	Left-Center 1	395
Center 1	8	Left-Center 2	406
Center 2	8	Center 1	419
Center 3	8	Center 2	419
Right 1	8	Rt-Center 1	387
Right 2	37	Rt-Center 2	355
Right 3	37	Right 2	322
		Right Pole	289
Foul Grnd	1		

Crosley Field, Cincinnati, Ohio

An abandoned brickyard was chosen in 1884 as the site for the home park of the American Association Reds. But on Opening Day that first season, the wooden grandstands collapsed and killed one fan. The facility was rebuilt, and it served as the home field for the Reds for the next 86 years. When the ballpark was rebuilt, the owners decided to paint the center field wall black and, in doing so, provided the first hitter's background in 1885.

This field was known primarily for its inside-the-park home runs. In 1901, 50 inside-the-parkers were hit (a record) with Sam Crawford collecting a dozen of those. Between 1900 and 1955, more than 350 inside-the-park home runs were hit.

In 1925, the Reds added 5,000 seats (mostly field boxes) and moved home plate 20 feet closer to the fences. Between 1946 and 1960, the team periodically experimented with installing a screen atop the right field fence to shorten the home run distance.

Crosley Field was the site of the first Major League night game. General Manager Larry McPhail asked the League's permission to install the lights as a means for generating bigger crowds. The Depression was causing financial strains throughout the League and officials agreed to the installment of lights. The first night game was played May 24, 1935.

HOME TO: REDS—NL (1890-1970)
SURFACE: Grass
WIND: Prevailing crosswind that blows out almost two-thirds of the time at an average of 15 m.p.h.
FENCES:

HEIGHTS		**DISTANCES**	
Left 1	18	Left Pole	328
Left 2	18	Left 2	355
Left 3	18	Left-Center 1	387
Center 1	18	Left-Center 2	383
Center 2	18	Center 1	386
Center 3	18	Center 2	386
Right 1	18	Rt-Center 1	387
Right 2	12	Rt-Center 2	387
Right 3	12	Right 2	363
		Right Pole	342
Foul Grnd	1		

Old Comiskey Park, Chicago, Illinois

The fact that Comiskey Park is a pitcher's park is not surprising, since owner Charles Comiskey enlisted the aid of his ace pitcher, Ed Walsh, in designing the park. Walsh was part of a committee that also included architect Zachary Davis and his assistant. Davis dispatched Walsh and the assistant to Forbes Field and Shibe Park to get fresh ideas on designing Davis' first Major League ballpark. The designer stole such innovations as ramps for the fans when he drew up the plans for Comiskey. The original outfield dimensions were 362 feet down the lines and 420 feet to dead center field. The stadium was in use more than a month before the first home run was hit here. Although Walsh has received much of the credit for the immense outfields, Comiskey himself was known to favor large parks.

Old Comiskey Park featured showers for fans in the center field bleachers.

Between the 1926 and 1927 seasons, Comiskey enlarged his stadium to accommodate more fans. Wooden bleachers in the outfield were replaced with concrete stands. The outfield pavilions were double-decked. Shortly after the renovations were completed in 1927, Babe Ruth hit a blast that cleared the right field roof and landed in a parking lot outside the stadium. That shot cleared a roof that stood 75 feet tall and was 360 feet from home plate. Two years later, Lou Gehrig lifted a homer over the right field roof. In all, more than 30 home runs cleared the roof during the life of the stadium.

In 1934, the White Sox decided to help their slugger, Al Simmons, hit more home runs at Comiskey Park. Home plate was moved out 14 feet to shorten the distances to the fences. But Simmons was gone the next year and home plate was then moved back to its original position. After 1949, an inner fence cut down the distance to straightaway center field.

Comiskey goundskeepers were known for creative caretaking to benefit the home team. In 1967, an area in front of home plate was referred to as Camp Swampy. The groundskeepers would soak the area with water on the days that White Sox sinkerball pitchers were on the mound. On days when opposing sinkerballers were pitching, the groundskeepers would pack the area with clay, douse it with gasoline, and burn it to harden the soil. The bullpen mounds for opposing teams were often lowered or raised from the ten-inch height limit in order to throw off the rhythm of opposing pitchers.

The height of the grass was cut to benefit White Sox players. During the late 1960s, the grass in front of shortstop was cut long because the White Sox were playing shortstops with limited range. The grass in front of second base was cut short to benefit the White Sox second basemen with more range. When the White Sox were playing a defensively poor outfield, the grass was cut long to keep doubles from turning into triples. When the team had good bunters, extra paint was added to the foul lines to cause more balls to roll into fair territory. The foul lines in the outfield were originally flattened fire hoses painted white.

HOME TO: WHITE SOX–AL (1912-1990)
SURFACE: Grass
WIND: Prevailing out to left averaging 15 m.p.h.
FENCES:

HEIGHTS		**DISTANCES**	
Left 1	9	Left Pole	352
Left 2	7	Left 2	400
Left 3	9	Left-Center 1	400
Center 1	9	Left-Center 2	352
Center 2	9	Center 1	352
Center 3	9	Center 2	352
Right 1	9	Rt-Center 1	352
Right 2	9	Rt-Center 2	352
Right 3	9	Right 2	352
		Right Pole	352
Foul Grnd	1		

Shibe Park (Connie Mack Stadium), Philadelphia, Pennsylvania

Built in 1909 and named for A's stockholder Ben Shibe, this was the first concrete-and-steel stadium in the Major Leagues. Over the next five years, Comiskey Park, Ebbets Field, Forbes Field, Fenway Park, Braves Field, and Wrigley Field were all built with concrete and steel. The construction of Shibe Park marked the end of the wooden ballpark era.

From 1934 to 1956, the right field wall stood 50 feet tall, 13 feet taller than the Green Monster at Fenway Park. The wall was a corrugated iron fence that caused strange hops for balls hit off its surface. The right field and left field walls met at a right angle in center field. Originally, the distance to dead center field was a massive 515 feet, but that was decreased in 1969 to less than 470 feet. The entire outfield was characterized by numerous slopes.

In the first 25 years of this ballpark's history, people living on 20th Street beyond the right field fence could sit in their front bedrooms (or on their roofs) and watch games over the small 12-foot fence. Connie Mack sued to prevent the residents from viewing games for free, but lost the battle in court. In

1935, he increased the height of the right field fences to between 20 and 40 feet.

This park at one time featured the highest pitcher's mound in the Major Leagues at 20 inches.

HOME TO: ATHLETICS–AL (1909-1954); PHILLIES–NL (1938-1970)
SURFACE: Grass
WIND: Prevailing out to left
FENCES:

HEIGHTS		**DISTANCES**	
Left 1	12	Left Pole	333
Left 2	12	Left 2	367
Left 3	20	Left-Center 1	399
Center 1	20	Left-Center 2	433
Center 2	20	Center 1	467
Center 3	20	Center 2	467
Right 1	20	Rt-Center 1	430
Right 2	40	Rt-Center 2	395
Right 3	40	Right 2	362
		Right Pole	330
Foul Grnd	1		

Griffith Stadium, Washington, D.C.

Opening Day at Griffith Stadium traditionally featured a U.S. President throwing out the first ball. When the American Association Senators chose this oak forest as the site for their park in 1884, they cleared the trees and removed the stumps to construct a ballpark that hosted baseball for the next 70 years. In the 1890s, the right field fence was topped with barbed wire. Legend says that Wee Willie Keeler once stuck his arm through the barbed wire to make a game-winning catch. The effort cut his arm from the wrist to the elbow.

The barbed wire was eventually replaced with a 30-foot tall concrete wall. Because the right field foul line was the grandstand wall for about the last 15 feet into the corner, outfielders could not catch foul balls deep down the right field line. During routine maintenance in 1956, the outfield fences were measured and workers discovered that the distance to the right field fence had mysteriously decreased by eight feet over the years. The wall in center field detoured around five houses and a huge tree, which overhung out onto the playing field. In Washington, saying "Meet me by the tree," referred to that oak tree beyond the center field fence.

A small box in center field, called the Dog House, was used to hold the flagpole. During one game, a Senator player hit a ball that rolled into the Dog House because the groundskeeper had inadvertently left the door open. Philadelphia outfielder Socks Seybold tried to crawl into the small box to retrieve the ball. He got stuck, and the Senator scored on an inside-the-park home run.

Mickey Mantle hit one of the longest home runs in baseball history out of this park. A public relations man for the Yankees said the blast was measured at 565 feet. But despite this blast, Griffith Stadium was predominantly a pitcher's park.

HOME TO: SENATORS–AL (1903-1961)
SURFACE: Grass
WIND: Prevailing out to left about 90 percent of the time
FENCES:

HEIGHTS		DISTANCES	
Left 1	12	Left Pole	356
Left 2	12	Left 2	383
Left 3	12	Left-Center 1	409
Center 1	12	Left-Center 2	416
Center 2	12	Center 1	421
Center 3	12	Center 2	421
Right 1	12	Rt-Center 1	427
Right 2	31	Rt-Center 2	434
Right 3	31	Right 2	381
		Right Pole	328
Foul Grnd	1		

Baltimore Memorial Stadium, Baltimore, Maryland

The old Memorial Stadium (also known as Baltimore Stadium) was an oval, like the Los Angeles Coliseum, with a baseball diamond in the middle. The facility was torn down in 1950 to make way for Memorial Stadium. An unfinished Memorial Stadium opened its doors in 1954. The new facility was a double-decked horseshoe shape designed to accommodate both baseball and football games.

Down the line the distance to the fences is short, but the distance sharply increases toward the power alleys. Because of this sharp angle, balls hit into the corners often bounce toward center field, which cuts down on the number of triples hit here. Early in 1954, hedges were used as fences in center field. By the summer of that year, a wire fence was constructed to replace the hedges. In 1958, Harvey Kuenn cut his face when he climbed the fence trying to catch a home run. Canvas padding was then added to the top six feet of the fence. The walls in left field and right field, which were constructed of concrete and plywood, were padded in 1977 after Curt Blefary injured his hip chasing a fly ball into the wall.

A picnic area in the upper deck of Baltimore Stadium during the 1960s was called Oriole Landing.

HOME TO: ORIOLES–IL (1944-1949); moved to Memorial Stadium (1950-1953); AL (1954-Present)
SURFACE: Bluegrass
WIND: Prevailing out to left
FENCES:

HEIGHTS		DISTANCES	
Left 1	14	Left Pole	308
Left 2	7	Left 2	359
Left 3	7	Left-Center 1	384
Center 1	7	Left-Center 2	397
Center 2	7	Center 1	410
Center 3	7	Center 2	410
Right 1	7	Rt-Center 1	397
Right 2	7	Rt-Center 2	384
Right 3	14	Right 2	359
		Right Pole	308
Foul Grnd	2		

Wrigley Field, Chicago, Illinois

Although owner William Wrigley had lights ready to be installed in his ballpark in 1940, he donated them to the war effort. In 1988, Wrigley Field became the last Major League stadium to install lights for night baseball.

Because the park is located at 600 feet above sea level, and because of the strong wind blowing out over Lake Michigan, more home runs than usual are hit here. In the old days, players would smell the air when they arrived at the ballpark. If they could smell stockyards, they knew that the wind was blowing out.

It is more difficult to hit a homer down the lines here than 50 feet into the field of play because the bleachers protrude out over the outfield. The bleachers were constructed where the outfield used to be. The bleachers start out narrow and rise to a peak in center field, giving the appearance of a boomerang atop the outfield fences. The characteristic ivy-covered brick outfield walls were decorated in 1937 with eight huge Chinese elm trees and potted plants on the bleacher stair steps. The plants and trees eventually died. The grandstands down the lines butt up against the field of play, eliminating any significant foul area.

The marker for the farthest distance to hit a homer is actually not even in the park. A sign on top of a house across Sheffield Avenue reads "495."

HOME TO: CUBS–NL (1920-Present)
SURFACE: Bluegrass and clover
WIND: Prevailing out to left averaging 15 m.p.h.
FENCES:

HEIGHTS		DISTANCES	
Left 1	11	Left Pole	354
Left 2	11	Left 2	370
Left 3	11	Left-Center 1	355
Center 1	11	Left-Center 2	384
Center 2	11	Center 1	399
Center 3	11	Center 2	399
Right 1	11	Rt-Center 1	387
Right 2	11	Rt-Center 2	359
Right 3	11	Right 2	367
		Right Pole	353
Foul Grnd	1		

Braves Field, Boston, Massachusetts

The original dimensions of Braves Field were 402 feet down the lines and 550 feet to dead center field. The ballpark hosted baseball for ten years before anyone hit a home run. For the first 12 years of its existence, Braves Field boasted the largest outfield in the Major Leagues. While the original dimensions were still in effect, only seven balls ever cleared the outfield fences in the air. Because of the great expanse in the outfield, Braves Field was the site of more than 200 inside-the-park homers. During the 1920s, the park became known as the last great place to hit inside-the-park round-trippers. During one game in the 1920 season, George Kelley hit two of visiting New York's four inside-the-park home runs.

In 1928, the fences were shortened with the construction of bleacher seats in the outfield.

HOME TO: BRAVES–NL (1912-1952)
SURFACE: Grass
WIND: Prevailing out to left
FENCES:

HEIGHTS		DISTANCES	
Left 1	20	Left Pole	336
Left 2	20	Left 2	350
Left 3	12	Left-Center 1	365
Center 1	12	Left-Center 2	376
Center 2	12	Center 1	389
Center 3	12	Center 2	389
Right 1	12	Rt-Center 1	371
Right 2	12	Rt-Center 2	355
Right 3	8	Right 2	336
		Right Pole	319
Foul Grnd	1		

Municipal Stadium, Kansas City, Missouri

Originally a frog pond, swimming hole, and ash heap, Municipal Stadium was constructed in the early 1920s. The Kansas City Monarchs of the Negro League were its primary tenants during the first three decades. The fences in the old days featured two rows of signs. One row ran along the base of the fence and defined the home run distances. The other row of signs, running above and behind the first, featured various advertising.

The fence heights and distances for Municipal Stadium were changed more often than any other Major League ballpark. The first change came with the double-decking of tall, deep grandstands and the construction of bleachers in the outfield. The grandstands were supported by huge steel beams that caused several sight obstructions for the fans. A light tower at the base of the left-center field wall was in the field of play.

When Charles O. Finley owned the Kansas City Athletics, he installed a zoo beyond the right field fence. The menagerie included a mule named Charley O, sheep, pheasants, monkeys, rabbits, and a dog. For a time under Finley's control, the stadium featured a mechanical rabbit named Harvey that would pop up behind home plate to deliver fresh baseballs to the umpire. Finley even installed an underground compressed air system that would "automatically" dust off home plate.

At one point, Finley decided that in order to field a winning ball club he had to imitate the outfield dimensions of Yankee Stadium. He constructed a "Pennant Porch" down the right field line that reduced the home run distance to 296 feet. The league did not approve of the construction and, in fact, passed a rule that no new fences could be built less than 325 feet from home plate. Finley's experiment lasted only two exhibition games before the Pennant Porch was dismantled.

HOME TO: ATHLETICS–AL (1955-1967); ROYALS–AL (1969-1972)
SURFACE: Grass
WIND: Prevailing out to left
FENCES:

HEIGHTS		**DISTANCES**	
Left 1	10	Left Pole	244
Left 2	10	Left 2	332
Left 3	10	Left-Center 1	443
Center 1	10	Left-Center 2	425
Center 2	10	Center 1	399
Center 3	10	Center 2	399
Right 1	10	Rt-Center 1	425
Right 2	10	Rt-Center 2	450
Right 3	10	Right 2	392
		Right Pole	335
Foul Grnd	1		

Sportsman's Park, St. Louis, Missouri

Sportsman's Park housed Major League baseball for 90 years, longer than any other stadium. If you count the years when the site was just a field used for games in the 1860s, baseball was played at this site for more than a century. Fires kept destroying the old park. A fire in 1891 burned the facility to the ground and marked the end of a St. Louis team in the American Association. It was rebuilt over the next two years and baseball resumed at the park in 1893. Smaller fires damaged the park over the next few years and portions had to be rebuilt. Finally, in 1898, a fire broke out during a game, resulting in hundreds of fans being either burned or trampled.

The site was not used as a ballpark from 1898 to 1902. The new St. Louis Browns of the American League took up residency in 1902 and the Cardinals moved into the stadium to become tenants of the Browns in 1920. St. Louis became a city with one ballpark and two Major League franchises for the next 22 years.

When a Cardinal hitter would clobber a home run at Sportsman's Park, the Busch Eagle would flap its wings.

In 1908, the old ballpark was reinforced with concrete and steel. A second deck was constructed behind the infield section of the stands in 1909 and extended down the lines to the foul poles in 1925. Right-center field featured a pavilion behind the power alley, where Babe Ruth once hit four homers in a game. A wire screen was installed in front of the pavilion from 1929 to 1955 to protect the fans. A local newspaper displayed an advertisement on the right-center field wall that would show the picture of the star of the previous game. Just to the right of the advertisement, league standings were posted.

In 1953, August Busch bought the stadium from the Browns. He wanted to rename the stadium Budweiser Stadium, but the league opposed the new name.

HOME TO: BROWNS–AL (1909-1953); CARDINALS–NL (1920-1966)
SURFACE: Grass
WIND: Prevailing out to left
FENCES:

HEIGHTS		DISTANCES	
Left 1	11	Left Pole	350
Left 2	11	Left 2	362
Left 3	11	Left-Center 1	376
Center 1	11	Left-Center 2	398
Center 2	11	Center 1	421
Center 3	11	Center 2	421
Right 1	11	Rt-Center 1	388
Right 2	11	Rt-Center 2	354
Right 3	11	Right 2	332
		Right Pole	309
Foul Grnd	1		

Ebbets Field, Brooklyn, New York

Ebbets Field was once described by noted baseball writer Roger Kahn as "a narrow cockpit of iron and concrete along a steep cobblestone slope." The stadium was, in fact, built on a hill, resulting in a slope from the lower right field to a slightly higher center field. With the scoreboard (which was built after 1930) jutting at a 45-degree angle about five feet into right field, the wall and the scoreboard created more than 280 different angles. A 3 x 30-foot sign advertising Schaefer Beer sat on top of the scoreboard and was used to deliver the official scorer's decisions. The "E" would light up for an error and the "H" would light up for a hit. Children could sneak a peak at their favorite ballplayers by watching the game through a gap under a metal gate in right-center field.

Charles Ebbets chose a land-filled marsh for the site of his ballpark in 1908. The area was a couple of blocks from an Italian ghetto near Flatbush Avenue. Ebbets spent three-quarters of a million dollars to build his park. He painted the brick wall enclosing the stadium olive green and planted vines to cover the walls.

The grandstands at Ebbets Field were extremely close to the playing field, so the bullpens had to be squeezed in between the foul lines and the stands. When double-decked grandstands were constructed all the way around left field to straightaway center field, this became a power hitter's park. The second deck in center field hung out over the field. The foul poles were 347 feet from home plate, but the power alleys were not much farther. The deepest part of the park stood less than 400 feet from home plate. The right field fence sloped back away from the field for the first 15 feet and then rose straight up for another 15 feet. The screen installed atop the fence was considered in the playing field.

Ebbets Field was where Jackie Robinson broke into Major League baseball.

HOME TO: DODGERS–AL (1913-1957)
SURFACE: Grass
WIND: Prevailing out to left
FENCES:

HEIGHTS		DISTANCES	
Left 1	10	Left Pole	347
Left 2	10	Left 2	353
Left 3	10	Left-Center 1	357
Center 1	10	Left-Center 2	372
Center 2	10	Center 1	388
Center 3	10	Center 2	388
Right 1	10	Rt-Center 1	366
Right 2	38	Rt-Center 2	344
Right 3	38	Right 2	320
		Right Pole	296
Foul Grnd	1		

Polo Grounds, New York, New York

In an effort to promote water drainage, the field at the Polo Grounds was sloped in a "turtle back" fashion from just beyond the infield down about a foot and a half for about 20 feet into the outfield, and then back up again. However, the deepest part of the outfield was sloped so steeply that a manager standing on the dugout steps could see only the top half of his players' bodies at the walls in the outfield. The ground at the walls was actually eight feet lower than at the infield. The right field wall sloped gradually from about ten feet at the foul poles to about 12 feet at the bleachers in right-center field. The left field wall sloped from a little more than 16 feet at the pole to about 18 feet in left-center field, then dropped to 16 feet, 14 feet, and finally 12 feet at the bleachers.

In the 1914 season, the right-center field wall featured two odd bends. Home runs were easier to hit over the 280-foot right field fence than over the 257-foot left field fence because the second deck in left field hung over the field. The protrusion was about 20 feet, but because of the angle of the overhang, a flyball hit 250 feet to left field would go out.

The right field wall was constructed of concrete, and balls bouncing off this mass would take crazy hops. The left field wall was interrupted with a corrugated iron door, which also caused some crazy hops. Left field was the sun field, and the overhang caused outfielders to temporarily lose sight of fly balls that narrowly missed going into the stands above the overhang. Instead of painting numerals on the walls to denote home run distances, tin or steel markers were placed along the bottom of the outfield walls. Balls hitting these markers would bounce crazily, stop dead at the marker, or roll along the base of the wall.

The cavernous outfield with all its obstacles and crazy hops made the Polo Grounds a pitcher's dream park.

HOME TO: GIANTS–NL (1911-1957); YANKEES–AL (1913-1922); METS–NL (1962)
SURFACE: Grass
WIND: Prevailing out to left
FENCES:

HEIGHTS		**DISTANCES**	
Left 1	17	Left Pole	280
Left 2	12	Left 2	441
Left 3	12	Left-Center 1	447
Center 1	12	Left-Center 2	424
Center 2	12	Center 1	471
Center 3	12	Center 2	471
Right 1	12	Rt-Center 1	424
Right 2	11	Rt-Center 2	452
Right 3	11	Right 2	434
		Right Pole	257
Foul Grnd	22		

Forbes Field, Pittsburgh, Pennsylvania

Pirates owner Barney Dreyfuss chose a plot of farmland not far from Pittsburgh's classiest suburbs as the home for his new ballpark. A ravine ran through the land and the site had to be filled before construction could begin. Dreyfuss wanted his park to reflect the class of the neighborhood, so he installed elevators, electric lights, telephones, and ramps, and he provided maids in the ladies' rooms.

Forbes Field was never known as a home run hitter's park. But it was considered a triples hitter's park. From 1900 to 1983, the Pirates led the league in triples 40 times. Balls that were hit beyond or in between fielders would roll a long way in the outfield. The outfielders had to run long distances to chase down the balls and then throw to deep cutoff men in a relay to the infield.

This was the first stadium to install foam padding on outfield walls. The padding was installed on the concrete walls in right field and right-center field. The left field and center field walls were originally wooden barriers, but were replaced with ivy-covered brick walls in 1946. When grandstands were constructed in right field in 1925, the distance to the foul pole was reduced by more than 75 feet. A screen was constructed over the right field fence in 1932, but during the years of World War II, repairs could not be made to the screen. It deteriorated badly during those years. The roof over right field stood 86 feet high. The third base grandstand stood between home plate and fans sitting in the upper confines of the left field bleachers, thus preventing them from watching any action at the plate. The first inner fence was built in 1947 to induce home runs, and it reduced the home run distance in left field by 30 feet. The area between the original fence and the inner fence was known for a while as Greenberg Gardens, in honor of Hank Greenberg, and later as Kiner's Korner, in honor of Ralph Kiner.

In May of 1935, Babe Ruth arrived in town with the Boston Braves. At the age of 41, Ruth hit three homers in one game. The last homer of the day was number 714 for Babe's career, and it cleared the right field roof, which had never been done. Ruth then retired from baseball.

Forbes Field is named for General John Forbes, who was a British general responsible for capturing Fort Duquesne and renaming it Fort Pitt during the French and Indian War.

HOME TO: PIRATES–NL (1909-1970)
SURFACE: Grass
WIND: Prevailing out to left
FENCES:

HEIGHTS		DISTANCES	
Left 1	12	Left Pole	335
Left 2	12	Left 2	392
Left 3	12	Left-Center 1	450
Center 1	12	Left-Center 2	425
Center 2	12	Center 1	399
Center 3	12	Center 2	399
Right 1	12	Rt-Center 1	387
Right 2	24	Rt-Center 2	375
Right 3	24	Right 2	336
		Right Pole	299
Foul Grnd	1		

Astrodome, Houston, Texas

Judge Roy Hoffheinz got his idea for a domed stadium while visiting the Colosseum in Rome. He looked up the history of the Colosseum and learned that slaves would cover the facility with a papyrus roof on hot days. The idea seemed to fit the hot, muggy climate of Gulf Coast summers in Houston.

The Harris County Domed Stadium was constructed to replace the old Colt Stadium, an interim facility within a mile of the new site that was home to the National League's Colt .45s. The original plan for the new stadium was to have real grass and a clear glass roof that would allow sunshine to beam down on the field. The glare from the glass made playing the outfield a dangerous position in the domed confines, so the glass was painted. The grass died and Hoffheinz turned to the Monsanto Corporation for a synthetic grass, originally called Chemgrass. The first Major League game to be played on an artificial surface took place on April 8, 1966.

Because Houston was the headquarters for NASA and because the Mercury astronauts were enjoying huge popularity when the stadium opened, the Houston team was renamed the Astros and the turf became known as Astroturf.

The power alleys in the Astrodome were originally 390 feet, but were decreased in 1985. The original dirt floor was replaced in 1987 with concrete. Ground rules in the park stipulate that any ball hitting a suspended speaker in fair territory is a fair ball and should be played either where it lands or where it is touched by a player. A ball hitting a speaker in foul territory is a foul ball.

The Astrodome is the best pitcher's park in baseball history. In 1981, the Astros' pitching staff allowed 2.08 runs per game at home (both earned and unearned), which broke a record of 2.28 runs per game set by the 1906 White Sox. The ball does not carry well indoors at the Astrodome.

Although it is a stadium that protects the field from all outside elements, the Astrodome has suffered one rainout. In 1976, a storm in Houston was so bad that no one could get to the ballpark.

HOME TO: ASTROS–NL (1965-Present)
SURFACE: Artificial turf
FENCES:

HEIGHTS		DISTANCES	
Left 1	10	Left Pole	339
Left 2	10	Left 2	356
Left 3	10	Left-Center 1	372
Center 1	10	Left-Center 2	389
Center 2	10	Center 1	405
Center 3	10	Center 2	405
Right 1	10	Rt-Center 1	389
Right 2	10	Rt-Center 2	372
Right 3	10	Right 2	356
		Right Pole	339
Foul Grnd	1		

Chavez Ravine, Los Angeles, California

Originally the home of both the National League Dodgers and the American League Angels, Chavez Ravine was built in a ravine marked with hills, gullies, and washes. Construction workers had to move 8 million cubic yards of earth before construction could begin. The Dodgers called the park Dodger Stadium while the Angels, eager to retain their own identity, referred to the facility as Chavez Ravine.

A pronounced pitcher's park with deep power alleys and a large foul territory, Chavez Ravine is known for its high pitcher's mound. The mound was lowered five inches in 1963. Sandy Koufax proved how much of a pitcher's park this really is by compiling a home record of 63-14 from 1962 to 1966.

Despite its reputation, in one game during the 1979 season, eight homers were poked with the home team Dodgers collecting six round trippers. Willie Stargell is the only player to ever hit a homer over the roof of this park, and he did it twice (1969 and 1973).

HOME TO: DODGERS–NL (1962-Present); ANGELS–AL (1961-1966)
SURFACE: Grass
WIND: Prevailing out to left
FENCES:

HEIGHTS		DISTANCES	
Left 1	8	Left Pole	329
Left 2	8	Left 2	333
Left 3	8	Left-Center 1	385
Center 1	8	Left-Center 2	400
Center 2	8	Center 1	400
Center 3	8	Center 2	385
Right 1	8	Rt-Center 1	333
Right 2	8	Rt-Center 2	329
Right 3	8	Right 2	329
		Right Pole	329
Foul Grnd	1		

Baker Bowl, Philadelphia, Pennsylvania

Nicknamed "The Hump," this stadium was constructed on an elevated piece of ground that actually had a railroad tunnel underneath the outfield. The site was a dump before the ballpark was constructed.

A fire in 1894 caused severe damage to the original facility. A steel grandstand was erected that year to replace the one that had burned. The new grandstand was the first cantilevered structure ever used in a Major League ballpark. Tragedy again struck the Baker Bowl in 1903 when the left field grandstands collapsed, killing 12 and injuring more than 230 fans.

Left-handed hitters loved this park. The right field foul pole was a scant 270 feet from home plate. The outfield fences changed angles frequently, which caused odd bounces off the walls. The center field wall was the foundation for a mortar-and-stone building that contained the clubhouses. The right field wall was made of iron, and when balls would bounce off it, they would leave dents. Atop the right field wall was a screen. Balls hitting either the dented wall or the screen often would bounce unpredictably. For awhile, a 15-foot wide bicycle track rimmed the outfield.

The 1930 Phillies boasted a team batting average of .370, but the pitching staff had an ERA of 6.70 (the highest team ERA ever recorded). Chuck Klein hit .383 with 170 RBI and 40 homers that year. He once hit a ball through a rust spot in the right field wall for a ground rule double. The team finished last with a 52-102 record.

The Baker Bowl clubhouse in center field housed a swimming pool in its basement prior to World War I.

Baker Bowl became the site of baseball history in 1923 when 11-year-old Reuben Berman retrieved a foul ball in the stands and refused to return the ball. The youngster was sent to a detention facility overnight. A judge later ruled that fans could keep balls landing in the stands. This was a landmark decision because it meant that foul balls no longer had to be returned.

HOME TO: PHILLIES–NL (1904-1938)
SURFACE: Grass
WIND: Prevailing out to left
FENCES:

HEIGHTS		DISTANCES	
Left 1	6	Left Pole	335
Left 2	6	Left 2	355
Left 3	10	Left-Center 1	375
Center 1	10	Left-Center 2	391
Center 2	10	Center 1	407
Center 3	10	Center 2	407
Right 1	10	Rt-Center 1	373
Right 2	37	Rt-Center 2	340
Right 3	37	Right 2	306
		Right Pole	271
Foul Grnd	1		

Other Ballparks

The remaining ten ballparks that are included with the EWBII program include some facilities that were used only a short time or that served as interim stadiums while new stadiums were being built. Others are facilities still in use today. The following are the remaining stadiums and their specifications.

Minnesota Metropolitan Stadium, Minneapolis, Minnesota

HOME TO: TWINS–AL (1960-1980)
SURFACE: Grass
WIND: Prevailing out to left
FENCES:

HEIGHTS		DISTANCES	
Left 1	8	Left Pole	329
Left 2	8	Left 2	346
Left 3	8	Left-Center 1	365
Center 1	8	Left-Center 2	388
Center 2	8	Center 1	411
Center 3	8	Center 2	411
Right 1	8	Rt-Center 1	388
Right 2	8	Rt-Center 2	365
Right 3	8	Right 2	346
		Right Pole	329
Foul Grnd	1		

Royals Stadium, Kansas City, Missouri

HOME TO: ROYALS–AL (1973-Present)
SURFACE: Artificial turf
WIND: Prevailing out to left
FENCES:

HEIGHTS		DISTANCES	
Left 1	12	Left Pole	319
Left 2	12	Left 2	349
Left 3	12	Left-Center 1	370
Center 1	12	Left-Center 2	390
Center 2	12	Center 1	409
Center 3	12	Center 2	409
Right 1	12	Rt-Center 1	390
Right 2	12	Rt-Center 2	370
Right 3	12	Right 2	357
		Right Pole	329
Foul Grnd	11		

RFK Stadium, Washington, D.C.

HOME TO: SENATORS–AL (1962-1971)
SURFACE: Grass
WIND: Prevailing out to left constantly at an average of 11 m.p.h.
FENCES:

HEIGHTS		DISTANCES	
Left 1	8	Left Pole	335
Left 2	8	Left 2	356
Left 3	8	Left-Center 1	379
Center 1	8	Left-Center 2	395
Center 2	8	Center 1	409
Center 3	8	Center 2	409
Right 1	8	Rt-Center 1	395
Right 2	8	Rt-Center 2	379
Right 3	8	Right 2	356
		Right Pole	335
Foul Grnd	1		

Sick's Stadium, Seattle, Washington

HOME TO: PILOTS–AL (1969)
SURFACE: Grass
WIND: Prevailing out to left constantly at an average of 15 m.p.h.
FENCES:

HEIGHTS		DISTANCES	
Left 1	8	Left Pole	325
Left 2	8	Left 2	345
Left 3	8	Left-Center 1	365
Center 1	8	Left-Center 2	382
Center 2	8	Center 1	399
Center 3	8	Center 2	399
Right 1	8	Rt-Center 1	382
Right 2	8	Rt-Center 2	365
Right 3	8	Right 2	345
		Right Pole	325
Foul Grnd	1		

Los Angeles Coliseum, Los Angeles, California

HOME TO: DODGERS–NL (1958-1961)
SURFACE: Grass
WIND: Prevailing out to left
FENCES:

HEIGHTS		DISTANCES	
Left 1	40	Left Pole	250
Left 2	40	Left 2	284
Left 3	12	Left-Center 1	319
Center 1	12	Left-Center 2	371
Center 2	12	Center 1	424
Center 3	12	Center 2	424
Right 1	12	Rt-Center 1	431
Right 2	8	Rt-Center 2	440
Right 3	8	Right 2	397
		Right Pole	354
Foul Grnd	1		

County Stadium, Milwaukee, Wisconsin

HOME TO: BRAVES–NL (1953-1965); BREWERS–AL (1970-Present)
SURFACE: Bluegrass
WIND: Prevailing out to left
FENCES:

HEIGHTS		DISTANCES	
Left 1	4	Left Pole	319
Left 2	4	Left 2	343
Left 3	6	Left-Center 1	367
Center 1	6	Left-Center 2	385
Center 2	6	Center 1	401
Center 3	6	Center 2	401
Right 1	6	Rt-Center 1	385
Right 2	10	Rt-Center 2	367
Right 3	10	Right 2	340
		Right Pole	315
Foul Grnd	1		

Colt Stadium, Houston, Texas

HOME TO: COLT .45s–NL (1962-1964)
SURFACE: Grass
WIND: Prevailing out to left
FENCES:

HEIGHTS		DISTANCES	
Left 1	8	Left Pole	356
Left 2	8	Left 2	374
Left 3	8	Left-Center 1	395
Center 1	8	Left-Center 2	406
Center 2	8	Center 1	419
Center 3	8	Center 2	419
Right 1	8	Rt-Center 1	406
Right 2	8	Rt-Center 2	395
Right 3	8	Right 2	374
		Right Pole	356
Foul Grnd	1		

Seals Stadium, San Francisco, California

HOME TO: GIANTS–NL (1958-1959)
SURFACE: Grass
WIND: Prevailing out to left
FENCES:

HEIGHTS		DISTANCES	
Left 1	12	Left Pole	339
Left 2	12	Left 2	355
Left 3	12	Left-Center 1	369
Center 1	12	Left-Center 2	385
Center 2	12	Center 1	399
Center 3	12	Center 2	399
Right 1	12	Rt-Center 1	397
Right 2	4	Rt-Center 2	395
Right 3	4	Right 2	374
		Right Pole	356
Foul Grnd	1		

Parc Jarry, Montreal, Quebec

HOME TO: EXPOS–NL (1969-1976)
SURFACE: Grass
WIND: Prevailing out to left averaging 15 m.p.h.
FENCES:

HEIGHTS		DISTANCES	
Left 1	6	Left Pole	339
Left 2	6	Left 2	360
Left 3	6	Left-Center 1	379
Center 1	6	Left-Center 2	397
Center 2	6	Center 1	416
Center 3	6	Center 2	416
Right 1	6	Rt-Center 1	397
Right 2	6	Rt-Center 2	379
Right 3	6	Right 2	360
		Right Pole	339
Foul Grnd	1		

Down on the Field

Using the information you have culled from previous chapters to formulate your team philosophy, and using the information here to design your home park, you are now ready to begin formulating a managerial strategy. For that, you'll need to meet a few more legends.

HOF - 1937
CONNIE MACK
PHILADELPHIA ATHLETICS – MANAGER
HOF - 19
JOHN McGRAW
NEW YORK GIANTS – MANAGER
1928
HOF - 1957
JOE McCARTHY
NEW YORK YANKEES – MANAGER
1935

CHAPTER 12

Molding the Perfect Manager

"There are only two kinds of managers. Winning managers and ex-managers."

–Gil Hodges, after being hired to manage the New York Mets

By now you have that look that says you've about had your fill of administrative duties. You look like someone who could use a break from behind that desk and a breath of fresh air. Perhaps now would be a good time to lay down your pencil, put away the stat sheets, roll up the ballpark blueprints, and head back down to the dugout.

As a rookie manager in this league, you may find managing a team of Hall of Fame ballplayers to be difficult. Sometimes the best substitute for experience is to pattern yourself after role models. Fortunately, this league has some of the best managerial role models the game has ever known. By tapping into the experiences of half a dozen managers who themselves are Hall of Fame caliber, you might be able to bypass some of the problems you'll face as a rookie skipper in this league.

You are about to meet a group of managers whose styles are varied, but whose common thread is success. By learning how these men achieved immortality, you can better formulate the strategies necessary to achieve your own success on the ball field. After you have established your team's strategies, you can use the Commissioner II utility to tell EWBII how to run your ball club.

Skippers from the Past

The styles and strategies of several legendary baseball managers have been programmed into EWBII to run a team automatically. Before you can understand how these managers are programmed, you should first learn a little about their careers.

The managers are presented in the chronological order in which they appeared in the Major Leagues. You should note how managerial styles have adjusted to the changing conditions of the game.

Connie Mack ("The Tall Tactician")

Always dapper and always in control, Connie Mack managed the Philadelphia Athletics for more than 50 years. During that half-century, Mack won nine pennants, five World Championships, and 3776 games, the most wins ever compiled by a Major League manager. The tall, lanky (he was 6'1" but weighed a slight 150 pounds) master tactician was easily recognized in the dugout. He was the last manager to wear a suit and tie while managing his troops.

Connie Mack was born during the Civil War in East Brookfield, Massachusetts, and grew up in poverty. At the age of 16 he was forced to be the breadwinner for his family when his father, a Union soldier, died. He played baseball for Brookfield's top-rated town team and signed a minor league contract with Meriden as a catcher for $90 a month.

Baseball during Mack's playing days was a game in which the batter told the pitcher where to throw and was allowed seven balls and four strikes. Mack was always regarded as a good fielder and excellent handler of pitchers. He was called up to Washington in the National League in 1886.

In 1890, Mack moved to Buffalo in the fledgling Brotherhood League. This was his first opportunity to become financially involved in big league baseball. He invested heavily in the young franchise, but the league soon folded. He was picked up by Pittsburgh of the National League, where he played every position except pitcher and third base. He suffered an ankle injury in 1893 that reduced his effectiveness and eventually contributed to the end of his 11-year playing career after the 1896 season. Mack wound up his playing days with a respectable .251 career batting average.

Mack assumed the role of player-manager for his Pittsburgh ball club in 1894. His success was limited, as the team finished in the second division for the next couple of years.

After his retirement as a player, he managed in the minor leagues from 1897 to 1900. He was then offered the manager's position with the Philadelphia Athletics in the newly formed American League in 1901. Part of his compensation was 25 percent of the team ownership.

Players and managers of the older National League eschewed the fledgling American League. In fact, rival National League manager John McGraw once taunted Mack by saying that "the American League's got a white elephant in Philadelphia." Always one to capitalize on a situation, Mack then called his team the White Elephants, and even adopted the pachyderm as its mascot. Philadelphia finished in fourth place its inaugural season and jumped to first place the following year.

The Oakland Athletics still use the elephant as their mascot, 90 years after Connie Mack adopted it for the Philadelphia Athletics.

Eventually, Mack assumed total ownership of the Athletics. His only business investment was in the game of baseball. Lacking other sources of income, he relied solely on gate receipts and concession sales. Unfortunately, this placed his club in several financial binds over the years. His financial troubles resulted in his dismantling two of the greatest teams ever.

In the five-year span from 1910 to 1914, his Athletics won four pennants. At the end of that 1914 season, the newly formed Federal League began luring some of his best players away. He was forced to sell some of his remaining stars in order to pay his bills. The Athletics plummeted from first place to last place and languished in the cellar for the next seven years. He gradually built up his team to field another collection of stars. From 1925 to 1933, his club never finished lower than third place. But the financial burdens of the Depression and high salary demands of his players forced him once again to sell off his stars.

Connie Mack's Philadelphia Athletics seemed to either finish a season on top or in the cellar. The A's finished first nine times and second seven times, but ended up dead last 17 times.

Mr. Mack, as his players always called him, insisted on a clean-cut image for the players on his team. He would not tolerate any carousing or carrying on by his players. For 50 years he was baseball's most steadfast image, wearing a stiff collar and tie, standing in the dugout waving his ever-present scorecard to position his players. Even before scouting reports on opposing teams became more common (Mack also kept statistics on his own players), he gained a reputation for his uncanny ability to anticipate where opposing batters would hit the ball. He seldom ventured into the clubhouse except for his traditional pregame meetings, in which he insisted that his players review strategy and their opponent's tactics.

Mr. Mack preferred college-educated players on his teams because they "put intelligence and scholarship into the game." Because of his experience as a catcher, his teams were noted for their ability to steal their opponent's signs. Sometimes his players would hold up at second base after hitting a clear triple just so they could relay signs to the next batter to keep the rally alive. Mack believed that pitching is 75 percent of the game of baseball.

Mack was elected to the Hall of Fame in 1937. He retired from baseball 13 years later with a career winning percentage of .484.

John McGraw ("The Little Napoleon")

In John McGraw's eyes, all baseball players were created equal. He had no superstars, no stars, no mediocre players. His teams consisted of players who were willing to be subjected to his iron hand. On the field, his authority was unquestioned. In the record books, his success is undeniable.

Two of McGraw's teams, the 1925 and 1927 Giants, featured seven future Hall of Fame players. During his 33 years as a big league manager, he managed such Hall of Famers as Roger Bresnahan, Hugh Jennings, Christy Mathewson, Casey Stengel, Carl Hubbel, Frankie Frisch, and Rogers Hornsby, to name just a few. He would not tolerate any dissension. In fact, he traded Frankie Frisch for revolting against his authority, and he traded Rogers Hornsby for apparently going after his job. He established 24 records as a Major League skipper, 13 of which are still unbroken after more than 50 years.

McGraw was the epitome of a hands-on manager. He led by example and would often step to the plate or go out on the field to show his team how to make a play. He followed his hard-nosed, feisty style as a player with a managerial dictatorship that made him one of the most successful managers in the history of the game.

As a youngster growing up in Truxton, New York, McGraw was forced to live with relatives after his family split up during a diphtheria epidemic. His relationship with his father was strained. His father, a railroad laborer, considered his son's playing baseball a disgraceful waste of time. Once he beat the young McGraw for shattering windows in a church located in right-center field of a sandlot field. But McGraw refused to give up the game and instead learned to hit to left field, a skill that benefitted him as a professional known for his prowess at the hit-and-run play.

As a player, John McGraw posted a career on-base percentage (.465) that places him second only to Ted Williams (.483) on the all-time list.

While in his teens, McGraw quit school to sell candy for a railroad company. He was pitching for a local team, the Truxton Grays, and a few other popular teams in the area when he was spotted by a scout and signed to a minor league contract for $40 a month. While playing in the minor leagues, he was converted from a pitcher to a third baseman. In August 1891, he made it to the Major Leagues at age 18 when he signed with the Baltimore Orioles of the fledgling American Association. The following year, the Orioles were admitted to the National League.

As a Major League ballplayer, McGraw became famous as a gutsy performer who would play with pain. He once played for weeks with a splintered collarbone. Batting behind future Hall of Famer Wee Willie Keeler, McGraw perfected the hit-and-run play. He and Keeler gained reputations for handling the bat exceptionally well. Both would stand in the box and foul off a dozen or more pitches until the pitcher finally served up a fat one or simply walked them.

The Baltimore Orioles of the 1890s were a team characterized by their stretching of the rules to the limits of dirty play. McGraw himself, who often sharpened his spikes before games, was a leader on a team that would block, trip, and generally obstruct base runners while the umpire followed the flight of the ball. On the field he was a master strategist. He ended his playing career in 1906 with an excellent lifetime batting average of .334.

McGraw began his career as a manager while still enjoying success as a player. At age 26, he was appointed player-manager of the Orioles in 1899. He served that double duty only one season before he was traded to the National League St. Louis club. He played only one season in St. Louis before he rejoined the Orioles (now in the American League) as a player-manager.

In the middle of the 1902 season, he jumped back over to the National League when he became a player-manager with the New York Giants. He remained with the Giants for the next 30 years. When he arrived in New York, he turned a second-division team into a contender. In 1904, his team won 106 games and the pennant, but he and owner John T. Brush refused to play the Red Sox in the World Series. In 1905, the Giants took their second consecutive pennant with a 105-48 record and agreed to play the A's in the Fall Classic. They whipped the A's in five games behind Christy Mathewson's three shutouts. In 1906, McGraw displayed his characteristic brazen style when he had "Champions of the World" emblazoned on his team's jerseys.

In 1916, John McGraw's New York Giants won 26 games in a row, making him the only manager ever to win that many consecutive games. The Giants also posted a 17-game winning streak that season. But despite the two streaks, McGraw's team finished the season in fourth place.

McGraw displayed his feisty attitude and fiery temper to his players, his opponents, umpires, and fans. He once got into a fight with Pirates manager Fred Clarke. He was fined a whopping $1500 for slugging umpire Bill "Lord" Byron. "The only road to popularity is to win," he once said. "The man who loses gracefully loses easily. Sportsmanship and easy-going methods are all right, but a good hard fight brings out the crowds."

The "long-ball game" popularized by Babe Ruth in the 1920s never appealed to McGraw. As a manager, he loved the running game and stealing bases. His 1911 club stole a record 347 bases. McGraw's ideal game was when he scored the most runs on the fewest hits. He thought raw speed had little to do with good baserunning. His system was based on ballplayers who could think. He disdained conservative baseball as bad baseball. He preferred the hit-and-run play to the sacrifice and he hated the squeeze play (a good pitcher can always throw wide, he would say). He is credited with inventing the cutoff play from the outfield during the 1922 season. He insisted on signalling players at bat and on the field before every pitch of a ball game and would not tolerate those who ignored his signals.

McGraw was friends with Giants coach Wilbert Robinson for more than 30 years. Their friendship ended when McGraw accused Robinson of missing a sign and costing the Giants a game. McGraw once fined outfielder Red Murray for missing a bunt sign with a runner on second. Murray had swung away on a high-and-tight fastball that most certainly would have been impossible to bunt and deposited it in the outfield bleachers.

McGraw managed more years, more games, and won more pennants than any other National League skipper in history. His .589 winning percentage ranks in the all-time top ten. He and rival Connie Mack were the first managers to be elected to the Hall of Fame in 1937.

Joe McCarthy ("Marse Joe")

Some baseball historians contend that Joe McCarthy was simply in the right spot at the right time. They claim that throughout his managerial career he was always blessed with great teams and that he was not a great manager. But the statistics belie that theory. He managed for 24 years in the Major Leagues and always finished in the first division. He was the first manager to win pennants in both the American League and the National League. He posted a 29-9 record in World Series competition. His .614 winning percentage after 3500 games as a manager has never been equalled and his six seasons of winning more than 100 games is also a record.

While it may be true that McCarthy was blessed with some great teams, he had a great understanding of the psychology of handling the superstars. McCarthy could spot talent and he knew how to realize the full potential of that talent. He took a chance on a minor league player named Joe DiMaggio, who played his way into the Hall of Fame. He picked up Ellis Kinder, a castoff pitcher with Boston, and turned him into a 23-game winner.

McCarthy would memorize the box scores. He always knew who was hot and who was not. McCarthy never ordered DiMaggio to steal bases for fear he would injure his knees and hinder his play in the outfield. He wisely never took the bat out of Lou Gehrig's hands by ordering him to sacrifice bunt. McCarthy was the ideal player's manager, even though he himself never played in the Major Leagues.

When he was growing up in Philadelphia during the 1880s, McCarthy was a devoted follower of Connie Mack and the Philadelphia Athletics. His father died when he was a teenager and he was forced to work in a textile factory to support his mother. He suffered a broken kneecap while playing sandlot baseball, an injury that may have kept him from making it to the big leagues.

Joe McCarthy's pennant-winning clubs never felt the pressure of a tight race. The nine pennant-winning clubs he managed finished their seasons nine or more games ahead of the second-place team. Five of his teams missed winning the pennant by four games or fewer.

McCarthy did play minor league ball for 12 years, and in 1919 he became the player-manager for the Louisville club of the American Association. In 1925, his club collected 102 victories. His accomplishments were noticed by William Wrigley, owner of the Chicago Cubs, and in 1926 Wrigley hired the 39-year-old McCarthy to manage the Cubs. McCarthy joined a ball club that had finished dead last in 1925. Under his guidance, the Cubs finished in the first division the next four seasons, culminating with the pennant in 1929.

At the end of that season he faced his idol Connie Mack and the Philadelphia Athletics in the World Series. The Cubs lost the series and Wrigley forced McCarthy to resign under pressure.

The Yankees signed McCarthy and after two years as the Yankee skipper, he collected a pennant and a World Series triumph over Wrigley's Cubs. From 1932 to 1941, McCarthy's Yankees won seven World Series championships.

McCarthy's basic philosophy was to always have a good double-play combination. Defense was stressed on teams that featured Babe Ruth, Gehrig, and DiMaggio. He considered his pitcher a fifth infielder and insisted that all his pitchers be good fielders.

Joe McCarthy was inducted into the Hall of Fame in 1957.

Casey Stengel ("The Ol' Perfessor")

As any fan is aware, Casey Stengel was one of the most colorful characters ever to step onto a baseball field. His days as a player and as a manager were punctuated with timeless quips and mischievous shenanigans. Underneath the guise of class clown, Stengel possessed enough guile to get elected to the Hall of Fame.

When he was born in Kansas City, Missouri, in 1890, Stengel's parents named him Charles. He acquired the nickname "KC" because of his birthplace, and later in life sportswriters began spelling out his nickname until he finally became known simply as Casey.

Stengel's brother, Grant, was the athlete of the family and was the early favorite to have a career in baseball. Casey was a bowlegged, jug-eared youngster seldom picked by his neighborhood pals to play in sandlot pickup games. But the popular Grant refused to participate in the games unless his younger brother could play.

Casey was not a good student. Some of his problems in school were caused by the fact that he was left-handed. One teacher in particular tried unsuccessfully to convert him into a right-handed student. He played varsity baseball at Central High School and graduated with good enough grades to be accepted at Western Dental College in Kansas City. He showed more interest in playing pranks, however, than he did in his pursuit of a dental career. Again, most of his disinterest in schooling was attributable to the fact that all of the dental equipment at the college was for right-handed students. Once he was given the opportunity to play professional baseball, Stengel dropped the idea of becoming a dentist.

He signed a contract for $135 a month to pitch for the Kansas City Blues of the American Association in 1910. After two years with the Blues, he was converted from a pitcher to an outfielder.

In 1912 he was purchased by Brooklyn of the National League and hit .316 his first month with the club. "I broke in 4 for 4 and folks thought I was the next Ty Cobb. It took them about four days to get over that," Stengel recounted. The next season the 22-year-old hit .272 with 7 home runs and 43 RBI. During the off-season, he joined his former high school coach in piloting the University of Mississippi baseball team. Stengel talked so much about his off-season college exploits that his Brooklyn teammates began calling him "Perfessor."

Casey loved to clown around on the ball field. At one of his first spring training camps, Stengel found a manhole cover over some water pipes in the lush outfield grass. Stengel managed to squeeze himself down past the surface, but still maintain a vantage point for the action on the field. When a fly ball was hit in his direction, his teammates wondered where he had gone. Casey then sprung from the hole holding the metal cover over his head and made the catch.

In 1937, the Dodgers paid Casey Stengel not *to manage the Bums from Brooklyn. The following year he was hired as the skipper of the Boston Braves. During his nine years as a manager for the Dodgers and the Braves, his teams never finished higher than fifth place.*

In 1914 he batted .316, but began showing lapses in concentration except during late-season "must" games and in postseason play. In spite of his many pranks and antics (which fit in well with this team), Brooklyn won the pennant in 1916. Although Stengel batted .364 in the World Series, Babe Ruth's Red Sox took the World Championship. Following the 1917 season, Stengel became a journeyman player.

John McGraw's Giants signed him in 1921. His stint with the Giants would influence him later in his career. McGraw platooned him against right-handed pitchers. He hit .368 for McGraw in 1922 and .339 in 1923. The Giants won the pennant both seasons, and Stengel starred in the 1923 World Series with a .417 batting average and two homers in six games. He concluded his playing days with the Boston Braves in 1925, compiling a career batting average of .284.

In 1934, Casey was hired to be the manager of the National League Brooklyn Dodgers. His managerial records with the Dodgers (1934-1936) and then with the Boston

Braves (1938-1943) were less than noteworthy. After the 1943 season, he managed in the minors for the next five years.

While managing Oakland's Pacific Coast League team, Casey marveled at the bridges in the Bay Area. "Every manager wants to jump off a bridge sooner or later, and it's very nice for an old man to know he doesn't have to walk 50 miles to find one," he said.

In 1948 the Yankees hired him for $35,000 a year to replace Bucky Harris, whom management had blamed for finishing third with a club predicted to win the pennant the previous year. During a rash of injuries on his club in 1949, Casey began platooning such aging stars as Phil Rizzuto, Tommy Henrich, Charlie Keller, and Johnny Lendell. The season came down to the final two games when the Yankees erased a one-game Red Sox lead to take the pennant. The Yankees then lost the World Series to their cross-town rivals in Brooklyn in five games.

While piloting the New York Mets in 1964, Casey Stengel became the only manager ever to go 32 innings in one day without winning a game. In May of that season, his Mets dropped the first game of a doubleheader to the San Francisco Giants in regulation time and then lost the nightcap in 23 innings at Shea Stadium.

During 1949, Stengel began to rely on his relief pitching, theorizing that it was more important to win than to give complete games to his starters. He never pitched his left-handed ace, Whitey Ford, in more than 33 games in a season. He decided to spot-start him rather than use him as a part of the regular pitching rotation. In World Series competition he would often put his starters in the bullpen. Casey always insisted that his pitchers concentrate on location rather than speed. He always encouraged pitchers to learn the sinkerball because it enticed the batters to hit ground balls. "Never heard of anyone gettin' home runs on ground balls," he said.

Casey always insisted that his hitters merely make contact with the ball rather than try to hit it out of the park. He rarely ordered steals or sacrifices to score runs. He loved a good double-play combination. He was the first great manager to achieve success by extensively platooning his ballplayers.

During his 25 years as a Major League manager, Stengel was the most successful skipper in the American League. He was elected to the Hall of Fame in 1966.

Leo Durocher ("The Lip")

When Leo Durocher was 12 years old, his family opened a boarding house in his hometown of Springfield, Massachusetts. Two blocks away lived Rabbit Maranville, a future Hall of Fame second baseman. Durocher's father became good friends with Maranville, and Rabbit would often talk to Leo about baseball. Maranville gave Durocher his first baseball glove (which Durocher later used in his own Major League career). Although Leo listened intently to the wisdom of Maranville, he seemed to shun all other authority. He punched a teacher while he was in the ninth grade and was expelled from school.

Durocher went to work for an electric company, but was signed to a minor league contract after trying out for the Hartford team of the Eastern League. Hartford sold Durocher to the Yankees in 1925. Three years later, Durocher made the Major League squad as a loudmouthed shortstop. Despite the fact that he was small in stature, Durocher would stand up to anyone. He once almost got into a fight with Ty Cobb after he allegedly insulted the Georgia Peach. He once snarled at Babe Ruth for stealing time from him in the batting cage. But Yankee skipper Miller Huggins liked Durocher and told him that as long as he used his head he would have a place in baseball.

The Yankee front office was not as fond of Durocher, however. When Huggins died in 1929, the Yankees shipped Durocher to the Cincinnati Reds. He spent three seasons with the Reds before the St. Louis Cardinals picked him up early in the 1933 season. Durocher coined the phrase "the Gashouse Gang" to describe his Cardinal team that consisted of such stars as Dizzy Dean, Joe Medwick, Frankie Frisch, and Pepper Martin. The Cards won the World Series in 1934. Durocher was appointed captain of the team the following season.

At the end of the 1937 season, the Brooklyn Dodgers traded four players to St. Louis to get Durocher. With three weeks left in a miserable, losing 1938 season, the Dodgers told manager Burleigh Grimes that his contract would not be renewed. The front office asked Grimes if he had a replacement in mind. Grimes recommended Durocher.

At age 33, Durocher became the player-manager of the Dodgers. During his first full season at the helm in 1939, the Dodgers finished in third place behind the Cincinnati Reds and Durocher was named Manager of the Year. He said it was easier to manage from the field than from the dugout. The two things a manager did, he said, were to place fielders and take out a pitcher. Managing was easiest from the field because he was in the middle of the action and could tell much easier when a pitcher was losing it.

As the starting shortstop for the National League in the 1938 All-Star game, Leo Durocher laid down a bunt in the eighth inning. Because of a wild throw to first base and the right fielder playing out of position, Durocher circled the bases for the only bunt home run in All-Star history.

The Dodgers played hard-nosed baseball. They were a team with a blue-collar mentality in which Durocher fit well. The team prided itself on its ability to steal signs, ride opposing players from the bench, and throw high hard ones to batters. The Dodgers finished second in 1940, but they won the pennant in 1941 with a 100-54 season mark.

Although he tried to retire as a player in 1942, World War II claimed several of the team's players, and Durocher was forced play on a part-time basis in the 1943 and 1945 seasons. As a manager only in 1946, he established himself as a shrewd strategist best known for his quick hook with pitchers. Although the Giants finished last that year, Durocher's Dodger pitching staff had fewer complete games than the Giants, primarily because Dodger reliever Hugh Casey had a great year (11-5, 1.98 ERA).

During an interview with reporters in the summer of 1946, Durocher was making a point about how scrappy he wanted his ball club. He was discussing his favorite player, Eddie Stanky, who was known as a battler with a feisty temperament. In that interview, he pointed to his cross-town rivals, managed by Mel Ott. "Take a look at them," he said. "All nice guys. They'll finish last. Nice guys. Finish last." This became Durocher's most famous quote.

During that 1946 season, Durocher was involved in numerous nasty arguments with umpires. He kicked dirt on some umpires' shoes and even threw a wet towel at one.

Long-standing allegations of his involvement with undesirable elements, compounded by his public accusation that a Yankee official was consorting with gamblers, ultimately led to his suspension for the 1947 season.

By 1948, the Dodgers were fed up with Durocher, and they fired him about the time the Giants fired Ott. The Giants hired Durocher and the Lip immediately began cleaning house. He traded Johnny Mize and Sid Gordon. He picked up scrappy players like Alvin Dark and Stanky to play on a team that became known for its use of the hit-and-run, sacrifice bunt, and suicide squeeze. With the Giants, Durocher fell in love with the element of surprise. During his years with the Giants, Durocher managed such greats as Willie Mays and was on the losing end of that famous Yankees-Giants subway World Series known as the "Miracle at Coogan's Bluff" (when Bobby Thompson hit his famous "shot heard around the world").

"What makes a good manager? Players are Number One. Players make the manager all the time," Durocher said. "If you have a ball club that can go out early and get, say, six runs, you try to add four more—three more. You can afford to gamble—hit and run, things like that. The other manager has to catch up. You eliminate his hit-and-run, his bunting. He has to have every man swing. He can't play for one run. He has to get a lot back.

"A manager becomes important in a one-run game. That's where strategy comes in. You have to know who's coming up next. Who's hitting. What your team can do. That's where a manager's thoughts come in. When you're playing for that one run, that's when a manager is important."

Leo Durocher retired from baseball in 1973.

Walter Alston ("Smokey")

Only John McGraw and Connie Mack ever managed their same teams for as long as Walter Alston. During Alston's 23-year managerial career with the Dodgers, he always worked on one-year contracts and came close to being fired more than a dozen times. In all, he won seven pennants and finished in the second division only three times. Alston led the Dodgers to two World Championships (1963 and 1965), and he won his last pennant in 1974.

Alston attributed his love for baseball to his father. His parents were sharecroppers in Darrtown, Ohio, (population 153) until harsh economic conditions forced his father to take a job with Ford Motor Company. In his autobiography, Alston said that next to farming, his dad loved baseball more than anything else.

While pursuing a degree at the College of Education at Miami of Ohio, Alston starred in baseball and basketball. Frank Rickey (the brother of Branch Rickey) saw Alston play baseball and offered him a $125-a-month contract with the St. Louis Cardinals. Alston had strong wrists and forearms that he used to hit the ball a country mile, but he couldn't touch the breaking stuff. He languished in the minors until age 32, when the Cards called him up in 1936.

On the roster of Walter Alson's famous 1955 Dodgers was a 27-year-old pitcher who posted an unimpressive 0-0 record with a whopping 13.50 ERA. That pitcher was Tommy Lasorda, who would succeed Alston as the Dodger skipper more than 20 years later.

Alston's Major League career lasted for one game. He had one at-bat against Lonnie Warneke of the Cubs, but failed miserably at the plate. He had two chances in the field while playing first base, one of which he made and the other he bobbled. Alston was shipped right back to the minors after the game.

In 1940, the Cards appointed Alston player-manager of his minor league team. In 1944 he retired as a player. When Alston retired, Branch Rickey, who was an executive with the Dodgers, hired him as a minor league manager in the Dodger organization. His managerial record was spotty, but he did win two pennants with the Trenton, New Jersey, club of the Inter-State league during the early 1950s. His big break came in 1953, when the Dodgers fired Chuck Dressen over a contract dispute and offered the job to Alston.

During his first season as the Dodgers skipper, the Bums from Brooklyn were predicted to be a pennant winner, but finished the season in second place. Alston had managed no fewer than 17 members of that club in the minor leagues. In 1955, with such stars as Jackie Robinson, Roy Campanella,

Don Newcombe, and Duke Snider, Alston's Dodgers finished 13 1/2 games ahead of the second-place Boston Braves.

The seventh game of the 1955 World Series against his cross-town rivals, the Yankees, exemplified Alston's conservative managerial style. The Dodgers led 1-0 in the sixth with Johnny Podres on the mound for the Bums. Pee Wee Reese led off the Dodgers' sixth with a single, and Alston ordered Snider to sacrifice him over. Snider was safe at first on an error. So Alston ordered Campanella to sacrifice, which he executed successfully to put runners on second and third with one out. Gil Hodges lofted a sacrifice fly to make the score 2-0. In the bottom of the inning, Alston moved Junior Gilliam from left field to second base and put the faster Sandy Amoros in left. The Yankees had runners on first and second with nobody out and Yogi Berra at the plate. Alston shifted Amoros to left center where Berra usually placed his most powerful hits. Podres got Berra to hit a bad pitch down the foul line, apparently destined to score the two runners. Amoros raced after the ball, caught it on the dead run, whirled and threw the ball back to the infield and doubled the runner at first to kill the rally. Alston's insurance run in the top of the inning and his defensive replacement in the bottom of the inning earned him a Series-ending 2-0 win.

When Walter Alston's Brooklyn Dodgers won the World Championship in 1955, it marked the first time since 1890 they had come close to winning in post-season competition. It would be the only championship the team would celebrate in Brooklyn.

The following year the Dodgers again faced the Yankees in the World Series, but this time came up short after battling for seven games. The Bums had aged as a team. Robinson retired, Reese was 38 years old, Campanella was plagued with injuries, and the Dodgers began to falter. But Alston began using the Dodger farm system to rebuild his team.

The Dodgers finished third in 1957 during their "swan song season" at Ebbets Field. At the end of the 1957 season, the team moved west to Los Angeles. In 1958, the Dodgers finished seventh and Alston was almost fired. However, in 1959 the team boasted such stars as Don Drysdale and a rookie named Maury Wills. The new Los Angeles Dodgers played in a makeshift stadium until a new one could be built. In their second year, the new Dodgers beat the Braves in a two-game playoff to take the pennant, and then won the World Series from the Chicago White Sox. Alston recognized that he no longer had a power-hitting ball club and shifted his strategy to fit a faster team, behind the great pitching of Drysdale and Sandy Koufax.

Alston was known as an ultra-conservative manager. In his later years as the Dodger skipper, he almost always went by the book on left-right platoon combinations.

Walter Alston was elected to the Hall of Fame in 1983.

The Edit Managers Utility

With a perspective on these great managers from baseball history, you can use the Edit Managers utility from the Commissioner II program to establish strategies and tendencies for the manager of your ball club. When you invoke the Edit Managers utility from the main menu of the Commissioner II program, you see the screen shown in Figure 12-1. The names of the managers on the left side of the screen represent the managers for teams in your current league. (See Chapter 10, "The Commissioner's Tools," for a complete discussion on current leagues.)

This utility provides two modes of editing. The Quick Edit mode enables you to establish managerial tendencies for 19 separate categories shown on the right side of the screen. The Zoom In mode allows you to fine-tune these tendencies by supplying you with various subcategories in the 19 tendencies provided in the Quick Edit mode.

Quick Edit Mode

The Quick Edit mode is a brief version of the Edit Managers utility. When you highlight the name of a manager on the left side of the screen, his tendencies for the 19 major categories are displayed on the right side of the screen.

For most of the categories, you have six options to characterize a manager's tendencies. These options are Never, Rarely, Sometimes, Average, Often, and Very Often. The

Figure 12-1.

The opening screen for the Edit Managers utility (Quick Edit mode)

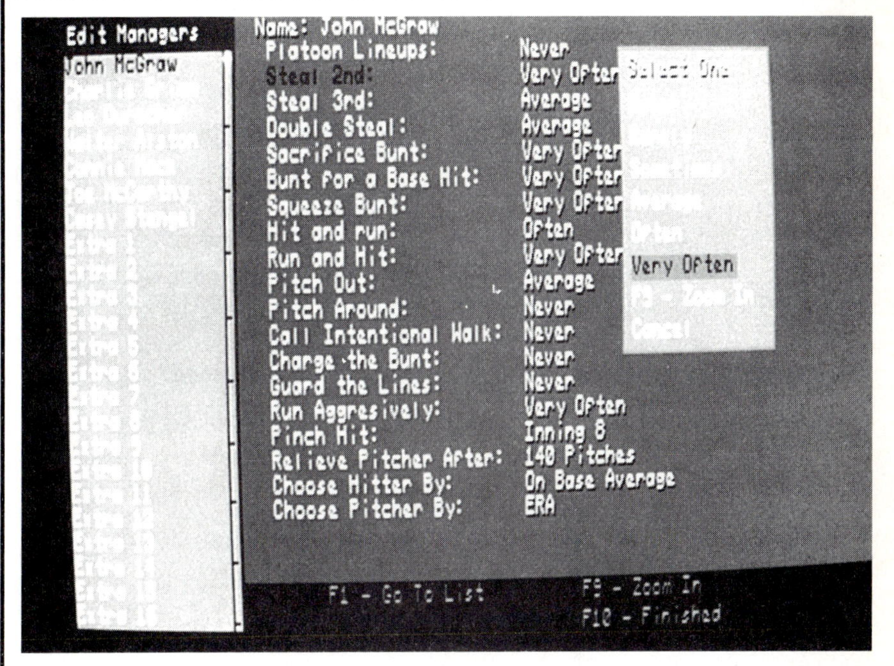

categories in which you can use these options include Platoon Lineup, Steal 2nd, Steal 3rd, Double Steal, Sacrifice Bunt, Bunt for Base Hit, Squeeze Bunt, Hit and Run, Run and Hit, Pitch Out, Pitch Around, Call Intentional Walk, Charge the Bunt, Guard the Lines, and Run Aggressively.

For the Pinch Hit category, you are asked to enter the earliest inning your manager will send in a pinch hitter (4th, 5th, 6th, 7th, 8th, or 9th inning). For the Relieve Pitcher After category, you are asked to supply the minimum number of pitches a starter can throw before being replaced (100, 110, 120, 130, 140, or 150 pitches). In the Choose Hitter By category, you are asked which statistic your manager will consider most important when judging hitters. Your choices are batting average (BA), on-base average (OBA), and slugging average (SA). Similarly, for the "Choose Pitcher By" category, you are asked which statistic your manager will consider most important when judging pitchers. Here your choices are earned run average (ERA), batting average for a batter (BA Batters Faced), strikeout-to-walk ratio (SO/Walks), ground-ball-to-flyball ratio (Grounders/Flies), and home runs per batters faced (HR/Batter Faced).

Table 12-1, located at the end of this chapter, shows the tendencies for each of the seven managers supplied with the EWBII progam. The major categories that you edit in the Quick Edit mode are listed in major sections of the table. Under each major category heading are thick black boxes indicating the tendencies as they are represented in the Quick Edit mode. The majority of the table, however, is data entered through the Zoom In mode.

Zoom In Mode

This mode allows you to fine-tune the strategies of your manager by providing more than 65 questions about the major categories you see in the Quick Edit mode (see Figure 12-2). Most of the questions ask for percentages to indicate how often a particular decision will be made. Use the following percentages for the six options you use in the Quick Edit mode:

Never	0-5%
Rarely	6-30%
Sometimes	31-45%
Average	46-60%
Often	61-75%
Very Often	76-100%

To use the Zoom In mode, highlight the name of the manager you want to edit and press F1. Highlight a category from the Quick Edit list on the right side of the screen and press F9. A separate screen appears for each of the Quick Edit categories. Each screen contains several questions about the categories. To answer the question, scroll down to the answer area on the screen and enter the information in the highlighted area. While you are in the Zoom In mode, you can scroll to

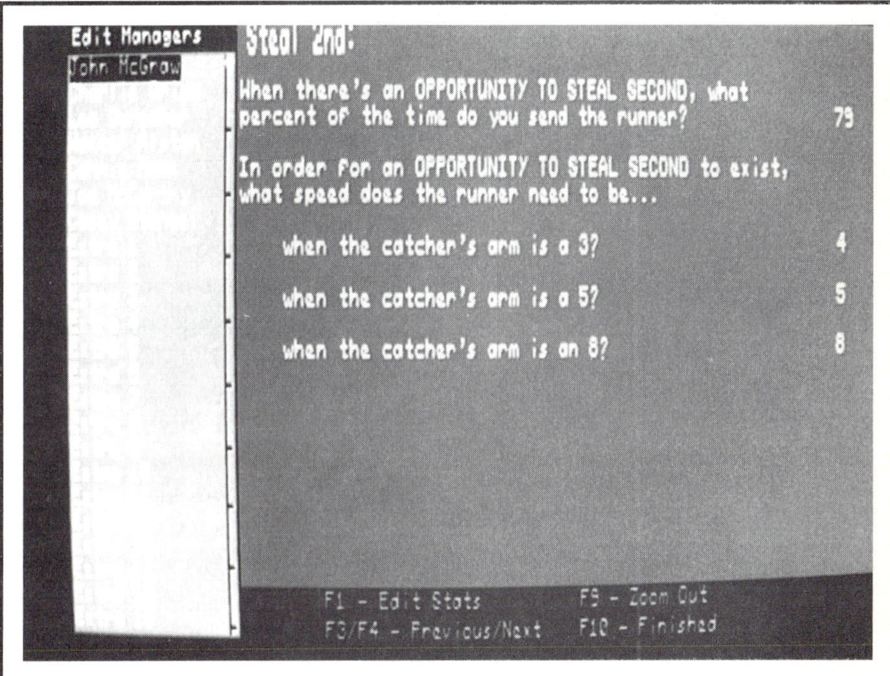

Figure 12-2.

The screen for the Zoom In mode of the Edit Managers utility

the next category by pressing F4, and you can scroll to the previous category by pressing F3. To exit the Zoom In mode, press F9 (Zoom Out).

Each question in the "Zoom In" mode is answered with a number. Some of the questions request percentages, some request player's EWBII ratings (such as for Arm or Power), and some ask for an inning.

The EWBII program provides 25 "extra" managers that you can edit for your team. Be careful if you edit the tendencies for one of the seven managers supplied with the program. If you change a tendency for one of these managers, the default settings are overwritten.

Who's in the Other Dugout?

If you use the Edit Managers utility to program the managers for all the teams in your league, each franchise owner can be assured of individual strategies being followed when games are played in the Super fast stat game mode (see Chapter 2 for a discussion of game modes). If you play games against the computer and not against another League team, then you are playing against Earl Weaver himself. Earl does not appear in the manager's profiles supplied with the Edit Manager's utility. A bit of research, however, can give you some insight to the strategies behind one of the most successful managers ever to grace a Major League dugout.

Table 12-1.

Index to Managerial Strategies

Platoon Lineup

What percent do you platoon your players?

McGraw	Grimm	Durocher	Alston	Mack	McCarthy	Stengel
Never	Avg	Rarely	Never	Avg	Rarely	Very Often
0	50	20	0	50	20	80

Steal 2nd

When there's an opportunity to steal second, what percent of the time do you send the runner?

McGraw	Grimm	Durocher	Alston	Mack	McCarthy	Stengel
Very Often	Avg.	Never	Often	Very Often	Avg.	Rarely
79	50	0	64	79	50	20

In order for the opportunity to steal second to exist, what speed does the runner need to be

when the catcher's arm is a 3?

McGraw	Grimm	Durocher	Alston	Mack	McCarthy	Stengel
4	5	8	5	4	5	5

when the catcher's arm is a 5?

McGraw	Grimm	Durocher	Alston	Mack	McCarthy	Stengel
5	7	8	6	5	7	8

when the catcher's arm is an 8?

McGraw	Grimm	Durocher	Alston	Mack	McCarthy	Stengel
8	8	9	8	8	8	9

Steal 3rd

When there's an opportunity to steal third, what percent of the time do you send the runner?

McGraw	Grimm	Durocher	Alston	Mack	McCarthy	Stengel
Avg.	Rarely	Never	Avg.	Rarely	Rarely	Never
50	20	0	50	20	20	0

Table 12-1.

Index to Managerial Strategies (continued)

Steal 3rd (*continued*)

In order for the opportunity to steal third to exist, what speed does the runner need to be

when the catcher's arm is a 3?

McGraw	Grimm	Durocher	Alston	Mack	McCarthy	Stengel
7	8	8	7	8	8	8

when the catcher's arm is a 5?

McGraw	Grimm	Durocher	Alston	Mack	McCarthy	Stengel
8	9	9	8	9	9	9

when the catcher's arm is an 8?

McGraw	Grimm	Durocher	Alston	Mack	McCarthy	Stengel
10	10	10	10	10	10	10

Double Steal

When there's an opportunity for a double steal, with runners at first and third, what percent of the time do you send the runners?

McGraw	Grimm	Durocher	Alston	Mack	McCarthy	Stengel
Avg	Never	Never	Rarely	Avg	Never	Never
50	0	0	19	50	0	0

In order for the opportunity for a double steal to exist,

what is the minimum speed of the runner at first?

McGraw	Grimm	Durocher	Alston	Mack	McCarthy	Stengel
6	7	7	7	6	7	7

what is the minimum speed of the runner at third?

McGraw	Grimm	Durocher	Alston	Mack	McCarthy	Stengel
4	6	6	5	4	6	6

what is the first inning you consider this double steal?

McGraw	Grimm	Durocher	Alston	Mack	McCarthy	Stengel
7	9	9	9	7	9	9

Sacrifice Bunt

Given a sacrifice bunt situation, what percent of the time do you call this play?

McGraw	Grimm	Durocher	Alston	Mack	McCarthy	Stengel
Very Often	Never	Rarely	Never	Avg	Never	Never
80	0	20	0	50	0	0

What is the earliest inning you would consider calling for a sacrifice bunt?

McGraw	Grimm	Durocher	Alston	Mack	McCarthy	Stengel
3	7	7	7	5	7	7

In order for a sacrifice bunt situation to come up, what is the minimum bunt rating for a

Weak hitter?

McGraw	Grimm	Durocher	Alston	Mack	McCarthy	Stengel
3	7	6	7	4	7	7

Normal hitter?

McGraw	Grimm	Durocher	Alston	Mack	McCarthy	Stengel
6	10	10	10	8	10	10

RBI hitter?

McGraw	Grimm	Durocher	Alston	Mack	McCarthy	Stengel
8	10	10	10	10	10	10

Home Run hitter?

McGraw	Grimm	Durocher	Alston	Mack	McCarthy	Stengel
8	10	10	10	10	10	10

Table 12-1.

Index to Managerial Strategies (continued)

Bunt for Base Hit

Given a bunt for base hit situation, what percent of the time do you call this play?

McGraw	Grimm	Durocher	Alston	Mack	McCarthy	Stengel
Very Often	Rarely	Never	Avg	Often	Rarely	Never
77	19	0	50	66	19	0

In order for a bunt for base hit situation to exist,

what must the minimum speed of the batter be?

McGraw	Grimm	Durocher	Alston	Mack	McCarthy	Stengel
4	8	8	6	5	8	8

what must the minimum bunt rating of the batter be?

McGraw	Grimm	Durocher	Alston	Mack	McCarthy	Stengel
5	7	7	6	6	7	7

what can the minimum power rating of the batter be?

McGraw	Grimm	Durocher	Alston	Mack	McCarthy	Stengel
8	4	3	6	7	4	3

Squeeze Bunt

Given a squeeze bunt situation (with less than two outs), what percent of the time do you call this play?

McGraw	Grimm	Durocher	Alston	Mack	McCarthy	Stengel
Very Often	Never	Never	Rarely	Often	Never	Never
80	0	0	21	66	0	0

In order for a squeeze bunt situation to exist

what must the minimum speed of the runner on third be?

McGraw	Grimm	Durocher	Alston	Mack	McCarthy	Stengel
4	9	9	8	5	9	9

what must the minimum bunt rating of the batter be?

McGraw	Grimm	Durocher	Alston	Mack	McCarthy	Stengel
3	7	7	6	3	7	7

what must the minimum power rating of the batter be?

McGraw	Grimm	Durocher	Alston	Mack	McCarthy	Stengel
3	1	1	1	2	1	1

When the bases are loaded or there are two outs, what percent of the time do you call a "surprise" squeeze?

McGraw	Grimm	Durocher	Alston	Mack	McCarthy	Stengel
80	0	0	20	65	0	0

Table 12-1.

Index to Managerial Strategies (continued)

Hit and Run

Given a hit and run situation, what percent of the time do you call this play?

McGraw	Grimm	Durocher	Alston	Mack	McCarthy	Stengel
Often	Never	Never	Never	Avg	Rarely	Never
66	0	0	0	49	16	0

In order for you to consider a hit and run situation exists, what's the minimum hit and run rating for a

	McGraw	Grimm	Durocher	Alston	Mack	McCarthy	Stengel
Weak hitter?	7	9	9	9	7	9	9
Normal hitter?	5	9	9	9	6	8	9
RBI hitter?	6	8	8	8	6	7	8
Home Run hitter?	7	10	10	10	8	10	10

Run and Hit

Given a sacrifice bunt situation, what percent of the time do you call this play?

McGraw	Grimm	Durocher	Alston	Mack	McCarthy	Stengel
Very Often	Rarely	Never	Rarely	Often	Never	Rarely
80	19	0	19	64	0	19

For a run and hit situation to exist, what's the minimum hit and run rating for a

	McGraw	Grimm	Durocher	Alston	Mack	McCarthy	Stengel
Weak hitter?	6	9	9	9	7	9	9
Normal hitter?	4	7	8	7	5	8	7
RBI hitter?	5	9	9	9	6	9	9
Home Run hitter?	7	9	9	9	8	9	9

What's the minimum speed of the base runner?

McGraw	Grimm	Durocher	Alston	Mack	McCarthy	Stengel
6	8	9	8	7	9	8

Table 12-1.

Index to Managerial Strategies (continued)

Pitch Out

Given a pitch out situation, what percent of the time do you call for a pitch out?

McGraw	Grimm	Durocher	Alston	Mack	McCarthy	Stengel
Avg	Avg	Avg	Avg	Avg	Avg	Avg
51	51	51	51	51	51	51

In order for a pitch out situation to exist, what's the maximum number of balls that can be called on the hitter?

2	2	2	2	2	2	2

In order for a pitch out situation to exist, what's the minimum speed of the base runner

when the catcher's arm is a 3?

6	6	6	6	6	6	6

when the catcher's arm is a 5?

7	7	7	7	7	7	7

when the catcher's arm is an 8?

9	9	9	9	9	9	9

Pitch Around

Given a pitch around situation, what percent of the time do you tell your pitcher to pitch around?

Never	Rarely	Rarely	Never	Never	Avg	Avg
0	20	20	0	0	50	50

Intentional Walk

Given an intentional walk situation, what percent of the time do you call for one?

Never	Rarely	Avg	Never	Rarely	Often	Avg
0	20	50	0	20	65	50

Table 12-1.

Index to Managerial Strategies (continued)

Charge the Bunt

Given a charge the bunt situation, what percent of the time do your fielders charge?

McGraw	Grimm	Durocher	Alston	Mack	McCarthy	Stengel
Never	Never	Never	Never	Never	Never	Never
0	0	0	0	0	0	0

For a charge the bunt situation to exist, what's the minimum bunt rating for a

Weak hitter?

7	7	7	7	7	7	7

Normal hitter?

9	9	9	9	9	9	9

RBI hitter?

10	10	10	10	10	10	10

Home Run hitter?

10	10	10	10	10	10	10

Guard the Lines

Given a guard the lines situation, what percent of the time do your infielders guard the lines

Never	Never	Never	Never	Never	Never	Never
0	0	0	0	0	0	0

What's the earliest inning you consider guarding the lines?

9	9	9	9	9	9	9

How many runs ahead does your team have to be in order for you not to bother to guard the lines?

1	1	1	1	1	1	1

Run Aggressively

What percentage of the time do you call for aggressive base running?

Very Often	Avg	Rarely	Rarely	Very Often	Often	Never
80	50	20	20	80	65	0

What's the earliest inning you call for aggressive base running?

1	3	5	5	1	2	6

How many runs ahead does the other team have to be before you call for aggressive base running?

0	1	2	2	0	1	3

Table 12-1.

Index to Managerial Strategies (continued)

Pinch Hit

What's the earliest inning you pinch hit for a fielder

	McGraw	Grimm	Durocher	Alston	Mack	McCarthy	Stengel
What's the earliest inning you pinch hit for a fielder	8	5	5	4	9	6	9
when your team is behind?	8	5	6	4	9	6	9
when your team is tied?	8	6	7	6	8	7	8
when your team is ahead?	9	7	8	7	9	8	9
when your team is losing by more than 3 runs?	6	4	5	3	7	5	7
when the score is tied?	9	7	8	7	9	8	9
Assume your pitcher averages 100 pitches and is ahead. What's the most number of pitches you let him throw before you pinch hit for him?	130	100	110	100	140	110	140
What's the first inning you put in a pinch runner?	9	7	8	7	9	8	9

Relieve Pitcher After

	McGraw	Grimm	Durocher	Alston	Mack	McCarthy	Stengel
If your pitcher averages 100 pitches and is ahead, what's the most number of pitches you let him throw?	140	150	110	100	140	110	120
What's the most number of runs you let a pitcher give up in one inning?	5	6	4	3	5	4	4
What's the earliest inning you consider bringing in a reliever, even if the pitcher in the game is not tired?	7	8	4	3	7	4	5
What's the earliest inning you consider bringing in a closer?	8	9	7	6	8	7	7

Table 12-1.

Index to Managerial Strategies (continued)

Choose Hitter By

	McGraw	Grimm	Durocher	Alston	Mack	McCarthy	Stengel
	OBA	BA	OBA	OBA	BA	SA	SA
Which stat do you wish to use to define a hitter's types? 1) Batting Avg. 2) On Base Avg. 3) Slugging Avg.	2	1	2	2	1	3	3
A weak hitter has an average less than	300	250	300	300	250	350	350
A normal hitter has an average less than	350	275	350	350	275	400	400
An RBI hitter has an average greater than	400	300	400	400	300	450	450
A Home Run hitter has an average greater than	300	230	300	300	230	450	450
and more home runs last season than	20	15	20	20	15	15	15
Choose these stats in priority order for your hitters (1 is highest priority, 5 is lowest priority, 0 is never)							
Batting average	2	1	2	2	1	3	3
Home runs per at bat	5	5	5	5	5	2	2
On base average	1	4	1	1	4	4	4
Slugging Average	4	3	4	4	3	1	1
Speed	3	2	3	3	2	5	5

Table 12-1.

Index to Managerial Strategies (continued)

Choose Pitcher By

	McGraw	Grimm	Durocher	Alston	Mack	McCarthy	Stengel
	ERA	SO/BB	BA(Batter)	ERA	SO/BB	BA(Batter)	BA(Batter)

Choose these stats in priority order for your starters (1 is highest priority, 5 is lowest priority, 0 is never)

	McGraw	Grimm	Durocher	Alston	Mack	McCarthy	Stengel
ERA	1	4	3	1	4	3	3
BA of batters faced	2	2	1	2	2	1	1
Strike out to walk ratio	3	1	2	3	1	2	2
Ground ball to fly ball ratio	5	5	4	5	5	4	4
Home runs per batter faced	4	3	5	4	3	5	5

Choose these stats in priority order for your middle relievers

	McGraw	Grimm	Durocher	Alston	Mack	McCarthy	Stengel
ERA	1	5	2	1	5	2	2
BA of batters faced	2	4	1	2	4	1	1
Strike out to walk ratio	3	1	3	3	1	3	3
Ground ball to fly ball ratio	5	2	5	5	2	4	5
Home runs per batter faced	4	3	4	4	3	5	4

Choose these stats in priority order for your closers

	McGraw	Grimm	Durocher	Alston	Mack	McCarthy	Stengel
ERA	1	3	3	1	3	3	3
BA of batters faced	3	2	1	3	2	1	1
Strike out to walk ratio	2	1	2	2	1	2	2
Ground ball to fly ball ratio	5	4	4	5	4	4	4
Home runs per batter faced	4	5	5	4	5	5	5

HOF - 1947
FRANKIE FRISCH
ST. LOUIS CARDINALS – 2ND BASE
HOF - 19
DIZZY DEAN
ST. LOUIS CARDINALS – PITCHER
1934
HOF - 1985
ENOS SLAUGHTER
ST. LOUIS CARDINALS – OUTFIELD
1938

CHAPTER 13

Earl's Strategy

"I'm 420 games over .500. That's ten years of 100-60 and then some. So that's gonna stay there. On my tombstone, just write: 'The sorest loser that ever lived.'"

–Earl Weaver, 1986

The Earl Weaver Baseball II program is patterned after a winner. Weaver's career in professional baseball was a showcase for a mediocre ballplayer and a most successful manager whose .583 winning percentage at the Major League level is in the all-time top ten. As the manager for the Orioles, Weaver posted more than 2500 victories and lost less than 1500 games. His Orioles were a dynasty in the 1970s, a team that won six division titles, four pennants, and one World Championship. Together with pitching coach George Bamberger, Weaver managed 22 20-game winners and six Cy Young award winners.

Throughout his 20 years in the minor leagues as a player, player-manager, and manager, and throughout his 17 years as a Major League skipper, Earl Weaver only had one losing season. After he was called out of retirement midway through the 1985 season, Weaver's Orioles won only 71 games in 1986. He retired for good the following year.

The EWBII program is patterned after Earl and the way he managed the game. While you play EWBII, ask for Earl's advice in key situations, and a dialog box will appear with a recommendation from him on what to do. To understand how Earl would manage a certain team and to understand how he would manage in key situations, you should first become familiar with some background on the namesake for EWBII. With that background, you can then examine his managerial strategies for situations that occur while playing EWBII.

Earl's Early Years

As a youngster growing up in St. Louis in the early 1930s, Weaver idolized his two hometown teams, the Cardinals and the Browns. At age five, his parents presented him with a uniform that had Dizzy Dean's famous "Me 'n' Paul" saying emblazoned on the back. He had no doubt that one day he would be a Major League ballplayer.

Weaver met his first big league ballplayers at age 6. Both the Cards and the Browns played their home schedules at Sportsman's Park. His father handled the dry cleaning for both Major League teams, and he would take his son with him to the clubhouses to pick up or deliver uniforms. Earl's rich uncle took the youngster to several ball games a year and Earl went to several more games as a member of the Knothole Gang.

"Even when I was playing ball I could get to the park after my games by the fifth or sixth inning. So throughout my childhood I sat in the stands and studied baseball day after day, second-guessing one of the game's greatest managers, Billy Southworth of the Cardinals, and wondering why...a smooth-swinging switch-hitter like Roy Cullenbine of the Browns could never hit to the opposite field," Weaver said.

As a 13-year-old, Earl began high school in 1944. The Cardinals won their third successive pennant that season, and the Browns won their first ever. It was an all-St. Louis World Series, and Earl would see all six games from the bleachers. The Browns won two of the first three games, but the Cardinal pitching came back, and the Redbirds won the final three games.

Earl's Playing Career

Earl played second base as a freshman at Beaumont High School and played in a summer American Legion league. He celebrated two state championships with those teams. As World War II was raging during those years, Missouri was a prime area for scouts looking for raw talent to fill out rapidly depleting Major League rosters. Fifty minor leagues were in operation. Teams would sign large numbers of kids, hoping for a few gems. A Major League rule prohibiting the signing of prospects before their high school class graduation was waived during World War II and, in fact, that's how Joe Nuxhall pitched for the Cincinnati Reds at age 15.

George Sisler, Jr., a scout with the Dodgers, saw some of Earl's games and sought the permission of Earl's parents for him to play professional baseball. Earl's father told Sisler that the youngster would love to play professional ball, but he hadn't yet celebrated his 14th birthday. Sisler confessed he didn't realize Earl was so young, but that he would be keeping an eye on him.

Weaver's father was a close friend of Freddie Hofmann, a coach with the St. Louis Browns. Earl's father wanted him to play with the Browns because of his friendship with Hofmann and with Bill DeWitt, the owner of the team. Just before Earl's high school graduation, the elder Weaver asked Hofmann for an assessment of Earl's chances in pro ball. Hofmann admitted that Earl would probably be no better than a minor league Class A ballplayer. Walter Shannon, who was in charge of the lower minor leagues for the Cardinals, watched Earl play most of his high school games and constantly encouraged him. Earl went through several tryouts with both the Cardinals and the Browns during the next three years.

Upon his high school graduation, Earl and his father went to the Browns front offices to talk to DeWitt, who offered Earl a contingency contract to play minor league ball. That meant agreeing to play for a monthly salary and collecting a bonus at the end of five months. Earl recalled stories of youngsters who signed such contracts only to be cut before the end of the five-month period, thus never collecting the bonus money. He refused DeWitt's offer. Earl and his father then walked down the hall to the Cardinals' offices, where the Cards offered Earl a Class B minor league contract for $175 a month and a $1500 signing bonus. Earl agreed to the terms.

At age 17, Earl Weaver boarded a bus and headed for the Cardinals' minor league training camp. Following spring training, he was assigned to a Class D club in West Frankfort, Illinois. He quickly established himself as a hustling ballplayer who knew that at 5'6" and 170 pounds he was too small to become a power hitter. He did hit .268 and scored 96 runs, a performance that earned him a promotion to C ball for the 1949 season. That year, the 18-year-old Weaver hit .282 with more than 100 walks. He decided that as a little guy he would do whatever he could to get on base. Throughout his minor league career, Weaver never struck out more than 35 times a season.

Earl Weaver once said, "It's what you learn after you know it all that counts."

Earl made the All-Star team that season and was promoted to a Class B ball club. For the third year in a row, his team finished first, and for the second year in row, Weaver made the All-Star team with a .276 average. He tried out for Class AA the following spring, but was sent back to play with Omaha of the Class A Western League. The manager of that club was George Kissell, who later coached in the Major Leagues for the Cardinals. Earl learned strategies and fundamentals from Kissell that stayed with him throughout his baseball career. Such Kissell strategies as the cutoff-and-relay system and the double steal (where the opposing pitcher holds the ball while he decides whether to make a play on a runner stealing second or a runner stealing home) were later modified and incorporated into the Baltimore Orioles system.

For contractual reasons, the Cardinals bought out Earl's minor league options and invited him the next year to the Major League spring training camp in Florida. Despite a good camp (where he got to play with some of the heros of his childhood), the Cardinals sent him down to the minor league Class AA club in Houston. Over the next few years, he bounced around from Class AA ball (New Orleans) and to Class A ball (Knoxville). He was beginning to realize that Freddie Hofmann's assessment of his talent was accurate.

Earl's Managing Career

While playing for the independent Knoxville club, Earl was offered the job of player-manager, which he gladly accepted. While he was managing the club, the Orioles sent an assistant from their farm system to investigate the possibility of Knoxville becoming an Oriole farm team. The assistant sent a good report on Weaver (the manager) back to the front office. That winter, the director of the Orioles' farm system offered Earl a job managing one of the Class D minor league clubs.

"I was excited," Earl said. "I had crossed the paths of a lot of former players who had made a decent living by staying in this game they loved and had learned so much about. Many of the most successful managers had been mediocre ballplayers like myself, because those of us with limited abilities had to think more and play smart baseball to sustain a professional playing career on any level."

Earl learned to look for young talent way up in the minor league system. That way he could put together winning clubs and, at the same time, help the parent club. He decided in 1960 that his days as a player were about over and played himself less and less. He did make one more appearance in the field five years later when his second baseman hurt his leg in the ninth inning of a game and Earl went in for the final three outs.

In the fall of 1960, Earl began managing Instructional League teams in Arizona. The following year he was named the director of the Orioles central spring training camp and was assigned responsibility of establishing a system of techniques and fundamentals to be used by every club in the organization below the Triple A level.

The Baltimore Orioles, under skipper Hank Bauer, won the World Championship by sweeping the Dodgers in the 1966 Fall Classic. The following season, the Birds finished in the second division. Over the previous five seasons, Weaver's minor league clubs had finished in first or second place. In 1963, 1965, and 1967, Weaver's team lost the pennant on the last day of the season. In 1964 and 1966, his team won the pennant on the last day.

Oriole General Manager Harry Dalton fired Bauer's coaching staff (but not Bauer) following the 1967 debacle and replaced them with men that Weaver had recommended. He hired Weaver as the Orioles first-base coach to begin the 1968 season. By the All-Star break midway through the season, the Orioles were 12 games behind the Tigers. The front office fired Bauer and named Weaver as the new manager of the Orioles.

The Orioles played .700 ball the second half of the season under Weaver, but didn't close the gap on the Tigers (who eventually won the pennant, 12 games ahead of the Orioles). The Orioles fielded an outfield consisting of Paul Blair, Merv Rettenmund, and Frank Robinson that season, and an infield anchored by Brooks Robinson, Dave Johnson, and Boog Powell, with Elrod Hendricks behind the plate. Following the end of the season, Dalton asked Earl what was needed to win the pennant in 1969. Earl recommended solid starting pitching, which thus began Weaver's building of a formidable pitching staff.

Earl Weaver was constantly listening to his pitching ace Jim Palmer complain about various physical ailments. When Palmer told Weaver he had a problem with the ulna nerve in his arm, Weaver thought he made up a new ailment. Later, when Weaver was experiencing swelling in his hand, he consulted a doctor who told him he had an ulna nerve problem. "I must've caught it from Jim Palmer," Weaver said.

During that first half-season as the Orioles' manager, Weaver convinced the front office to finally institute an idea he had formulated over the years. He wanted statistics on players' performances against every pitcher in the league and how each of his pitchers had fared against every batter they faced. The new reports included the types of every pitch thrown by an Oriole, the location, and where the ball landed when it was hit. Advance scouts would tell Weaver the tendencies of opposing pitchers and how they pitched in different situations.

For the next 17 years as manager of the Orioles, Weaver would conduct pregame meetings with his pitching coach, pitchers, and catchers to discuss the opposing starting lineup and how to pitch to each batter. He would pass along the information about opposing pitchers to his hitters so they knew what to look for. Weaver became the master of the pregame statistical scouting reports on opponents. This scouting became an integral part of the Weaver managerial strategy.

Earl's Strategy

If you rely on Earl's strategy while playing EWBII, you should know his tendencies in certain situations. While playing games in the manage-only mode, you select strategies by pressing the SPACEBAR and selecting from the options shown in offensive and defensive strategy menus (see Chapter 2, "Playing the Game," for complete details on playing EWBII). If you have selected the Auto Strategy Menus option in the Ground Rules menu, these strategy options will appear automatically on the screen.

If you play games against the computer, Earl will be your opposing manager. Decisions by the computer in key situations reflect how the developers of EWBII programmed Earl's strategies into the game. Remember, if you need advice in certain situations, you can always ask Earl by selecting the Earl option from the strategy menus. To be an effective manager in EWBII, you should be familiar with Earl's stated philosophies and strategies. An effective way to understand how Earl manages a game is to examine several of the options in the strategy menus to see how Earl views each strategy.

Offense

The offensive strategy menu consists of such options as Lineup (how to set your batting order, who to pinch hit, and so on in the Lineup screen described in Chapter 2), Bunt (telling the batter to bunt), H&R, (the hit-and-run play), R&H (the run-and-hit play), Take (instructing the hitter to try to get a base on balls), steal options (second, third, and home), D steal (for the double-steal play), and Squeeze (the squeeze bunt play).

Lineup

Earl admits that the first inning is the only inning a manager can really set a batting order that will be followed exactly as he wants. Earl agrees with a discussion in Chapter 9 about various positions in the batting order serving specific functions to the offensive strategy of the team.

Because you want as many men on base as possible when the cleanup hitter steps into the box, you want your first three slots in the batting order to consist of good on-base hitters. The leadoff hitter, according to Earl, should be someone who has a high on-base percentage, who can draw 70 or more walks a season, and who hits for a high average. Some managers will use a good bunter as the second hitter in the lineup so that he can bunt over the leadoff man. Earl doesn't like to use the bunt that often, so he often looks for a good contact hitter, one who can execute the run-and-hit play. The third man in the lineup must not only be able to get on base, but also drive in some runs. The fifth spot needs to be a power hitter so that the pitcher cannot pitch around the cleanup hitter.

Weaver's managerial strategies rely heavily on statistics showing how hitters fare against individual pitchers. Using the same lineup against all pitchers may be acceptable, but you must be able to make adjustments in your lineup to account for slumps and weaknesses against various pitchers. If no statistics are available on how your hitters do against individual pitchers, then you must determine how the opposing pitcher has performed against other clubs. For example, if your team is facing a pitcher who is a poor fielder or has trouble holding on runners, load the top of your lineup with speedy players.

Since the days of Casey Stengel in the 1950s, platooning has become an offensive weapon favored by many managers, including Weaver. As discussed in Chapter 6, right-handed hitters perform best against left-handed pitchers and vice versa because it is easier to hit a ball breaking toward you than away from you. This all boils down to getting the right hitter to the plate at the right time.

During his first half-season as the manager of the Orioles, Weaver had outfielder Curt Blefary (a left-handed hitter who had difficulty hitting left-handed pitching), catcher Andy Etchebarren (a right-handed hitter who had difficulty hitting right-handed pitching), and outfielder Paul Blair (a right-handed hitter who was excellent defensively). The Orioles acquired outfielder Don Buford from the White Sox, a switch hitter who was excellent at getting on base, running the bases, and stealing bases, but only adequate defensively. One of Weaver's first moves as a manager was to platoon Blair and

Reggie Jackson once ignored Weaver's edict that no base runner could steal on his own. With a lefty on the mound and left-handed hitter Lee May at the plate, Jackson stole second. The pitcher walked May and the following pinch hitter made the inning-ending out. When Jackson returned to the dugout, Weaver said, "Yeah, you stole. That opens first base. The left-hander walks May. Then I've got to bring in a right-handed pinch hitter. I had the gun loaded with May. You take the bat out of his hands and make me waste another player. That's what the stolen base got us." Jackson never ran on his own again as an Oriole.

Blefary, play Buford all the time in leadoff spot, and platoon Etchebarren with Elrod Hendricks, a left-handed hitting catcher.

When a team begins losing games 1-0, 2-1, or 3-2, you need to add some punch to your lineup. Earl believes it is bad for a team when a pitcher takes the mound with the notion that he has to throw a shutout to win. Good bench players can supply that needed punch. When teams are not hitting, they are simply not going to win.

Weaver always had a definite recipe in mind when putting together his Major League roster. "You should have 9 pitchers and 16 position players available. The ideal situation is to have a right-handed hitting catcher, left-handed hitting catcher, and a catcher who can go behind the plate and play other positions. Then you'll need one starter each at first base, second base, shortstop, and third base, and two utility infielders to back them up. That makes nine. Now you can either have seven outfielders or six outfielders and a third utility infielder. That's the way I would select if I was selecting off the roster. Ideally, I'd have four right-handed hitting infielders, three left-handed hitting infielders, and as many switch hitters as I can get in there."

Weaver considers bench players as offensive weapons rather than as defensive replacements. "A manager is always weighing a player's defense against his offense to determine if he should be in the lineup," Weaver says. "I don't think the occasional extra base that could be given up is worth sacrificing much offense for, however. The players who are your regulars are more than likely pretty good defensive ballplayers, so on my bench I emphasized hitting. The bench guys are around for offense. They'll step into the lineup if some of your nine guys on the field aren't producing offensively."

The Bunt

Weaver has often said the most precious possessions on offense are the 27 outs you are allowed in a 9-inning game. He doesn't like the sacrifice bunt because in essence you are giving up one of three outs in an inning and making things harder on yourself. As a manager, you must be sure that the one or two runs you are bunting for will win a ball game. If this is not the case, then it doesn't make much sense to call for a bunt.

Bunting in the second or third inning makes no sense to Earl because you don't know that early in a ball game how many runs a pitcher will give up. You can, of course, use the ERA of the opposing pitcher to see how many runs he usually gives up in a 9-inning game. You must be conscious of which hitter you ask to bunt and who follows that hitter in the order. After all, the opposing pitcher can always walk the following hitters (in effect taking the bats out of their hands) if you use the bunt to advance a runner to scoring position.

"The fact is that it is easier to score a man from first with no outs than it is to bring him home from second with two outs. I also believe you can score a runner from second with none out easier than you can score him from third with one out. The only time to sacrifice is when the hitter appears to have no chance of advancing the runner," Earl says.

Bunting is not the key to success, according to Earl. "The Yankees didn't bunt when they won nine pennants in ten years. The '69, '70, and '71 Orioles didn't bunt while winning pennants. The '72 Orioles didn't bunt, either, and then Chan Keith wrote a four-part series on why we finished five games out of first and said, in essence, we lost because we didn't bunt. There are more games won on two-run and three-run homers than on sacrifice bunts. And it don't take no philosopher or genius to make that comment."

Hit-and-Run/Run-and-Hit

In Earl Weaver's mind, the hit-and-run is the worst play in baseball. The runner is going half speed to second base and watching to see if the ball has even been hit by the batter. If the batter fails to connect, the runner is thrown out 90 percent of the time. The batter, on the other hand, is forced to swing at anything thrown to him in order to protect the runner. The hit-and-run puts everyone at a disadvantage, according to Earl.

The hit-and-run play is giving the opposition an out. The only good thing Earl sees about the hit-and-run is that it keeps you out of double plays. But compared to the times caught stealing, the weak ground balls, and the line-drive double plays that often result from the hit-and-run play, that advantage quickly disappears.

A better variation of this play (and one favored by Weaver) is the *run-and-hit.* In this play, the runner is running full speed in an effort to steal second base and the hitter has the option of swinging at a good pitch or letting a bad pitch go by. With a right-handed hitter at the plate, this play opens up the right side of the infield because the second baseman will cover second on the steal attempt. The run-and-hit play also affords the runner the luxury of choosing on which pitch to run and when he has a good jump off first base.

Bases on Balls

Sometimes a walk can win a ball game. If a batter leads off an inning with a walk when you are two runs down, you could be tied with just one swing of the bat. This is just the kind of scenario that Earl loves.

A manager must use a batter's on-base percentage to gauge when to order the hitter to take pitches in order to get a base on balls. Earl is fond of citing two of his players as examples for how valuable a walk can be. In 1982, Glenn Gulliver played 50 games for the Orioles, hit a meager .200, but drew 37 walks. Projected over the course of a season, he would have walked 120 times. Don Buford (another favorite example of Earl's) hit .318 on an Oriole club that had a .273 team batting average in 1980, but also drew 78 walks. In both cases, the walks were almost as important to the club as each player's hits.

Earl notes that a player who can draw the walk adds another dimension to batting in the leadoff or No. 2 spot in the order.

Stolen Bases

Weaver sticks by the book when it comes to steals. In order for a steal to be an effective offensive weapon, the runner must be successful 75 percent of the time. The runner must be aware of who is at the plate and who is waiting on-deck so that a pitcher cannot walk a dangerous hitter to occupy an open base. Earl doesn't like to put on the steal sign with two outs and a power hitter at the plate. He notes that a double will score a fast runner from first base, whereas using the stolen base to get a runner into scoring position might allow the pitcher to pitch around the power hitter.

Like the bunt, Earl views the stolen base as a play for one run. It can improve your chances to score a runner, but it also makes things tougher for the hitter. Not only can the pitcher not give the batter any good pitches to hit (because he can walk him without advancing another runner), the first baseman is no longer holding a runner on first base, thus closing one of the holes on the right side of the infield.

Earl says that speed is a tremendous asset to any ball club. But any team should be built with power hitters first, and the speed added around them. In 1973, the American League Eastern Division champion Orioles posted a 97-65 record. That team only hit 119 home runs all year and Earl Williams led the club with 22. This was a team built on speed. The Orioles that year stole 140 bases and were caught stealing only 64 times. This team won fewer games than any of the division-winning teams managed by Earl Weaver.

The importance of stealing depends on the team and the stadium in which the team plays its home games. Earl says that Tiger Stadium and Fenway Park are bad stadiums in which to steal (because they are such hitter's parks), but Yankee Stadium and Baltimore Stadium are just the opposite.

The Double Steal

Earl does not like to use this play unless you have two outs in an inning with runners on first and third. This play (which Earl learned while playing in the minors for George Kissell) is designed to get one run and should only be used in close games. Weaver liked to use the double steal in extra innings, but would not use it in, say, the eighth inning unless his team was ahead by two and needed an insurance run.

This is a very dangerous play. The key to success with the double steal is to make the pitcher play the runner on first base and forget about the runner on third long enough for him to score. The double steal seems to be more effective with a lefty on the mound because from the stretch position, the pitcher faces the runner on first and can only glance over his shoulder at the runner on third. After the pitcher has completed checking the runners, the man at first takes a big enough lead to be picked off. The runner on third breaks for home the second the pitcher takes his eye away from third (in effect, the runner on third is moving before the throw to first). If the pitcher throws to first, the runner going home cannot be caught and will cross the plate before the guy at first is tagged out.

Because it will only work against certain pitchers, the double steal is not a good percentage play.

The Squeeze Play

The *suicide squeeze bunt* (bunting the ball with a runner bearing down on the plate from third base) is the most dangerous play in baseball, according to Weaver. It can win or lose a game right then and there. The opposing team has no way to defend against a squeeze bunt, but everything must work precisely in order for it to be successful. The play fails when the runner breaks too early, when the batter misses the sign, when the batter fails to make contact with the ball, or when the batter doesn't bunt the ball in fair territory on the ground. Because of all these chances for things to go wrong, Earl prefers the base hit or a sacrifice fly ball to get the runner home from third.

"Some managers liked to try a squeeze bunt or suicide squeeze almost any time they found themselves with a man on third, less than two outs, and a mediocre hitter up," Earl says. "I disagree, because a slow groundball or a flyball can get that run in, so why give up an out when you've got the chance for a bigger inning? I don't believe in giving away an out at any time. (You've only got 27 in a nine-inning game, why cut that number?) The only occasion that might call for a squeeze bunt is late in a game when your hitter is known to strike out a lot against the pitcher on the mound."

Defense

For more than a dozen of the years that Weaver managed the Orioles, the team finished either first or second in fielding percentage. In all, players on his teams won 30 Gold Gloves. Weaver always insisted that fielding was more than simply catching the ball. The defensive players must know when the opposition will bunt, when a runner will steal, how the pitcher is throwing, and how the batter is hitting.

To achieve this defensive success and to win ball games, Earl kept certain types of players in mind for certain defensive spots in his lineups. He also expressed definite opinions on the positioning of his fielders.

Infield

The first baseman and the third baseman traditionally represent offensive power hitters for a club. The first baseman, according to Earl, does not have to be specifically right-handed or specifically left-handed, although a left-hander does have an easier throw to second base. The third baseman does not need to be speedy, but a strong arm is an asset for the longest throw in the infield.

Up the middle, Earl insists on a good double-play combination because the DP is a team's best defensive weapon. Any time the opposition has a runner on first base with less than two outs, the infielders should be looking to turn a double play. Both the shortstop and second baseman have a considerable amount of ground to cover, so they must be aware of a batter's tendencies. As an example, if the batter is a left-handed, dead pull hitter, the second baseman must guard the hole between first base and second base.

Outfield

The key to a good defensive outfield is speed, according to Weaver, but you expect your outfielders to be solid hitters at the plate. Earl discouraged his outfielders from playing at a shallow depth because that would allow runners to go from first to third (or even score) on a ball hit to medium depth in the outfield. The shallow outfield also runs the risk of allowing line drives to roll all the way to the fence for extra-base hits. Thus, the shallow outfield tends to give up a double or a triple in an effort to cut off a bloop single.

The center fielder should be the player with the most speed in the outfield. Earl does not think a certain type of player fits in better in right field than in left field. A good arm in right field, however, does allow the outfielder to throw out a runner going from first to third on a single (the throw from right field to third base is one of the longest throws on the diamond). Because he does not think an occasional base hit is worth sacrificing much offense for (except in late innings when protecting a lead), Earl's strategy is to fill the left field and right field positions with power hitters rather than defensive specialists.

Catcher

A good arm for a catcher is definitely an asset, but a pitcher who will watch the runner on base is really the best defense against stolen bases. Earl notes that a team with plenty of left-handed pitching will help any catcher when it comes to thwarting stolen bases. Weaver suggests carrying three catchers on your squad so that you can pinch hit for a weaker hitting catcher in the late innings and still have a replacement on the bench in case of an injury.

Defensive Shifts

Positioning your players defensively obviously assumes some knowledge about the tendencies of opposing hitters. A few defensive plays, however, are put on to counteract an offensive strategy.

Some managers prefer to move their first basemen and third basemen closer to the foul lines in late innings of a close game. Guarding the lines often does prevent extra-base hits, but it also opens up holes for singles to scoot through the infield. The manager must weigh whether a dribbling seeing-eye single is less damaging than an extra-base hit before he orders his corner infielders to guard the lines.

If you are expecting the batter to bunt, you can order your corner infielders to charge the plate as the middle infielders move to cover different positions when the play unfolds. With a runner on first base and the batter squaring around to bunt, the first baseman and third baseman should charge the plate. The second baseman then covers first and the shortstop covers second. With runners on first and second in a bunting situation, either the first baseman or the third baseman should charge the plate, but not both. If the first baseman charges, the second baseman covers first, the shortstop covers second, and the third baseman covers his bag at third. If the third baseman charges, the shortstop covers third, the second baseman covers his bag at second, and the first baseman covers first.

In some situations with a runner on third, a manager might choose to move his infield in. Playing the infield in increases the chances for throwing out the runner trying to score from third. However, the infield now has less range and more routine ground balls may turn into singles.

Earl Weaver was the only manager in history to have 20-game winners on his pitching staff for 13 consecutive seasons. They included Jim Palmer, Dave McNally, Mike Cuellar, Pat Dobson, Mike Torrez, Wayne Garland, Mike Flanagan, Steve Stone, and Scott McGregor.

Pitching

To Earl Weaver (and most successful baseball managers), pitching is the most important, most delicate, and most challenging part of the game. As Earl once said, "The only thing that matters is what happens on that little hump out in the middle of the field." Weaver's championship teams were always stocked with potential 20-game winners in the starting rotation and workhorses in the bullpen.

The Starting Rotation

Earl prefers the four-man starting rotation. If you have four pitchers who are winning, you can get them to the mound more often with a four-man rotation, and that translates into more wins for the team. With a five-man rotation, the starts you give your fifth starter take away from the four pitchers who are better than him. Earl says the key to winning 20 games a season is for a pitcher to work between 250 and 300 innings per year. Earl used his fifth starter in doubleheaders and when he wanted to vary his rotation. A fifth starter can also be used in long relief.

Weaver gained a reputation his first season as "Captain Hook" when it came to yanking his starting pitchers. His propensity for going to the bullpen at even the slightest sign of trouble on the mound contributed heavily to this reputation. His cardinal rule about pitching was to never leave a starting pitcher in to lose a game. If your starting pitcher is getting hammered in the second inning and the game is getting out of hand, pull him. If the score is 2-1 or 1-0, stick with the starter if he is still throwing well. If you're ahead 4-1 and the starter has two men on and the winning run at the plate, you have to go to the bullpen. From the seventh inning on, you should never let your starting pitcher face the winning run at the plate.

One sure sign that a pitcher is tiring is when he issues a walk to lead off an inning. Another sign of tiring is when hitters batting low in the order begin to pull pitches. If you see either of these signs, you'd better have someone warming up in the bullpen.

The Bullpen

Earl's basic philosophy about his relief corps is that it takes care of itself. He says to stick with whoever has the hot hand, but be careful not to overuse your relief pitchers. Too much work in one game can ruin a relief pitcher's effectiveness for as long as a week afterward. Contrary to many of today's top managers, Earl places little importance on left/right combinations when deciding on a reliever. He does encourage using statistics showing a hitter's performance against an individual pitcher as a better tool for your decision on who to bring in.

Where Fantasy Becomes Reality

Earl Weaver's credo for managing the championship Orioles teams was simple: strong arms and long, long hits. "In my first spring training as a major-league manager I...made clear to everyone my offensive philosophy. Basically, I liked to get a couple-three men on base and have someone hit the ball out of the park," he said.

According to Earl, the key to being a good manager is player evaluation. He learned this tenet while playing and managing in the minor leagues where his teams often played with different lineups from season to season. That evaluation extends to the opposition as well as your own team. Once you understand the talent on your ball club and the caliber of your competition, you can formulate strategies to win ball games.

Throughout this book, you have become familiar with the incredible talent available in the player pool for the Hall of Fame League. You have seen the personal side of the superstars, and learned of the feats that have immortalized them. You have learned how to cross the time line of baseball history to compare players from all eras. You have learned what it takes to field a winning ball club and how to select your team in a competitive draft. With this basic knowledge, you now have a solid background for playing EWBII and enjoying the national pastime year-round.

In a 1986 article for *Advertising Age,* Bob Garfield wrote, "Everybody has an idea of what makes the national game so enduring a phenomenon. People talk about baseball's strategy, culture, statistical tidiness. Some like its color, its folklore, its excruciating tension.

"All true I suppose. But the big thing is misery–misery in the quest for redemption, which curiously enough is the story of life. And therein lies the lure of the game. Baseball is a metaphor for our existence on earth."

With Earl Weaver Baseball, you can experience the mesmerizing enjoyment of playing the game of baseball. With all you have learned in this book, you can turn the fantasies of youth into reality. With the Hall of Fame League, your dreams can now come true.

HOF - 19
JOE SEWELL
CLEVELAND INDIANS – SHORTSTOP
1922
HOF - 1956
JOE CRONIN
PITTSBURGH PIRATES – 2ND BASE
75 YEARS AGO
WORLD CHAMPS
DUTCH LEONARD
BOSTON RED SOX – PITCHER
1916

CHAPTER A

Hitters' Actual & Normalized Statistics

Table A-1.

Hitters' Actual and Normalized Statistics

		YR	G	AB	R	H	BA	2B	3B	HR	RBI	BB	K	SB	CS	BAT RUNS	STL RUNS	FLD RUNS	TTL PLYR RTG
OUTFIELD																			
RUTH	L	1920	142	458	158	172	.376	36	9	54	137	148	80	14	14				
		AL		498		172	.345	49	9	54		89	77			101	-3	-1	97
DELAHANTY	R	1896	123	499	131	198	.397	44	17	13	126	62	22	37					
		NL		522		198	.379	47	17	13		50	22			64	5	19	88
COBB	L	1911	146	591	147	248	.420	47	24	8	127	44	34	83					
		AL		606		248	.409	49	24	8		35	34			67	13	7	87
SPEAKER	L	1913	141	520	94	189	.363	35	22	3	71	65	22	46					
		AL		497		189	.380	38	22	3		52	21			58	6	22	86
WILLIAMS, T.	L	1941	143	456	135	185	.406	33	3	37	120	145	27	2	4				
		AL		492		185	.376	45	3	37		87	26			88	-1	-4	83
JACKSON, J.	L	1912	152	572	121	226	.395	44	26	3	90	54	29	35					
		AL		553		226	.409	46	26	3		43	28			68	4	9	81
SHECKARD	L	1903	139	515	99	171	.332	29	9	9	75	75	54	67					
		NL		501		171	.341	32	9	9		60	51			40	10	31	81
HENDERSON, R.	R	1990	143	489	119	159	.325	33	3	28	61	97	60	65	10				
		AL		472		159	.337	41	3	28		28	58			59	14	6	79
MANTLE	S	1957	144	474	121	173	.365	28	6	34	94	146	75	16	3				
		AL		477		173	.363	40	6	34		88	68			83	2	-7	78
MUSIAL	L	1948	155	611	135	230	.376	46	18	39	131	79	34	7					
		NL		636		230	.362	49	18	39		63	34			73	-1	5	77
SEYMOR	L	1905	149	581	95	219	.377	40	21	8	121	51	39	21					
		NL		545		219	.402	42	21	8		41	36			65	1	6	72
THOMPSON	L	1895	119	538	131	211	.392	45	21	18	165	31	11	27					
		NL		572		211	.369	46	21	18		25	12			57	3	12	72
MAYS	R	1955	152	580	123	185	.319	18	13	51	127	79	60	24	4				
		NL		607		185	.305	21	13	51		63	61			53	5	14	72
CLARKE	L	1897	128	518	120	202	.390	30	13	6	67	45	34	57					
		NL		504		202	.401	32	13	6		36	33			57	8	6	71
KLEIN	L	1930	156	648	158	250	.386	59	8	40	170	54	50	4					
		NL		771		250	.324	61	8	40		43	58			42	-2	30	70
DIMAGGIO	R	1939	120	462	108	176	.381	32	6	30	126	52	20	3	0				
		AL		492		176	.358	34	6	30		42	21			62	1	6	69
DAWSON	R	1981	103	394	71	119	.302	21	3	24	64	35	50	24	4				
		NL		379		119	.314	22	3	24		28	47			42	9	17	68
YASTRZEMSKI	L	1968	157	539	90	162	.301	32	2	23	74	119	90	13	6				
		AL		480		162	.338	42	2	23		71	75			56	0	11	67
GUERRERO	R	1985	137	487	99	156	.320	22	2	33	87	83	68	12	4				
		NL		469		156	.333	26	2	33		66	64			59	1	6	66
KELLEY	R	1896	131	519	148	189	.364	31	19	8	101	91	19	87					
		NL		531		189	.356	39	19	8		55	18			49	13	4	66
JACKSON	L	1969	152	549	123	151	.275	36	3	47	118	114	142	13	5				
		AL		510		151	.296	46	3	47		68	124			61	1	3	65
HEILMANN	R	1923	144	524	121	211	.403	44	11	18	115	74	40	8	7				
		AL		552		211	.382	47	11	18		59	41			66	-2	0	64

Table A-1.

Hitters' Actual and Normalized Statistics (continued)

		YR	G	AB	R	H	BA	2B	3B	HR	RBI	BB	K	SB	CS	BAT RUNS	STL RUNS	FLD RUNS	TTL PLYR RTG
ROBINSON, F.	R	1966	155	576	122	182	.316	34	2	49	122	87	90	8	5				
		AL		548		182	.332	38	2	49		70	84			69	-1	-4	64
KALINE	R	1967	131	458	94	141	.308	28	2	25	78	83	47	8	2				
		AL		430		141	.328	32	2	25		66	43			56	1	7	64
SMITH, E.	L	1896	122	484	121	175	.362	21	14	7	94	74	18	33					
		NL		485		175	.361	24	14	7		59	18			48	4	12	64
STARGELL	L	1973	148	522	106	156	.299	43	3	44	119	80	129	0	0				
		NL		512		156	.305	46	3	44		64	123			61	0	1	62
SIMMONS, A.	R	1930	138	554	152	211	.381	41	16	36	165	39	34	9	2				
		AL		617		211	.342	43	16	36		31	37			55	2	5	62
KEELER	L	1897	129	564	145	239	.424	27	19	1	74	35	12	64					
		NL		571		239	.419	28	19	1		28	12			56	9	-3	62
FLICK	L	1900	138	545	106	200	.367	32	16	11	110	56	40	35					
		NL		543		200	.368	34	16	11		45	39			50	4	7	61
COLAVITO	R	1958	143	489	80	148	.303	26	3	41	113	84	89	0	2				
		AL		488		148	.303	30	3	41		67	86			56	-1	6	61
MAGEE, S.	R	1910	140	519	110	172	.331	39	17	6	123	94	36	49					
		NL		468		172	.368	47	17	6		56	31			60	7	-7	60
GOSLIN	L	1928	135	456	80	173	.379	36	10	17	102	48	19	16	3				
		AL		488		173	.355	38	10	17		38	20			51	4	5	60
AARON	R	1962	156	592	127	191	.323	28	6	45	128	66	73	15	7				
		NL		613		191	.312	31	6	45		53	74			46	0	13	59
CEDENO	R	1973	139	525	86	168	.320	35	2	25	70	41	79	56	15				
		NL		514		168	.327	37	2	25		33	76			38	10	11	59
DONLIN	L	1903	126	496	110	174	.351	25	18	7	67	56	37	26					
		NL		502		174	.347	27	18	7		45	37			40	3	15	58
OTT	L	1929	150	545	138	179	.328	37	2	42	151	113	38	6					
		NL		605		179	.296	47	2	42		68	39			44	-1	15	58
CRAWFORD	L	1903	137	550	88	184	.335	23	25	4	89	25	28	18					
		AL		500		184	.368	24	25	4		20	25			42	1	14	57
CLEMENTE	R	1969	138	507	87	175	.345	20	12	19	91	56	73	4	1				
		NL		494		175	.354	22	12	19		45	70			50	1	6	57
FOSTER	R	1977	158	615	124	197	.320	31	2	52	149	61	107	6	4				
		NL		638		197	.309	34	2	52		49	109			46	-1	12	57
KINER	R	1947	152	565	118	177	.313	23	4	51	127	98	81	1					
		NL		591		177	.299	31	4	51		59	79			49	-2	9	56
MEDWICK	R	1937	156	633	111	237	.374	56	10	31	154	41	50	4					
		NL		655		237	.362	58	10	31		33	51			57	-2	1	56
WILLIAMS, K.	L	1923	147	555	106	198	.357	37	12	29	91	79	32	18	17				
		AL		605		198	.327	40	12	29		63	34			49	-5	12	56
GWYNN	L	1987	157	589	119	218	.370	36	13	7	54	82	35	56	12				
		NL		611		218	.357	39	13	7		66	35			42	8	5	55
WYNN	R	1965	157	564	90	155	.275	30	7	22	84	84	126	43	4				
		NL		523		155	.296	34	7	22		67	115			34	11	9	54
RAINES	S	1985	150	575	115	184	.320	30	13	11	41	81	60	70	9				
		NL		556		184	.331	33	13	11		65	57			38	14	2	54

Table A-1.

Hitters' Actual and Normalized Statistics (continued)

		YR	G	AB	R	H	BA	2B	3B	HR	RBI	BB	K	SB	CS	BAT RUNS	STL RUNS	FLD RUNS	TTL PLYR RTG
PARKER	L	1977	159	637	107	215	.338	44	8	21	88	58	107	17	19				
		NL		662		215	.325	46	8	21		46	109			32	-6	27	53
HAMILTON	L	1895	123	517	166	201	.389	22	6	7	74	96	30	97					
		NL		538		201	.374	30	6	7		58	29			45	12	-5	52
MINOSO	R	1954	153	568	119	182	.320	29	18	19	116	77	46	18	11				
		AL		569		182	.320	32	18	19		62	45			41	-1	12	52
LYNN	L	1979	147	531	116	177	.333	42	1	39	122	82	79	2	2				
		AL		563		177	.314	45	1	39		66	81			52	-1	1	52
WANER, P.	L	1936	148	585	107	218	.373	53	9	5	94	74	29	7					
		NL		601		218	.363	56	9	5		59	29			45	-1	8	52
ROSE	S	1969	156	627	120	218	.348	33	11	16	82	88	65	7	10				
		NL		618		218	.353	37	11	16		70	63			47	-3	7	51
STAUB	L	1969	158	549	89	166	.302	26	5	29	79	110	61	3	4				
		NL		526		166	.316	35	5	29		66	55			47	-2	5	50
WINFIELD	R	1979	159	597	97	184	.308	27	10	34	118	85	71	15	9				
		NL		604		184	.305	31	10	34		68	70			41	-1	10	50
MURCER	L	1972	153	585	102	171	.292	30	7	33	96	63	67	11	9				
		AL		531		171	.322	33	7	33		50	60			49	-2	3	50
WILSON, H.	R	1930	155	585	146	208	.356	35	6	56	190	105	84	3					
		NL		695		208	.299	44	6	56		63	92			48	-2	4	50
JOHNSON	R	1939	150	544	115	184	.338	30	9	23	114	99	59	15	5				
		AL		582		184	.316	38	9	23		59	59			38	2	10	50
BARFIELD	R	1986	158	589	107	170	.289	35	2	40	108	69	146	8	8				
		AL		603		170	.282	38	2	40		55	146			32	-2	20	50
CAREY	S	1917	155	588	82	174	.296	21	12	1	51	58	38	46					
		NL		521		174	.334	23	12	1		46	33			23	6	20	49
LEZCANO	R	1982	138	470	73	136	.289	26	6	16	84	78	69	2	1				
		NL		449		136	.303	29	6	16		62	64			35	0	13	48
WHEAT	L	1924	141	566	92	212	.375	41	8	14	97	49	18	3	4				
		NL		585		212	.362	43	8	14		39	18			44	-2	5	47
ASHBURN	L	1951	154	643	92	221	.344	31	5	4	63	50	37	29	6				
		NL		656		221	.337	33	5	4		40	37			18	4	24	46
CLARK, J.	R	1978	156	592	90	181	.306	46	8	25	98	50	72	1	2				
		NL		571		181	.317	48	8	25		40	68			38	-2	10	46
RICE	R	1978	163	677	121	213	.315	25	15	46	139	58	126	7	5				
		AL		687		213	.310	27	15	46		46	126			42	-1	5	46
POWELL	L	1964	134	424	74	123	.290	17	0	39	99	76	91	0	0				
		AL		433		123	.284	20	0	39		61	90			47	0	-2	45
KELLER	R	1941	140	507	102	151	.298	24	10	33	122	102	65	6	4				
		AL		524		151	.288	33	10	33		61	62			41	-1	4	44
WILLIAMS, B.	L	1965	162	645	115	203	.315	39	6	34	108	65	76	10	1				
		NL		640		203	.317	42	6	34		52	74			40	2	2	44
SNIDER	L	1954	149	584	120	199	.341	39	10	40	130	84	96	6	6				
		NL		629		199	.316	43	10	40		67	100			51	-2	-9	40
HAFEY	R	1928	138	520	101	175	.337	46	6	27	111	40	53	8					
		NL		556		175	.315	48	6	27		32	56			37	-1	1	37

Table A-1.

Hitters' Actual and Normalized Statistics (continued)

		YR	G	AB	R	H	BA	2B	3B	HR	RBI	BB	K	SB	CS	BAT RUNS	STL RUNS	FLD RUNS	TTL PLYR RTG
AVERILL	L	1936	152	614	136	232	.378	39	15	28	126	35	35	3	3				
		AL		679		232	.342	40	15	28		28	38			41	-1	-9	31
SLAUGHTER	L	1939	149	604	95	193	.320	52	5	12	86	44	53	2					
		NL		636		193	.303	54	5	12		35	55			16	-3	14	27
BROCK	L	1971	157	640	126	200	.313	37	7	7	61	61	107	64	19				
		NL		612		200	.327	40	7	7		49	101			23	7	-10	20
SS/2B																			
APPLING	R	1936	138	526	111	204	.388	31	7	6	128	85	25	10	6				
		AL		597		204	.342	35	7	6		68	27			32	-1	17	48
CHAPMAN	R	1917	156	563	98	170	.302	28	13	2	36	61	65	52					
		AL		552		170	.308	31	13	2		49	63			16	8	22	46
YOUNT	R	1982	156	635	129	210	.331	46	12	29	114	54	63	14	3				
		AL		633		210	.332	48	12	29		43	62			46	2	-3	45
PECKINPAUGH	R	1919	122	453	89	138	.305	20	2	7	33	59	37	10					
		AL		457		138	.302	22	2	7		47	36			14	-1	31	44
SMITH, O.	S	1984	124	412	53	106	.257	20	5	1	44	56	17	35	7				
		NL		399		106	.266	22	5	1		45	16			-1	8	36	43
FREGOSI	R	1964	147	505	86	140	.277	22	9	18	72	72	87	8	3				
		AL		478		140	.293	25	9	18		58	81			29	1	12	42
JACKSON, T.	R	1927	127	469	67	149	.318	29	4	14	98	32	30	8					
		NL		487		149	.306	30	4	14		26	31			18	-1	25	42
BANKS	R	1959	155	589	97	179	.304	25	6	45	143	64	72	2	4				
		NL		608		179	.294	28	6	45		51	73			39	-2	5	42
SEWELL	L	1923	153	553	98	195	.353	41	10	3	109	98	12	9	6				
		AL		572		195	.341	49	10	3		59	12			35	-1	5	39
MARANVILLE	R	1914	156	586	74	144	.246	23	6	4	78	45	56	28					
		NL		554		144	.260	25	6	4		36	52			-12	4	46	38
BANCROFT	S	1921	153	606	121	193	.318	26	15	6	67	66	23	17	10				
		NL		624		193	.309	29	15	6		53	23			17	-1	17	33
APARICIO	R	1969	156	599	77	168	.280	24	5	5	51	66	29	24	4				
		AL		614		168	.274	27	5	5		53	29			-4	5	28	29
3B/1B																			
WILLIAMS, J.	R	1899	152	617	126	219	.355	28	27	9	116	60	53	26					
		NL		615		219	.356	31	27	9		48	52			45	2	5	52
ROSEN	R	1953	155	599	115	201	.336	27	5	43	145	85	48	8	7				
		AL		612		201	.328	31	5	43		68	48			54	-2	0	52
MOLITOR	R	1987	118	465	114	164	.353	41	5	16	75	69	67	45	10				
		AL		490		164	.335	44	5	16		55	68			45	9	-5	49
MELTON	R	1971	150	543	72	146	.269	18	2	33	86	61	87	3	3				
		AL		517		146	.282	21	2	33		49	82			27	-1	23	49
MATHEWS	L	1954	138	476	96	138	.290	21	4	40	103	113	61	10	3				
		NL		490		138	.282	31	4	40		68	58			47	1	0	48
NETTLES	L	1971	158	598	78	156	.261	18	1	28	86	82	56	7	4				
		AL		595		156	.262	21	1	28		66	54			12	0	36	48
ZIMMERMAN	R	1912	145	557	95	207	.372	41	14	14	99	38	60	23					
		NL		574		207	.361	43	14	14		30	61			45	2	0	47

Table A-1.

Hitters' Actual and Normalized Statistics (continued)

		YR	G	AB	R	H	BA	2B	3B	HR	RBI	BB	K	SB	CS	BAT RUNS	STL RUNS	FLD RUNS	TTL PLYR RTG
ROBINSON, B.	R	1967	158	610	88	164	.269	25	5	22	77	54	54	1	3				
		AL		555		164	.295	27	5	22		43	49			21	-2	27	46
COLLINS, J.	R	1901	138	564	108	187	.332	42	16	6	94	34	32	19					
		AL		555		187	.337	43	16	6		27	31			30	1	15	46
GROH	R	1917	156	599	91	182	.304	39	11	1	53	71	30	15					
		NL		516		182	.353	42	11	1		57	26			39	0	4	43
BOYER, K.	R	1960	151	552	95	168	.304	26	10	32	97	56	77	8	7				
		NL		577		168	.291	28	10	32		45	79			30	-2	15	43
EVANS	L	1973	161	595	114	167	.281	25	8	41	104	124	104	6	3				
		NL		613		167	.272	35	8	41		74	99			35	0	6	41
SS																			
DAVIS	S	1899	108	416	68	140	.337	21	5	1	57	37	18	34					
		NL		410		140	.341	23	5	1		30	17			22	5	57	84
JENNINGS	R	1896	130	521	125	209	.401	27	9	0	121	68	11	70					
		NL		552		209	.379	30	9	0		54	11			41	9	33	83
WAGNER	R	1905	147	548	114	199	.363	32	14	6	101	54	49	57					
		NL		517		199	.385	34	14	6		43	46			53	8	18	79
DAHLEN	R	1896	125	474	137	167	.352	30	19	9	74	64	36	51					
		NL		512		167	.326	33	19	9		51	38			37	8	24	69
RIPKEN	R	1984	162	641	103	195	.304	37	7	27	86	71	89	2	1				
		AL		630		195	.310	40	7	27		57	86			33	0	35	68
BARTELL	R	1937	128	516	91	158	.306	38	2	14	62	40	38	5					
		NL		518		158	.305	40	2	14		32	38			19	-2	42	59
BOUDREAU	R	1948	152	560	116	199	.355	34	6	18	106	98	9	3	2				
		AL		579		199	.344	42	6	18		59	9			44	0	9	53
WALLACE	R	1901	134	550	69	178	.324	34	15	2	91	20	48	15					
		NL		516		178	.345	35	15	2		16	45			25	0	27	52
VAUGHN	L	1938	148	541	88	174	.322	35	5	7	68	104	21	14					
		NL		534		174	.326	44	5	7		62	19			31	0	18	49
CRONIN	R	1930	154	587	127	203	.346	41	9	13	126	72	36	17	10				
		AL		645		203	.315	44	9	13		58	38			26	-1	24	49
HARRAH	R	1975	151	522	81	153	.293	24	1	20	93	98	71	23	9				
		AL		498		153	.307	32	1	20		59	64			32	2	13	47
TINKER	R	1908	157	548	67	146	.266	22	14	6	68	32	21	30					
		NL		487		146	.300	23	14	6		26	19			11	5	29	45
3B																			
SCHMIDT	R	1981	102	354	78	112	.316	19	2	31	91	73	71	12	4				
		NL		359		112	.312	22	2	31		58	69			63	1	31	95
BRETT	L	1980	117	449	87	175	.390	33	9	24	118	58	22	15	6				
		AL		457		175	.383	35	9	24		46	22			74	1	4	79
MCGRAW	R	1899	117	399	140	156	.391	13	3	1	33	124	10	73					
		NL		389		156	.401	23	3	1		74	9			60	9	2	71
DEVLIN	R	1906	148	498	76	149	.299	23	8	2	65	74	32	54					
		NL		438		149	.340	26	8	2		59	28			34	8	27	69
SANTO	R	1966	155	561	93	175	.312	21	8	30	94	95	78	4	5				
		NL		545		175	.321	29	8	30		57	72			46	-2	25	69

Table A-1.

Hitters' Actual and Normalized Statistics (continued)

		YR	G	AB	R	H	BA	2B	3B	HR	RBI	BB	K	SB	CS	BAT RUNS	STL RUNS	FLD RUNS	TTL PLYR RTG
CLIFT	R	1937	155	571	103	175	.306	36	7	29	118	98	80	8	5				
		AL		615		175	.285	44	7	29		59	81			28	-1	37	64
BAKER, F.	L	1912	149	577	116	200	.347	40	21	10	130	50	43	40					
		AL		559		200	.358	42	21	10		40	41			48	6	9	63
BELL	R	1982	148	537	62	159	.296	27	2	13	67	70	50	5	4				
		AL		525		159	.303	30	2	13		56	48			21	-1	36	56
DECINCES	R	1982	153	575	94	173	.301	42	5	30	97	66	80	7	5				
		AL		584		173	.296	45	5	30		53	79			34	-1	23	56
BOGGS	L	1987	147	551	108	200	.363	40	6	24	89	105	48	1	3				
		AL		566		200	.353	49	6	24		63	46			57	-2	0	55
BRADLEY, B.	R	1903	136	536	101	168	.313	36	22	6	68	25	45	21					
		AL		484		168	.347	37	22	6		20	40			40	2	13	55
KILLEBREW	R	1969	162	555	106	153	.276	20	2	49	140	145	84	8	2				
		AL		540		153	.283	32	2	49		87	75			53	1	-9	45
2B																			
LAJOIE	R	1910	159	591	145	227	.384	51	7	4	125	60	26	27					
		AL		523		227	.434	54	7	4		48	23			72	2	22	96
COLLINS, E.	L	1910	153	583	81	188	.322	16	15	3	81	49	41	81					
		AL		518		188	.363	18	15	3		39	36			35	13	31	79
CHILDS	L	1896	132	498	106	177	.355	24	9	1	106	100	18	25					
		NL		531		177	.333	32	9	1		60	18			27	2	46	75
FRISCH	S	1927	153	617	112	208	.337	31	11	10	78	43	10	48					
		NL		655		208	.318	33	11	10		34	10			16	7	46	69
HORNSBY	R	1924	143	536	121	227	.424	43	14	25	94	89	32	5	12				
		NL		570		227	.398	47	14	25		71	33			81	-5	-8	68
ROBINSON, J.	R	1951	153	548	106	185	.338	33	7	19	88	79	27	25	8				
		NL		556		185	.333	36	7	19		63	27			42	3	20	65
MORGAN	L	1975	146	498	107	163	.327	27	6	17	94	132	52	67	10				
		NL		496		163	.329	38	6	17		79	47			49	11	5	65
GRICH	R	1983	120	387	65	113	.292	17	0	16	62	76	62	2	4				
		AL		375		113	.301	20	0	16		61	58			35	-2	25	58
CAREW	L	1974	153	599	86	218	.364	30	5	3	55	74	49	38	16				
		AL		583		218	.374	33	5	3		59	47			40	1	16	57
SANDBERG	R	1984	156	636	114	200	.314	36	19	19	84	52	101	32	7				
		NL		655		200	.305	38	19	19		42	102			26	5	21	52
HUGGINS	S	1905	149	564	117	154	.273	11	8	1	38	103	48	27					
		NL		506		154	.304	20	8	1		62	41			13	2	35	50
SCHOENDIENST	S	1953	146	564	107	193	.342	35	5	15	79	60	23	3	3				
		NL		607		193	.318	38	5	15		48	24			25	-1	24	48
GEHRINGER	L	1936	154	641	144	227	.354	60	12	15	116	83	13	4	1				
		AL		714		227	.318	64	12	15		66	14			32	1	15	48
HUBBARD	R	1985	142	439	51	102	.232	21	0	5	39	56	54	4	3				
		NL		440		102	.232	23	0	5		45	53			-17	-1	58	40
DOERR	R	1949	139	541	91	167	.309	30	9	18	109	75	33	2	2				
		AL		595		167	.281	33	9	18		60	35			17	-1	23	39

Table A-1.

Hitters' Actual and Normalized Statistics (continued)

		YR	G	AB	R	H	BA	2B	3B	HR	RBI	BB	K	SB	CS	BAT RUNS	STL RUNS	FLD RUNS	TTL PLYR RTG
HERMAN	R	1935	154	666	113	227	.341	57	6	7	83	42	29	6					
		NL		685		227	.331	59	6	7		34	29			22	-1	18	39
MAZEROSKI	R	1963	142	534	43	131	.245	22	3	8	52	32	46	2	0				
		NL		511		131	.256	23	3	8		26	44			-14	1	48	35
EVERS	L	1913	136	446	81	127	.285	20	5	3	49	50	14	11					
		NL		429		127	.296	22	5	3		40	13			9	-1	21	29
1B																			
CASH	L	1961	159	535	119	193	.361	22	8	41	132	124	85	11	5				
		AL		541		193	.357	32	8	41		74	79			75	0	5	80
FOXX	R	1933	149	573	125	204	.356	37	9	48	163	96	93	2	2				
		AL		588		204	.347	45	9	48		58	90			72	-1	5	76
GEHRIG	L	1927	155	584	149	218	.373	52	18	47	175	109	84	10	0				
		AL		633		218	.344	61	18	47		65	85			76	3	-6	73
SISLER	L	1920	154	631	137	257	.407	49	18	19	122	46	19	42	17				
		AL		698		257	.368	51	18	19		37	21			50	2	14	66
MCCOVEY	L	1969	149	491	101	157	.320	26	2	45	126	121	66	0	0				
		NL		484		157	.324	36	2	45		73	60			71	0	-5	66
ALLEN, R.	R	1972	148	506	90	156	.308	28	5	37	113	99	126	19	8				
		AL		474		156	.329	36	5	37		59	111			65	1	-4	62
FOURNIER	L	1915	126	422	86	136	.322	20	18	5	77	64	37	21	16				
		NL		374		136	.364	23	18	5		51	32			58	-4	2	56
CAMILLI	L	1937	131	475	101	161	.339	23	7	27	80	90	82	6					
		NL		506		161	.318	27	7	27		72	84			48	-1	7	54
GREENBURG	R	1938	155	556	144	175	.315	23	4	58	146	119	92	7	5				
		AL		620		175	.282	33	4	58		71	94			48	-1	6	53
TENNEY	L	1902	134	489	88	154	.315	18	3	2	30	73	24	21					
		NL		428		154	.360	21	3	2		58	21			37	1	14	52
HERNANDEZ	L	1979	161	610	116	210	.344	48	11	11	105	80	78	11	6				
		NL		637		210	.330	51	11	11		64	79			35	0	16	51
TERRY	L	1932	154	643	124	225	.350	42	11	28	117	32	23	4					
		NL		664		225	.339	43	11	28		26	23			40	-2	12	50
MURRAY	S	1984	162	588	97	180	.306	26	3	29	110	107	87	10	2				
		AL		566		180	.318	35	3	29		64	79			42	2	6	50
MIZE	L	1939	153	564	104	197	.349	44	14	28	108	92	49	0					
		NL		588		197	.335	52	14	28		55	48			55	-2	-4	49
MATTINGLY	L	1984	153	603	91	207	.343	44	2	23	110	41	33	1	1				
		AL		595		207	.348	46	2	23		33	32			41	0	7	48
CHANCE	R	1903	125	441	83	144	.327	24	10	2	81	78	29	67					
		NL		420		144	.343	27	10	2		62	27			40	11	-3	48
ALLISON	R	1964	149	492	90	141	.287	27	4	32	86	92	99	10	1				
		AL		477		141	.296	35	4	32		55	90			44	2	2	48
CEPEDA	R	1967	151	563	91	183	.325	37	0	25	111	62	75	11	2				
		NL		537		183	.341	40	0	25		50	70			46	2	-1	47
KLUSZEWSKI	L	1954	149	573	104	187	.326	28	3	49	141	78	35	0	2				
		NL		626		187	.299	31	3	49		62	37			44	-1	-3	40

Table A-1.

Hitters' Actual and Normalized Statistics (continued)

		YR	G	AB	R	H	BA	2B	3B	HR	RBI	BB	K	SB	CS	BAT RUNS	STL RUNS	FLD RUNS	TTL PLYR RTG
YORK	R	1940	155	588	105	186	.316	46	6	33	134	89	88	3	2				
		AL		665		186	.280	50	6	33		71	96			29	0	5	34
BOTTOMLEY	L	1928	149	576	123	187	.325	42	20	31	136	71	54	10					
		NL		616		187	.304	45	20	31		57	56			44	-1	-13	30
C																			
FISK	R	1972	131	457	74	134	.293	28	9	22	61	52	83	5	2				
		AL		429		134	.312	30	9	22		42	77			44	0	19	63
TORRE	R	1966	148	546	83	172	.315	20	3	36	101	60	61	0	4				
		NL		543		172	.317	23	3	36		48	59			42	-2	12	52
CAMPENELLA	R	1951	143	505	90	164	.325	33	1	33	108	53	51	1	2				
		NL		518		164	.317	35	1	33		42	51			43	-1	8	50
CARTER	R	1982	154	557	91	163	.293	32	1	29	97	78	64	2	5				
		NL		559		163	.292	35	1	29		62	63			31	-2	20	49
BENCH	R	1972	147	538	87	145	.270	22	2	40	125	100	84	6	6				
		NL		500		145	.290	30	2	40		60	74			46	-2	4	48
FREEHAN	R	1964	144	520	69	156	.300	14	8	18	80	36	68	5	1				
		AL		501		156	.311	16	8	18		29	65			21	1	24	46
MCFARLAND	R	1899	96	324	59	108	.333	22	10	1	57	36	27	9					
		NL		318		108	.340	24	10	1		29	26			34	-1	13	46
COCHRANE	L	1933	130	429	104	138	.322	30	4	15	60	106	22	8	6				
		AL		426		138	.324	39	4	15		64	20			47	-1	0	46
MUNSON	R	1973	147	519	80	156	.301	29	4	20	74	48	64	4	6				
		AL		510		156	.306	31	4	20		38	62			26	-2	21	45
HARTNETT	R	1928	120	388	61	117	.302	26	9	14	57	65	32	3					
		NL		405		117	.289	29	9	14		52	32			32	-3	14	43
BAILEY	L	1956	118	383	59	115	.300	8	2	28	75	52	50	2	0				
		NL		406		115	.283	10	2	28		42	51			30	1	12	43
HOWARD	R	1961	129	446	64	155	.348	17	5	21	77	28	65	0	3				
		AL		458		155	.338	18	5	21		22	66			36	-3	9	42
MCCARVER	L	1967	138	471	68	139	.295	26	3	14	69	54	32	8	8				
		NL		453		139	.307	28	3	14		43	30			26	-2	17	41
SIMMONS, T.	S	1973	161	619	62	192	.310	36	2	13	91	61	47	2	2				
		NL		597		192	.322	39	2	13		49	45			24	-1	18	41
BERRA	L	1956	140	521	93	155	.298	29	2	30	105	65	29	3	2				
		AL		546		155	.284	32	2	30		52	30			27	0	13	40
PORTER	L	1979	157	533	101	155	.291	23	10	20	112	121	65	3	4				
		AL		538		155	.288	33	10	20		73	61			31	-2	9	38
ROMANO	R	1961	142	509	76	152	.299	29	1	21	80	61	60	0	0				
		AL		517		152	.294	32	1	21		49	60			23	0	15	38
DICKEY	L	1933	130	478	58	152	.318	24	8	14	97	47	14	3	4				
		AL		483		152	.315	26	8	14		38	14			27	-2	12	37
BURGESS	L	1954	108	345	41	127	.368	27	5	4	46	42	11	1	5				
		NL		369		127	.344	29	5	4		34	11			34	-4	4	34
BRESNAHAN	R	1906	124	405	58	114	.281	22	4	0	46	81	36	25					
		NL		354		114	.322	25	4	0		65	31			32	3	-1	34
LOMBARDI	R	1938	129	489	60	167	.342	30	1	19	95	40	14	0					
		NL		495		167	.337	32	1	19		32	14			36	-3	-3	30
FERRELL	R	1932	117	386	67	118	.306	30	4	3	65	56	12	2	3				
		AL		414		118	.285	32	4	3		45	12			11	-1	11	21

HOF - 1968
JOE MEDWICK
ST. LOUIS CARDINALS – OUTFIELD
HARRY HEILMANN
DETROIT TIGERS – OUTFIELD
1926
HOF - 1952
PAUL WANER
PITTSBURGH PIRATES – OUTFIELD
1926

CHAPTER B

Hitters Versus Left-Handed & Versus Right-Handed Pitching

Table B-1.

Hitters Versus Left-Handed and Versus Right-Handed Pitching

	SL %	OB %	ISO PWR	OTS %	VS LEFT AB	H	2B	3B	HR	BB	K	SL %	OB %	BAT RNS	VS RIGHT AB	H	2B	3B	HR	BB	K	SL %	OB %	BAT RNS
OUTFIELD																								
RUTH	.869	.463	.514	.402	135	44	14	3	15	25	20	.807	.431	94	310	114	35	6	39	64	51	.895	.476	118
DELAHANTY	.608	.434	.229	.264	157	62	15	5	4	16	7	.631	.451	72	365	136	32	12	9	34	15	.599	.426	61
COBB	.609	.441	.199	.269	182	70	14	7	2	9	10	.571	.414	53	424	178	35	17	6	26	24	.625	.453	72
SPEAKER	.563	.439	.183	.247	150	53	11	6	1	15	6	.527	.412	45	347	136	27	16	2	37	15	.579	.451	63
WILLIAMS, T.	.706	.470	.330	.332	147	52	13	1	10	22	7	.660	.438	73	345	133	32	2	27	65	19	.725	.483	94
JACKSON, J.	.603	.451	.194	.272	166	64	13	7	1	11	8	.566	.424	55	387	162	33	19	2	32	20	.618	.463	73
SHECKARD	.495	.412	.154	.204	155	48	9	3	3	19	14	.465	.385	28	346	123	23	6	6	41	37	.509	.424	45
HENDERSON, R.	.615	.409	.278	.252	144	50	13	1	9	20	17	.639	.427	67	328	109	28	2	19	38	37	.604	.402	55
MANTLE	.686	.462	.324	.317	145	54	13	2	11	30	21	.717	.480	92	332	119	27	4	23	58	47	.673	.454	79
MUSIAL	.680	.419	.318	.285	192	65	14	5	11	17	10	.635	.392	59	444	165	35	13	28	46	24	.699	.431	79
SEYMOR	.600	.444	.198	.266	162	61	12	6	2	11	10	.562	.416	52	383	158	30	15	6	30	26	.617	.455	71
THOMPSON	.618	.395	.249	.244	171	59	13	6	5	7	3	.579	.371	44	401	152	33	15	13	18	9	.634	.406	62
MAYS	.635	.370	.330	.235	183	58	7	4	16	20	19	.661	.384	61	424	127	14	9	35	43	42	.623	.364	49
CLARKE	.551	.441	.151	.243	155	57	9	4	2	12	9	.516	.413	44	349	145	23	9	4	24	24	.567	.453	62
KLEIN	.580	.360	.256	.209	228	70	17	2	11	11	16	.544	.339	30	543	180	44	6	29	32	42	.595	.369	46
DIMAGGIO	.635	.408	.277	.259	147	55	11	2	9	13	7	.660	.425	71	345	121	23	4	21	29	14	.624	.401	59
DAWSON	.579	.361	.265	.209	112	37	7	1	7	8	15	.598	.375	48	267	82	15	2	17	20	32	.571	.355	39
YASTRZEMSKI	.577	.423	.240	.244	143	45	12	1	6	19	21	.538	.395	43	337	117	30	1	17	52	54	.594	.434	62
GUERRERO	.607	.415	.274	.252	141	49	8	1	10	21	20	.631	.432	67	328	107	18	1	23	45	44	.596	.408	55
KELLEY	.546	.416	.190	.227	157	58	12	6	2	17	6	.561	.431	56	374	131	27	13	6	38	12	.539	.410	47
JACKSON	.674	.379	.378	.255	152	42	13	1	13	19	35	.632	.357	49	358	109	33	2	34	49	89	.692	.388	66
HEILMANN	.605	.442	.223	.267	167	66	15	3	6	20	13	.629	.460	74	385	145	32	8	12	39	28	.595	.434	62
ROBINSON, F.	.676	.408	.344	.276	164	57	12	1	15	22	26	.707	.425	78	384	125	26	1	34	48	58	.663	.400	65
KALINE	.585	.417	.257	.244	132	44	10	1	8	24	13	.606	.436	64	298	97	22	1	17	42	30	.576	.409	52
SMITH, E.	.512	.430	.151	.220	146	49	7	4	2	17	5	.479	.405	36	339	126	17	10	5	42	13	.525	.441	52
STARGELL	.665	.382	.360	.254	153	44	13	1	12	17	35	.621	.359	48	359	112	33	2	32	47	88	.684	392	66
SIMMONS, A.	.638	.373	.296	.238	184	66	13	5	11	9	12	.663	.389	63	433	145	30	11	25	22	25	.627	.367	51
KEELER	.540	.446	.122	.241	168	67	8	5	0	5	3	.506	.416	42	403	172	20	14	1	23	9	.555	.458	61
FLICK	.551	.417	.183	.230	161	56	10	4	3	11	11	.516	.390	38	382	144	24	12	8	34	28	.566	.428	56
COLAVITO	.628	.387	.325	.243	147	46	9	1	13	22	27	.653	.402	63	341	102	21	2	28	45	59	.617	.381	52
MAGEE, S.	.579	.435	.211	.252	140	53	15	5	2	19	10	.600	.453	67	328	119	32	12	4	37	21	.570	.427	56
GOSLIN	.578	.401	.223	.232	150	49	11	3	5	12	6	.540	.377	39	338	124	27	7	12	26	14	.595	.412	57
AARON	.602	.366	.290	.220	184	59	10	2	14	18	23	.625	.381	54	429	132	21	4	31	35	51	.592	.360	43
CEDENO	.552	.367	.225	.203	156	52	11	1	8	12	23	.571	.381	45	358	116	26	1	17	21	53	.544	.361	36
DONLIN	.515	.400	.168	.206	151	49	8	5	2	12	10	.483	.374	28	351	125	19	13	5	33	27	.528	.411	45
OTT	.588	.367	.292	.216	184	50	13	1	12	21	11	.549	.346	33	421	129	34	1	30	47	28	.605	.376	49
CRAWFORD	.540	.392	.172	.212	150	52	7	7	1	5	7	.507	.368	30	350	132	17	18	3	15	18	.554	.403	48
CLEMENTE	.564	.408	.209	.230	150	54	7	4	6	17	22	.580	.425	57	344	121	15	8	13	28	48	.556	.401	47
FOSTER	.612	.358	.303	.219	190	61	10	1	16	15	34	.637	.371	54	448	136	24	1	36	34	75	.602	.353	43
KINER	.625	.363	.325	.227	177	55	10	1	16	19	25	.650	.378	57	414	122	21	3	35	40	54	.614	.357	46
MEDWICK	.622	.392	.261	.244	198	74	18	3	10	12	16	.646	.410	65	457	163	40	7	21	21	35	.612	.385	53
WILLIAMS, K.	.577	.391	.250	.226	179	56	11	3	8	15	10	.542	.366	36	426	142	29	9	21	48	24	.592	.401	53
GWYNN	.498	.419	.142	.209	184	61	11	4	2	19	10	.467	.394	31	427	157	28	9	5	47	25	.512	.430	47

Table B-1.

Hitters Versus Left-Handed and Versus Right-Handed Pitching (continued)

					VS LEFT										VS RIGHT									
	SL %	OB %	ISO PWR	OTS %	AB	H	2B	3B	HR	BB	K	SL %	OB %	BAT RNS	AB	H	2B	3B	HR	BB	K	SL %	OB %	BAT RNS
WYNN	.513	.376	.217	.193	158	48	10	2	7	23	35	.525	.392	40	365	107	24	5	15	44	80	.508	.369	32
RAINES	.497	.401	.166	.199	164	56	10	4	3	21	17	.506	.416	43	392	128	23	9	8	44	40	.493	.394	35
PARKER	.514	.369	.190	.190	199	61	13	2	6	12	31	.482	.346	21	463	154	33	6	15	34	78	.528	.378	37
HAMILTON	.491	.435	.117	.213	163	57	8	2	2	16	8	.460	.408	33	375	144	22	4	5	42	21	.504	.446	50
MINOSO	.540	.387	.220	.209	173	56	10	6	6	22	14	.555	.400	47	396	126	22	12	13	40	31	.533	.381	39
LYNN	.607	.386	.292	.234	169	50	13	0	11	18	23	.568	.364	40	394	127	32	1	28	48	58	.623	.396	57
WANER, P.	.511	.420	.148	.214	179	61	16	3	1	16	8	.480	.395	33	422	157	40	6	4	43	21	.524	.430	49
ROSE	.525	.419	.173	.220	184	67	11	3	5	24	19	.538	.438	54	434	151	26	8	11	46	44	.520	.410	44
STAUB	.567	.392	.252	.222	156	47	10	1	8	17	15	.532	.370	36	370	119	25	4	21	49	40	.582	.401	52
WINFIELD	.557	.375	.253	.209	183	57	9	3	11	24	22	.574	.391	48	421	127	22	7	23	44	48	.550	.368	38
MURCER	.596	.380	.274	.227	158	48	9	2	9	13	17	.557	.357	37	373	123	24	5	24	37	43	.613	.390	54
WILSON, H.	.621	.358	.322	.222	207	65	14	2	17	19	29	.647	.372	55	488	143	30	4	39	44	63	.610	.352	44
JOHNSON	.532	.379	.215	.202	176	57	12	3	7	21	18	.545	.396	44	406	127	26	6	16	38	41	.526	.372	35
BARFIELD	.550	.342	.269	.188	180	52	12	1	12	18	45	.567	.354	37	423	118	26	1	28	37	101	.544	.337	29
CAREY	.431	.388	.097	.167	157	53	7	4	0	18	10	.433	.406	28	364	121	16	8	1	28	23	.430	.380	21
LEZCANO	.502	.387	.199	.194	137	42	9	2	5	22	20	.511	.403	41	312	94	20	4	11	40	44	.498	.381	33
WHEAT	.535	.402	.173	.215	175	60	12	2	4	10	5	.503	.378	33	410	152	31	6	10	29	13	.549	.412	49
ASHBURN	.421	.375	.084	.158	192	62	9	1	1	9	10	.396	.353	7	464	159	24	4	3	31	27	.431	.384	22
CLARK, J.	.561	.362	.244	.203	171	56	15	2	8	13	21	.579	.375	45	400	125	33	6	17	27	47	.553	.356	36
RICE	.595	.353	.285	.210	206	66	9	5	14	15	39	.617	.367	49	481	147	18	10	32	31	87	.585	.348	39
POWELL	.601	.372	.317	.224	131	35	6	0	11	17	25	.565	.351	36	302	88	14	0	28	44	65	.617	.382	52
KELLER	.578	.362	.289	.209	156	47	10	3	10	19.	19	.596	.377	48	368	104	23	7	23	42	43	.570	.356	38
WILLIAMS, B.	.561	.368	.243	.207	196	57	12	2	10	17	21	.526	.347	29	444	146	30	4	24	35	53	.576	.378	45
SNIDER	.607	.382	.290	.232	188	56	12	3	11	18	28	.569	.359	39	441	143	31	7	29	49	72	.623	.392	56
HAFEY	.568	.352	.253	.200	165	54	15	2	8	10	17	.588	.366	44	391	121	33	4	19	22	39	.559	.346	34
AVERILL	.569	.368	.228	.209	203	65	11	4	8	8	11	.532	.346	30	476	167	29	11	20	20	27	.585	.377	47
SLAUGHTER	.460	.340	.157	.156	185	54	15	1	3	8	15	.432	.321	6	451	139	39	4	9	27	40	.472	.347	20
BROCK	.449	.377	.122	.169	183	56	11	2	2	14	28	.421	.355	13	429	144	29	5	5	35	73	.461	.386	27
SS/2B																								
APPLING	.453	.409	.112	.185	179	62	10	2	2	25	8	.458	.426	38	418	142	25	5	4	43	19	.451	.401	30
CHAPMAN	.421	.364	.113	.154	168	51	9	4	1	20	19	.423	.378	20	384	119	22	9	1	29	44	.421	.358	14
YOUNT	.583	.374	.252	.218	191	65	15	4	9	15	19	.602	.388	52	442	145	33	8	20	28	43	.575	.368	43
PECKINPAUGH	.406	.367	.104	.149	138	41	7	1	2	19	11	.406	.382	18	319	97	15	1	5	28	25	.406	.360	12
SMITH, O.	.354	.340	.089	.120	115	31	7	1	0	15	5	.348	.354	2	284	75	15	4	1	30	11	.357	.334	-2
FREGOSI	.496	.369	.203	.183	148	43	8	3	6	22	25	.507	.382	35	330	97	17	6	12	36	56	.491	.363	27
JACKSON, T.	.471	.341	.165	.161	142	45	9	1	4	8	9	.479	.353	22	345	104	21	3	10	18	22	.468	.336	16
BANKS	.582	.349	.287	.203	184	56	9	2	14	17	23	.603	.363	46	424	123	19	4	31	34	50	.572	.343	36
SEWELL	.478	.403	.137	.192	174	55	14	3	1	17	3	.448	.377	23	398	140	35	7	2	42	9	.491	.414	40

Table B-1.

Hitters Versus Left-Handed and Versus Right-Handed Pitching (continued)

					VS LEFT										VS RIGHT									
	SL %	OB %	ISO PWR	OTS %	AB	H	2B	3B	HR	BB	K	SL %	OB %	BAT RNS	AB	H	2B	3B	HR	BB	K	SL %	OB %	BAT RNS
MARANVILLE	.348	.305	.088	.106	164	42	7	2	1	14	15	.341	.315	-11	390	102	18	4	3	22	37	.351	.301	-13
BANCROFT	.432	.363	.123	.157	191	58	9	5	2	23	7	.435	.379	22	433	135	20	10	4	30	16	.431	.356	15
APARICIO	.358	.331	.084	.119	179	50	8	1	1	18	9	.352	.345	-1	435	118	19	4	4	35	20	.360	.326	-5
3B/1B																								
WILLIAMS, J.	.537	.403	.181	.216	185	68	9	8	3	16	16	.551	.418	51	430	151	22	19	6	32	36	.531	.396	42
ROSEN	.606	.396	.277	.240	185	63	10	2	13	22	15	.627	.411	61	427	138	21	3	30	46	33	.596	.389	51
MOLITOR	.543	.402	.208	.218	151	51	14	2	5	21	21	.556	.419	52	339	113	30	3	11	34	47	.537	.394	42
MELTON	.521	.345	.239	.180	155	45	6	1	10	16	25	.535	.357	33	362	101	15	1	23	33	57	.515	.339	25
MATHEWS	.605	.369	.324	.223	146	39	9	1	11	18	16	.568	.348	36	344	99	22	3	29	50	42	.621	.378	52
NETTLES	.443	.336	.181	.149	178	44	6	0	8	18	15	.416	.316	3	417	112	15	1	20	48	39	.454	.344	16
ZIMMERMAN	.557	.392	.196	.218	169	64	13	4	4	8	19	.574	.407	52	405	143	30	10	10	22	42	.550	.386	43
ROBINSON, B.	.482	.346	.186	.167	169	50	8	2	7	17	15	.491	.360	26	386	114	19	3	15	26	34	.477	.340	19
COLLINS, J.	.505	.368	.168	.186	167	57	13	5	2	11	10	.515	.382	36	388	130	30	11	4	16	21	.501	.361	28
GROH	.483	.417	.130	.201	153	56	13	3	0	18	8	.490	.433	44	363	126	29	8	1	39	18	.479	.410	37
BOYER, K.	.541	.342	.250	.185	174	52	9	3	10	15	24	.557	.354	36	403	116	19	7	22	30	55	.534	.337	28
EVANS	.557	.351	.285	.195	186	47	10	2	12	22	28	.522	.332	24	427	120	25	6	29	52	71	.573	.359	40
SS																								
DAVIS	.428	.386	.087	.165	123	42	7	2	0	12	5	.431	.400	26	287	98	16	3	1	18	12	.427	.380	20
JENNINGS	.465	.434	.087	.202	167	64	9	3	0	21	3	.473	.452	47	385	145	21	6	0	33	8	.462	.426	38
WAGNER	.540	.432	.155	.233	155	61	11	4	2	16	14	.555	.450	60	362	138	23	10	4	27	32	.534	.424	49
DAHLEN	.517	.387	.191	.200	155	51	10	6	3	19	12	.529	.402	43	357	116	23	13	6	32	26	.512	.380	35
RIPKEN	.524	.367	.214	.192	186	60	12	2	8	18	26	.538	.382	40	444	135	28	5	19	39	60	.518	.360	31
BARTELL	.470	.345	.165	.163	155	48	12	1	4	12	12	.477	.359	24	363	110	28	1	10	20	26	.467	.339	17
BOUDREAU	.531	.404	.187	.215	176	61	13	2	6	23	3	.545	.422	51	403	138	29	4	12	36	6	.524	.396	41
WALLACE	.482	.365	.137	.176	159	54	11	5	1	10	14	.491	.379	31	357	124	24	10	1	6	31	.479	.358	23
VAUGHN	.466	.396	.140	.184	158	49	12	1	2	16	5	.437	.374	21	376	125	32	4	5	46	14	.478	.405	36
CRONIN	.471	.371	.157	.175	194	62	13	3	4	21	12	.479	.386	31	451	141	31	6	9	37	26	.468	.365	23
HARRAH	.497	.381	.189	.189	148	47	10	0	6	19	20	.507	.395	38	350	106	22	1	14	40	44	.492	.374	30
TINKER	.442	.335	.142	.148	146	44	7	4	2	10	6	.445	.346	15	341	102	16	10	4	16	13	.441	.331	10
3B																								
SCHMIDT	.644	.408	.332	.262	110	35	7	1	10	20	22	.673	.423	71	249	77	15	1	21	38	47	.631	.401	59
BRETT	.657	.439	.275	.289	140	49	10	3	7	15	6	.614	.413	60	317	126	25	6	17	31	16	.677	.451	80
MCGRAW	.485	.497	.084	.241	116	48	7	1	0	25	3	.491	.518	67	273	108	16	2	1	49	6	.482	.488	57
DEVLIN	.450	.419	.110	.188	132	45	8	2	1	22	8	.455	.435	40	306	104	18	6	1	37	20	.448	.411	32
SANTO	.569	.385	.248	.219	160	54	9	2	9	17	22	.588	.401	53	385	121	20	6	21	40	50	.561	.379	43
CLIFT	.521	.347	.236	.181	186	54	14	2	9	20	25	.532	.359	33	429	121	30	5	20	39	56	.516	.342	26
BAKER, F.	.562	.401	.204	.225	169	56	12	6	3	12	12	.527	.376	36	390	144	30	15	7	28	29	.577	.411	54
BELL	.442	.370	.139	.164	159	48	9	1	4	21	15	.447	.383	25	366	111	21	1	9	35	33	.440	.364	19
DECINCES	.544	.355	.248	.193	175	53	14	2	9	18	24	.560	.368	40	409	120	31	3	21	35	55	.537	.349	31
BOGGS	.588	.418	.235	.246	173	56	14	2	7	19	13	.549	.391	44	393	144	35	4	17	44	33	.605	.430	63
BRADLEY, B.	.552	.373	.205	.206	146	52	11	7	2	8	12	.568	.390	47	338	116	26	15	4	12	28	.545	.366	37
KILLEBREW	.623	.383	.339	.238	162	48	10	1	15	27	23	.648	.397	61	378	105	22	1	34	60	52	.612	.377	50

Table B-1.

Hitters Versus Left-Handed and Versus Right-Handed Pitching (continued)

					VS LEFT										VS RIGHT									
	SL %	OB %	ISO PWR	OTS %	AB	H	2B	3B	HR	BB	K	SL %	OB %	BAT RNS	AB	H	2B	3B	HR	BB	K	SL %	OB %	BAT RNS
2B																								
LAJOIE	.586	.482	.152	.282	155	70	17	2	1	16	7	.606	.503	81	368	157	37	5	3	32	16	.578	.473	69
COLLINS, E.	.473	.408	.110	.193	155	53	5	4	1	10	10	.445	.382	24	363	135	13	11	2	29	26	.485	.418	40
CHILDS	.434	.401	.101	.174	159	50	9	3	0	16	5	.409	.377	17	372	127	23	6	1	44	13	.445	.411	32
FRISCH	.447	.351	.129	.157	195	63	10	3	3	13	3	.451	.365	21	460	145	23	8	7	21	7	.445	.345	14
HORNSBY	.661	.465	.263	.307	171	71	15	4	8	23	10	.690	.485	90	399	156	32	10	17	48	23	.649	.456	76
ROBINSON, J.	.526	.401	.193	.211	167	57	11	2	6	22	8	.539	.418	49	389	128	25	5	13	41	19	.520	.393	39
MORGAN	.533	.421	.204	.224	152	46	11	2	5	23	13	.500	.394	37	344	117	27	4	12	56	34	.547	.432	54
GRICH	.483	.399	.182	.193	114	35	6	0	5	21	18	.491	.415	41	261	78	14	0	11	40	40	.480	.392	33
CAREW	.463	.431	.089	.200	172	61	9	1	1	14	13	.436	.403	28	411	157	24	4	2	45	34	.475	.443	44
SANDBERG	.509	.347	.203	.177	198	61	12	6	6	16	31	.520	.360	31	457	139	26	13	13	26	71	.504	.342	24
HUGGINS	.381	.380	.077	.145	149	46	6	2	0	21	12	.376	.394	17	357	108	14	6	1	41	29	.383	.374	12
SCHOENDIENST	.470	.368	.152	.173	186	59	11	2	5	20	7	.478	.383	30	421	134	27	3	10	28	17	.467	.361	22
GEHRINGER	.504	.376	.186	.189	212	64	18	3	4	17	4	.472	.354	21	502	163	46	9	11	49	10	.517	.385	37
HUBBARD	.319	.303	.087	.097	130	30	7	0	1	16	15	.308	.315	-15	310	72	16	0	4	29	38	.324	.298	-17
DOERR	.457	.347	.177	.159	177	51	10	3	5	20	11	.463	.360	22	418	116	23	6	13	40	24	.455	.341	15
HERMAN	.465	.363	.134	.169	206	69	18	2	2	14	9	.471	.377	27	479	158	41	4	5	20	20	.463	.357	20
MAZEROSKI	.361	.292	.104	.105	152	39	7	1	2	10	13	.355	.302	-12	359	92	16	2	6	16	31	.363	.288	-15
EVERS	.392	.356	.096	.140	127	36	6	1	1	10	4	.370	.336	-1	302	91	16	4	2	30	9	.401	.364	12
1B																								
CASH	.674	.434	.317	.293	163	54	9	2	12	21	22	.632	.408	61	378	139	23	6	29	53	57	.692	.445	80
FOXX	.699	.406	.352	.284	176	64	14	3	15	18	28	.733	.423	82	412	140	31	6	33	40	62	.685	.398	68
GEHRIG	.721	.405	.376	.292	188	61	17	5	13	17	24	.676	.380	62	445	157	44	13	34	48	61	.740	.416	82
SISLER	.574	.400	.206	.230	206	72	14	5	5	8	6	.539	.374	38	492	185	37	13	14	29	15	.589	.411	56
MCCOVEY	.686	.413	.362	.283	148	44	10	1	13	22	17	.642	.388	58	336	113	26	1	32	51	43	.706	.424	77
ALLEN, R.	.661	.403	.332	.267	145	49	11	2	12	21	35	.690	.422	74	329	107	25	3	25	38	76	.649	.395	61
FOURNIER	.561	.440	.197	.247	108	38	6	5	1	11	9	.528	.412	45	266	98	17	13	4	40	23	.574	.451	63
CAMILLI	.559	.403	.241	.225	155	45	8	2	8	22	24	.523	.379	36	351	116	19	5	19	50	60	.575	.414	54
GREENBURG	.629	.356	.347	.224	185	55	10	1	18	21	29	.654	.369	56	435	120	23	3	40	50	65	.619	.351	45
TENNEY	.437	.436	.077	.191	131	43	6	1	1	18	6	.412	.409	26	297	111	15	2	1	40	15	.448	.448	42
HERNANDEZ	.497	.391	.167	.194	189	59	14	3	3	16	22	.466	.366	23	448	151	37	8	8	48	57	.510	.401	40
TERRY	.564	.364	.225	.205	199	63	12	3	8	8	6	.528	.343	28	465	162	31	8	20	18	17	.579	.373	45
MURRAY	.544	.387	.226	.211	171	56	11	1	9	22	24	.561	.404	49	395	124	24	2	20	42	55	.537	.380	39
MIZE	.614	.392	.279	.240	177	55	15	4	8	16	13	.576	.368	43	411	142	37	10	20	39	35	.630	.402	60
MATTINGLY	.547	.382	.200	.209	177	58	13	1	6	9	9	.514	.360	30	418	149	33	1	17	24	23	.562	.391	46
CHANCE	.470	.427	.127	.201	128	44	8	3	1	23	8	.477	.444	46	292	100	19	7	1	39	19	.467	.420	38
ALLISON	.587	.368	.291	.216	143	44	11	1	10	17	28	.608	.381	51	334	97	24	3	22	38	62	.577	.363	41
CEPEDA	.554	.397	.213	.220	163	57	12	0	8	17	22	.571	.411	52	374	126	28	0	17	33	48	.547	.391	43
KLUSZEWSKI	.593	.362	.294	.215	191	53	9	1	14	19	10	.555	.343	33	435	134	22	2	35	43	27	.610	.370	49
YORK	.521	.349	.242	.182	199	57	15	2	10	24	29	.533	.363	34	466	129	35	4	23	47	67	.517	.343	26
BOTTOMLEY	.593	.363	.289	.215	189	53	13	6	9	17	16	.556	.340	32	427	134	32	14	22	40	40	.609	.373	49

Table B-1.

Hitters Versus Left-Handed and Versus Right-Handed Pitching (continued)

					VS LEFT										VS RIGHT									
	SL %	OB %	ISO PWR	OTS %	AB	H	2B	3B	HR	BB	K	SL %	OB %	BAT RNS	AB	H	2B	3B	HR	BB	K	SL %	OB %	BAT RNS
C																								
FISK	.579	.374	.266	.216	131	42	9	3	7	14	24	.595	.386	50	298	92	21	6	15	28	53	.571	.368	42
TORRE	.568	.372	.251	.212	162	53	7	1	11	16	18	.586	.388	49	381	119	16	2	25	32	41	.560	.366	39
CAMPENELLA	.580	.368	.263	.213	154	51	11	0	10	13	16	.597	.383	50	364	113	24	1	23	29	35	.572	.361	40
CARTER	.514	.362	.222	.186	167	50	11	0	9	21	19	.527	.378	37	392	113	24	1	20	41	44	.508	.356	28
BENCH	.599	.366	.309	.219	148	45	9	1	12	18	23	.622	.380	53	352	100	21	1	28	42	51	.589	.360	43
FREEHAN	.482	.349	.171	.168	147	48	5	2	5	8	20	.490	.361	26	354	108	11	6	13	21	45	.479	.344	20
MCFARLAND	.486	.395	.146	.192	93	33	7	3	0	9	8	.495	.412	40	225	75	17	7	1	20	18	.482	.388	32
COCHRANE	.540	.412	.216	.223	127	39	11	1	4	16	6	.504	.385	35	299	99	28	3	11	48	14	.555	.424	53
MUNSON	.500	.354	.194	.177	153	48	10	1	6	13	19	.510	.367	31	357	108	21	3	14	25	43	.496	.348	24
HARTNETT	.508	.370	.219	.188	121	36	9	3	4	17	10	.521	.384	37	284	81	20	6	10	35	22	.503	.364	29
BAILEY	.525	.350	.242	.184	124	32	3	1	8	13	14	.492	.328	19	282	83	7	1	20	29	37	.540	.360	35
HOWARD	.538	.369	.199	.198	138	48	6	2	6	8	20	.551	.384	42	320	107	12	3	15	14	46	.532	.362	34
MCCARVER	.475	.367	.168	.174	137	39	8	1	4	13	8	.445	.347	15	316	100	20	2	10	30	22	.488	.376	30
SIMMONS, T.	.458	.373	.137	.171	181	58	12	1	4	20	14	.464	.388	29	416	134	27	1	9	29	31	.456	.366	22
BERRA	.514	.346	.230	.178	164	44	9	1	8	14	8	.482	.326	16	382	111	23	1	22	38	22	.528	.355	31
PORTER	.499	.373	.210	.186	165	44	9	3	6	21	17	.467	.349	20	373	111	24	7	14	52	44	.513	.384	36
ROMANO	.481	.355	.187	.171	151	46	10	0	6	15	18	.490	.367	28	366	106	22	1	15	34	42	.477	.350	21
DICKEY	.489	.365	.174	.178	144	43	7	2	4	10	4	.458	.344	17	339	109	19	6	10	28	10	.501	.373	31
BURGESS	.482	.400	.138	.192	108	36	8	1	1	7	3	.454	.374	23	261	91	21	4	3	27	8	.493	.410	39
BRESNAHAN	.416	.427	.094	.178	106	34	8	1	0	24	9	.415	.446	37	248	80	17	3	0	41	22	.417	.419	30
LOMBARDI	.521	.378	.183	.197	148	51	10	0	6	12	4	.534	.394	42	347	116	22	1	13	20	10	.515	.371	33
FERRELL	.404	.355	.119	.144	124	35	10	1	1	17	4	.403	.369	15	290	83	22	3	2	28	8	.405	.349	9

HOF - 1954
BILL TERRY
NEW YORK GIANTS – 1ST BASE
75 YEARS A
LEAGUE LEA
HEINIE GROH
WALKS, N.L. – 84
1916
HOF - 1974
JIM BOTTOMLEY
ST. LOUIS CARDINALS – 1ST BASE
1929

CHAPTER C

Hitters' EWBII Ratings & Fielding Ratings

Table C-1.

Hitters' EWBII Ratings and Fielding Ratings

	PWR	H/R	BNT	RN	RG	AR	DUR	FA1	FA2	E	PO	AST
OUTFIELD												
RUTH	10	3	2	4	4	3	9	.952	.746	17	343	13
DELAHANTY	6	8	8	8	7	8	8	.985	.746	7	445	28
COBB	5	10	10	10	5	5	9	.967	.746	13	380	18
SPEAKER	5	10	9	10	8	8	9	.989	.746	5	464	31
WILLIAMS, T.	9	3	4	3	3	3	9	.944	.746	19	324	10
JACKSON, J.	5	8	8	8	6	5	10	.972	.746	12	399	21
SHECKARD	4	9	8	10	10	9	9	.998	.746	1	511	39
HENDERSON, R.	8	8	7	10	5	5	9	.967	.746	13	380	18
MANTLE	9	5	4	6	3	2	9	.939	.746	20	315	8
MUSIAL	9	5	5	5	5	4	10	.963	.746	14	371	17
SEYMOR	5	7	7	7	5	5	10	.967	.746	13	380	18
THOMPSON	7	7	7	7	6	6	8	.975	.746	11	408	23
MAYS	9	6	5	7	6	7	10	.978	.746	10	417	24
CLARKE	4	10	9	10	5	5	8	.967	.746	13	380	18
KLEIN	7	3	4	3	9	10	10	.997	.746	2	501	37
DIMAGGIO	8	4	5	4	5	5	8	.967	.746	13	380	18
DAWSON	7	6	6	8	7	7	8	.983	.746	8	436	27
YASTRZEMSKI	7	3	3	4	6	6	10	.975	.746	11	408	23
GUERRERO	8	3	3	4	5	5	9	.967	.746	13	380	18
KELLEY	5	9	10	10	5	4	8	.963	.746	14	371	17
JACKSON	10	3	1	5	4	5	10	.960	.746	15	361	15
HEILMANN	6	4	5	4	4	3	9	.952	.746	17	343	13
ROBINSON, F.	10	2	2	3	3	3	10	.944	.746	19	324	10
KALINE	7	3	4	4	5	5	8	.967	.746	13	380	18
SMITH, E.	4	7	8	7	6	6	8	.975	.746	11	408	23
STARGELL	10	2	1	3	4	4	10	.956	.746	16	352	14
SIMMONS, A.	8	5	5	6	5	4	9	.963	.746	14	371	17
KEELER	3	10	10	10	3	4	8	.948	.746	18	333	11
FLICK	5	7	7	8	5	6	9	.970	.746	12	389	20
COLAVITO	9	2	2	3	3	8	9	.967	.746	13	380	18
MAGEE, S.	6	9	8	10	3	2	9	.939	.746	20	315	8
GOSLIN	6	6	6	6	5	4	9	.963	.746	14	371	17
AARON	8	3	3	4	6	7	10	.978	.746	10	417	24
CEDENO	6	8	6	10	6	6	9	.975	.746	11	408	23
DONLIN	4	6	7	7	7	6	8	.980	.746	9	427	26
OTT	8	3	3	3	7	6	10	.980	.746	9	427	26
CRAWFORD	5	7	7	7	6	7	9	.978	.746	10	417	24
CLEMENTE	6	4	4	5	3	8	9	.967	.746	13	380	18
FOSTER	9	2	2	3	6	6	10	.975	.746	11	408	23
KINER	9	2	2	3	5	6	10	.970	.746	12	389	20
MEDWICK	7	3	4	3	4	4	10	.956	.746	16	352	14
WILLIAMS, K.	7	3	4	3	6	6	9	.975	.746	11	408	23
GWYNN	4	8	8	9	5	4	10	.963	.746	14	371	17
WYNN	6	7	5	10	6	5	10	.972	.746	12	399	21
RAINES	4	8	9	10	4	5	10	.960	.746	15	361	15
PARKER	5	2	2	3	9	9	10	.995	.746	3	492	36

Table C-1.

Hitters' EWBII Ratings and Fielding Ratings (continued)

	PWR	H/R	BNT	RN	RG	AR	DUR	FA1	FA2	E	PO	AST
HAMILTON	3	9	10	10	3	3	8	.944	.746	19	324	10
MINOSO	6	5	5	6	6	6	10	.975	.746	11	408	23
LYNN	8	2	2	3	4	4	9	.956	.746	16	352	14
WANER, P.	4	3	5	3	5	6	10	.970	.746	12	389	20
ROSE	5	3	4	3	5	6	10	.970	.746	12	389	20
STAUB	7	2	3	3	5	5	10	.967	.746	13	380	18
WINFIELD	7	3	4	4	6	5	10	.972	.746	12	399	21
MURCER	8	2	3	3	4	5	10	.960	.746	15	361	15
WILSON, H.	9	2	2	3	5	4	10	.963	.746	14	371	17
JOHNSON	6	5	4	6	6	5	10	.972	.746	12	399	21
BARFIELD	7	2	1	3	8	7	10	.987	.746	6	455	30
CAREY	2	7	8	8	8	7	10	.987	.746	6	455	30
LEZCANO	5	3	3	4	6	6	9	.975	.746	11	408	23
WHEAT	5	3	5	3	5	4	9	.963	.746	14	371	17
ASHBURN	2	5	7	6	8	9	10	.991	.746	4	473	33
CLARK, J.	7	2	3	3	6	5	10	.972	.746	12	399	21
RICE	8	4	2	5	5	4	10	.963	.746	14	371	17
POWELL	9	2	2	3	3	4	9	.948	.746	18	333	11
KELLER	8	3	3	4	5	4	9	.963	.746	14	371	17
WILLIAMS, B.	7	4	4	5	4	4	10	.956	.746	16	352	14
SNIDER	8	2	2	3	2	3	10	.934	.746	20	305	7
HAFEY	7	2	3	3	4	4	9	.956	.746	16	352	14
AVERILL	6	4	5	4	2	3	10	.934	.746	20	305	7
SLAUGHTER	4	2	3	3	7	6	10	.980	.746	9	427	26
BROCK	3	7	6	9	2	2	10	.929	.746	21	296	5
SS/2B												
APPLING	3	3	5	3	5	6	9	.963	.970	29	282	492
CHAPMAN	3	7	7	9	6	6	10	.969	.975	24	291	496
YOUNT	7	5	5	6	4	3	10	.948	.957	39	257	482
PECKINPAUGH	3	2	4	3	7	6	8	.975	.979	20	301	500
SMITH, O.	2	7	7	9	7	7	8	.977	.981	18	306	502
FREGOSI	5	4	3	5	5	5	9	.960	.967	31	277	490
JACKSON, T.	4	3	4	3	6	6	8	.969	.975	24	291	496
BANKS	8	2	2	3	4	5	10	.954	.962	35	267	486
SEWELL	4	4	6	4	4	5	10	.954	.962	35	267	486
MARANVILLE	2	5	5	6	8	8	10	.985	.988	12	321	508
BANCROFT	3	5	6	5	5	6	10	.963	.970	29	282	492
APARICIO	2	5	6	6	6	7	10	.972	.977	22	296	498
3B/1B												
WILLIAMS, J.	5	6	7	7	5	4	10	.923	.984	36	129	331
ROSEN	8	3	4	3	4	4	10	.911	.981	40	123	325
MOLITOR	6	7	6	9	3	3	8	.892	.978	47	116	317
MELTON	7	2	2	3	7	8	10	.965	.992	18	149	353
MATHEWS	9	4	3	5	4	4	9	.911	.981	40	123	325
NETTLES	5	2	3	3	9	9	10	.987	.997	7	162	367
ZIMMERMAN	5	5	6	6	4	4	9	.911	.981	40	123	325
ROBINSON, B.	5	2	3	3	8	7	10	.969	.993	16	152	356

Table C-1.

Hitters' EWBII Ratings and Fielding Ratings (continued)

	PWR	H/R	BNT	RN	RG	AR	DUR	FA1	FA2	E	PO	AST
COLLINS, J.	4	5	6	6	6	6	9	.945	.988	27	139	342
GROH	3	5	6	5	4	5	10	.917	.983	38	126	328
BOYER, K.	7	2	3	3	6	6	10	.945	.988	27	139	342
EVANS	8	3	2	4	5	4	10	.923	.984	36	129	331
SS												
DAVIS	2	6	8	7	9	9	7	.993	.746	6	335	514
JENNINGS	2	9	10	9	7	7	8	.977	.746	18	306	502
WAGNER	4	9	8	10	5	6	9	.963	.746	29	282	492
DAHLEN	5	9	8	10	6	6	8	.969	.746	24	291	496
RIPKEN	6	2	3	3	7	7	10	.977	.746	18	306	502
BARTELL	4	3	4	3	8	7	8	.983	.746	14	316	506
BOUDREAU	5	3	5	3	5	4	10	.957	.746	33	272	488
WALLACE	4	5	6	6	6	7	9	.972	.746	22	296	498
VAUGHN	4	4	5	4	6	5	10	.966	.746	26	286	494
CRONIN	4	3	5	4	6	6	10	.969	.746	24	291	496
HARRAH	5	4	4	5	5	5	10	.960	.746	31	277	490
TINKER	4	7	7	8	7	6	10	.975	.746	20	301	500
3B												
SCHMIDT	9	4	2	5	8	9	8	.979	.746	11	157	361
BRETT	8	6	6	6	4	5	8	.917	.746	38	126	328
MCGRAW	2	9	10	9	4	5	8	.917	.746	38	126	328
DEVLIN	3	8	8	9	8	7	10	.969	.746	16	152	356
SANTO	7	2	3	3	7	8	10	.965	.746	18	149	353
CLIFT	6	3	3	4	9	10	10	.992	.746	4	165	369
BAKER, F.	6	8	7	9	5	5	10	.928	.746	33	131	333
BELL	4	2	4	3	9	9	10	.987	.746	7	162	367
DECINCES	7	2	2	3	7	7	10	.960	.746	20	147	350
BOGGS	6	3	4	3	4	4	9	.911	.746	40	123	325
BRADLEY, B.	6	7	6	8	6	5	9	.939	.746	29	136	339
KILLEBREW	9	3	2	4	3	2	10	.885	.746	49	113	314
2B												
LAJOIE	4	6	7	6	6	6	10	.975	.746	22	358	516
COLLINS, E.	3	9	10	10	7	7	10	.981	.746	17	365	532
CHILDS	2	5	7	6	8	9	9	.990	.746	9	374	553
FRISCH	3	7	8	8	8	9	10	.990	.746	9	374	553
HORNSBY	7	3	5	3	3	3	9	.952	.746	39	338	467
ROBINSON, J.	5	5	6	6	6	5	10	.972	.746	24	356	510
MORGAN	6	9	7	10	4	5	9	.962	.746	31	347	489
GRICH	5	1	2	2	6	7	8	.977	.746	20	361	521
CAREW	2	5	6	6	5	6	10	.970	.746	26	354	505
SANDBERG	5	6	5	8	6	6	10	.975	.746	22	358	516
HUGGINS	2	5	6	6	7	8	10	.984	.746	15	367	537
SCHOENDIENST	4	3	5	3	6	6	9	.975	.746	22	358	516
GEHRINGER	5	4	5	4	5	6	10	.970	.746	26	354	505
HUBBARD	2	2	2	3	9	10	9	.996	.746	4	381	569
DOERR	5	2	4	3	6	6	9	.975	.746	22	358	516
HERMAN	3	3	5	3	6	5	10	.972	.746	24	356	510

Table C-1.

Hitters' EWBII Ratings and Fielding Ratings (continued)

	PWR	H/R	BNT	RN	RG	AR	DUR	FA1	FA2	E	PO	AST
MAZEROSKI	3	3	4	4	9	8	9	.992	.746	7	376	559
EVERS	2	3	5	4	6	6	9	.975	.746	22	358	516
1B												
CASH	9	3	3	4	5	5	10	.985	.746	17	999	84
FOXX	10	2	2	3	5	5	10	.985	.746	17	999	84
GEHRIG	10	5	4	6	3	2	10	.977	.746	24	999	78
SISLER	6	7	7	7	7	7	10	.991	.746	10	999	90
MCCOVEY	10	2	2	3	3	2	10	.977	.746	24	999	78
ALLEN, R.	9	4	2	6	3	3	10	.978	.746	23	999	79
FOURNIER	5	5	6	6	4	5	8	.983	.746	19	999	82
CAMILLI	7	2	3	3	5	6	8	.986	.746	16	999	85
GREENBURG	10	2	2	3	5	6	10	.986	.746	16	999	85
TENNEY	2	5	6	5	7	7	9	.991	.746	10	999	90
HERNANDEZ	4	4	4	5	7	8	10	.992	.746	9	999	91
TERRY	6	3	5	3	7	6	10	.990	.746	11	999	89
MURRAY	6	3	3	4	5	6	10	.986	.746	16	999	85
MIZE	8	3	4	3	3	3	10	.978	.746	23	999	79
MATTINGLY	5	3	5	3	5	6	10	.986	.746	16	999	85
CHANCE	3	9	9	10	3	3	8	.978	.746	23	999	79
ALLISON	8	3	2	5	4	5	10	.983	.746	19	999	82
CEPEDA	6	3	4	4	4	3	10	.980	.746	21	999	80
KLUSZEWSKI	8	3	3	3	3	4	10	.979	.746	22	999	79
YORK	7	2	2	3	5	5	10	.985	.746	17	999	84
BOTTOMLEY	8	5	4	6	1	1	10	.972	.746	30	999	73
C												
FISK	7	4	3	5	6	7	8	.985	.746	17	999	122
TORRE	7	2	3	2	5	6	10	.980	.746	22	999	103
CAMPENELLA	7	2	3	3	5	5	9	.979	.746	23	999	96
CARTER	6	2	2	2	6	7	10	.985	.746	17	999	122
BENCH	9	2	2	3	4	5	9	.976	.746	26	999	84
FREEHAN	5	4	4	5	7	7	9	.988	.746	14	999	135
MCFARLAND	4	4	5	5	6	6	6	.982	.746	20	999	109
COCHRANE	6	3	4	3	4	4	8	.974	.746	28	999	77
MUNSON	5	2	3	3	7	7	9	.986	.746	16	999	128
HARTNETT	6	2	3	3	6	6	8	.982	.746	20	999	109
BAILEY	7	3	3	4	5	6	8	.980	.746	22	999	103
HOWARD	5	2	3	3	5	5	8	.979	.746	23	999	96
MCCARVER	4	3	4	3	6	6	9	.983	.746	19	999	116
SIMMONS, T.	4	3	4	3	6	7	10	.985	.746	17	999	122
BERRA	6	2	4	3	6	6	9	.982	.746	20	999	109
PORTER	6	2	3	3	5	5	10	.979	.746	23	999	96
ROMANO	5	2	3	3	6	6	9	.983	.746	19	999	116
DICKEY	5	3	5	3	5	6	8	.980	.746	22	999	103
BURGESS	4	2	5	2	4	5	7	.976	.746	26	999	84
BRESNAHAN	2	5	5	6	4	4	8	.972	.746	30	999	71
LOMBARDI	5	1	5	1	3	4	8	.971	.746	31	999	65
FERRELL	3	3	4	3	5	6	8	.980	.746	22	999	103

HOF - 19
MAX CAREY
PITTSBURGH PIRATES – OUTFIELD
1925
75 YEARS AGO
LEAGUE LEADER
ZACH WHEAT
SLUGGING AVG., N.L. – .461
HOF - 1955
GABBY HARTNETT
CHICAGO CUBS – CATCHER
1930

Pitchers' Actual & Normalized Statistics

Table D-1.

Pitchers' Actual and Normalized Statistics

		YR	W	L	TG	GS	CG	IP	H	HR	BB	K	ERA	ER	PIT RNS	BAT RNS	FLD RNS	TTL PLYR RTNG
STARTERS																		
R	WOOD	1912	34	5	43	38	35	344	267	2	82	258	1.91	73				
		AL						243					1.94	52	69	9	2	80
R	JOHNSON	1913	36	7	48	36	29	346	232	9	38	243	1.14	44				
		AL						261					1.96	57	69	9	0	78
R	MATHEWSON	1909	25	6	37	33	26	275	192	2	36	149	1.15	35				
		NL						237					2.04	54	66	8	2	76
R	FERRELL	1935	25	14	41	38	31	322	336	16	108	110	3.52	126				
		AL						236					2.30	60	58	16	1	75
R	LEMON	1948	20	14	43	37	20	294	231	12	129	147	2.82	92				
		AL						239					2.23	59	60	12	3	75
L	WHITE	1906	18	6	28	24	20	219	160	2	38	95	1.52	37				
		AL						193					2.00	43	68	6	1	75
R	BENDER	1910	23	5	30	25	25	250	182	1	47	155	1.58	44				
		AL						203					2.13	48	64	9	1	74
R	CUPPY	1896	25	14	46	40	35	358	388	8	75	86	3.12	124				
		NL						241					1.97	53	69	4	1	74
R	WALSH	1910	18	20	45	36	33	370	242	4	61	258	1.26	52				
		AL						249					2.01	56	67	4	3	74
R	WALTERS	1939	27	11	39	36	31	319	250	15	109	137	2.29	81				
		NL						244					2.19	59	62	11	1	74
R	NICHOLS	1897	31	11	46	40	37	368	362	9	68	127	2.64	108				
		NL						247					1.88	52	71	2	0	73
L	SPAHN	1953	23	7	35	32	24	266	211	14	70	148	2.10	62				
		NL						249					2.00	55	68	4	1	73
R	LYONS	1939	14	6	21	21	16	173	162	7	26	65	2.76	53				
		AL						194					2.04	44	66	6	0	72
R	RUSIE	1897	28	10	38	37	35	322	314	6	87	135	2.54	91				
		NL						245					1.94	53	70	1	1	72
L	GOMEZ	1937	21	11	34	34	25	278	233	10	93	194	2.33	72				
		AL						247					1.82	50	73	-1	-1	71
L	GROVE	1931	31	4	41	30	27	289	249	10	62	175	2.06	66				
		AL						252					1.79	50	74	-2	-1	71
L	GUIDRY	1978	25	3	35	35	16	274	187	13	72	248	1.74	53				
		AL						250					1.92	53	70	0	1	71
R	ALEXANDER	1915	31	10	49	42	36	376	253	3	64	241	1.22	51				
		NL						248					1.98	54	68	0	2	70
L	BRECHEEN	1948	20	7	33	30	21	233	193	6	49	149	2.24	58				
		NL						236					1.94	51	70	0	0	70
R	CHESBRO	1904	41	12	55	51	48	455	338	4	88	239	1.82	92				
		AL						239					2.07	55	65	4	1	70
R	FELLER	1939	24	9	39	35	24	297	227	13	142	246	2.85	94				
		AL						240					2.06	55	66	4	0	70
R	GRIMES	1920	23	11	40	33	25	304	271	5	67	131	2.22	75				
		NL						239					2.27	60	59	10	1	70
L	HUBBELL	1933	23	12	45	33	22	309	256	6	47	156	1.66	57				
		NL						248					2.04	56	66	1	3	70
L	LEONARD,D	1914	19	5	36	25	17	225	139	3	60	176	0.96	24				
		AL						215					1.86	44	72	-1	-1	70
R	PETERS	1963	19	8	41	30	13	243	192	9	68	189	2.33	63				
		AL						233					2.25	58	60	10	0	70
R	WILLIS	1899	27	8	41	38	35	343	277	6	117	120	2.49	95				
		NL						241					1.86	50	72	-2	0	70
R	JOSS	1908	24	11	42	35	29	325	232	2	30	130	1.16	42				
		AL						248					2.05	56	66	2	1	69
L	KOUFAX	1965	26	8	43	41	27	336	216	26	71	382	2.04	76				
		NL						250					2.08	58	65	5	-1	69
L	LEE	1941	22	11	35	34	30	300	258	18	92	130	2.37	79				
		AL						246					2.13	58	64	5	0	69
R	MAYS	1917	22	9	35	33	27	289	230	1	74	91	1.74	56				
		AL						236					2.24	59	60	6	3	69
R	NEWCOMBE	1955	20	5	34	31	17	234	222	35	38	143	3.19	83				
		NL						244					2.69	73	46	24	-1	69

Table D-1.

Pitchers' Actual and Normalized Statistics (continued)

		YR	W	L	TG	GS	CG	IP	H	HR	BB	K	ERA	ER	PIT RNS	BAT RNS	FLD RNS	TTL PLYR RTNG
L	NEWHOUSER	1946	26	9	37	34	29	293	215	10	98	275	1.94	63				
		AL						243					1.95	53	69	-1	1	69
R	TAYLOR	1902	23	11	36	33	33	325	271	2	43	83	1.33	48				
		NL						247					2.12	58	64	4	1	69
R	GRIFFITH	1898	24	10	38	38	36	326	305	1	64	97	1.88	68				
		NL						244					1.96	53	69	-2	1	68
R	LUQUE	1923	27	8	41	37	28	322	279	2	88	151	1.93	69				
		NL						245					2.04	55	66	2	0	68
L	PARNELL	1949	25	7	39	33	27	295	258	8	134	122	2.78	91				
		AL						236					2.04	53	66	2	0	68
R	PASCUAL	1959	17	10	32	30	17	239	202	10	69	185	2.64	70				
		AL						239					2.26	60	59	7	2	68
R	RUFFING	1938	21	7	31	31	22	247	246	16	82	127	3.32	91				
		AL						241					2.26	60	60	9	-1	68
L	WADDELL	1905	27	10	46	34	27	329	231	5	90	287	1.48	54				
		AL						245					1.91	52	70	-2	0	68
R	YOUNG	1901	33	10	43	41	38	371	324	6	37	158	1.63	67				
		NL						253					2.03	57	67	1	0	68
R	BRIDGES	1933	14	12	33	28	17	233	192	8	110	120	3.09	80				
		AL						235					2.09	55	65	2	0	67
R	BROWN	1909	27	9	50	34	32	343	246	1	53	172	1.31	50				
		NL						244					2.06	56	66	1	0	67
L	CARLTON	1972	27	10	41	41	30	346	257	17	87	310	1.98	76				
		NL						245					2.12	58	64	4	-1	67
L	SHANTZ	1952	24	7	33	33	27	280	230	21	63	152	2.48	77				
		AL						245					2.09	57	65	1	1	67
L	TUDOR	1985	21	8	36	36	14	275	209	14	49	169	1.93	59				
		NL						249					2.08	58	65	2	0	67
R	ALLEN	1936	20	10	36	31	19	243	234	5	97	165	3.44	93				
		AL						238					1.98	52	68	-3	1	66
R	HUTCHINSON	1947	18	10	33	25	18	220	211	14	61	113	3.03	74				
		AL						235					2.52	66	51	14	1	66
R	RYAN	1981	11	5	21	21	5	149	99	2	68	140	1.69	28				
		AL						235					2.52	66	51	14	1	66
R	CICOTTE	1917	28	12	49	35	29	347	246	2	70	150	1.53	59				
		AL						242					2.15	58	63	2	0	65
R	COOMBS	1910	31	9	45	38	35	353	248	0	115	224	1.30	51				
		AL						236					2.13	56	63	3	-1	65
R	DEAN	1934	30	7	50	33	24	312	288	14	75	195	2.65	92				
		NL						243					2.13	58	63	3	-1	65
L	DOWNING	1963	13	5	24	22	10	176	114	7	80	171	2.56	50				
		AL						157					1.97	34	69	-3	-1	65
R	DRYSDALE	1964	18	16	34	29	9	321	242	15	68	237	2.19	78				
		NL						244					2.25	61	60	4	1	65
L	LOPAT	1950	18	8	35	32	15	236	244	19	65	72	3.47	91				
		AL						240					2.29	61	58	7	0	65
L	MCDOWELL	1965	17	11	42	35	14	273	178	9	132	325	2.18	66				
		AL						235					2.02	53	67	-2	0	65
R	MCGINNITY	1904	35	8	51	44	38	408	307	8	86	144	1.61	73				
		NL						247					2.08	57	65	-1	1	65
R	PASSEAU	1940	20	13	46	31	20	281	259	8	59	124	2.50	78				
		NL						242					2.26	61	59	6	0	65
R	RUCKER	1912	18	21	45	34	23	298	272	6	72	151	2.20	73				
		NL						242					2.16	59	62	2	1	65
R	SHOCKER	1920	20	10	38	28	22	246	224	10	70	107	2.71	74				
		AL						242					2.15	58	63	2	0	65
L	ANTONELLI	1954	21	7	39	37	18	259	209	22	94	152	2.29	66				
		NL						244					2.13	58	63	0	1	64
L	COOPER,W	1916	12	11	42	23	16	246	189	4	74	111	1.87	51				
		NL						224					2.10	52	64	0	0	64
R	FABER	1921	25	15	43	39	32	331	293	10	87	124	2.47	91				
		AL						246					2.03	56	67	-3	0	64

Table D-1.

Pitchers' Actual and Normalized Statistics (continued)

		YR	W	L	TG	GS	CG	IP	H	HR	BB	K	ERA	ER	PIT RNS	BAT RNS	FLD RNS	TTL PLYR RTNG
L	FORD,W	1958	14	7	30	29	15	219	174	14	62	145	2.01	49				
		AL						233					2.15	56	63	1	0	64
R	HARDER	1934	20	12	44	29	17	255	246	6	81	91	2.61	74				
		AL						242					2.12	57	64	-1	1	64
R	LEEVER	1903	25	7	36	34	30	284	255	2	60	90	2.06	65				
		NL						241					2.00	53	68	-4	0	64
L	MCNALLY	1968	22	10	35	35	18	273	175	24	55	202	1.95	59				
		AL						229					2.20	56	61	4	-1	64
L	PIERCE	1955	15	10	33	26	16	206	162	16	64	157	1.97	45				
		AL						242					2.11	57	64	0	0	64
R	REULBACH	1905	18	14	34	29	28	292	208	2	73	152	1.42	46				
		NL						245					1.95	53	69	-5	0	64
R	SCOTT	1986	18	10	37	37	7	275	182	17	72	306	2.23	68				
		NL						246					2.07	57	65	-2	1	64
R	VANCE	1924	28	6	35	34	30	309	238	11	77	262	2.16	74				
		NL						248					2.06	57	66	-2	0	64
R	GARVER	1950	13	18	37	31	22	260	264	18	108	85	3.39	98				
		AL						236					2.29	60	58	4	1	63
R	GIBSON	1968	22	9	34	34	28	305	198	11	62	268	1.12	38				
		NL						252					2.23	62	60	4	-1	63
R	HORLEN	1964	13	9	32	28	9	211	142	11	55	138	1.88	44				
		AL						199					2.15	47	63	-1	1	63
L	LEIBRANDT	1985	17	9	33	33	8	238	223	17	68	108	2.68	71				
		AL						242					2.22	60	61	0	2	63
R	PERRY,G	1972	24	16	41	40	29	343	253	17	82	234	1.92	73				
		NL						242					2.17	58	62	0	1	63
R	WYNN	1956	20	9	38	35	18	278	233	19	91	158	2.72	84				
		AL						242					2.27	61	59	4	0	63
L	CANDELARIA	1977	20	5	33	33	6	231	197	29	50	133	2.34	60				
		NL						249					2.33	64	57	5	0	62
R	MALONEY	1966	16	8	32	32	10	225	174	18	90	216	2.80	70				
		NL						219					2.30	56	58	4	0	62
R	REUSCHEL	1977	20	10	39	37	8	252	233	13	74	166	2.79	78				
		NL						238					2.26	60	59	2	1	62
R	RICHARD	1977	18	12	36	36	13	267	212	18	104	214	2.97	88				
		NL						235					2.38	62	55	6	1	62
R	SEAVER	1971	20	10	36	35	21	286	210	18	61	289	1.76	56				
		NL						249					2.30	63	58	4	0	62
R	DAVIS	1934	19	17	51	31	18	274	283	14	60	99	2.96	90				
		NL						241					2.26	61	59	-1	3	61
L	POLLET	1946	21	10	40	32	22	266	228	12	86	107	2.10	62				
		NL						241					2.20	59	61	0	0	61
R	STIEB	1985	14	13	36	36	8	265	206	22	96	167	2.48	73				
		AL						244					2.26	61	59	0	2	61
L	TANANA	1977	15	9	31	31	20	241	201	19	61	205	2.54	68				
		AL						247					2.21	61	61	0	0	61
R	TROUT	1946	17	13	38	32	23	276	244	11	97	151	2.35	72				
		AL						238					2.34	62	57	3	1	61
R	WARNEKE	1932	22	6	35	32	25	277	247	12	64	106	2.37	73				
		NL						244					2.17	59	62	-1	0	61
L	JOHN	1977	20	7	31	31	11	220	225	12	50	123	2.78	68				
		NL						239					2.32	62	58	1	1	60
R	BLACKWELL	1947	22	8	33	33	23	273	227	10	95	193	2.47	75				
		NL						241					2.20	59	61	-4	2	59
R	BUNNING	1967	17	15	40	40	16	302	241	18	73	253	2.29	77				
		NL						242					2.32	62	57	2	-1	58

Table D-1.

Pitchers' Actual and Normalized Statistics (continued)

		YR	W	L	TG	GS	SV	IP	H	HR	BB	K	ERA	ER	PIT RNS	BAT RNS	FLD RNS	TTL PLYR RTNG
RELIEVERS																		
R	ECKERSLEY	1990	4	2	63	0	48	73	41	2	4	73	0.61	5				
		AL						73					1.69	14	77	0	-3	74
R	SUTTER	1977	7	3	62	0	31	107	69	5	23	129	1.35	16				
		NL						110					1.86	23	72	0	1	73
L	OROSCO	1983	13	7	62	0	17	110	76	3	38	84	1.47	18				
		NL						114					1.99	25	68	3	1	72
L	BURGMEIER	1980	5	4	62	0	24	99	87	3	20	54	2.00	22				
		AL						108					1.99	24	68	0	3	71
L	HERNANDEZ	1984	9	3	80	0	32	140	96	6	36	112	1.93	30				
		AL						139					1.88	29	72	0	-1	71
L	MCGRAW	1980	5	4	57	0	20	92	62	3	23	75	1.47	15				
		NL						91					1.89	19	71	0	0	71
L	MOSSI	1954	6	1	40	5	7	93	56	5	39	55	1.94	20				
		AL						91					1.90	19	71	0	-1	70
R	ABERNATHY	1967	6	3	70	0	28	106	63	1	41	88	1.27	15				
		NL						101					1.92	22	70	-3	2	69
L	HILLER	1973	10	5	65	0	38	125	89	7	39	124	1.44	20				
		AL						139					1.97	30	69	0	0	69
L	HRABOSKY	1975	13	3	65	0	22	97	72	3	33	82	1.67	18				
		NL						102					2.03	23	67	3	-2	68
L	MONGE	1979	12	10	76	0	19	131	96	9	64	108	2.40	35				
		AL						149					2.00	33	68	0	0	68
L	RIGHETTI	1986	8	8	74	0	46	107	88	4	35	83	2.44	29				
		AL						115					1.97	25	69	0	-1	68
R	GOSSAGE	1977	11	9	72	0	26	133	78	9	49	151	1.62	24				
		NL						136					2.04	31	66	2	-1	67
R	KERN	1979	13	5	71	0	29	143	99	5	62	136	1.57	25				
		AL						165					2.00	37	68	0	-1	67
R	LINZY	1965	9	3	57	0	21	82	76	2	23	35	1.43	13				
		NL						96					2.35	25	57	4	6	67
R	MCDANIEL	1960	12	4	65	2	26	116	85	8	24	105	2.09	27				
		NL						114					2.15	27	63	3	1	67
L	PERRANOSKI	1969	9	10	75	0	31	120	85	4	52	62	2.10	28				
		AL						120					2.00	27	68	-2	1	67
R	KINDER	1953	10	6	69	0	27	107	84	8	38	39	1.85	22				
		AL						125					2.30	32	58	8	0	66
R	QUISENBERRY	1983	5	3	69	0	45	139	118	6	11	48	1.94	30				
		AL						145					2.08	34	65	0	1	66
L	SCURRY	1982	4	5	76	0	14	104	79	3	64	94	1.73	20				
		NL						122					2.15	29	63	3	0	66
R	FINGERS	1981	6	3	47	0	28	78	55	3	13	61	1.04	9				
		AL						82					2.10	19	65	0	0	65
R	REGAN	1966	14	1	65	0	21	117	85	6	24	88	1.62	21				
		NL						117					2.16	28	63	0	1	64
R	SMITH	1983	4	10	66	0	29	103	70	5	41	91	1.66	19				
		NL						109					2.19	27	62	0	1	63
R	WILHELM	1954	12	4	57	0	7	111	77	5	52	64	2.11	26				
		NL						119					2.02	27	67	-5	1	63
L	LAVELLE	1977	7	7	73	0	20	118	106	4	37	93	2.06	27				
		NL						134					2.04	30	66	-5	1	62
R	MARSHALL	1972	14	8	65	0	18	116	82	3	47	95	1.78	23				
		NL						117					2.19	28	62	0	0	62
R	TEKULVE	1983	7	5	76	0	18	99	78	1	36	52	1.64	18				
		NL						106					2.11	25	64	-3	1	62
R	GARBER	1978	6	5	65	0	25	117	84	12	24	85	2.15	28				
		NL						117					2.26	29	60	0	1	61
R	MURPHY	1974	10	10	70	0	20	123	97	6	51	47	1.90	26				
		AL						136					2.33	35	57	2	2	61
R	GRANT	1970	8	3	80	0	24	135	112	10	32	58	1.87	28				
		AL						148					2.42	40	54	4	1	59

75 YEARS AG
WORLD CHAM
BABE RUTH
BOSTON RED SOX – PITCHER
1916
WES FERRELL
BOSTON RED SOX – PITCHER
ALL TIME
LEADER
ADDIE JOSS
2ND LOWEST CAREER ERA – 1.89
1908

CHAPTER E

Pitchers Versus Left-Handed & Versus Right-Handed Hitting

Table E-1.

Pitchers Versus Left-Handed and Versus Right-Handed Hitting

	OVERALL		VS. LEFT							VS. RIGHT						
	OPP BA	OPP OB%	AB	H	HR	BB	K	OPP BA	OPP OB%	AB	H	HR	BB	K	OPP BA	OPP OB%
STARTERS																
WOOD	.133	.180	405	55	3	24	84	.136	.184	436	57	3	25	98	.130	.177
JOHNSON	.100	.123	419	43	13	11	85	.103	.126	451	44	14	12	98	.098	.121
MATHEWSON	.144	.174	401	60	4	15	59	.150	.180	430	60	5	15	69	.140	.169
FERRELL	.160	.212	407	67	5	28	37	.165	.218	436	68	5	28	44	.156	.207
LEMON	.144	.220	404	60	4	40	56	.149	.225	434	61	5	41	64	.141	.215
WHITE	.149	.186	203	29	3	9	26	.143	.179	477	72	7	22	58	.151	.188
BENDER	.155	.198	348	56	2	19	58	.161	.204	373	56	3	19	68	.150	.191
CUPPY	.141	.175	406	59	4	17	27	.145	.180	436	60	5	17	31	.138	.170
WALSH	.130	.169	415	56	7	20	81	.135	.175	444	56	8	20	93	.126	.164
WALTERS	.144	.204	412	61	5	32	49	.148	.209	443	62	6	33	56	.140	.200
NICHOLS	.126	.157	409	53	6	15	39	.130	.160	439	54	6	16	46	.123	.154
SPAHN	.162	.207	266	42	2	15	43	.158	.203	625	102	5	36	96	.163	.209
LYONS	.150	.177	330	51	3	11	34	.155	.182	355	52	3	11	39	.146	.172
RUSIE	.134	.178	410	57	4	22	48	.139	.183	439	57	5	23	55	.130	.173
GOMEZ	.141	.196	257	35	2	17	53	.136	.190	606	87	4	42	119	.144	.199
GROVE	.142	.178	263	36	3	11	47	.137	.172	618	89	6	28	106	.144	.181
GUIDRY	.153	.204	264	39	2	17	70	.148	.199	621	96	5	40	156	.155	.206
ALEXANDER	.148	.186	421	64	3	20	74	.152	.190	452	65	4	21	85	.144	.182
BRECHEEN	.165	.204	253	41	1	12	47	.162	.200	595	99	4	29	104	.166	.205
CHESBRO	.144	.188	404	60	5	22	58	.149	.192	434	61	6	23	68	.141	.184
FELLER	.129	.211	399	53	4	42	92	.133	.215	428	54	4	43	107	.126	.206
GRIMES	.166	.207	415	71	5	22	48	.171	.213	445	72	5	22	55	.162	.201
HUBBELL	.179	.207	270	47	2	9	39	.174	.201	636	115	5	23	86	.181	.209
LEONARD, D	.124	.179	220	26	4	14	52	.118	.171	516	65	10	36	116	.126	.183
PETERS	.167	.220	406	70	2	28	84	.172	.226	433	70	3	29	97	.162	.214
WILLIS	.113	.176	393	46	5	31	39	.117	.182	422	46	6	31	45	.109	.170
JOSS	.154	.175	424	67	5	11	46	.158	.179	455	68	6	12	53	.149	.171
KOUFAX	.153	.199	264	39	4	14	88	.148	.191	622	97	11	36	196	.156	.202
LEE	.163	.213	263	42	3	16	33	.160	.208	619	102	9	40	74	.165	.215
MAYS	.173	.224	414	74	2	28	34	.179	.231	442	74	3	28	40	.167	.217
NEWCOMBE	.187	.215	435	84	9	16	69	.193	.222	465	84	9	16	80	.181	.208
NEWHOUSER	.146	.209	255	36	3	20	71	.141	.204	599	89	6	48	157	.149	.212
TAYLOR	.162	.188	427	71	5	14	29	.166	.193	457	72	5	14	34	.158	.183
GRIFFITH	.161	.195	421	70	1	18	34	.166	.200	451	70	1	19	39	.155	.189
LUQUE	.161	.207	423	70	1	25	53	.165	.212	453	71	1	26	62	.157	.203
PARNELL	.159	.232	251	39	1	23	30	.155	.226	591	95	4	57	68	.161	.235
PASCUAL	.169	.221	417	73	3	29	86	.175	.229	446	73	3	29	99	.164	.215
RUFFING	.159	.210	415	68	5	27	57	.164	.215	445	69	5	28	67	.155	.205
WADDELL	.128	.184	252	31	5	17	66	.123	.178	591	77	12	41	148	.130	.187
YOUNG	.158	.176	435	71	5	10	50	.163	.182	466	71	5	10	58	.152	.170
BRIDGES	.135	.216	393	55	4	42	56	.140	.223	422	55	4	42	65	.130	.209
BROWN	.165	.200	423	72	2	19	56	.170	.206	454	73	2	19	66	.161	.195
CARLTON	.170	.219	265	44	3	16	68	.166	.214	621	107	6	39	152	.172	.221
SHANTZ	.160	.202	262	41	4	13	41	.156	.196	613	99	11	33	92	.162	.204
TUDOR	.173	.207	269	45	3	11	47	.167	.200	634	111	7	28	106	.175	.210
ALLEN	.146	.208	404	61	2	33	75	.151	.215	432	61	2	33	87	.141	.202
HUTCHINSON	.176	.223	413	75	7	25	56	.182	.228	443	76	7	26	65	.172	.217

Table E-1.

Pitchers Versus Left-Handed and Versus Right-Handed Hitting (continued)

	OVERALL		VS. LEFT							VS. RIGHT						
	OPP BA	OPP OB%	AB	H	HR	BB	K	OPP BA	OPP OB%	AB	H	HR	BB	K	OPP BA	OPP OB%
RYAN	.154	.238	253	40	0	29	64	.158	.245	272	41	1	29	75	.151	.233
CICOTTE	.162	.206	418	70	4	24	49	.167	.213	448	70	4	24	56	.156	.199
COOMBS	.165	.233	410	70	0	37	69	.171	.239	438	70	0	38	81	.160	.227
DEAN	.156	.197	417	67	5	22	70	.161	.203	447	68	5	22	82	.152	.192
DOWNING	.145	.238	164	23	1	19	47	.140	.230	387	57	3	48	106	.147	.241
DRYSDALE	.172	.214	427	76	4	23	83	.178	.220	457	76	5	24	97	.166	.208
LOPAT	.184	.226	263	47	3	14	23	.179	.220	619	115	9	34	50	.186	.228
MCDOWELL	.149	.242	248	36	2	30	87	.145	.237	580	87	4	72	193	.150	.244
MCGINNITY	.131	.174	412	56	9	22	40	.136	.180	441	56	10	22	47	.127	.168
PASSEAU	.180	.216	427	79	3	20	50	.185	.221	458	80	3	21	57	.175	.211
RUCKER	.160	.202	417	69	5	23	57	.165	.209	447	69	6	23	66	.154	.196
SHOCKER	.140	.189	407	59	8	25	49	.145	.194	437	59	8	26	56	.135	.184
ANTONELLI	.166	.226	262	42	3	20	44	.160	.220	616	104	8	48	99	.169	.229
COOPER,W	.160	.220	239	37	3	18	31	.155	.214	561	91	8	43	70	.162	.222
FABER	.150	.194	419	65	4	24	43	.155	.201	449	65	5	24	49	.145	.188
FORD,W	.175	.224	253	43	3	16	48	.170	.219	594	105	6	38	106	.177	.226
HARDER	.166	.214	420	72	2	27	40	.171	.221	450	72	3	27	46	.160	.208
LEEVER	.153	.192	412	65	3	20	35	.158	.197	442	66	4	21	41	.149	.188
MCNALLY	.159	.205	244	38	5	14	52	.156	.202	573	92	13	33	117	.161	.206
PIERCE	.152	.203	256	38	5	16	57	.148	.199	600	92	13	39	127	.153	.205
REULBACH	.142	.194	414	61	3	27	59	.147	.200	443	61	4	28	69	.138	.189
SCOTT	.145	.200	416	62	5	29	127	.149	.204	447	63	6	30	147	.141	.195
VANCE	.147	.193	421	64	5	25	97	.152	.200	451	64	6	25	113	.142	.187
GARVER	.167	.228	411	71	4	33	36	.173	.234	439	71	5	34	41	.162	.222
GIBSON	.166	.208	438	75	5	24	102	.171	.214	469	76	5	24	119	.162	.203
HORLEN	.160	.212	344	57	3	23	60	.166	.218	367	57	4	24	70	.155	.207
LEIBRANDT	.186	.231	266	48	3	15	34	.180	.224	626	118	7	37	76	.188	.234
PERRY,G	.160	.209	417	69	5	27	76	.165	.216	447	69	5	27	89	.154	.203
WYNN	.162	.218	418	70	5	31	64	.167	.225	448	70	6	31	74	.156	.211
CANDELARIA	.179	.215	271	47	6	12	44	.173	.208	639	116	13	30	99	.182	.218
MALONEY	.153	.228	374	59	5	37	97	.158	.234	402	60	6	38	113	.149	.223
REUSCHEL	.175	.224	418	75	3	27	73	.179	.229	447	76	4	28	84	.170	.219
RICHARD	.169	.239	409	71	5	39	87	.174	.246	439	72	5	39	101	.164	.232
SEAVER	.171	.211	436	77	6	23	117	.177	.218	465	77	6	23	135	.166	.205
DAVIS	.177	.212	424	77	5	19	40	.182	.217	454	78	6	20	47	.172	.207
POLLET	.176	.230	262	45	3	18	30	.172	.225	615	109	9	44	67	.177	.232
STIEB	.161	.223	421	70	6	35	71	.166	.230	451	70	6	35	83	.155	.216
TANANA	.171	.214	266	44	5	14	65	.165	.207	628	109	12	35	145	.174	.217
TROUT	.175	.233	418	75	4	33	60	.179	.239	447	76	5	33	70	.170	.227
WARNEKE	.165	.205	423	72	5	22	43	.170	.211	454	73	5	22	50	.161	.200
JOHN	.206	.241	269	54	2	12	42	.201	.235	634	132	6	30	92	.208	.244
BLACKWELL	.171	.230	421	74	3	33	79	.176	.236	451	75	3	34	91	.166	.225
BUNNING	.173	.219	424	76	6	26	94	.179	.227	454	76	6	26	109	.167	.213

Table E-1.

Pitchers Versus Left-Handed and Versus Right-Handed Hitting (continued)

	OVERALL		VS. LEFT							VS. RIGHT						
	OPP BA	OPP OB%	AB	H	HR	BB	K	OPP BA	OPP OB%	AB	H	HR	BB	K	OPP BA	OPP OB%
RELIEVERS																
ECKERSLEY	.127	.138	121	16	1	1	34	.132	.139	130	16	1	2	39	.123	.136
SUTTER	.132	.175	183	25	1	10	62	.137	.181	197	25	2	10	71	.127	.169
OROSCO	.153	.217	121	18	1	10	27	.149	.214	283	44	1	23	60	.155	.219
BURGMEIER	.176	.210	117	20	1	5	18	.171	.205	276	49	1	12	41	.178	.212
HERNANDEZ	.147	.198	146	21	1	9	34	.144	.194	343	51	3	22	77	.149	.200
MCGRAW	.147	.197	96	14	1	6	23	.146	.196	224	33	2	14	51	.147	.197
MOSSI	.125	.209	93	11	1	10	17	.118	.204	219	28	3	23	37	.128	.211
ABERNATHY	.139	.217	169	24	0	17	39	.142	.220	183	25	1	18	45	.137	.214
HILLER	.149	.204	146	21	2	10	43	.144	.199	344	52	4	24	95	.151	.207
HRABOSKY	.152	.213	108	16	1	8	27	.148	.207	253	39	2	20	59	.154	.216
MONGE	.137	.219	155	21	2	16	38	.135	.216	363	50	5	38	85	.138	.219
RIGHETTI	.163	.219	123	19	1	9	28	.154	.212	289	48	1	21	61	.166	.223
GOSSAGE	.124	.197	225	29	3	21	71	.129	.203	241	29	3	21	83	.120	.191
KERN	.135	.208	276	38	2	26	73	.138	.212	296	39	2	27	84	.132	.204
LINZY	.189	.232	171	33	0	10	19	.193	.238	184	34	1	10	22	.185	.227
MCDANIEL	.153	.193	195	31	2	10	48	.159	.200	209	31	3	10	55	.148	.187
PERRANOSKI	.157	.236	127	19	1	13	19	.150	.229	300	48	2	31	43	.160	.239
KINDER	.146	.204	212	32	3	16	21	.151	.211	227	32	3	16	25	.141	.198
QUISENBERRY	.173	.187	254	45	2	4	23	.177	.190	272	46	2	5	27	.169	.184
SCURRY	.159	.253	129	19	1	16	34	.147	.241	304	48	2	39	76	.158	.254
FINGERS	.169	.199	143	25	1	5	30	.175	.203	153	25	1	6	34	.163	.195
REGAN	.166	.206	203	35	2	10	41	.172	.211	218	35	2	11	47	.161	.201
SMITH	.153	.225	186	29	2	18	44	.156	.230	200	30	2	18	52	.150	.220
WILHELM	.146	.227	201	30	1	22	32	.149	.233	217	31	2	22	37	.143	.222
LAVELLE	.183	.233	147	26	1	9	33	.177	.224	345	64	2	23	73	.186	.236
MARSHALL	.162	.237	202	34	1	20	44	.168	.243	217	34	1	21	52	.157	.231
TEKULVE	.172	.234	186	33	0	15	26	.177	.239	198	33	1	16	30	.167	.229
GARBER	.150	.189	199	31	5	10	39	.156	.196	214	31	5	10	46	.145	.183
MURPHY	.171	.239	238	42	2	22	24	.176	.246	254	42	2	22	28	.165	.232
GRANT	.182	.222	262	49	3	14	30	.187	.228	281	50	4	14	34	.178	.217

TRIVIA
RED RUFFING
CAREER COMEBACK PLAYER
BURLEIGH GRIMES
PITTSBURGH PIRATES – PITCHER
1928
75 YEARS AGO
WORLD CHAMPS
CARL MAYS
BOSTON RED SOX – PITCHER
1916

CHAPTER F

Pitchers' EWBII Ratings, Fielding Ratings, & Batting Statistics

Table F-1.

Pitchers' EWBII Ratings, Fielding Ratings, and Batting Statistics

	HR/PA	S	C	F	B	H	DUR	FA	BATTING STATS BA	AB	H	HR
STARTERS												
WOOD	.007	8	7	8	6	6	9	.887	.270	100	27	6
JOHNSON	.030	8	10	7	6	4	9	.821	.290	100	29	6
MATHEWSON	.010	6	10	7	6	6	9	.896	.270	100	27	6
FERRELL	.011	3	7	7	8	4	9	.840	.340	100	34	10
LEMON	.010	5	3	6	7	7	9	.905	.300	100	30	7
WHITE	.014	4	9	6	5	5	9	.849	.250	100	25	4
BENDER	.007	6	8	7	6	5	9	.849	.270	100	27	6
CUPPY	.010	3	9	8	5	5	9	.849	.220	100	22	3
WALSH	.017	7	9	8	5	7	9	.915	.220	100	22	3
WALTERS	.012	4	5	8	7	5	9	.858	.300	100	30	7
NICHOLS	.014	4	10	8	4	4	9	.821	.200	100	20	2
SPAHN	.007	6	7	7	5	5	9	.849	.230	100	23	3
LYONS	.008	4	10	6	5	3	9	.812	.250	100	25	4
RUSIE	.010	4	8	8	4	5	9	.849	.200	100	20	2
GOMEZ	.007	7	6	7	3	3	9	.802	.150	100	15	1
GROVE	.010	6	9	7	3	3	9	.812	.130	100	13	1
GUIDRY	.007	9	7	6	4	5	9	.849	.190	100	19	1
ALEXANDER	.008	7	9	8	4	6	9	.887	.190	100	19	1
BRECHEEN	.006	6	8	6	4	4	9	.840	.190	100	19	1
CHESBRO	.012	5	8	9	5	5	9	.849	.220	100	22	3
FELLER	.009	8	3	7	5	4	9	.821	.230	100	23	3
GRIMES	.011	4	8	7	6	5	9	.849	.290	100	29	6
HUBBELL	.007	5	10	6	4	6	9	.896	.190	100	19	1
LEONARD, D	.018	8	6	5	3	2	9	.783	.130	100	13	1
PETERS	.006	8	6	5	6	3	9	.812	.290	100	29	6
WILLIS	.013	4	5	8	3	4	9	.830	.110	100	11	1
JOSS	.012	4	10	7	4	5	9	.849	.200	100	20	2
KOUFAX	.016	10	8	7	5	3	9	.812	.230	100	23	3
LEE	.013	4	7	8	5	4	9	.821	.250	100	25	4
MAYS	.005	3	7	7	5	7	9	.905	.250	100	25	4
NEWCOMBE	.019	6	10	6	10	3	9	.802	.430	100	43	14
NEWHOUSER	.010	9	5	7	3	5	9	.849	.150	100	15	1
TAYLOR	.011	3	10	8	5	5	9	.858	.220	100	22	3
GRIFFITH	.002	3	9	8	3	4	9	.840	.130	100	13	1
LUQUE	.002	5	7	7	4	4	9	.830	.200	100	20	2
PARNELL	.005	4	4	7	4	4	9	.821	.200	100	20	2
PASCUAL	.007	8	6	6	6	6	9	.877	.260	100	26	5
RUFFING	.011	5	7	7	6	3	9	.812	.270	100	27	6
WADDELL	.019	9	6	7	3	4	9	.821	.130	100	13	1
YOUNG	.011	4	10	8	4	4	9	.830	.190	100	19	1
BRIDGES	.009	5	3	6	4	4	9	.840	.200	100	20	2
BROWN	.004	5	9	7	4	4	9	.821	.190	100	19	1
CARLTON	.010	9	7	8	5	3	9	.812	.230	100	23	3
SHANTZ	.016	5	8	7	4	5	9	.849	.190	100	19	1
TUDOR	.011	6	9	6	4	4	9	.840	.200	100	20	2
ALLEN	.004	7	5	6	2	4	9	.840	.090	100	9	0
HUTCHINSON	.015	5	7	6	7	5	9	.849	.330	100	33	9
RYAN	.002	9	2	4	5	3	9	.812	.250	100	25	4
CICOTTE	.009	4	8	7	4	4	9	.821	.200	100	20	2

Table F-1.

Pitchers' EWBII Ratings, Fielding Ratings, and Batting Statistics (continued)

	HR/PA	S	C	F	B	H	DUR	FA	BATTING STATS BA	AB	H	HR
COOMBS	.000	6	4	8	5	2	9	.783	.220	100	22	3
DEAN	.011	6	8	6	4	3	9	.812	.200	100	20	2
DOWNING	.006	9	1	5	2	3	9	.812	.070	100	7	0
DRYSDALE	.010	7	8	5	5	4	9	.840	.220	100	22	3
LOPAT	.013	3	8	5	6	4	9	.840	.260	100	26	5
MCDOWELL	.006	10	1	5	3	4	9	.840	.110	100	11	1
MCGINNITY	.021	4	8	8	3	4	9	.840	.150	100	15	1
PASSEAU	.006	4	9	5	5	4	9	.830	.250	100	25	4
RUCKER	.012	5	8	6	4	4	9	.840	.200	100	20	2
SHOCKER	.018	4	7	6	4	4	9	.821	.200	100	20	2
ANTONELLI	.012	6	5	6	4	5	9	.849	.190	100	19	1
COOPER,W	.013	4	5	5	4	3	9	.812	.190	100	19	1
FABER	.010	4	8	7	2	4	9	.830	.090	100	9	0
FORD,W	.010	6	7	6	4	4	9	.840	.190	100	19	1
HARDER	.005	4	7	5	3	4	9	.840	.150	100	15	1
LEEVER	.008	3	8	7	2	4	9	.821	.070	100	7	0
MCNALLY	.021	7	7	6	5	3	9	.793	.220	100	22	3
PIERCE	.020	8	7	5	4	3	9	.812	.190	100	19	1
REULBACH	.008	5	7	7	1	3	9	.812	.030	100	3	0
SCOTT	.012	10	6	5	3	5	9	.849	.110	100	11	1
VANCE	.012	9	7	8	3	4	9	.821	.130	100	13	1
GARVER	.010	3	5	6	5	4	9	.840	.220	100	22	3
GIBSON	.010	9	8	8	5	3	9	.793	.230	100	23	3
HORLEN	.009	7	7	4	3	5	9	.868	.130	100	13	1
LEIBRANDT	.011	4	7	5	4	5	9	.868	.190	100	19	1
PERRY,G	.011	7	7	7	4	5	9	.849	.190	100	19	1
WYNN	.012	6	6	6	5	4	9	.830	.220	100	22	3
CANDELARIA	.020	6	9	5	5	3	9	.812	.230	100	23	3
MALONEY	.013	9	3	5	5	4	9	.821	.220	100	22	3
REUSCHEL	.008	6	7	5	4	5	9	.858	.200	100	20	2
RICHARD	.011	8	4	5	5	5	9	.858	.250	100	25	4
SEAVER	.013	10	8	6	5	4	9	.840	.230	100	23	3
DAVIS	.012	4	9	5	3	7	9	.905	.150	100	15	1
POLLET	.013	4	6	6	4	4	9	.840	.190	100	19	1
STIEB	.013	6	5	5	4	6	9	.877	.190	100	19	1
TANANA	.018	8	8	6	4	4	9	.840	.190	100	19	1
TROUT	.010	5	5	6	5	5	9	.868	.220	100	22	3
WARNEKE	.011	4	8	7	3	4	9	.821	.150	100	15	1
JOHN	.008	5	9	5	4	5	9	.849	.190	100	19	1
BLACKWELL	.006	7	5	7	2	5	9	.868	.070	100	7	0
BUNNING	.013	8	7	6	4	3	9	.793	.200	100	20	2

Table F-1.

Pitchers' EWBII Ratings, Fielding Ratings, and Batting Statistics (continued)

	HR/PA	S	C	F	B	H	DUR	FA	BA	AB	H	HR
									BATTING STATS			
RELIEVERS												
ECKERSLEY	.008	10	10	1	4	1	9	.746	.190	100	19	1
SUTTER	.008	10	8	2	4	5	9	.849	.190	100	19	1
OROSCO	.005	8	5	2	5	5	9	.849	.220	100	22	3
BURGMEIER	.005	5	9	1	4	7	9	.905	.190	100	19	1
HERNANDEZ	.008	8	7	2	4	3	9	.802	.190	100	19	1
MCGRAW	.009	8	7	1	4	4	9	.821	.190	100	19	1
MOSSI	.012	6	3	2	4	3	9	.793	.190	100	19	1
ABERNATHY	.003	8	3	2	2	6	9	.877	.090	100	9	0
HILLER	.011	10	6	2	4	4	9	.821	.190	100	19	1
HRABOSKY	.008	8	5	1	5	2	9	.765	.220	100	22	3
MONGE	.012	8	3	2	4	4	9	.821	.190	100	19	1
RIGHETTI	.005	8	6	2	4	3	9	.802	.190	100	19	1
GOSSAGE	.012	10	4	2	4	3	9	.802	.200	100	20	2
KERN	.006	10	4	2	4	3	9	.812	.190	100	19	1
LINZY	.003	4	8	1	5	10	9	.990	.220	100	22	3
MCDANIEL	.012	9	8	2	4	5	9	.849	.200	100	20	2
PERRANOSKI	.006	5	3	2	3	5	9	.849	.110	100	11	1
KINDER	.013	4	6	2	6	4	9	.821	.260	100	26	5
QUISENBERRY	.007	4	10	2	4	5	9	.868	.190	100	19	1
SCURRY	.004	8	1	2	4	4	9	.821	.200	100	20	2
FINGERS	.007	8	10	1	4	4	9	.821	.190	100	19	1
REGAN	.009	8	8	2	4	5	9	.849	.190	100	19	1
SMITH	.009	9	4	1	4	5	9	.849	.190	100	19	1
WILHELM	.006	6	2	2	1	5	9	.849	.030	100	3	0
LAVELLE	.006	8	7	2	1	5	9	.849	.030	100	3	0
MARSHALL	.004	8	3	2	4	4	9	.821	.190	100	19	1
TEKULVE	.002	5	5	1	2	5	9	.849	.090	100	9	0
GARBER	.023	7	8	2	4	5	9	.849	.190	100	19	1
MURPHY	.007	4	4	2	4	5	9	.868	.200	100	20	2
GRANT	.012	4	8	2	5	5	9	.849	.230	100	23	3

HOF - 1966
CASEY STENGEL
BOSTON BRAVES – OUTFIELD
CHICAGO
CHIEF BENDER
CHICAGO WHITE SOX – COACH
1926
MOST VALUABLE PLAYER
ROGER PECKINPAUGH
A.L. MVP – LEAGUE AWARD
1925

CHAPTER G

Selected Bibliography

20th Century Baseball Chronicle. New York: Beekman House, 1991.

Alexander, Charles. *Our Game: An American Baseball History.* New York: Henry Holt and Company, 1991.

Alston, Walter, and S. Burick. *Alston and the Dodgers.* New York: Doubleday and Company, 1966.

Astor, Gerald. *The Baseball Hall of Fame 50th Anniversary Book.* New York: Prentice-Hall Press, 1988.

Cantaneo, David. *Peanuts and Crackerjack.* Nashville: Rutledge Hill Press, 1991.

Cleveland, Charles B. *The Great Baseball Managers.* New York: Thomas Crowell Company, 1950.

Cobb, Ty, with Al Stump. *My Life in Baseball.* New York: Doubleday and Company, 1961.

Dickson, Paul. *Baseball's Greatest Quotations.* New York: Harper Collins Publishers, 1991.

Durocher, Leo. *Nice Guys Finish Last.* New York: Universe Books, 1975.

Einstein, Charles, ed. *The Fireside Book of Baseball, Volume IV.* New York: Simon and Schuster, 1987.

Flood, Curt, with Richard Carter. *The Way It Is.* New York: Trident Press, 1971.

Golenbock, Peter. *How to Win at Rotisserie Baseball.* New York: Vintage Books, 1987.

Honig, Donald. *The Man in the Dugout.* Chicago: Follett Publishing Company, 1977.

Hopper, Joe, and Craig Carter. *Baseball Trivia 2.* St. Louis: The Sporting News, 1987.

James, Bill. *The Bill James Historical Baseball Abstract.* New York: Villard Books, 1988.

Koppett, Leonard. *The New Thinking Fan's Guide to Baseball.* New York: Simon and Shuster, 1991.

Mann, Steve. *The Baseball Superstats 1989.* New York: McGraw-Hill, 1989.

Mead, William B. *The Explosive Sixties.* Alexandria, Va.: Redefinition, Inc., 1990.

Mercurio, John A. *Record Profiles of Baseball's Hall of Famers.* New York: Harper and Row, 1990.

Nuwer, Hank. *Strategies of the Great Baseball Managers.* New York: Franklin Watts, 1988.

Okkonen, Marc. *Baseball Uniforms of the 20th Century.* New York: Sterling Publishing Co., 1991.

Okrent, Daniel, and Steve Wulf. *Baseball Anecdotes.* New York: Oxford University Press, 1989.

Reichler, Joseph, ed. *The Baseball Encyclopedia.* New York: MacMillan Publishing Co., 1985.

Ritter, Lawrence, and Donald Honig. *The Image of Their Greatness.* New York: Crown Publishers, Inc., 1984.

Shatzkin, Mike, ed. *The Ballplayers: Baseball's Ultimate Biographical Reference.* New York: William Morrow & Company, 1990.

Snyder, John. *Play Ball: Great Moments & Dubious Achievements in Baseball History.* San Francisco: Chronicle Books, 1991.

Thorn, John, and Pete Palmer, eds. *Total Baseball, Second Edition.* New York: Warner Books, 1991.

Thorn, John, and Pete Palmer, eds. *Total Baseball.* New York: Warner Books, 1989.

Thorn, John. *The Relief Pitcher.* New York: E. P. Dutton, 1979.

Waggoner, Glen, and Robert Sklar, eds. *Rotisserie League Baseball.* New York: Bantam Books, 1987.

Weaver, Earl. *Winning.* Edited by John Sammis. New York: William Morrow & Company, 1972.

Weaver, Earl, with Berry Stainback. *It's What You Learn After You Know It All That Counts.* New York: Doubleday and Company, 1982.

Weaver, Earl, with Terry Pluto. *Weaver on Strategy.* New York: Collier Books, 1984.

Zagaris, Michael, and John Hickey. *Oakland A's.* San Francisco: Chronicle Books, 1991.

Index

C

D

M

N

O

P

Q

R

S

T

U

V

W

Y

Z